ORAL INTERPRETATION OF LITERATURE:
an annotated bibliography with multimedia listings

by

Howard D. Doll

THE SCARECROW PRESS, INC.
METUCHEN, N.J., & LONDON
1982

Library of Congress Cataloging in Publication Data

Doll, Howard D., 1937-
   Oral interpretation of literature.

   Includes index.
   1. Oral interpretation--Bibliography.   I. Title.
Z6514.S7D64   [PN4145]   016.8085'4   82-3344
ISBN 0-8108-1538-9   AACR2

Manufactured in the United States of America

CONTENTS

ASSOCIATE EDITORS

ANDERSON, ROBERT G. Mississippi State University. Mississippi State, MS

BEATY, RAY C. Vice-President, Reddy Communications, Inc. New York, NY

BENJAMIN, ROBERT L. San Diego St. University. San Diego, CA

BENNETT, SUZANNE. University of North Dakota. Grand Forks, ND

BRENEMAN, LUCILLE. University of Hawaii. Honolulu, HI

CALDWELL, WINIFRED A. University of Rhode Island. Kingston, RI

CHAPMAN, WAYNE A. University of Arkansas at Little Rock. Little Rock, AR

CHARD, GEORGE. West Georgia College. Carrollton, GA

COWAN, MARLENE S. Towson State University. Towson, MD

CRANNELL, KENNETH C. Emerson College. Boston, MA

CROUCH, ISABEL M. New Mexico State University. Las Cruces, NM

GRAY, JOHN. University of Arkansas. Little Rock, AR

GREENE, MARK. Dayton, OH

HAAS, RICHARD. Ann Arbor, MI

HAUSHALTER, WILLIAM. Central Michigan University. Mount Pleasant, MI

HUNSINGER, PAUL. University of Denver. Denver, CO

KLEINAU, MARION. Southern Illinois University. Carbondale, IL

LONG, BEVERLY WHITAKER. University of North Carolina. Chapel Hill, NC

MATTINGLY, ALETHEA S. University of Arizona Tucson, AZ

McCOARD, WILLIAM. University of Southern California. Los Angeles, CA

McCURDY, FRANCES. University of Missouri. Columbia, MO

McDONNELL, WILLIAM E. University of Wisconsin. Eau Claire, WI

McGEEVER, CHARLES. Baylor University. Waco, TX

OVERSTREET, ROBERT. Auburn University. Auburn, AL

PATTISON, SHERON D. Indiana State University. Terre Haute, IN

PEARSE, JAMES. Baylor University. Waco, TX

PHILLIPS, JEAN. University of Texas. Austin, TX

POST, ROBERT. University of Washington. Seattle, WA

QUEENER, LEA G. Memphis State University. Memphis, TN

REYNOLDS, JERRY D. Louisiana College. Pineville, LA

SIMPSON, VERA. Texas Tech University. Lubbock, TX

SPEER, JEAN H. Virginia Polytechnic Institute. Blacksburg, VA

THOMPSON, DAVID. University of Houston. Houston, TX

VALENTINE, KRISTIN B. Arizona State University. Tempe, AZ

WAISMAN, CHARLOTTE. Salt Lake City, UT

WIGLEY, JOSEPH. Pennsylvania State University. University Park, PA

WILLIAMS, DAVID A. University of Arizona. Tuscon, AZ

PREFACE

The impetus for this bibliography came from a visit in 1970 to the University of Utah. While there I met two Oral Interpretation scholars, David Williams and Richard Haas. Haas and Williams had compiled an annotated bibliography of oral interpretation articles contained in the major Speech Communication journals from 1911 to the late 1960s. I obtained a copy.

Early the next year, at the University of North Carolina, Paul D. Brandes and I began work on an up-to-date, annotated bibliography that would meet the following needs: 1) keep the Haas-Williams bibliography current; 2) add to each up-dated bibliography two previous years of related scholarship; 3) expand the areas covered to fields of scholarship outside Speech Communication; and 4) computerize the entries for indexing by a program called KWIC (Key Word in Context). Through the devotion and hard work of many Associate Editors, a computerized bibliography was produced yearly and published in the North Carolina Journal of Speech Communication.

In 1976 a graduate thesis by John W. Creagh gave us an expanded base for covering articles in a wide range of subject areas from 1900 to 1976, and the process of annotating these articles was begun with grants from the University of North Carolina Research Council and sanctions and support from the Speech Communication Association. That same year, the Interpretation Division of SCA funded the Index to Studies in Oral Interpretation 1911-1976, edited by Lee Hudson. The Index served as a source for additional entries as did the Supplement to the Index published a few years later.

In addition to these excellent sources, Brooks, Bahn and Okey's The Communicative Act of Oral Interpretation, the SCA's Bibliographic Annual, Readers Theatre News, Literature in Performance and supportive information from Kristin Valentine and Kristin Marshall (as well as input from the Associate Editors) gave the annotated bibliography more breadth.

This bibliography contains over 4200 entries, plus an appendix of recorded literature. Ninety-nine percent of the entries in the categories of Journals, Chapters in Books, Specialized Periodicals, Filmstrips and Videotapes are annotated. Books, Theses and Dissertations, and Recordings are not annotated due to their general unavailability.

In selecting entries for inclusion the editor used the following criteria: 1) the entry was perceptually relevant to Oral Interpretation; 2) the entry dealt in some way with aural or oral qualities of literature; 3) the entry was an example of the type of research an oral interpretation scholar was likely to be engaged in; and 4) the entry could be concisely stated in about 25-30 words. Criterion three was left deliberately vague in order to give the Associate Editors choice in selecting from those entries more traditionally associated with English Literature. To have exhaustively surveyed the fields of Literary Criticism, Folklore, Aesthetics and other related areas would have been impossible.

The major purpose of compiling this bibliography then was to produce a representative survey of related and relevant scholarship. It is hoped that this work will be used to stimulate research in Oral Interpretation and that it will serve to guide interested scholars to topic areas of interest in the many fields of art and literature which interest the performer of literature.

ACKNOWLEDGMENTS

This bibliography is the work of many minds and many hours of dedicated scholarship.

In completing the work, I must give special recognition to David Williams and Richard Haas, Paul Brandes, Carroll Arnold, Beverly Long and the Associate Editors listed.

The undergraduate and graduate students who contributed to the bibliography in significant fashion must also be recognized:

Wanda Diefes, Janet Sherman, Frankie Jenkins, Patricia Moylan, Jan Ceropski, Sam Crawford, Stacey Cox, Anne Nipper, Caspar Thomson, and Janis Waldrop.

Most special and most sacrificing throughout this project was my wife, Anne. I will never be able to repay the encouragement and sustenance she provided, nor will I ever be able to make up the lost pleasures of which she was deprived in seeing this book through to its completion. It is, in a real sense, her book too.

H. D. D.
Chapel Hill, NC
November 1981

LIST OF JOURNALS SURVEYED

Abstracts of English Studies
Akademie der Wissenschaften
Alcor
Alpha Psi Omega Playbill
American Images: A Psycho-
    analytic Journal for the
    Arts and Sciences
American Literature
American Literature Abstracts
American Literature Realism
American Notes and Queries
American Quarterly
American Speech
Archives des Lettres Modernes
Arizona Quarterly
Art and Literature
Arte y Literatura
The Athenaeum
Australian Literary Studies

Ball State University Forum
The Beloit Poetry Journal
Bibliographical Society of Amer-
    ican Papers
Black Orpheus
Black Theatre
Black Theatre Bulletin
Blackwood's Magazine
The Bookman
Boston University Studies in
    English
British Journal of Aesthetics
Bucknell Review
Bucknell University Studies

California University Publica-
    tions
Cambridge Journal
Cambridge Quarterly
Canadian Literature
Catholic Theatre
Central States Speech Journal

The Chaucer Review
Chicago Review
Childhood Education
Christian Century
Church Today
Classical Review
Colby Library Quarterly
College Composition and Com-
    munication
College English
College Language Association
    Journal
Communication Association of
    the Pacific
Communication Education
Communication Monographs
Communication Quarterly
Communication Technology for
    the Mass Media
The Communicator
Comparative Literature
Comparative Literature Studies
Compatero and the Humanities
Concerning Poetry
The Conch
Contemporary Literature
Criterion
The Critic: An Illustrated
    Monthly Review of Literature,
    Art, and Life
The Critical Quarterly
The Critical Survey
Criticism
Criticism: A Quarterly for Lit-
    erature and the Arts
Critique: Studies in Modern
    Fiction
Current Literature

The Dial: A Fortnightly Journal
    of Criticism and Discussion
    of Literature and the Arts

Discourse: A Review of Dramatic Literature and the Theatrical Arts
Drama
Drama and Theatre
Drama Critique
Drama Magazine
Drama Review
Drama Survey
Drama II
Dramatics
Dramatika

Early American Literature
Edinburgh Review or Critical Journal
Educational Theatre Journal
Elementary English
Elementary School Journal
Encore: The Voice of Vital Theatre
English
English Association Essays and Studies
English Dance and Song
English Institute; Selected Papers
English Institute Essays
English Journal
English Language Notes
English Literary Renaissance
English Literature History
English Literature in Transition
English Miscellany: A Symposium of History, Literature, and the Arts
English Quarterly
English Record
English Studies
English: The Magazine of the English Association
Essays and Studies on English
Essays in Criticism (Aylesbury, England)
Essays in Criticism (Oxford)
Explicator
Expression: Australian Quarterly
Expression: Poetry Quarterly

Florida Speech Communication Journal
Folklore

Folklore Forum
Gambit
Grade Teacher

Hollins Critic
Human Communication Research
Humanities in the South
Huntington Library Quarterly

Illinois Schools Journal
Illinois Speech and Theatre Journal
Illinois Speech News
Indiana Speech Journal
Information Literaire
Inside Education
Interchange
International Journal of American Linguistics
International Theatre Magazine
Interpretation: A Journal of Bible and Theology

James Joyce Quarterly
Journal of Aesthetics and Art Criticism
Journal of American Folklore
Journal of Applied Behavior Science
Journal of Arizona Communication and Theatre
Journal of Biblical Literature
Journal of Black Poetry
Journal of Black Studies
Journal of Broadcasting
Journal of Commonwealth Literature
Journal of Communication
Journal of Communication Association of the Pacific
Journal of Creative Behavior
Journal of Education
Journal of Educational Measurement
Journal of Educational Psychology
Journal of English and Germanic Philology
Journal of Experimental Education
Journal of Experimental Research
Journal of General Education

Journal of Linguistics
Journal of Medieval and Renaissance Studies
Journal of Modern Literature
Journal of Narrative Technique
Journal of Reading
Journal of Savants
Journal of the American Forensics Association
Journal of the Wisconsin Communication Association
Journal of William Morris Society

Keats-Shelley Journal
Kentucky Association of Communication Arts
Kentucky Folklore Record
Kentucky Journal of Communication Arts
Kenyon Review

Language
Language and Speech
Language and Style
Language Quarterly
Latin American Theatre Review
The Laurel Review
Learning; Magazine for Certain Teaching
Library Quarterly
Lingua
Linguistic Inquiry
Linguistics: An International Review
The Literary Review
Literature and Psychology

Medieval Studies
Medium Aevum
The Michigan Academician
Michigan Academy of Arts and Science and Letters
Michigan Alumnus: Quarterly Review
Michigan History
Mississippi Quarterly
Modern Australian Literature
Modern Drama
Modern Fiction Studies
Modern International Drama
Modern Language Association
Modern Language Journal

Modern Language Notes
Modern Language Quarterly
Modern Language Review
Modern Language Review--Monographs
Modern Philosophy
Monographs for Experimental Research in Theatre

National Association of Educational Broadcasters Newsletter
National Education Association News
National Institute of Social and Behaviorial Science
New: American and Canadian Poetry
New England Review
New Literary History
New Testament Studies
New Theatre Magazine
New York Review of Books
New York State Speech Association Reports
New Yorker
New Zealand Journal of Educational Studies
Nineteenth Century Fiction
Northeast Modern Language Association
Notes and Queries
Novel: A Forum on Fiction

Ohio State Speech Journal
Ohio State University Theatre Collection Bulletin: Research and Theatre History
Oral English

Pacific Speech
Papers in Linguistics
Papers on Language and Literature
Performing Arts in Canada
Performing Arts in Review
Philological Quarterly
Philosophy and Rhetoric
Players Magazine
Plays and Players
Poet and Critic
Poetica
Poetics: International Review for Theory of Literature

Poetlore
Poetry
Poetry Australia
Poetry Bag
Poetry Magazine
Poetry Northwest
Poetry Review
Prairie Schooner
Publication of the Modern Language Association

Quarterly Checklist of Linguistics
Quarterly Journal of Speech
Quarterly Review of Literature
Quartet Magazine of the Arts

Reading Research Quarterly
Renaissance Quarterly
Resources for American Literary Studies
Resources in Education
The Review: A Magazine of Poetry and Criticism
The Review of English Literature
Review of the English Studies

St. Louis Quarterly
School Activities
School Arts
Scholastic Teacher
Scholastic Voice
Seventeenth Century News Letter
Sewanee Review
Shakespeare Quarterly
Shakespeare Survey
Southern Folklore Quarterly
Southern Poetry Review
Southern Review
Southern Speech Communication Journal
Southwest Film Teachers Journal
Southwest Folklore
Speculum
Speech and Drama
Speech Communication in Business and Industry
Stand: A Quarterly Review of Literature and the Arts
Studies in Bibliography

Studies in Black Literature
Studies in English Literature
Studies in Literary Imagination
Studies in Philology
Studies in Short Fiction
Studies in the Novel
Studies in the Renaissance
Studies in the Twentieth Century
Style

Tennessee Studies in Literature
Texas Speech Association Newsletter
Texas Studies in Literature and Language
Theatre-Arts
Theatre Notebook
Theatre Research/Recherches Theatrales
Theatre World
Thoth
The Times Literary Supplement
The Toastmaster
Transatlantic
Triquarterly
Tulane Studies in English
Twentieth Century Literature

University of Toronto Quarterly
The University Review

Victorian Newsletter
Victorian Poetry
Victorian Studies

Western American Literature
Western Journal of Speech Communication
Wisconsin Communication Association
World Theatre

Xavier

Yale Review
Yale Theatre

RECORD OF SPEECH COMMUNICATION JOURNALS
WITH INITIATION DATES AND NAME CHANGES

QUARTERLY JOURNAL OF SPEECH

From 1911 through 1915: PUBLIC SPEAKING REVIEW

From Volume 1 (Apr. 1915) to Volume 3 (Oct. 1917): QUAR-
TERLY JOURNAL OF PUBLIC SPEAKING

From Volume 4 (Jan. 1918) to Volume 13 (Nov. 1927): QUAR-
TERLY JOURNAL OF SPEECH EDUCATION

From Volume 14 (Feb. 1928) to Present: QUARTERLY JOUR-
NAL OF SPEECH

COMMUNICATION MONOGRAPHS

From Volume 1 (1953) to Volume 42 (Nov. 1975): SPEECH
MONOGRAPHS

From Volume 43 (Mar. 1976) to Present: COMMUNICATION
MONOGRAPHS

SOUTHERN SPEECH COMMUNICATION JOURNAL

From Volume 1 (Oct. 1935) to Volume 7 (Mar. 1942): SOUTH-
ERN SPEECH BULLETIN

From Volume 8 (Sept. 1942) to Volume 36 (Summer 1971):
SOUTHERN SPEECH JOURNAL

From Volume 37 (Fall 1971) to Present: SOUTHERN SPEECH
COMMUNICATION JOURNAL

WESTERN JOURNAL OF SPEECH COMMUNICATION

From Volume 1 (Mar. 1937) to Volume 39 (Summer 1975):
WESTERN SPEECH

From Volume 39 (Spring 1975) to Volume 40 (Fall 1976):
WESTERN SPEECH COMMUNICATION

From Volume 41 (Winter 1977) to Present: WESTERN JOURNAL
OF SPEECH COMMUNICATION

CENTRAL STATES SPEECH JOURNAL

From Volume 1 (Nov. 1949) to Present: CENTRAL STATES
SPEECH JOURNAL

COMMUNICATION QUARTERLY

From Volume 1 (Apr. 1953) to Volume 23 (Fall 1975): TODAY'S
SPEECH

From Volume 24 (Winter 1976) to Present: COMMUNICATION QUARTERLY

COMMUNICATION EDUCATION

From Volume 1 (Jan. 1952) to Volume 24 (Nov. 1975): SPEECH TEACHER

From Volume 25 (Jan. 1976) to Present: COMMUNICATION EDUCATION

JOURNAL OF THE AMERICAN FORENSICS ASSOCIATION

From Volume 1 (Jan. 1964) to Present: JOURNAL OF THE AMERICAN FORENSICS ASSOCIATION

ORAL INTERPRETATION BIBLIOGRAPHY

BOOKS

1700-1799

1 Mason, John. Essays on Poetical and Prosaic Numbers and
   Elocution. London: Buckland and Waugh, 1761.

2 Scott, William. Lessons in Elocution. Phila: W. Young,
   1796.

3 Enfield, William. The Speaker. Hudson, NY: Ashbel Stoddard,
   1798.

1800-1899

4 Kirkham, Samuel. An Essay on Elocution. Baltimore: J. E.
   Woods, 1834.

5 Bronson, C. P. Elocution: Or Mental and Vocal Philosophy.
   Louisville: Morton & Griswold, 1845.

6 Mandeville, Henry. The Elements of Reading and Oratory.
   NY: D. Appleton, 1850.

7 Logoure, Ernest. Art of Reading. Phila: Claxton, 1879.

8 Vance, J. J. The Philosophy of Emphasis. Baltimore: J. B.
   Piet, 1881.

9 Ross, W. T. Voice Culture and Elocution. NY: Baker Pub.
   Co. , 1890.

10 Kimball, M. P. B. Textbook of Elocution. Boston: Leach,
   1892.

11 Corson, Hiram. The Voice and Spiritual Education. London:
   Macmillan, 1896.

1

12 Curry, S. S. Imagination and Dramatic Instinct. Boston: Expression Co. , 1896.

13 Chamberlain, W. B. Principles of Vocal Expression. Chicago: Scott-Foresman, 1897.

1901

14 Mitchell, W. B. School and College Speaker. NY: Holt-Rinehart.

1902

15 Lee, G. C. Principles of Public Speaking. 2nd ed. NY: Putnam.

1905

16 Breare, W. H. Elocution: Its First Principles. London: n. p.

17 Gott, John. Reading: An Address.... London: Christian Knowledge Society.

18 Hasluck, A. Elocution and Gesture. n. p. : Methuen Pub. Co.

1906

19 Flint, MacHenry. Natural Elocution in Speech and Song. Edinburgh: Blackie and Son.

20 Palmer, Erastus, & L. W. Sammis. The Principles of Oral English. NY: Macmillan.

1907

21 Curry, S. S. The Province of Expression. Magnolia, Mass: Expression Co.

1908

22 Everts, K. J. The Speaking Voice. NY: Harper.

23 Hasluck, S. L. The Elements of Elocution and Gesture. London: Simkin and Marshall.

1909

24　Burrell, A. E.　Clear Speaking and Good Reading.　London: Longman's and Co.

25　Forsyth, J.　Forsyth's Elocution:　Select Readings and Recitations.　Paisley, n. p. :　A. Gardner.

26　Phillips, A. E.　Natural Drills in Expression.　Chicago:　The Newton Co.

1910

27　Curry, S. S.　Foundations of Expression.　Magnolia, Mass: Expression Co.

1911

28　Betts, G. A.　Recitation.　NY:　Houghton Mifflin.

29　Bolenius, E. M.　Teaching of Oral English.　Phila:　J. B. Lippincott.

30　Brown, I. H.　Standard Elocution.　Chicago:　Laird and Co.

31　Editors.　Century Series of Readings, Recitations and Dialogs. 5 vols.　Lebanon:　March Bros.

32　Everts, K. J.　Vocal Expression.　NY:　Harper & Brothers.

33　Gib, C.　Vocal Science and Art.　NY:　Chas. Scribner's Sons.

34　Gordon, H. E.　Vocal Expression in Speech.　Chicago:　Ginn & Co.

35　Kirton, J. W. , ed.　Standard Comic Reciter.　NY:　Platt & Peck Co.

36　Kirton, J. W. , ed.　Standard Popular Reciter.　NY:　Platt & Peck Co.

37　Kleiser, G.　How to Read and Declaim.　NY:　Funk & Wagnalls Co.

38　Knowles, A.　Oral English.　NY:　D. C. Heath.

39　Lawrence, E. G.　Lawrence Reader and Speaker.　Chicago: A. C. McClurg & Co.

40　Mackay, F. F.　Vocal Gymnastic.　NY:　F. F. Mackay.

41 March, G. O., ed. With Trumpet and Drum. Lebanon: March Bros.

42 March, G. O., comp. Worthwhile Pieces. Lebanon: March Bros.

43 Minshall, E. Handbook of Elocution. London: Murray Br Mus 011805 DF.

44 Powers, L. T. Practice Book 4th ed. Boston: Leland Powers School.

45 Vickers, G. M. Book of Selection for Home and School Entertainment. Phila: National Pub. Co.

1912

46 Bissell, K. L. Practical Lessons in Voice Training and Reading. NY: Devinne.

47 Curry, S. S. Little Classic, with Initiative Steps in Vocal Training for Oral English. Boston: Expression Co.

48 Edgerly, M. Edgerly Natural Reader, Speaker and Conversationalist. Hopewell: Ralston Co.

49 Fenno, F. H. Art of Rendering. NY: R. F. Fenno & Co.

50 Foster, J. E. Ten Lessons in Elocution. Washington: Durham.

51 Marsland, C. Interpretive Reading. NY: Longmans, Green & Co.

52 Rogers, C. K. English Diction for Singers and Speakers. London: G. G. Harrap.

1913

53 Bagley, L., & G. Goodes. The Student's Elocution Book. London: Simkin & Marshall.

54 Biddle, E. F. Fifty Practical Lessons in Reading and Public Speaking. Phila: E. F. Biddle.

55 Cumnock, R. M., ed. Choice Readings for Public and Private Entertainments, with Elocutionary Advice. Chicago: A. C. McClurg & Co.

56 Curry, S. S. Spoken English. Boston: Expression Co.

57 Dickens, C. Dickens Reciter. NY: E. P. Dutton.

58 Emerson, C. W. Evolution of Expression. 29th ed. 4 vol.
Boston: Emerson College of Oratory Pub.

59 Jennings, H. Everybody's Guide to Art of Public Speaking and
Elocution. London: Brindley & Howe. Br Mus 11805 A
40.

60 Noyes, E. C., comp. Basic Principles in Oral English. Vol. 1.
Boston: E. C. Noyes Sym. Chamber.

61 Powers, L. T., ed. Practice Book, Leland Powers School.
Boston: Groom & Co.

62 Williams, P. Elements of Expression, Vocal and Physical.
3rd ed. Atchison: St. Benedict's Col.

1915

63 Brewer, J. Oral English. Chicago: Ginn & Co.

64 Clark, S. H. Interpretation of the Printed Page. NY: Row,
Peterson.

65 Curry, S. S. Smile. Boston: Boston Sch. of Expression.

66 Graves, A. P. & G. P., eds. Reciter's Treasury of Irish
Verse and Prose. NY: E. P. Dutton.

67 Winter, I. L. Public Speaking: Principle and Practice Rev.
NY: Macmillan.

1916

68 Brewer, J. M. Oral English: Directions and Exercises.
Boston: n. p. Br Mus 011805 FF 23.

69 Kerfoot, J. B. How to Read. Boston: Houghton Mifflin.

70 Lewis, C. L. A Handbook of American Speech. Chicago:
Scott-Foresman.

71 Morse, E. Principles of Expression. St. Louis: Morse Sch.
of Expression.

72 Powers, L. T. Fundamentals of Expression. 2nd ed. Boston: Groom & Co.

73 Powers, L. T., ed. Practice Book. Boston: Groom & Co.

1917

74 Bassett, L. E. Handbook of Oral Reading. Boston: Houghton Mifflin Co.

75 McCale, F., comp. Pieces That Have Won Prizes. Chicago: G. W. Noble.

76 Phillips, A. E. Natural Drills in Expression with Selections. Chicago: Newton Co.

77 Powers, L. T. Talks on Expression. Boston: T. Groom & Co.

78 Shurter, E. D., ed. Winning Declamations and How to Speak Them. Chicago: G. W. Noble.

79 Winans, J. A. Public Speaking. NY: Century.

1918

80 Andrews, C. E. Writing and Reading of Verse. Chicago: Daniel Appleton & Co.

81 Barthel, D. The Student's Class Book of Elocution. St. Meinrad, Ind: St. Meinrad's Abbey.

82 Case, C. B., comp. Wartime and Patriotic Selections for Recitation and Reading. Chicago: Shrewsbury Publis. Co.

83 Clapp, J. M. Reading: War-Time Suggestions. Charleston, Ill: East. Ill. St. Norman Sch.

84 Jones, E. D., comp. Patriotic Pieces from the Great War. Phila: Penn Pub. Co.

85 Norlie, O. M. Principles of Expressive Reading. Boston: Gorham Press.

86 Pelsma, J. R. Oral Reading and Public Speaking. Boston: Gorham Press.

87 Shurter, E. D. Oral English and Public Speaking. Chicago: Row, Peterson, & Co.

88 Shurter, E. D. Patriotic Selections for Supplementary Reading. NY: L. A. Noble.

89 Wilson, A. J. Emphasis in the Book of Common Prayer: An Essay in Elocution. London: n. p. Br Mus 011805 E 63.

1919

90   Bolenius, E. M.   Teacher's Manual of Silent and Oral Read-
     ing.   Boston: Houghton Mifflin Co.

91   Brown, G. J.   The Art of Reading in Public.   Edinburgh:
     n. p.   Br Mus 011805 H 7.

92   Faxon, G. B. , ed.   Pieces and Plays for Special Days.
     Danville, NY: F. A. Owen Pub. Co.

93   Haas, F. B. , comp.   Standard Selections for Declamation.
     Phila: Franklin Pub. Co.

94   Hunter, A.   A Guide to Eloquence and Acting.   London: C.
     Gorley.   Br Mus 011805 E 52.

95   Kinzie, R.   The Speech-Reading Club of Philadelphia.   Wash. ,
     DC: Volta Bureau.

96   McHale, F.   Pieces That Have Won Prizes in Speaking Con-
     tests.   Boston: L. A. Noble.

97   Miles, H.   The Colonial Elocutionist and Reciter.   Cape
     Town: n. p.   Br Mus 011805 C 63.

1920

98   Bolenius, E. M.   The Teaching of Oral English.   3rd ed.
     Phila: J. B. Lippincott Co.

99   Gilbert, E. C.   Social Recitations.   Chicago: E. C. Gilbert.

100 Johnson, G. E.   Modern Literature for Oral Interpretation.
     NY: Century Co.

101 Norris, H. J.   Popular Recitations.   Chicago: Regan Pub.
     Corp.

102 Shurter, E. D.   New Patriotic Selections for Reading and
     Speaking.   Boston: L. A. Noble.

1921

103 Deming, N. H. , & K. I. Bemis, eds.   Pieces for Every Day
     the Schools Celebrate.   NY: L. A. Noble.

104 Faxon, G. B.   Popular Recitations and How to Recite Them.
     Chicago: Hall & McCreary.

105 Hare, W. B.   Brand New Monologues and Readings in Prose and Verse.   Boston: Walter H. Baker & Co.

106 Hare, W. B.   Readings and Monologues a la mode.   NY: T. S. Denison & Co.

107 Hatch, R. H.   Robert H. Hatch's Recitals.   NY: E. S. Werner & Co.

108 Hilliard, E.   Elements of Elocution.   2nd ed.   n. p.:   E. Hilliard.

109 Lysnes, O.   Select Readings and Recitations.   2nd ed.   Minneapolis: Augsburg Pub. Co.

110 Shurter, E. D., ed.   Selections of American Citizenship. Austin: Univ. of Texas.

111 Tobin, B. I.   Recitations, Drills and Plays for Children. Boston: Walter H. Baker & Co.

1922

112 Fogerty, E.   The Speaking of English Verse.   NY: E. P. Dutton & Co.

113 Johnson, G. E.   Dialects for Oral Interpretation.   NY: Century Co.

114 Mathay, J.   The Art of the Spoken Word.   Glasgow Festival Booklets.   BR Mus WP 7603/12.

115 Pearson, P. M.   Practical Uses of Literature.   Chicago: La Salle Ext Univ.

116 Stone, C. R.   Silent and Oral Reading.   NY: Houghton Mifflin Co.

117 Tallcott, R. A.   The Art of Acting and Public Reading.   NY: Bobbs-Merrill Co.

118 Tallcott, R. A.   The Art of Acting and Public Reading. Indianapolis: n. p.   Br Mus 011795 A 45.

1923

119 Cowan, Milton.   Pitch and Intensity Characteristics of Stage Speech.   Iowa City: n. p.   Br Mus 20031 K 3.

120 Cumnock, R. M., ed.   Choice Readings for Public and Private Entertainment and for the Use of Schools, Colleges,

and Public Readers: With Elocutionary Advice. Chicago: A. C. McClurg & Co.

121 Hopps, M. The Spoken Word on Stage and Platform. London: U. of London Press.

122 Tassin, Algernon. The Oral Study of Literature. NY: Alfred A. Knopf.

1924

123 Arnold, J. G. Pieces with Pep. Harrisburg: Handy Book Corp.

124 Baldwin, C. S. Ancient Rhetoric and Poetic. Boston: Houghton Mifflin.

125 Burt, E. R., ed. The Speaker and Recitations for All Occasions. NY: E. J. Globe.

126 Cumnock, R. M. Cumnock's School Speaker: Rhetorical Recitations for Boys and Girls. Rev. ed. Chicago: A. C. McClurg & Co.

127 Gaige, G., comp. Recitations Old and New, for Boys and Girls. NY: Appleton.

128 Lovejoy, M. I., & E. Adams, comps. Pieces for Every Month of the Year. Boston: L. A. Noble.

129 Pertwee, E. G., comp. Reciter's Treasury of Verse. Rev. ed. NY: E. P. Dutton & Co.

130 Shriner, S. V., comp. Sara Shriner's Selections. Phila: Penn Pub. Co.

1925

131 Campbell, J. A., ed. Songs, Stories, Recitations Given at the Clover Club. Chicago: Nickerson & Collins Co.

132 Drummond, A. M., ed. A Course of Study in Speech Training and Public Speaking for Secondary Schools. NY: Century.

133 Morley, J. Practical Elocution. England: Dunbar. Br Mus 11795 DF 16.

134 Tassin, Algernon. The Oral Study of Literature. 2nd ed. NY: Alfred A. Knopf.

<u>1926</u>

135 Baswell, G. T. The Place of Oral Reading in the Elementary
School. Improvement in the Teaching of Reading. Bureau
of Research Monograph I. Baltimore: Dept. of Educ.

136 Burrell, Arthur. Clear Speaking and Group Reading. London: Longmans.

137 Crandell, I. J. Voice and Gesture, with Selections for
Dramatic Reading. Chicago: The Dramatic Pub. Co.

138 Johnson, G. E., comp. Modern Literature for Oral Interpretation. NY: Century Co.

139 Johnson, G. E. Modern Literature for Oral Interpretation,
A Practice Book for Vocal Expression. NY & London:
Century Co.

140 Lanham, C. B. Monologues, Skits and Sketches--Dramatic
Readings. Kansas City: O. D. Burton.

141 Smith, W. P. Oral English for Secondary Schools. NY:
Macmillan.

<u>1927</u>

142 Adams, F. A., & E. McCarrick, comps. Highdays and
Holidays. NY: E. P. Dutton & Co.

143 Barthel, D. Student's Class Book of Elocution. 2nd ed.
St. Meinrad, Ind: St. Meinrad Abbey Press.

144 Blackstone, H., comp. New Pieces That Will Take Prizes
in Speaking Contests. Chicago: G. W. Noble.

145 Curry, S. S. Foundations of Expression: Studies and Problems for Developing the Voice, Body, and Mind in Reading
and Speaking. Boston: The Expression Co.

146 Curry, S. S. Lessons in Vocal Expression. Course 1:
Processes of Thinking in the Modulation of the Voice.
28th ed. Boston: The Expression Co.

147 Curry, S. S. The Province of Expression: A Search for
Principles Underlying Adequate Methods of Developing
Dramatic and Oratoric Delivery. New ed. Boston: The
Expression Co.

148 Dunlop, Knight. The Role of Eye-Muscles and Mouth-Muscles
in the Expression of the Emotions. Worcester, Mass:
Clark Univ.

149 Gaige, C., comp. & ed. Recitations for Younger Children. Chicago: Daniel Appleton & Co.

150 Le Row, C. B., comp. Pieces for Every Occasion. Chicago: G. W. Noble.

151 O'Neill, R. M. The Science and Art of Speech and Gesture. London: Daniel. Br Mus 011805 I 21.

152 Patry, R. I. Elocution for Teachers and Students. London: Allen and Unwin. Br Mus 011805 G 72.

153 Shurter, E. D., & D. E. Watkins, comps. & eds. Poems for Oral Interpretation. Chicago: G. W. Noble.

154 Whitaker, L. C. Spoken Thought: A Textbook on Vocal Expression for Use in High Schools, Normal Schools and Colleges. NY: A. S. Barnes & Co.

155 Woolbert, C. H. The Fundamentals of Speech: A Text Book on Delivery, with a Section on Speech Composition and Interpretative Reading. Rev. ed. NY & London: Harper & Brothers.

156 Woolbert, C. H., & S. E. Nelson. Art of Interpretative Speech. NY: Appleton-Century-Crofts.

1928

157 Ahrens, G., & B. R. Ford. Original Monologues and Recitations. Chicago: Fitzgerald Book Co.

158 Anonymous. Oxford Recitations. NY: Macmillan Co.

159 Avery, Elizabeth; Jane Dorsey; Vera Sickels. First Principles of Speech Training. NY: D. Appleton.

160 Burrell, Arthur. Clear Speaking and Good Reading. New ed. London: Longmans.

161 Cretcher, J. R. Michigan High School Declaimer. Lansing: Hallenbeck Co.

162 Curry, S. S. Foundations of Expression: Studies and Problems for Developing the Voice, Body and Mind in Reading and Speaking. New ed. Boston: The Expression Co.

163 Griscom, A. B., comp. Peace Crusaders. Phila: J. B. Lippincott Co.

164 Lowe, C. E. Cyclopaedic Handbook for Elocution and Literary Students. London: J. Williams. Br Mus 011805 K 20.

165 Maclure, V. The Practical Elocution Book. London: Harrap. Br Mus 011805 L 31.

166 Morgan, Anna, comp. Selected Readings, Designed to Impart to the Student an Appreciation of Literature in Its Wider Sense. 9th ed. Chicago: A. C. McClurg & Co.

167 Ridley, F. A Manual of Elocution for Teacher and Student. London: French. Br Mus 011805 H 64.

1929

168 Cumnock, R. M., comp. Choice Readings for Public and Private Entertainments and for Use in Schools, Colleges and Public Readers, with Elocutionary Advice. New & definitive ed. Chicago: A. C. McClurg & Co.

169 Drew, Alfred, & Barry Robinson. A Commentary on Prose and Verse Speaking: An Introduction to Technique. London: G. G. Harrap & Co.

170 Hollister, R. D., ed. Literature for Oral Interpretation. Ann Arbor: G. Wahr.

171 Hollister, R. D., ed. Literature for Oral Interpretation, with an Introduction and Notes. Ann Arbor: G. Wahr.

172 Lovejoy, M. I., & E. Adams, comps. Pieces for Every Month of the Year. Enlarg. ed. Chicago: G. W. Noble.

173 McCollum, E. M. Pieces and Plays for All Ages. NY: E. S. Werner & Co.

174 Southwick, J. Progressive Voice Culture, Including the Emerson System. Boston: Expression Co.

175 Tassin, Algernon. The Oral Study of Literature. 3rd rev. ed. NY: A. A. Knopf.

176 Tickell, S. P. Histrionics: The Simple Laws of Variation of Pitch in Speaking Discovered. London: Cirencester. Br Mus 011805 E 89.

1930

177 Babcock, M. M. Handbook for Teachers of Interpretation: A Textbook for Teachers and for Prospective Teachers of Oral Expression in High Schools and Colleges. NY: The University Pub. Co.

178 Babcock, M. M. Interpretative Selections for Colleges. NY: University Pub. Co.

179 Babcock, M. M. Interpretative Selections for Colleges, Each
    with a Basic Purpose. NY: University Pub. Co.

180 Babcock, M. M. Interpretative Selections for High Schools.
    NY: University Pub. Co.

181 Babcock, M. M. Interpretative Selections for High Schools:
    An Aim for Every Selection, Every Selection with an Aim.
    NY: University Pub. Co.

182 Curry, S. S. Foundations of Expression: Studies and Prob-
    lems for Developing the Voice, Body, and Mind in Reading
    and Speaking. New ed. Boston: The Expression Co.

183 Day, S. Favorite Characterizations. Chicago: Means &
    McLean.

184 Farma, W. J., ed. Prose, Poetry and Drama for Oral In-
    terpretation. NY: Harper & Brothers.

185 Gullan, M., and P. Gurrey. Poetry Speaking for Children.
    London: Methuen.

186 Hartley, H. W. Tests of the Interpretative Reading of Poetry
    for Teachers of English. NY: Columbia Univ.

187 Hollister, R. D. Modern Literature for Oral Interpretation.
    Rev. ed. NY & London: Century Co.

188 McHale, F. C., comp. Pieces That Have Won Prizes.
    Enlarg. ed. Chicago: G. W. Noble.

189 Patry, R. I. A Practical Handbook on Elocution. London:
    Allen and Unwin.

190 Southwick, J. Emerson Philosophy of Expression. Boston:
    Expression Co.

191 Southwick, J. The Emerson Philosophy of Expression: An
    Application to Character Education. Boston: Expression
    Co.

192 Stanistreet, G. M., ed. Recitations for Children. Phila:
    Penn Pub. Co.

193 Tanquay, D. M., et al. Best Pieces to Recite. Franklin,
    Ohio: Eldridge Entertainment House Inc.

194 Tassin, Algernon. The Oral Study of Literature. 4th ed.
    NY: A. A. Knopf.

1931

195 Deming, N. G. , & K. I. Bemis. Pieces for Every Day the
    Schools Celebrate. Enlarg. ed. Chicago: G. W. Noble.

196 Griffiths, W. H. Daily Studies in Speaking and Reading.
    London: Paxton.

197 Gullan, M. Choral Speaking. London: Methuen & Co.

198 Lanz, Henry. The Physical Basis of Rime: Essay on Aes-
    thetics of Sound. Calif: Stanford U. Press.

199 Kanner, L. Judging Emotions from Facial Expressions.
    Princeton, NJ & Albany, NY: Psychological Review Co.

200 Keppie, E. E. The Teaching of Choric Speech. Boston:
    The Expression Co.

201 Molins, W. J. El Expresionismo Americanista. Buenos
    Aires: L. J. Rosso.

202 Winans, J. A. , & H. H. Hudson. A First Course in Public
    Speaking, with Debating and Public Reading. NY & Lon-
    don: Century Co.

1932

203 Brown, H. The Essentials of Reading and Speaking. Boston:
    Rand Avery Supply Co.

204 Cecil, M. Breezy Episodes. NY: Samuel French.

205 Mulroy, M. D. The Improvement of Reading Through an
    Analysis of Errors in Oral Reading. Chicago: U. of
    Chicago.

206 Parrish, W. M. Reading Aloud: A Technique in the Inter-
    pretation of Literature. NY: Thomas Nelson & Sons.

207 Stevenson, B. E. , & E. S. Stevenson, comps. Days and
    Deeds. New ed. rev. and enlarged. Garden City, NY:
    Doubleday, Page & Co.

208 Tallcott, R. A. People We've Met. Chicago: Dramatic
    Pub. Co.

1933

209 Blake, W. H. Preliminary Study of the Interpretation of
    Bodily Expression. NY: Columbia Univ.

210 Bowman, C. Critique of the Curry Principles of Training in Expression. Boston: Expression Co.

211 Hopps, M. Spoken Word: On Stage and Platform. London: Univ. of London Press.

212 Johnson, G. E. Dialects for Oral Interpretation. NY: Century.

213 Tickell, S. P. Speech and Movement: Corporal, Facial and Vocal Expression. London: Swindon Co. Br Mus 11804 DE 32.

1934

214 Anonymous. Werner's Readings and Recitations. NY: E. S. Werner & Co.

215 Bernard, J. Dramatic Recitals and How to Deliver Them. NY: Pitman.

216 Swann, Mona. Approach to Choral Speech. Boston: Expression Co.

217 Woolbert, C. H., & S. E. Nelson. Art of Interpretative Speech: Principles and Practices of Effective Reading. 2nd ed. NY: Appleton-Century-Crofts.

1935

218 Davis, E. H., & E. W. Mammen. The Spoken Word in Life and Art. Englewood Cliffs, NJ: Prentice-Hall.

219 Fuller, H. H., & A. T. Weaver. How to Read Aloud. n. p. : Silver.

220 Hamm, A. C., comp. Selections for Choral Speaking. Boston: Expression Co.

1936

221 Burns, D. T. Principles of Oral Interpretation. Boston: Expression Co.

222 Burns, D. T. Principles of Oral Interpretation: With Selections Old and New. Boston: Expression Co.

223 Dewitt, M. E. Dramaticules for Choric Recitation with Group Movement. Boston: Expression Co.

224 Dewitt, M. E., et al. Practical Methods in Choral Speaking.
Boston: Expression Co.

225 Farma, W. J., ed. Prose Poetry and Drama for Oral Interpretation. 2nd series. NY: Harper.

226 Gullan, M. Choral Speaking. 3rd rev. ed. Boston: Expression Co.

227 McLean, M. P. Oral Interpretation of Forms of Literature.
NY: E. P. Dutton.

228 Parrish, W. M. Reading Aloud: Technique in Interpretation
of Literature. NY: P. Dutton.

229 Robinson, M. P., & R. L. Thurston. Poetry Arranged for
the Speaking Choir. Boston: Expression Co.

230 Santayana, George. The Interpretation of Poetry. NY:
Charles Scribner's.

1937

231 Barksdale, E. C. Art and Science of Speech. n.p.: Naylor.

232 Craig, A. E. Speech Arts. Rev. ed. NY: Macmillan.

233 De Banke, Cecile. The Art of Choral Speaking. Boston:
Baker.

234 Edmonds, Paul. Essentials of Voice Technique: With Notes
on the Art of Speaking Verse and the Value of Elocution.
London: A. Hammond & Co.

235 Enfield, G. Verse Choir Values and Technique. Boston:
Expression Co.

236 Gough, H. B. Effective Speech: Complete Course. NY:
Harper & Brothers.

237 Gullan, M. Speech Choir. NY: Harper.

238 Gullan, M., & P. Gurry. Poetry Speaking for Children.
Boston: Expression Co.

239 Haney, G., ed. Declamatory Contest Readings. Evanston,
Ill: Northwestern Press.

240 Nichols, W. B. Speaking Poetry. London: Methuen.

241 Schoolfield, L. D. Better Speech and Better Reading. Boston: Expression Co.

1938

242 Newton, M. B. Unit Plan for Choral Reading. Boston: Expression Co.

243 Quaife, E. W. Oral Readings for Moderns. V. 1 & 2.
NY: Samuel French. (V. 3: 1940)

244 Runsey, H. St. James. Clear Speech for Stage, Platform
and Pulpit. London: F. Muller. Br Mus 11806 A 1.

245 Smith, M. Wings to Fly. Boston: Expression Co.

1939

246 Bates, G. D., & K. H. Bates. Literature for Interpretation.
Boston: Expression Co.

247 Body, A. H. The Music of Poetry. n. p. : Nelson's Music
Practice. Br Mus W. D. 5253-8.

248 Hicks, H. G., ed. Reading Chorus. NY: Noble.

249 Keppie, E. E. Choral Verse Speaking. Boston: Expression
Co.

250 Robinson, M. P., & R. L. Thurston. Poetry for Men to
Speak Chorally. Boston: Expression Co.

251 Robinson, M. P., & R. L. Thurston. Poetry for Women to
Speak Chorally. Boston: Expression Co.

252 Shipherd, M. M., & M. L. Rasmussen. Fundamentals of
Choric Arts. NY: Lyon & Healy Inc.

253 Smith, J. H. Reading of Poetry. Boston: Houghton Mifflin.

254 Tassin, Algernon. The Oral Study of Literature. 5th ed.
rev. NY: Alfred Knopf.

1940

255 Ashmun, H. E. Effective Public Reading. Englewood
Cliffs, NJ: Prentice-Hall.

256 Clark, S. H. Interpretation of the Printed Page. Rev. ed.
Englewood Cliffs, NJ: Prentice-Hall.

257 Gullan, M., & C. Sansom, comps. Poet Speaks Transatlantic.
London: Methuen.

258 Hollister, R. D. Literature for Oral Interpretation. Ann
Arbor: George Wahr.

259 Johnson, G. E. , ed. Studies in the Art of Interpretation.
NY: Appleton-Century.

260 Johnson, O. M. , ed. New Declamations for Seniors, Jun-
iors, and Sub-Juniors. NY: Upshaw.

1941

261 Cunningham, C. C. Literature as a Fine Art. NY: Thomas
Nelson & Sons.

262 Daniels, E. R. Art of Reading Poetry. NY: Farrar &
Rinehart.

263 Hamm, A. C. Choral Speaking Technique. Milwaukee:
Tower Press.

264 Lucus, H. M. , ed. Prose and Poetry of Today. NY: Singer.

265 Lyon, James. Notes on Choral Speaking. Toronto: Clark,
Irwin & Co.

266 Parrish, W. M. Reading Aloud. 2nd rev. ed. NY: Ronald
Press Co.

267 Robb, M. M. Oral Interpretation of Literature in American
Colleges and Universities. NY: H. W. Wilson.

1942

268 Blodgett, H. W. , & B. Johnson, eds. Readings for Our
Times. Boston: Ginn & Co.

269 Keefe, M. J. , ed. Choric Interludes. Boston: Expression
Co.

270 Keppie, E. E. , et al. Speech Improvement Through Choral
Speaking. Boston: Expression Co.

271 Lowrey, Sara, & G. E. Johnson. Interpretative Reading.
NY: Appleton-Century.

272 Sawyer, Ruth. The Way of the Storyteller. NY: Viking
Press.

1943

273 Cole, Wilton. Sound and Sense: A Handbook on Elocution.
London: George Allen.

274 Esdaile, Ernest. The Art of Speaking for Young People.
     London: Quality Press.

275 Hyatt, A. V. Place of Oral Reading in the School Program.
     NY: Columbia Univ.

276 Sergeant, F. I. Stepping Stones: Verse Speaking for Chil-
     dren Under Eight Years of Age. Glasgow: Blackie &
     Son, Br Mus 118068A.

1944

277 Hoffman, W. G., & R. L. Rogers. Effective Radio Speaking.
     NY: McGraw-Hill.

278 Schory, H. F. America Speaks. Danville, Ill: The Inter-
     state.

279 Seligman, M., & S. Fogle, eds. More Solo Readings for
     Radio and Class Work. NY: Dramatists Play Service,
     Inc.

1945

280 Anonymous. Fun with Poetry. Chicago: Scott, Foresman &
     Co.

281 Anonymous. Place of Oral Reading in the School Program
     1880-1941. NY: Teacher's Col.: Rpt.: NY: AMS
     Press.

282 Benson, H. M., comp. Choral Readings. Rock Island, Ill:
     Augustana Book Concern.

283 Blair, Walter, & J. C. Gerber. Better Reading. Chicago:
     Scott, Foresman & Co.

284 Brent, G. First Lessons in Elocution. London: G. G.
     Harrap & Co.

285 Bugbee, W. N. In Many Moods and Meters. NY: W. N.
     Bugbee Co.

286 Corp, G. M. Choral Speaking. Rev. ed. Milwaukee: Univ.
     of Wisconsin Ext. Div.

287 Drew, A., & Barry Robinson. Commentary on Prose and
     Verse Speaking. Boston: W. H. Baker Co.

288 Esdaile, Ernest. Elocution, the Mint of the Mouth. Lon-
     don: Quality Press.

289 Hemphill, E. I., ed. Choral Speaking and Speech Improvement. Darien, Conn.: Educational Pub. Co.

290 Hollister, R. D. Speaking Before an Audience. Ann Arbor: Braun-Brumfield.

291 Thomas, Wright, & S. G. Brown. Reading Poems. NY: Oxford Univ. Press.

292 Wilson, W. A., comp. Selected Memory Gems. NY: Bardeen's Inc.

293 Woolbert, C. H., & S. E. Nelson. The Art of Interpretative Speech. NY: Appleton-Century-Crofts & Co.

1946

294 Anonymous. Recitation Time. Franklin, Ohio: Eldridge Entertainment House, Inc.

295 Clark, Elizabeth. Stories to Tell and How to Tell Them. London: Univ. of London.

296 Craig, A. E. Speech Arts. 2nd rev. ed. Toronto: Macmillan.

297 Fisher, A. S., ed. Voice and Verse. Cambridge, Toronto: Macmillan Co.

298 Hamm, A. C. Choral Speaking Technique. Rev. ed. Milwaukee: Tower Press.

299 Hardendeen, J. E. Speech Quality and Interpretation. NY: Harper & Brothers.

300 Swann, Mona. An Approach to Choral Speech. 3rd ed. London: Macmillan.

1947

301 Bernard, J. Twenty-Four Lessons in Elocution. 3rd ed. NY: Pitman Pub. Corp.

302 Boone, Lester, ed. New Declamations: Modern Short Speeches on Current Subjects for Class Study and Speaking Contests. NY: Noble & Noble.

303 Crocker, Lionel, & L. M. Eich. Oral Reading. NY: Prentice-Hall, Inc.

304 Mosier, R. D. Making the American Mind: Social and Moral Ideas in the McGuffey Readers. NY: King's Crown Press.

305 Owen, M. G. So You Don't Like Choral Reading: Monograph on Language Arts. n. p. : Row Peterson.

1948

306 Anonymous. Joy Bell's Reciter. London: Pickering & Inglis.

307 Buford, R. Speech and Drama. Toronto: S. J. Reginald Saunders and Co.

308 Furber, D. Favourites of the Stars. NY: Samuel French Inc.

309 Paterson, T. W. Choice Reading and Select Recitations. 2 vols. Edinburgh: Oliver & Boyd, 1948-1949.

310 Paterson, T. W. Scot's Recitations, Readings and Sketches. 1st & 2nd ser. Edinburgh: Oliver & Boyd, 1948-1949.

311 Pertwee, E. G. , comp. Anthology for Verse Speakers. NY: Samuel French Inc.

312 Philip, F. Manual of Elocution for the Ministry. NY: Charles Scribner's Sons.

1949

313 Anonymous. Seeds of Kindness Reciter. Glasgow: Pickering & Inglis Ltd.

314 Brown, H. A. , & H. J. Heltman, eds. Let's-Read-Together Poems. Evanston, Ill: Row Peterson & Co.

315 Compere, M. S. , ed. Living Literature for Oral Interpretation. NY: Appleton-Century-Crofts, Inc.

316 Harley, A. B. Five-Minute Recitations Reprint. Edinburgh: Oliver & Boyd.

317 Lamar, N. N. How to Speak the Written Word. NY: Fleming Revell Co.

318 Nichols, W. B. Speaking of Poetry. 2nd ed. London: Dennis Dobson Ltd.

319 Paterson, T. W. Recitations. Edinburgh: Oliver & Boyd.

320 Powers, L. T. Fundamentals of Expression. Boston: H. M. Powers.

321 Swann, Mona, ed. Many Voices. London: Macmillan.

322 White, A. M., ed. Anthology of Choral Readings. NY: Girl Scouts.

1950

323 Church, Richard, ed. Poems for Speaking. London: J. M. Dent and Sons Ltd.

324 Eberhart, W. L., et al. Reading-Literature. 3 vols. Evanston, Ill: Row Peterson & Co.

325 Hollister, R. D. Literature for Oral Interpretation. Ann Arbor: George Wahr.

326 Leavis, F. R. New Bearings in English Poetry. London: Chatto and Windus.

327 Millet, F. B. Reading Poetry. NY: Harper.

1951

328 Cunningham, C. C. Making Words Come Alive. Dubuque: W. C. Brown & Co.

329 Gullan, Thomas, & C. Sansom, eds. The Poet Speaks. London: Methuen & Co.

330 Hamm, A. C. Choral Speaking Technique. 3rd ed. Milwaukee: The Tower Press.

331 Rehner, H. A. Dramatic Use of Oral Interpretation. Chicago: Bruce-Howard Pub. Co.

1952

332 Stageberg, N. C., & W. L. Anderson. Poetry as Experience. NY: American Book Co.

1953

333 Abney, L., & G. Rowe. Choral Speaking Arrangements for the Lower Grades. Magnolia, Mass.: Expression Co.

334 Babington, W. G., & E. N. Brown, eds. The Choir Speaks: A Choral Speaking Anthology. London: Methuen and Co.

335 Crump, G. H. Speaking Poetry. London: Methuen and Co.

336 Lowrey, Sara, & G. E. Johnson. Interpretative Reading. 2nd ed. NY: Appleton-Century-Crofts.

337 Mouat, L. H. A Guide to Effective Public Speaking. Boston: Heath.

338 Parrish, W. M. Reading Aloud. 3rd ed. NY: Ronald Press.

339 Rasmussen, Carrie. Choral Speaking for Speech Improvement. Magnolia, Mass: Expression Co.

1954

340 Henneke, B. G. Reading Aloud Effectively. NY: Rinehart.

1955

341 Crocker, Lionel, & L. M. Eich. Oral Reading. 2nd ed. Englewood Cliffs, NJ: Prentice-Hall.

342 Editors. Conference on Reading: Oral Aspects of Reading. Chicago: Univ. of Chicago Press.

343 Gullan, Thomas, & P. Gurrey. Poetry Speaking for Children. 3rd ed. London: Methuen and Co.

344 Hedde, W. G. American Speech. Phila: Lippincott.

345 McBurney, J. H., & E. J. Wrange. The Art of Good Speech. Englewood Cliffs, NJ: Prentice-Hall.

346 Robinson, H. M. Oral Aspects of Reading. Chicago: U. of Chicago Press.

1956

347 Aggertt, O. J., & E. R. Bowen. Communicative Reading. NY: Macmillan Co.

348 Dolman, John. The Art of Reading Aloud. NY: Harpers.

349 Howell, W. S. Logic and Rhetoric in England 1500-1700. Princeton, NJ: Princeton Univ. Press.

350 Woolbert, C. H., & S. E. Nelson. Art of Interpretative Speech. 4th ed. NY: Appleton-Century-Crofts.

1957

351 Frye, Northrop, ed. Sound and Poetry. NY: Columbia U. Press.

352 Gullan, M. Choral Speaking. 7th ed. London: Methuen & Co.

353 La Driere, Craig. Structure, Sound and Meaning: Sound and Poetry. NY: Columbia U. Press.

354 Laughton, Charles. How to Tell a Story. NY: McGraw-Hill.

1958

355 Geiger, Don. Oral Interpretation and Literary Study. San Francisco: P. Van Vloten.

356 Horner, A. M. Spoken Words. London: Phoenix House Ltd.

1959

357 Abney, L. Choral Speaking Arrangements for the Junior High. Rev. ed. Boston: Expression Co.

358 Bacon, W. A., & R. S. Breen. Literature as Experience. NY: McGraw-Hill.

359 Cobin, M. T. Theory and Technique of Interpretation. Englewood Cliffs, NJ: Prentice-Hall.

360 Lee, C. I. Oral Interpretation. 2nd ed. Boston: Houghton Mifflin.

361 Lynch, Gladys, & H. C. Crain. Projects in Oral Interpretation. NY: Henry Holt and Co.

362 Okey, L. L., & V. J. Horkan. A Guide to Speech for High Schools. NY: Noble & Noble.

1960

363 Rowe, K. T. A Theatre in Your Head. NY: Funk & Wagnalls.

364 Smith, J. F., & J. R. Linn. Skill in Reading Aloud. NY: Harper & Row.

1961

365 Bacon, W. A., & R. S. Breen. Literature for Interpretation. NY: Holt Rinehart and Winston.

366 Booth, W. A. The Rhetoric of Fiction. Chicago: U. of Chicago Press.

367 Brown, H. A., & H. J. Heltman, eds. Read-Together Poems. NY: Harper & Row.

368 Grimes, W. H., & A. S. Mattingly. Interpretation: Writer, Reader, Audience. San Francisco: Wadsworth Pub.

369 Henneke, B. G. Reading Aloud Effectively. NY: Holt-Rinehart.

370 Natchez, Gladys. Personality Patterns and Oral Reading. NY: Reading Institute of NYU.

1962

371 Bennett, G. C. Readers Theatre Comes to Church. Richmond, Va: John Knox.

372 Berry, Francis. Poetry and the Physical Voice. London: Routledge and K. Paul. Rev. by T. O. Sloan in QJS 50 (Feb. 1964) 92.

373 Fitzgerald, Burdette. World Tales for Creative Dramatics and Story Telling. Englewood Cliffs, NJ: Prentice-Hall.

374 Mouat, L. H. Reading Literature Aloud. NY: Oxford.

375 Rasmussen, Carrie. Let's Say Poetry Together and Have Fun. Minneapolis: Burgess.

1963

376 Aggertt, O. J., & E. R. Bowen. Communicative Reading. 2nd ed. NY: Macmillan.

377 Armstrong, Chloe, & P. D. Brandes. The Oral Interpretation of Literature. NY: McGraw-Hill.

378 Coger, L. I., & M. R. White, eds. Studies in Readers Theatre. San Francisco: S & F Press. Anthology of previously published articles on R. T., Rev., Jere Veilleux, Spch Tchr 13 (Sept. 1964) 244.

379 Geiger, Don. The Sound, Sense, and Performance of Literature. Chicago: Scott, Foresman.

380 Willcox, I. Reading Aloud with Elementary School Children. n.p.: Teachers Practical Press.

1964

381 Bamman, H. A.; M. A. Dawson; & R. J. Whitehead. Oral Interpretation of Children's Literature. Dubuque, Iowa: W. C. Brown.

382 Barfield, Owen. Poetic Diction: A Study in Meaning. NY: McGraw-Hill.

383 Brack, H. A. Effective Oral Interpretation for Religious Leaders. Englewood Cliffs, NJ: Prentice-Hall.

384 Buys, W. E., et al., eds. Contest Speaking Manual. Lincolnwood, Ill: National Textbook Co.

385 Crump, G. H. Speaking Poetry. London: Dobson Books Ltd.

386 Gross, H. S. Sound and Form in Modern Poetry: A Study of Prosody from Thomas Hardy to Robert Lowell. Ann Arbor: U. Michigan Press.

387 Hibbit, G. W., & R. A. Norman. Guide to Speech Training: Voice, Articulation and Oral Reading. NY: Ronald Press.

388 Streeter, D. C. A Speech Handbook for Teachers. Englewood Cliffs, NJ: Prentice-Hall.

389 Thompson, D. W., & Virginia Fredericks. Oral Interpretation of Fiction: A Dramatistic Approach. Minneapolis: Burgess.

390 White, M. R. From the Printed Page: Interpretation Assignment Handbook. Brooklyn: S & F Press.

391 Wise, Arthur. Reading and Talking in English. London: G. G. Harrap & Co.

1965

392 Black, Edwin. Rhetorical Criticism: A Study in Method. NY: Macmillan.

393 Cobin, M. T. Humorous Dramatic Interpretation. Skokie, Ill: National Textbook.

394 Cobin, M. T. Serious Dramatic Interpretation. Skokie, Ill: National Textbook.

395 Lee, C. I. Oral Interpretation. 3rd ed. Boston: Houghton Mifflin.

<u>1966</u>

396 Bacon, W. A. The Art of Interpretation. NY: Holt, Rinehart, & Winston, Inc.

397 Beloof, R. L. The Performing Voice in Literature. Boston: Little, Brown, and Co.

398 Campbell, P. N. Oral Interpretation. NY: Macmillan & Co.

399 Geeting, B. M. Interpretation for Our Time. Dubuque: W. C. Brown Co.

400 Hill, K. C. Interpreting Literature: History, Drama, Fiction, Philosophy, Rhetoric. Chicago: Univ. of Chicago Press.

401 Parrish, W. M. Reading Aloud. 4th ed. NY: Ronald Press Co.

402 Robb, M. M., & Lester Thonssen, eds. Chironomia by Gilbert Austin. Carbondale: So. Ill. Univ. Press.

403 Sloan, T. O., ed. The Oral Study of Literature. NY: Random House.

404 Walters, D. N. The Reader: An Introduction to Oral Interpretation. NY: Odyssey Press.

<u>1967</u>

405 Anderson, T. V. The Elements of Oral Reading. NY: Vantage Press.

406 Bertram, J. D. The Oral Experience of Literature: Sense, Structure, and Sound. Chicago: Science Research Associates.

407 Brooks, Keith; Eugene Bahn; & L. L. Okey. The Communicative Act of Oral Interpretation. Boston: Allyn and Bacon.

408 Campbell, P. N. The Speaking and the Speakers of Literature. Belmont, Calif: Dickenson.

409 Coger, L. I., & M. R. White. Readers Theatre Handbook. Glenview, Ill: Scott, Foresman, and Co.

410 Geiger, Don. The Dramatic Impulse in Modern Poetics. Baton Rouge: LSU Press.

411 Henry, M. W., ed. Creative Experiences in Oral Language: A Symposium. Champaign, Ill: National Council of Teachers of English.

412 Hunsinger, Paul. Communicative Interpretation: Speech Communication Series. Dubuque, Iowa: W. C. Brown & Co.

413 Thompson, D. W., & Virginia Fredericks. Oral Interpretation of Fiction: A Dramatistic Approach. 2nd ed. Minneapolis: Burgess Pub. Co.

414 Veilleux, Jere. Oral Interpretation: The Recreation of Literature. NY: Harper & Row.

1968

415 Armstrong, Chloe. Oral Interpretation of Biblical Literature. Minneapolis: Burgess Pub. Co.

416 Brooks, Keith. Literature for Listening: An Oral Interpreter's Anthology. Boston: Allyn & Bacon.

417 Gray, J. W., ed. Perspectives on Oral Interpretation: Essays and Readings. Minneapolis: Burgess Pub. Co.

418 Hedde, W. G. New American Speech. 3rd ed. Philadelphia: Lippincott.

419 Holland, J. B., & V. D. Sessions. Oral Interpretation Drill Book. Boston: Holbrook Press.

420 Pagela, G. G.; W. G. Pinney; & R. D. Stiff. Reading and Interpreting. Belmont, Calif: Wadsworth Pub. Co.

421 Robb, M. M. Oral Interpretation of Literature in American Colleges and Universities. Rev. ed. NY: Johnson Reprint Corp.

422 Scrivner, L. M. A Guide to Oral Interpretation. NY: Odyssey Press.

423 Sessions, V. D., & J. B. Holland. Your Role in Interpretation. Boston: Holbrook Press.

424 Sheridan, Thomas. A Course of Lectures on Elocution. NY: B. Blom.

425 Woolbert, C. H., & S. E. Nelson. The Art of Interpretative Speech. 5th ed. NY: Appleton-Century-Crofts.

1969

426 Beck, R. A. Group Reading: Readers Theatre for Interscholastic Speech Contestants. Skokie, Ill: National
Textbook Co.

427 Daniels, E. R. The Art of Reading Poetry. Freeport, NY:
Books for Libraries Press.

428 Fernandez, T. L. , ed. Oral Interpretation and the Teaching
of English: A Collection of Readings. Champaign, Ill:
National Council of Teachers of English.

429 Mulcahy, Betty. To Speak True. Oxford: Pergamon Press.

1970

430 Bahn, Eugene, & M. L. Bahn. A History of Oral Interpretation. Minneapolis: Burgess Pub. Co.

431 Evans, G. E. Where Beards Wag All: Relevance of the
Oral Tradition. London: Faver.

432 Gullan, M. The Speech Choir: With American Poetry and
English Ballads for Choral Reading. Freeport, NY:
Books for Libraries Press.

433 Heston, L. A. , ed. Man in the Dramatic Mode (Books 1-6).
Evanston, Ill: McDougal Littel.

434 Mattingly, A. S. , & W. H. Grimes. Interpretation: Writer,
Reader, Audience. 2nd ed. Belmont, Calif: Wadsworth
Pub. Co.

435 Sloan, T. O. Rhetoric and the Interpretation of Poetry.
Bethesda, Md: ERIC/NCTE.

1971

436 Bamman, H. A. ; M. A. Dawson; & R. J. Whitehead. Oral
Interpretation of Children's Literature. 2nd ed. Dubuque:
W. C. Brown Co.

437 Lee, C. I. Oral Interpretation. 4th ed. Boston: Houghton
Mifflin.

438 Maclay, J. H. Readers Theatre: Toward a Grammar of
Practice. NY: Random House.

439 Parry, Adam, ed. The Making of Homeric Verse: The
Collected Papers of Milman Parry. Oxford: Clarendon
Press. Rev. by Lee Hudson in QJS 59 (Dec. 1973) 481.

440 Walker, John. A Rhetorical Grammar (Reprint of 1822 Edition). Menston, England: Scolar Press.

1972

441 Aggertt, O. J., & E. R. Bowen. Communicative Reading. 3rd ed. NY: Macmillan.

442 Anonymous. Oral Interpretation in the Secondary School. Skokie, Ill: National Textbook Co.

443 Bacon, W. A. The Art of Interpretation. 2nd ed. NY: Holt, Rinehart, and Winston.

444 Bennett, G. C. Readers Theatre Comes to Church. Richmond, Va: John Knox Press.

445 Campbell, P. N. Rhetoric-Ritual: A Study of the Communicative and Aesthetic Dimension of Language. Belmont, Calif: Dickenson.

446 Collins, P. A. Reading Aloud: A Victorian Metier. Lincoln, n. p. : Tennyson Research Center.

447 Doyle, E. M. , & V. H. Floyd, eds. Studies in Interpretation I. Amsterdam: Rodopi N. V.

448 Fish, S. E. Self-Consuming Artifacts: The Experience of 17th Century Literature. Berkeley: U. California Press. Rev. by T. O. Sloan in QJS 59 (Dec. 1973) 477.

449 Hartley, H. W. Tests of the Interpretative Reading of Poetry for Teachers of English. NY: A. M. S. Press.

450 Maclay, J. H. , & T. O. Sloan. Interpretation: An Approach to the Study of Literature. NY: Random House. Rev. by R. J. Koperski in QJS 59 (Dec. 1973) 482.

1973

451 Cayer, R. I. ; Elmer Baker; & Jerome Green. Listening and Speaking in the English Classroom: A Collection of Readings. NY: Macmillan.

452 Coger, L. I. , & M. R. White. Readers Theatre Handbook: A Dramatic Approach to Literature. Rev. ed. Glenview, Ill: Scott Foresman.

453 Friedrich, G. W. , & W. D. Brooks. Teaching Speech Communication in the Secondary School. Boston: Houghton Mifflin. Rev. by Jerry Butler in Sthn Spch Comm J 41 (Fall 1976) 86.

454 Newcobe, P. J., & J. S. Yeast, eds. Choose an Objective in Speech Communication. Vero Beach, Fla: Media Tronics. Rev. by L. H. Clayton in Sthn Spch Comm J 41 (Summer 1976) 413-4.

455 Roloff, L. H. The Perception and Evocation of Literature. Glenview, Ill: Scott Foresman. Rev. by J. E. Popovich in Sthn Spch Comm J 41 (Spring 1976) 320-1; and by J. W. Carlsen in QJS 59 (Dec. 1973) 482.

1974

456 Bernstein, Melvin. The Collected Works of James Rush. Weston, Mass: M and S Press. Rev. by Jerry Tarver in Sthn Spch Comm J 41 (Winter 1976) 203-4.

457 Burack, A. S., & B. A. Crossley, eds. Popular Plays for Classroom Reading. Boston: Plays, Inc.

458 Gilbert, C. A. The Communicative Performance of Literature. NY: Macmillan.

459 Lee, C. I. Oral Reading of the Scriptures. Boston: Houghton Mifflin. Rev. by J. D. Blanton in Sthn Spch Comm J 41 (Winter 1976) 205-6.

460 Long, C. C. The Liberal Art of Interpretation. NY: Harper & Row.

1975

461 Bacon, W. A. Oral Interpretation and the Teaching of Literature in Secondary Schools. Urbana, Ill: ERIC.

462 Beasley, Marty. In the Lost Eye of God: A Play for Readers Theatre with Notes on the Use of Readers Theatre in the Church. n. p. : Broadman.

463 Boynton, R. W., & M. Mack, comps. Sounds and Silences: Poems for Performing. n. p. : Hoyden Books.

464 Brooks, Keith; Eugene Bahn; & L. L. Okey. The Communicative Act of Oral Interpretation. 2nd ed. Boston: Allyn & Bacon.

465 Brown-Azarowicz, M. F. A Handbook of Creative Choral Speaking. Minneapolis: Burgess.

466 Haas, Richard, & D. A. Williams, eds. The Study of Oral Interpretation: Theory and Comment. Indianapolis: Bobbs-Merrill.

467   Pickering, J. V.   Readers Theatre.   Encino, Calif: Dicken-
        son Pub.

468   Sessions, V. D., & J. B. Holland.   Your Role in Oral Inter-
        pretation.   2nd ed.   n. p. :   Holbrook Press.

469   Vohs, J. L., & G. P. Mohrmann.   Audiences Messages
        Speakers: An Introduction to Human Communication.   NY:
        Harcourt Brace Jovanovich.   Rev. by D. W. Zacharias
        in Sthn   Spch   Comm   J 41 (Spring 1976) 316-7.

470   Wilkinson, C. A.; C. I. Lee; & Bud Beyer.   Speaking of ...
        Communication/Interpretation/Theatre.   Glenview, Ill:
        Scott Foresman.   Rev. by M. P. Metcalf in Sthn   Spch
        Comm   J 41 (Spring 1976) 318-20.

1976

471   Gamble, T. K., & M. W. Gamble.   Oral Interpretation: The
        Meeting of Self and Literature.   Skokie, Ill: National
        Textbook.

472   Haas, Richard, et al.   Theatres of Interpretation.   Ann Ar-
        bor, Mich: Robert-Burton.

473   Hopkins, M. F., & B. W. Long.   Contemporary Speech: A
        Comprehensive Guide to Communication.   Skokie, Ill:
        National Textbook.

474   Jaynes, Julian.   Origin of Consciousness in the Breakdown of
        the Bicameral Mind.   Boston: Houghton Mifflin.

475   Trotter, Judy.   Beyond Borrowed Bathrobes: Guide to Read-
        ers Theatre Including Two Scripts for Youth and Adults.
        Cincinnati: Standard Press.

1977

476   Cohen, Edwin.   Oral Interpretation: The Communication of
        Literature.   Chicago: Science Research Assc.

477   Doyle, E. M., & V. H. Floyd, eds.   Studies in Interpreta-
        tion II.   Amsterdam, Netherlands: Editions Rodopi N. V.

478   Gilbert, C. A.   Communicative Performance of Literature.
        NY: Macmillan.

479   Lee, C. I., & F. J. Galati.   Oral Interpretation.   5th ed.
        Boston: Houghton Mifflin.

480 Long, B. W.; Lee Hudson; & P. R. Jeffrey. Group Performance of Literature. Englewood Cliffs, NJ: Prentice-Hall.

481 Silber, Robert. Technique of Interpretation with Readers Manuscripts. Dubuque, Iowa: Kendall/Hunt.

482 Valentine, K. B. Interlocking Pieces: Twenty Questions for Understanding Literature. Dubuque, Iowa: Kendall/Hunt.

483 Valentine, K. B., & Karen Nobel, eds. Duppies, Huldre and More: Oral Traditions in Selected Cultures. Tempe, Ariz: Lacuentista Pub. Co.

1978

484 Bowen, E. R.; O. J. Aggertt; & W. E. Rickert. Communicative Reading. 4th ed. NY: Macmillan.

485 Breen, R. S. Chamber Theatre. Englewood Cliffs, NJ: Prentice-Hall.

486 Riffaterre, Michael. Semiotics of Poetry. Bloomington, Ind: Indiana U. Press.

487 Smith, R. E. Fundamentals of Oral Interpretation: Modules in Speech Communication. Chicago: Science Research Associates.

1979

488 Eckroyd, D. H., & H. S. Wagner. Communicate Through Oral Reading. NY: McGraw-Hill.

1980

489 Gottlieb, M. R. Oral Interpretation. NY: McGraw-Hill.

490 Hudson, Lee. An Index to Studies in the Oral Interpretation of Literature 1911-1975. Rev. ed. Falls Church, Va: SCA.

491 Kleinau, Marion, & J. L. McHughes. Theatres for Interpretation. Sherman Oaks, Calif: Alfred Pub. Co.

492 Scrivner, L. M., & Dan Robinette. A Guide to Oral Interpretation. 2nd ed. NY: Odyssey Press.

CHAPTERS IN BOOKS

493 JOHNSON, G. E., ED. STUDIES IN THE ART OF INTER-
PRETATION. NY: APPLETON-CENTURY, 1940.

494 Johnson, G. E. Backgrounds for Interpretation, pp.
3-8. Necessity for background prep for those who would
work in field of speech training.

495 Marshman, J. T. The Mystery of Oral Interpretation, pp. 9-17. Reprint of article in Qtr J Spch 24
(Dec. 1938) 596-603. Spiritual element in lit as manifested by articulation and action.

496 Simon, C. T. Appreciation in Reading, pp. 18-28.
Factors in appreciation of lit and aids to increase appreciation.

497 Black, A. K. This Thing Called Dramatic, pp. 29-
36. Differentiates dramatic power from histrionic power;
focuses on dramatic power.

498 Pearson, P. M. Artistic Interpretation, pp. 37-43.
Reprint of article in QJS 2 (July 1916) 286-92. OI requires performer be sincere, present the beautiful and
produce in audience degree elation.

499 McLean, M. P. Oral Interpretation--A Recreative
Art, pp. 44-51. OI gives new life to material already
present.

500 Eich, L. M. Relation of Content, Form and Style
to Interpretative Reading, pp. 52-6. Reprint of article
in QJS 25 (Apr. 1939) 281-4. Indicates pedagogical emphasis to maintain OI's academic respectability.

501 Parrish, W. M. Interpretative Reading, pp. 57-65.
Reprint of article in QJS 13 (Apr. 1927) 160-8. Chief aim
and focus of OI should be to give skill in vocal interpretation of poetry.

502 Black, A. K. Speech as a Fine Art, pp. 66-76.
Comparative study of speech with other fine arts.

503 Rice, Phidelah. The Art of Impersonation in Play
Reading, pp. 79-84. Taking on personality not one's own
when performing a play.

504 Babcock, M. M. Interpretative Presentation vs. Im-
personative Presentation, pp. 85-93. Reprint of article in
QJS 2 (Jan. 1916) 18-25. Impersonation merely imitative;
interpretation translative.

505 Tallcott, R. A. The Place for Personation, pp. 94-
101. Reprint of article in QJS (Apr. 1916) 116-22. Argues for place for personation in answer to question of
its relevance.

506 Babcock, M. M. Impersonation Versus Interpretation, pp. 102-5. Reprint of article in QJS 2 (Oct. 1916)
340-3. The con's of impersonation.

507 Babcock, M. M. Interpretation or Impersonation, pp.
106-11. Difference between interpretation and impersonation.

508 Parrish, W. M. Impersonation and the Art of Interpretation, pp. 112-6. Mastery of the art of OI should be
governed by well-understood principles; OI should not pre-
tend to be the poet or the character whom he represents.

509 Curry, S. S. Personation and Participation, pp. 117-
23. Explains two attitudes of personation and participation
of dramatic sympathy which are universally present in all
forms of lit.

510 Johnson, G. E. Impersonation, A Necessary Technique, pp. 124-30. Mood of lit suffers if not given complete impersonation.

511 Tripp, W. B. Impersonation Versus Interpretation,
pp. 131-7. Suggestions for drawing the line between impersonation and interpretation.

512 Allen, A. H. The Impersonation of Plays, pp. 138-
52. Reprint of article in QJS 20 (Feb. 1934) 57-72. Impersonation as expressive technique.

513 Lowell, Amy. Poetry as a Spoken Art, pp. 153-61.
Suggests that poetry is art because art has changes and
variations and so does poetry.

514 Johnson, G. E. The Place and Importance of Interpretive Expression (Dramatic) in the Scheme of Education,
pp. 165-6. An outline of interpretative expression.

515 Pellegrini, A. M. The Aim and Educational Content
of Oral Reading, pp. 167-73. Reprint of article in QJS

28 (Dec. 1937) 643-7. Purpose of OI lies in audience's understanding of lit's worth.

516 Farma, W. J. Oral Reading: A Vital Educational Technique, pp. 174-7. Two main heads under which the content to be communicated by OI can be placed and gives suggestions for attaining them.

517 Rodigan, M. V. New Approaches to Aims in Interpretative Reading in Teachers Colleges, pp. 178-83. Dominant aim and content difference that interpretation reading must have from related courses.

518 Johnson, G. E. Teaching Values in Dialect Material, pp. 184-91. Dialect material aids in gaining a generous, general and sincere response because of appeal of material.

519 Kramer, Magdalene, & M. M. McCarthy. The Development of Personality, pp. 192-5. Essential aim of developing personality.

520 Johnson, G. E. Selection and Arrangement of Program Materials, pp. 196-200. Strategies for arranging programs.

521 Parrish, W. M. Concerning Taste, pp. 201-6. Varieties and kinds of taste.

522 Johnson, G. E. Extemporaneous Reading Contests and Methods of Judging Them, pp. 207-11. General suggestions intended to help person give more flexible and vital performance as well as criteria for judging contests.

523 Lloyd, M. P., & J. T. Marshman. Selection and Arrangement of Reading Material, pp. 212-18. Criteria for selecting and arranging material for most effective presentation.

524 Johnson, G. E. Dramatic Reading and Platform Art Critique, pp. 219-22. Outline of dramatic reading considerations.

525 Bailey, E. V. Standards of Criticism Applied to Oral Interpretation, pp. 223-8. Criticism appled to poetry; five elements selection of lit should contain.

526 Chamberlain, W. B., & S. H. Clark. Criticism, pp. 229-34. Discusses two classes of criticism.

527 Curry, S. S. Criticism, pp. 235-46. General and perceptive discussion of criticism.

528 SLOAN, T. O., ED. THE ORAL STUDY OF LITERATURE. NY: RANDOM HOUSE, 1966.

529 Beloof, R. L. A Reading of Robert Lowell's Where the Rainbow Ends, pp. 17-52. Examines kinds of literary works which attract explication. Comments on explicative problems frequently encountered and easily distinguished.

530 Long, C. C. Long Day's Journey Into Night as Aesthetic Object, pp. 53-93. Analysis of play with view to aesthetic effect on audience.

531 Chatman, Seymour. A Study of James Mason's Interpretation of "The Bishop Orders His Tomb," pp. 94-133. Analysis of poem line by line indicating how lines should be read. Claims poem can be meaningful only with closest reference to its full meaning.

532 Sloan, T. O. Persuasive Strategies in the Structure of John Donne's "Satire III," pp. 137-70. Rhetorical analysis of poem with reference to persona and audience.

533 Klyn, M. S. The Symbolic Act in Its Content, Chekhov's Ward No. 6, pp. 171-205. Uses intrinsic approach to one of Chekhov's plays and explicates the text in detail.

534 GRAY, J. W., ED. PERSPECTIVES ON ORAL INTERPRETATION: ESSAYS AND READINGS. MINNEAPOLIS: BURGESS, 1968.

535 Gray, J. W. The Process: Oral Interpretation as Communication, pp. 1-13. OI experience to be understood must be examined from three major concepts: encoder is attempting to communicate experience, message is complex of attitudes, encoder's goal is total response.

536 Veilleux, Jere. The Interpreter: The Nature of His Art, pp. 15-29. Examines OIer's role, language and audience.

537 Hart, M. B. The Writer: Poet's Thoughts on Oral Interpretation, pp. 31-43. Sees poet and interpreter as emphasizing different aspects of poetry when performed.

538 Armstrong, Chloe. The Literature: Choosing Materials for Oral Interpretation, pp. 45-54. Must consider literary value, audience and own skills when choosing.

539 Hendrix, J. A., & J. W. Gray. The Analysis: A Note on Value Orientation, pp. 55-63. Focus on recognizing writer's value system to improve accuracy of interpretation.

540   Horton, J. F.   The Response: A Discussion of Empathy, pp. 65-85.   Nature, function, definition and uses of empathy in OI performance.

541   Cobin, M. T.   The Criticism: The Teaching of Oral Interpretation, pp. 87-98.   Examination of basic nature of the critical function; offers suggestions for evaluating and guiding the performer.

542   Brandes, P. D.   The Research: A Behavioral Approach, pp. 99-119.   Contributions of expe-imental research; offers two studies as examples.

543   FERNANDEZ, T. L., ED.   ORAL INTERPRETATION AND THE TEACHERS OF ENGLISH.   CHAMPAIGN, ILL: NATIONAL COUNCIL OF TEACHERS OF ENGLISH, 1969.

544   Bacon, W. A.   The Act of Literature and the Act of Interpretation, pp. 1-7.   Literature and interpretation in the context with which teachers of English and Speech are concerned: Lit and OI thought of as serving the needs of students and of teachers on secondary level.

545   McCurdy, F. L.   Oral Interpretation as an Approach to Literature, pp. 9-16.   Discussion of several ways OI contributes to study of lit.

546   Neville, M. M.   Oral Interpretation as an Aid to the Understanding of Literature, pp. 17-20.   Emphasis on using oral reading as aid to one's own understanding of lit.

547   Bales, Allen.   Oral Interpretation: An Extension of Literary Study, pp. 21-7.   OI is extension of lit study by the fact that it utilizes the total range of lit study, that it stretches li† study to its fullest capacity, and it causes OI to exert him/herself to fullest extent.

548   Friederich, W. J.   Teaching Delivery Techniques of Oral Interpretation, pp. 29-36.   List of techniques for effective merging of technique with literature.

549   Hach, C. W.   A Supervisor Looks at Teaching of Literature in the High School, pp. 37-44.   Two major emphases in teaching lit are enjoyment and appreciation and reading with understanding.   OI helps teacher achieve both.   So does reading aloud to students.

550   Worrell, Elizabeth.   Readers Theatre and the Short Story, pp. 45-52.   Staging lit helps students understand and appreciate lit plus student involvement is strongly increased.

551 Doyle, V. G. Why Read to High School Students?, pp. 53-7. OI can help effect appreciation and understanding; makes students feel as if they, too, are experiencing the events.

552 Matthews, Dorothy. Uses of Oral Interpretation in Directing and Motivating the Outside Reading of High School Students, pp. 59-69. Special uses for OI for high school English teacher in motivating students to do outside reading and applying outside reading to inside oral activities.

553 Fernandez, T. L. Findings and Recommendations of the ISCPET Conference on Oral Interpretation, pp. 71-81. Guidelines for a course of study in OI specifically adapted to student preparing to teach English in secondary school.

554 DOYLE, E. M., & V. H. FLOYD, EDS. STUDIES IN INTERPRETATION I. AMSTERDAM: RODOPI, 1972. Rev. by B. W. Long in Qtr J Spch 59 (Dec. 1973) 480.

555 Floyd, V. H. Towards a Definition of Hubris, pp. 3-32. Hubris seen as both sin and virtue, as everlastingly ambiguous.

556 Loesch, K. T. The Shape of Sound: Configurational Rime in the Poetry of Dylan Thomas, pp. 33-66. Linguistic analysis of sound structure and function of structural elements in Thomas' poetry.

557 Queener, L. G. Contiguity Figures: An Index to the Language-World Relationship in Auden's Poetry, pp. 67-98. Relationship of language to reality it represents; Auden's language choices reveal his Weltanschauung.

558 Rude, R. V. Diagnosis and Dialect, pp. 99-122. Suggests dialectical approach as applicable to all lit and gives insight into archetype and symbol.

559 Doyle, E. M. Poet on Stage, pp. 123-36. Points up function of verse as poetic language, as contemporary speech, as character or as action; verse is integral part of verse drama.

560 Heston, L. A. The Interpreter and the Structure of the Novel, pp. 137-54. Usefulness of an approach to structure through narrator.

561 Maclay, J. H. The Interpreter and Modern Fiction: Problems of Point of View and Structural Tensiveness, pp. 155-70. Point of view critical to understanding novel, leads to understanding of work's narrative structure.

562 Wigley, J. A. Imagery and the Interpreter, pp. 171-90. Function of animal imagery in Absalom, Absalom!

563 Worrell, Elizabeth. The Unspoken Word, pp. 191-206. Problem of communication which sometimes breaks down, the failure of perception, lack of awareness of the word withheld as evidenced in Virginia Woolf's works.

564 Hadley, D. S. Oral Interpretation at the Chautauqua Institution and the Chautauqua School of Expression, 1874-1900, pp. 207-28. Historical examination of Chautauqua with emphasis on platform readers.

565 Hampton, P. E. Oral Interpretation as a Means of Instruction in Anglo-Saxon England, pp. 229-54. Historical examination of oral reading in English history: A. D. 597-887 with emphasis on monastic use of oral reading.

566 Mattingly, A. S. Art and Nature: The Mechanical School in England: 1761-1786, pp. 255-74. Background against which mechanical and natural schools may be understood with examination of mechanical school proponents, particular attention to concepts of art and nature.

567 Coger, L. I. Physical Actions and the Oral Interpreter, pp. 275-86. Concludes organic appreciation best for today's reader. Kinesics part of organic appreciation.

568 Geiger, Don. Poetry as Awareness of What?, pp. 287-308. Examination of poetry as illusion of life, analogues to life with consideration of dramatistic approach to lit.

569 Hunsinger, Paul. A Communication Model for Oral Interpretation, pp. 309-24. Representational model of OI with concern for pre-literary, literary performance and response process.

570 Long, C. C. The Poem's Text as a Technique of Performance in Public Group Readings of Poetry, pp. 325-40. Suggests a methodology for insuring choric or group performance of poetry growing from inner structure of piece itself rather than traditional or arbitrary conventions.

571 Sloan, T. O. Speaking Literature, pp. 341-62. Literature has a kind of permanent ongoing availability, a unique temporality making it different from rhetoric.

572 DOYLE, E. M. , & V. H. FLOYD, EDS. STUDIES IN INTERPRETATION II. AMSTERDAM: EDITIONS RODOPI, 1977.

573 Hargis, D. E. Socrates and the Rhapsode: Plato's
Ion, pp. 1-12. Student of OI should be acquainted with
concept of inspiration as espoused by Socrates, though
platonic proposition of absolute reason is unacceptable to
modernists.

574 Floyd, V. H. Point of View in Modern Drama, pp.
13-28. Point of view considered central structural problem of modern drama.

575 Espinola, J. C. Narrative Discourse in Virginia
Woolf's To the Lighthouse, pp. 29-44. Presence of narrative, as controlling force and speaking guide, serves
as semi-transparent envelope and surrounding presence,
plus conditions form of novel.

576 Strine, M. S. Narrative Strategy and Communicative
Design in Flannery O'Connor's The Violent Bear It Away,
pp. 45-58. Shifting point of view, conjectural commentary
and normative discourse seen as primary narrative devices
in novel.

577 Hudson, Lee. Poetics in Performance: The Beat
Generation, pp. 59-76. Beats placed poetry in oral dimension and reemphasized performance oriented poetics.

578 Gray, P. H. American Concrete: New Poetic, New
Performance, pp. 77-98. Concrete poetry within parameters of OI can help open up OI to accommodate a
similar open spirit in contemporary lit.

579 Crannell, K. C. A Metrical Analysis of Frost's
"The Hill Wife," pp. 99-114. Metrical analysis of "Hill
Wife."

580 Salper, D. R. Onomatopoeia, Gesture and Synaes-
thesia in the Perception of Poetic Meaning, pp. 115-24.
OI best approach to appreciating such values in poetry because reading aloud reinforces these values.

581 Brandes, P. D. A Critique of the Use of Reading
Aloud to Evaluate Daily Progress in Silent Reading, pp.
125-38. There are functional reasons for using oral
reading to measure silent reading ability; however, there
are at least five processes involved in silent reading and
these factors can distort ability to measure silent reading
through oral reading.

582 Kleinau, Marion, & T. L. Isbell. Roland Barthes
and the Co-Creation of Text, pp. 139-56. Reader in discovering poem's persona discovers himself and cultural
temporal ideological artifacts of others.

583 Haas, Richard. Phenomenology and the Interpreter's Interior Distance, pp. 157-66. Fullness of OI experience not just experience of performance but experience of act of performing; since performing is understanding, OI event emerging from the interior distance is experiencing understanding.

584 Henning, W. K. Interpretation as Revelatory Act: A Wheelwrightean Perspective, pp. 167-82. OI creative potential rests on three interactive assumptions: presential coalescent and perspectival characteristics of reality; synedochic nature of poetic object; open and imitative nature of poetic language.

585 Pattison, S. D. Rhetoric and Audience Effect/Kenneth Burke on Form and Identification, pp. 183-98. Burke's concept of form and identification used to illustrate lit designed to evoke response OI may become more efficient communicator by knowing how response is attained.

586 Williams, D. A. Audience Response and the Interpreter, pp. 199-206. View of communication as transactional but OI as communal; suggests audience's response be further investigated.

587 Hopkins, M. F. Sincerity and the Performing Artist: An Old Critical Concept Re-established, pp. 207-20. Toward a definition of modern use of the term and its value for OI.

588 Carlsen, J. W. Persona, Personality, and Performance, pp. 221-32. Investigation of persona in poetry through analysis of interplay among poem's voices.

589 Hardwick, M. R. The Interpreter's Responsibility to Selectivity, pp. 233-44. Suggests way to encourage total physical responsiveness for beginning readers' muscular thinking.

590 Doll, H. D. Nonverbal Communication and Oral Interpretation, pp. 245-66. Role of facial expression in OI.

591 Long, B. W. Evaluating Performed Literature, pp. 267-82. Process of evaluating performance aided by concentrating on text's certainties, encouraging probabilities, tolerating possibilities, and rejecting distortions.

592 Bowen, E. R. Adapting Novel for Production in Readers/Chamber Theatre, pp. 283-96. Experimental study designed to establish principles of common practice in adapting novels for RT/CT Productions.

593 Pearse, J. A. Montage: A Paradigm for Readers
Theatre, pp. 297-307. Montage provides paradigm for Rt
in two ways: first persistence of vision and second col-
lision if images work to reveal emotional content of text
by binding visual/verbal cues in audience's imagination.

594 HAAS, RICHARD, & D. A. WILLIAMS, EDS. THE STUDY
OF ORAL INTERPRETATION: THEORY AND COM-
MENT. INDIANAPOLIS: BOBBS-MERRILL, 1975.

595 Bacon, W. A. The Dangerous Shores: From Elocution to Interpretation, pp. 1-12. Reprint of article in
QJS 46 (Apr. 1960) 148-52. OI balance between lit,
criticism and performance techniques.

596 Haas, Richard, & D. A. Williams. Response to
W. A. Bacon's The Dangerous Shores: From Elocution
to Interpretation, pp. 9-11. Points out some dimensions
of Bacon's essay which could evoke good discussion:
Bacon emphasizes lit value over delivery; what about audience? Today's student functions as creative artist not always stressing lit.

597 Curry, S. S. Importance of Studying the History of
Elocution and Vocal Training, pp. 13-6. Reprint from
Proceedings of Nat'l Assc. of Elocutionists, 1895. Study
helps prevent mistakes, encourages appreciation, enables
one to understand own times, prevents egotism, broadens
mind and allows appreciation of changes in style.

598 Bowen, E. R. Response to S. S. Curry's The Importance of Studying the History of Elocution and Vocal
Training, pp. 16-7. Bowen finds Curry right in looking
back for perspective, but also finds him ambiguous and
inconsistent.

599 McCurdy, F. L. Response to Curry's The Importance
of Studying the History of Elocution and Vocal Training,
pp. 18-9. Finds Curry relevant in reference to past as
way of realizing relation of OI to other ways of knowing.

600 Haas, Richard, and D. A. Williams. Some Elocutionary Positions, pp. 22-9. Excerpts on elocutionary
theory by Ebenezer Porter, R. I. Fulton, T. C. Trueblood, Leland Porter, S. S. Curry, L. E. Bassett, C.
W. Emerson, J. W. Showmaker, and S. H. Clark.

601 Clark, S. H. The New Elocution, pp. 31-8. Reprint from Proceedings of Sixth Annual Meeting of the
Nat'l Assc. of Elocutionists, 1897. New motto for OI is:
Force out the expression through the thought; if the mental
action is right, the expression will be right.

602 Haas, Richard, & D. A. Williams. Response to S. H. Clark's The New Elocution, pp. 40-2. Notes how change in name focused OI on lit away from delivery, but that delivery continued to be a problem, i. e., confusion between acting and interpretation.

603 Williams, D. A. Impersonation: The Great Debate, pp. 43-57. Let's declare a moratorium on use of word impersonation. Popularity of OI due in part to variety of methods and styles which prevail.

604 Williams, D. A. Whatever Happened to Choral Reading?, pp. 58-70. Speech profession has overlooked dynamic interest which may have cost us a number of students for there is still a demand for CR, though not many are qualified to teach it, and few colleges offer it.

605 Dennis, R. B. One Imperative Plus, pp. 72-7. Reprint of article in QJS 8 (June 1922) 218-23. Need for oral English to be interpretation of life and not restricted to rules for rules' sake.

606 Bacon, W. A. Response to R. B. Dennis' One Imperative Plus, pp. 77-81. Agrees in general with Dennis on lack of rules but sees Dennis as too general in enthusiasm and optimism. One can permit all and end up with nothing.

607 Marshman, J. T. The Paradox of Oral Interpretation, pp. 82-5. Reprint of article in QJS 28 (Feb. 1942) 31-6. Extended definition of OI focusing on reader's subservience to lit.

608 Bolton, Janet. Response to J. T. Marshman's The Paradox of Oral Interpretation, pp. 85-91. Paradox Marshman posed not gone: Thrust today is inquiry rather than celebration, operational definition rather than metaphor. We are still searching. Marshman would approve.

609 Parrish, W. M. The Concept of Naturalness, pp. 93-101. Reprint of article in QJS 37 (Dec. 1951) 448-54. Naturalness to be approved, not when it feels natural to performer, but when it seems natural to audience.

610 Mattingly, A. S. Response to W. M. Parrish's The Concept of Naturalness, pp. 101-7. Imagination is sine qua non for OI as for poet. Through its power OI can create performance revelatory of poem, making seem real what is not actual, and showing as present what is absent. How best to acquire ability to do so or teach it may never be fully understood.

611 Parrish, W. M. Interpreting Emotion in Poetry, pp. 108-17. Reprint of article in Sthn Spch J 19 (Mar. 1954)

205-13. Proper study of elements of poetry will create proper emotion in performance.

612 Floyd, V. H. Response to W. M. Parrish's Interpreting Emotion in Poetry, pp. 118-24. OIer's response to poem is not passivity, but fully embodied one wherein one surrenders, looks, listens, receives and then gets oneself out of the way of the poem.

613 Haas, Richard, & D. A. Williams. Response to Parrish, pp. 124-9. Some areas of agreement with Parrish and Floyd. Asks performer to surrender to poem so as to gain the kind of realization of the work which occurs only when one can make some intimate, personal connection with it.

614 McCoard, W. B. How Conversational Is the Conversational Norm?, pp. 131-2. Reprint of article in Wstn Spch 16 (May 1952) 199-200. Concept helpful as long as one recognizes that reading situation is not natural but must seem so.

615 Bowen, E. R. Response to W. B. McCoard's How Conversational Is the Conversational Norm?, pp. 132-5. Term "controversial" is essentially meaningless; rather respond to the lit's demands.

616 Bolton, Janet. Response to McCoard, pp. 135-6. Unless OI is a friendly discussion or exchange of ideas about lit text, the phenomenon of conversation is not relevant.

617 Bowen, E. R. Response to Bolton, pp. 136-7. Most OI use communication norm in reading most forms of lit. most of the time--that is, if such a thing exists, but this cannot be proved.

618 Geiger, Don. Oral Interpretation and the New Criticism, pp. 139-49. Reprint of article in QJS 36 (Dec. 1950) 508-13. OI verifies a basic insight of new criticism into nature of lit structure and shows how to enlarge this insight.

619 Geiger, Don. Interpretation and the Locus of Poetic Meaning, pp. 150-65. A poet means what he says in text, but has no special province to explain his text's meaning. The locus of poetic meaning is in the communicative process which is completed in reading performance, whether silent or oral.

620 McCurdy, F. L. The Ultimate Commitment, pp. 166-78. Deals in problem of symbols in poetry. The OI must experience and reveal the symbolic in performance.

621 Carlson, E. W. Robert Frost on Vocal Imagination. The Merger of Form and Content, pp. 180-2. Reprint of an article in Amer Lit (Jan. 1962) 510-22. "The tones are closest to the form, especially where we start and where we end a poem. The form is inside when you begin and when you get through rolling it, the material is inside and the form is outside." (Quoting Frost).

622 McCurdy, F. L. Response to E. W. Carlson's Robert Frost on Vocal Imagination. The Merger of Form and Content, pp. 183-4. Over-riding concern is tone. The speaker is important in determining tone.

623 Mattingly, A. S. Response to Carlson/Frost, pp. 184-5. Interpreter seeks to let tone merge form and content.

624 Bacon, W. A. Response to Carlson/Frost, pp. 185-7. Perception not limited to a matter of tone, meter, rhyme, vowels, alliteration, assonance. Finds Frost's notion of meaning and form as one quite hopeless.

625 Geiger, Don. Response to Carlson/Frost, pp. 187-8. We may say that for OI the voice that he hears is his own when he identifies and faithfully reproduces the particular speech acts that emerge from the words of a poem and govern their meaning.

626 Haas, Richard, & D. A. Williams. Response to Carlson/Frost, pp. 189-90. Tone, despite its importance, is not the totality of a poem's meaning. Frost is wrong.

627 Haas, Richard. To Say in Words ... to Read Aloud, pp. 191-204. Need for expressive skills for today's OIer. Not usually available in most schools.

628 Breen, R. S. Chamber Theatre, pp. 207-11. Primary concern of Chamber Theatre is presentation on stage of narrative lit without sacrificing its narrative elements and stylistic demands of the lit.

629 Malone, Kemp. The Next Decade, pp. 212-4. Call for teachers to read texts aloud to make words come alive. May lead to different understanding of text.

630 Floyd, V. H. Response to Malone, pp. 214-5. Disagrees with Malone, reading aloud not to bring to life the literary object, but literary object experienced by reader in that unique moment when reader is seized by his/her text.

631 Bolton, Janet. Response to Malone, pp. 215-6. Malone nearsighted in recognition of oral tradition. Is

not behavioral engagement with text perhaps better viewed as means of exploring significant human experience?

632 Bowen, E. R. Response to Malone, pp. 216-8. Malone's idea of oralizing simply an old rediscovery. Let's hope we do more to convince others that OI is not just a dynamic approach to lit experience, but the only good one.

633 Bacon, W. A. Response to Malone, pp. 218-9. Sees results of the rediscovery of oralizing lit in renewed interest among English teachers along with oral English. We need to educate them better for this interest is not revolutionary.

634 Geiger, Don. Response to Malone, pp. 219-20. Appreciates Malone's remarks. Responsibility for further oral study rests with teachers and students of OI; we are advancing.

635 Bacon, W. A. The Dangerous Shores a Decade Later, pp. 221-8. The ultimate goal of education is to lead the performer outside himself, to bring him to experiences other than his own, to create in him a sense of the otherness of the other.

JOURNAL ARTICLES

1902

636 Editors. Recitation or Cantilation. <u>Nation</u> 74 (June 26) 501-
   2. Prefer poetry recited to chanted.

1905

637 Higginson, T. W. How a Child Learns the Music of Words.
   <u>Outlook</u> 79 (Jan. 28) 237-9. Child's natural affinity for
   rhyme and music aid to appreciating poetry.

1907

638 Editors. Pleasant Practice of Reading Aloud. <u>Nation</u> 85
   (Dec. 19) 559-60. Values of reading aloud.

639 Morse, J. H. Reading Aloud. <u>Independent</u> 62 (April) 942-4.
   Poet's and writer's ability to read aloud.

1909

640 Editors. Decline of Reading Aloud. <u>Independent</u> 66 (Apr. 15)
   824-6. Trends toward silent reading.

641 Gummere, F. B. Poetry and Elocution. <u>Nation</u> 89 (Nov. 11)
   453-4. Revive habit of reading aloud.

1910

642 Pier, Florida. Reading Aloud. <u>Harpers Weekly</u> 54 (July 9)
   25. Reading aloud for comprehension.

1911

643 Beecher, I. G. The Reader's Art. <u>Pub Spking Rev</u> 1 (Oct.)
   68-70.

644 Robinson, F. B. The Teaching of Reading in the Schools.
Pub Spking Rev 1 (Oct.) 50-2.

1912

645 Bassett, L. E. The Place of Declamation in the College
Curriculum. Pub Spking Rev 1 (Apr.) 238-41.

646 Bassett, L. E. The Teaching of Poetry in the Public
Schools. Pub Spking Rev 1 (May) 14-20.

647 Editors. The Teachings of Charles Wesley Emerson. Pub
Spking Rev 2 (Dec.) 110-2.

648 Fleagel, B. E. Oral English in the High School. Engl J 1
(Dec.) 611-18. Baltimore City College integrates classroom and street English.

649 Garns, J. S. Good Literature in High School Contests. Pub
Spking Rev 2 (Dec.) 112-4.

650 Gates, A. L. Should the Instructor Read for His Class?
Pub Spking Rev 1 (Jan.) 156-7.

651 Harris, A. M. The Place of Declamation in the College
Curriculum. Pub Spking Rev 1 (Jan.) 133-5.

652 Heagle, B. E. Oral English in the High School. Pub Spking
Rev 2 (Nov.) 84-9.

653 Immel, R. K. Shall the Teacher Recite for the Class?
Pub Spking Rev 2 (Nov.) 89-91.

654 Lardner, J. L. The Teaching of Reading in the Schools.
Pub Spking Rev 1 (Mar.) 198-202.

655 Lewis, C. L. Oral English Again. Pub Spking Rev 1 (Jan.)
145.

656 Lewis, C. L. Reading and Speaking in the Public Schools.
Pub Spking Rev 1 (Feb.) 161-7.

657 Thorn-Wright, Doris. Oral Reading in Its Relation to the
Study of Literature. Engl J 1 (Nov.) 557-61. Value of
oral interpretation of lit in lit class.

658 Tilroe, H. M. The Place of Declamation in the College
Curriculum. Pub Spking Rev 1 (Jan.) 136-8.

1913

659 Brown, F. E. Oral Story Telling. Pub Spking Rev 3 (Nov.)
23-4.

660 Christable, Abbott. Problems in the School Reading of Poetry. Pub Spking Rev 3 (Dec.) 102-7.

661 Clapp, J. M. Oral English in the College Course. Engl J
2 (Apr.) 18-33. Vocal elements in lit ignored.

662 Eaton, H. A. Reading Poetry Aloud. Engl J 2 (Mar.) 151-
7. Factors that determine quality of reading aloud.

663 Frank, M. M. Oral English in the Literature Class. Pub
Spking Rev 3 (Mar.) 199-202.

664 Gummere, F. B. Poetry and Elocution. Pub Spking Rev 2
(Jan.) 146-8.

665 Koopman, H. L. Two Ways of Reading: How to Cultivate
Eye and Ear for Different Kinds of Literature. Inde-
pendent 74 (May 15) 1082-4. Combo of eye motor audi-
tory-response method for reading efficiency.

666 Painter, L. G. Expressive Reading as a Vitalizing Force in
the Classroom Teaching of College English. Engl J 2
(Sept.) 428-36. Expressive reading should play a more
important role in teaching of literature.

667 Pintner, Rudolf. Oral and Silent Reading of Fourth Grade
Pupils. J Educ Psych 4 (June) 333-7. Oral reading re-
tards the reading process: children comprehend more
when reading silently.

668 Shurter, E. D. Oral English in the Schools. Pub Spking
Rev 2 (Jan.) 148-50.

669 Tassin, Algernon. Disclosures of a College Elocution Class.
Educ Rev 45 (May) 485-500. Equal emphasis on speaking
and writing correct English valued.

670 Thorn-Wright, Doris. Oral Reading and the Study of Literature. Pub Spking Rev 3 (Mar.) 198-9.

671 Winans, J. A. What Is Good Contest Literature? Pub
Spking Rev 2 (Feb.) 165-6.

1914

672 Breck, E. J. The Present Possibilities of Oral English in
High Schools. Engl J 3 (Jan.) 28-37. Increased need for
instructors of oral English.

673 Hollister, R. D. Interpretive Reading and Its Place in a
Department of Public Speaking. Pub Spking Rev 4 (Dec.)
104-13.

674 Johnson, G. E. Literature and Vocal Expression. Engl J
3 (Nov.) 533-7. Speaks from the teaching standpoint concerning standards in interpretive work, and the general
attitude of by far the greater majority of English teachers
toward teachers of vocal expression.

675 Lewis, C. L. The Neglected Side of English. Engl J 3
(May) 282-9. Oral instruction essential element in education.

676 Lynahan, M. M. Some Experience in Teaching Expression in
Country Schools. Pub Spking Rev 3 (Jan.) 140-3.

677 Robinson, F. B. Robert Irving Fulton, M. S. Pub Spking
Rev 3 (Mar.) 191-5.

678 Robinson, F. B. Robert McLean Cumnock. Pub Spking Rev
3 (Jan.) 127-31.

679 Robinson, F. B. Thomas Clarkson Trueblood. Pub Spking
Rev 3 (Feb.) 159-63.

680 Russell, L. M. Some Experiments in Oral English. Engl J
3 (Mar.) 176-80. Students participate in experiment using
reflectoscope.

681 Tenney, A. F. How to Read the Bible in the Public Schools.
Pub Spking Rev 3 (Feb.) 172-6.

1915

682 Babcock, M. M. Teaching Interpretation. Qrt J Pub Spking
1 (July) 173-6. Problem of OI teacher is to enable student to turn printed page into living, breathing experience
for both listener and interpreter.

683 Editorial. Elocution Redivivus. Qrt J Pub Spking 1 (Apr.)
77-8. Report of editorial in the English Journal which
states belief in cooperation between English and elocution.

684 Gaylord, J. S. Preparing literary material for public utterance. Qrt J Pub Spking 1 (Apr.) 38-43. Methods of
securing intimate personal mastery of message to be de-
livered when this message is gathered from a literary
masterpiece and is to be given either in language chosen
by speaker or in words of the author.

685 Lyman, R. L. Oral English in the High School. Qrt J Pub
Spking 1 (Oct.) 241-59. Article limited to oral composition, but before developing main point, author supports the
oral interpretation of lit.

686 Mead, C. D. Silent vs. Oral Reading with One Hundred
    Sixth Graders. J Educ Psychology 6 (June) 345-8. Silent
    reading superior to oral reading for comprehension.

687 Prichard, M. F. The Value of Storytelling in the High
    School Course. Engl J 4 (Mar.) 191-3. Emphasize en-
    joyment in art of storytelling.

688 Sharp, G. H. By Products of Reading Aloud. Home Pro-
    gress 4 (Jan.) 830-4. Values of reading aloud.

689 Woolbert, C. H. Theories of Expression: Some Criticisms.
    Qrt J Pub Spking 1 (July) 127-43. Attempt to clarify dif-
    ference in systems of expression by pointing out virtues
    and shortcomings: no one system is complete. All are
    needed, all are useful.

1916

690 Babcock, M. M. Impersonation Versus Interpretation. Qrt
    J Pub Spking 2 (Oct.) 340-3. Clarifies earlier article.
    Objection was not to doing of such stunts, but to the do-
    ing of them under misnomer of elocution, reading, inter-
    preting, public speaking and reciting.

691 Babcock, M. M. Interpretative Presentation Versus Imper-
    sonation Presentation. Qrt J Pub Spking 2 (Jan.) 18-25.
    Differentiates OI and impersonation. OI incorporates
    suggestion and imagination while impersonation is an ex-
    act, literal characterization.

692 Pearson, P. M. Artistic Interpretation. Qrt J Pub Spking
    2 (July) 286-92. OI is creative art. Includes three
    standards: sincerity, beauty and elation. Also there can
    be no OI without the collaboration of the audience.

693 Pintner, Rudolph, & A. R. Gilliland. Oral and Silent Read-
    ing. J of Educ Psych 7 (Apr.) 201-12. As children pro-
    gress in school, silent reading is more economical and
    best method in relation to time expended and information
    gained.

694 Tallcott, R. A. The Place for Personation. Qrt J Pub
    Spking 2 (Apr.) 116-22. Response to Babcock's article.
    Rather than accepting her terms, he expands concern to
    four terms: interpretative reading, impersonative read-
    ing, straight reading and acting. Also defends role of
    personation as expressive manner for orally interpreting lit.

695 Watkins, D. E. The Relation of the Speaker to His Litera-
    ture. Qrt J Pub Spking 2 (Jan.) 46-51. Should be a
    knowledge coordination between reader and lit.

696 Wilds, E. H. Public Speaking in the Early Colleges and
Schools. Qrt J Pub Spking 2 (Jan.) 31-8. Includes elocution practice and declamatory education practices in U. S.,
1636-1849.

1917

697 Clark, S. H. Some Neglected Aspects of Public Speaking.
Qrt J Pub Spking 3 (Oct.) 310-6. Three aspects of public
speaking which, if more carefully regarded than they are,
would greatly improve a speaker's efficiency. Also discusses several neglected factors in public speaking.

698 Dowd, M. H. Oral English in the High School. Qrt J Pub
Spking 3 (Jan.) 1-11. How to set up and administer a
course in oral English.

699 Duffey, W. R. The Foundation Course in Public Speaking at
the University of Texas. Qrt J Pub Spking 3 (Apr.) 163-
71. Use of OI and expression in public speaking course.

700 Editors. Report of the Committee on Oral Expression in
Secondary Schools. Qrt J Pub Spking 3 (Oct.) 317-26.
Aims of and means of attaining aims in curriculum for
grades 7-12 in OI.

701 Gaylord, J. S. Teaching Reading and Spelling as Functions
of Personality. Qrt J Pub Spking 3 (July) 265-72. Values
of self expression in OI.

702 Herring, B. F. A Special Course in Oral Expression for
High Schools. Qrt J Pub Spking 3 (Apr.) 140-52. Teachers of English can use Clark's interpretation of the
printed page for oral English exercises.

703 Herring, B. F. Storytelling in High Schools. Qrt J Pub
Spking 3 (Jan.) 37-47. Values of storytelling for stimulating interest in lit.

704 Lowie, R. H. Oral Tradition and History. J of Amer Folklore 30 (Apr.) 161-7. Argues fallacies of primitive oral
tradition used as facts.

705 Mead, C. D. Results in Silent vs. Oral Reading. J Ed
Psychology 8 (June) 367-8. Silent reading superior to
oral reading for comprehension.

706 Myra, L. M. Some Experiments in High School Oral English.
Engl J 6 (June) 399-401. How to teach English via topics
chosen by students.

707 Newcomb, C. M. The Educational Value of Expression.
Qrt J Pub Spking 3 (Jan.) 69-79. Voice and action human's chief means of expression.

708 Stratton, Clarence. The New Emphasis of Oral English.
Engl J 6 (Sept.) 463-71. Increased interest in oral English exam.

709 Swink, R. A. Vocal Expression in Perspective. Qrt J Pub
Spking 3 (Apr.) 185-90. Teaching oral expression through
perspective of whole subject.

710 Williams, C. B. Spoken English II at Smith College. Qrt J
Pub Spking 3 (July) 229-34. OI in beginning English
course.

711 Woolbert, C. H. Suggestions as to Methods in Research.
Qrt J Pub Spking 3 (Jan.) 12-26. Introduces research
topics for OI.

1918

712 Bain, F. H. The Bible, the Greeks, and Oral English.
Engl J 7 (Apr.) 245-50. Using Old Testament stories and
Iliad and Odyssey for oral reading to increase language
skills of high school students.

713 Craig, A. T. Sound Magic in Poetry. Poet Lore 29 (Winter)
596-605. Use of words to convey rhythm.

714 Forncrook, E. M. A Fundamental Course in Speech Training.
Qrt J Spch Educ 4 (May) 271-89. Use of OI in fundamental
course.

715 Newcomb, C. M. How to Stimulate the Imagination in Interpretative Reading. Qrt J Spch Educ 4 (Mar.) 135-49.
Search for methods to enable teachers to stimulate students in endeavors to interpret lit; several factors to be
considered.

716 Park, J. M. Oral English in the High School. Engl J 7
(Sept.) 452-6. Teacher's responsibility to emphasize
speaking well.

1919

717 Jones, E. E., & A. V. Lockhart. Study of Oral and Silent
Reading in the Elementary Schools of Evanston. Schl &
Society 10 (Nov. 15) 587-90. Graphical results of Kansas
silent reading test and Gray's oral reading test.

1920

718 Flemming, E. G.   A Study of Silent Reading in Speech
Classes.   Qrt J Spch Educ 6 (Nov.) 31-51.   Quantitative
study showing students in speech classes have weaknesses
in concentration, accuracy, and vocabulary.

719 Galinsky, Hans.   The Overseas Writer and the Literary Language of the Mother Country.   Jahrbuch für Amerikastudien
5 (1920) 34-65.   Singles out attitudes of a few American
writers who are caught up in that triangular relationship
of their craft with the tradition of literary British English
and the growth of American speech.

720 Herring, B. F.   Vocal Interpretation of Literature in High
Schools.   Qrt J Spch Educ 6 (Nov.) 52-8.   Early study
of OI in high school.

721 Johnson, G. E.   Education Through Reading Declamation.
Qrt J Spch Educ 6 (Feb.) 65-71.   Performing is explication.

722 Kaufman, Paul.   Getting a Hearing for Tennyson: A Natural
Method in the Teaching of Poetry.   Engl J 9 (Jan.) 25-7.
How sound and form assist sense.

1921

723 Blount, R. E.   The Chicago High School Literary Union.
Qrt J Spch Educ 7 (June) 258-60.   Changes in debate,
extemporaneous declamation and reading within Chicago
high school.

724 Bullowa, A. M.   Pantomime: Its Uses in the High School.
Qrt J Spch Educ 7 (June) 213-20.   Pantomime helps students convey thoughts, not mere words.

725 Duyn, M. V.   Call Your People America.   Senior Scholastic
44 (Feb. 21) 15.   A poem for choral speaking.   Very
patriotic.

726 Renshaw, A. T.   Modern Attention to Pantomimic Action.
Qrt J Spch Educ 7 (Feb.) 43-51.   Introduction to aspects
of pantomimic expression from view of practical demand
and supply.

727 Weeks, R. M.   Phrasal Prosody.   Engl J 10 (Jan.) 11-9.
Free-verse movement, by emphasizing a neglected rhythmic
possibility, brings a new and beautiful note to the com-
posite chord of the coming poetic harmony.   A discussion
of the rhythm of English.

728 Whitmire, L. G.   Oral Expression in Seattle High Schools.
Qrt J Spch Educ 7 (Nov.) 312-7.   Structuring three
courses in oral expression.

1922

729 Bullowa, A. M.   The Course of Study for Oral English in
Hunter College High School.   Qrt J Spch Educ 8 (Nov.)
354-63.   Seven-term program for use of oral English in
high school.

730 Bullowa, A. M.   The Reading-Telling Method in the Use of
the Short Story in Teaching Spoken English.   Qrt J Spch
Educ 8 (Feb.) 1-7.   Attention gained by reading-telling
method; lists stories.

731 Coleman, E. T.   Assignments in Beginning Oral English.
Qrt J Spch Educ 8 (Nov.) 311-22.   Rationale and suggestions for oral English in high school.

732 Dennis, R. B.   One Imperative Plus.   Qrt J Spch Educ 8
(June) 218-23.   Need for oral English to be interpretation
of life and not restricted by rules.

733 Hazard, L. L.   Dante in the Drama Class.   Poet Lore 33
(1922) 228-31.   Methods of applying Dante to dramatic
arts.

734 Monroe, Harriet.   Utterance of Poetry.   Poetry 19 (Feb.)
266-72.   Reading of poetry should be an easily accessible
delight instead of bore it usually is.   Defect chiefly to be
avoided is high sounding rotundity which most people as-
sume like a toga when they read poetry aloud.

735 Richardson, Eva.   Stories for the Classroom: A Bibliography.   Qrt J Spch Educ 8 (Feb.) 8-25.   Stories for grade
school or juvenile audiences.

736 Rousseau, L. G.   Speech Education in the Normal Schools--A
Survey.   Qrt J Spch Educ 8 (June) 209-17.   Status of
speech education in normal schools, 1921.   Interest is in
the number of different titles of courses in field of interpretative reading.

1923

737 Editors.   Spoken Verse.   Living Age 318 (Sept. 8) 475-6.
Values of reading aloud.

738 Hall, R. W.   Phonic Literature: A New Sound for a New
Age.   Engl J 62 (Mar.) 383-93.   Explores boundaries
between print and speech.

739 Lane, A. H. Literary Study as a Preparation for Oral Presentation. Qrt J Spch Educ 9 (Apr.) 181-7. Lit study
valuable aid in preparing student for OI.

740 Osmer, L. C. The Function of the Teacher's Taste in Oral
English. Qrt J Spch Educ 9 (Nov.) 340-4. Need for student's freedom of expression uninfluenced by teacher judgment and culture.

741 Pardoe, T. E. Language of the Body. Qrt J Spch Educ 9
(June) 252-7. Awkward body movement accompanied by
qualitative voice defects.

742 Tallcott, R. A. Teaching Public Reading. Qrt J Spch Educ
9 (Feb.) 53-66. Tallcott's method of teaching public reading.

743 Woodcock, G. M. Combining Oral English and Other English
in the High School. Qrt J Spch Educ 9 (Feb.) 19-24.
How to obtain greatest possible good from English courses
in shortest space of time.

1924

744 Bullowa, A. M. Pantomime: Its Value in Speech Education.
Qrt J Spch Educ 10 (Feb.) 53-60. Pantomime training in
high school needed.

745 Editors. Eulogy of Oral Reading. Elem Schl J 24 (May)
647-9. The case for oral reading.

746 Hudson, H. H. Rhetoric and Poetry. Qrt J Spch Educ 10
(Apr.) 143-54. Definitions of rhetoric and poetic based
on passages written by past authorities in rhetoric and
poetic.

747 McGrew, J. F. Criticism in the Classroom. Qrt J Spch
Educ 10 (Apr.) 154-7. Short section on evaluative criticism in OI.

748 McMillan, Carol. The Growing Academic Recognition of
Dramatic Production. Qrt J Spch Educ 10 (Feb.) 23-9.
Cites increasing number of drama courses in higher edu-
cation in U. S.

749 Parrish, W. M. Public Speaking and Reading--A Plea for
Separation. Qrt J Spch Educ 10 (June) 277-81. Notes
many differences between public speaking and OI and concludes two should be taught separately.

750 Thorpe, C. D. The Educational Function of High School
Dramatics. Qrt J Spch Educ 10 (Apr.) 116-27. Impor-

tance of intense study and performance of drama in high school.

1925

751 Bridge, W. H. The Place of Pantomime in the School Curriculum. Qrt J Spch Educ 11 (Nov.) 350-9. Pantomime source of better mental and physical well-being.

752 Cheeseman, Grace. The Concept of Naturalness as a Basis for Criticism. Qrt J Spch Educ 11 (Feb.) 37-45. As basis for criticism naturalness seems entirely inadequate and often injurious to student.

753 Fry, Dorothea. Learning Material for Oral Interpretation. Qrt J Spch Educ 11 (June) 253-8. Methods for learning for OI.

754 Harris, A. M. Fostering Oral English. Qrt J Spch Educ 11 (Apr.) 124-30. Lists three suggestions for acquiring fluent, forceful and effective use of oral English in prep schools.

755 Tallcott, R. A. Speech Training Through Acting Reading and Declamation. Qrt J Spch Educ 11 (Feb.) 8-17. Kinds of public practice and the order best presented to the beginning student.

756 Tassin, Algernon. Oral Reading as an Intelligence Test. Qrt J Spch Educ 11 (June) 258-66. Most people lack knowledge of how to read and how to comprehend what they hear.

1926

757 Barnes, John. Vital Capacity and Ability in Oral Reading. Qrt J Spch Educ 12 (June) 176-82. Lung capacity not related to effective oral performance.

758 Crocker, Lionel. The Voice Element in Prose: An Examination of Pater and Emerson. Qrt J Spch Educ 12 (Apr.) 168-75. Prose is written in silence for silent reading yet contains a voice and rhythm.

759 Miller, W. J. Motor Control and Ability in Interpretation. Qrt J Spch Educ 12 (Nov.) 334-7. Two forms of motor control were selected because of their elementary nature and comparative absence of uncontrolled factors.

760 Wilson, Helene. Some Statistics Concerning Interpretation Courses. Qrt J Spch Educ 12 (Nov.) 342-52. Aim and content of OI courses in academic settings in U. S.

1927

761 Embank, H. L. The Rhetorical Reader. Qrt J Spch Educ
13 (Nov.) 474-6. Review focuses on popularity of gesture and modernity of E. Porter's book.

762 Hannah, Robert. The Interpretation of the Prologue and Epi-
logue. Qrt J Spch Educ 13 (Apr.) 123-32. Historical
criticism of drama and pageants.

763 Hudson, H. H. Old Books. Qrt J Spch Educ 13 (Apr.) 209-
12. Review of Cockin's art of delivering written language:
Or an Essay on Reading.

764 Hudson, H. H. Lecture on the Analysis of Vocal Inflections:
An Analysis of the Principles of Rhetorical Delivery &
Lectures on Eloquence and Style. Qrt J Spch Educ 13
(June) 337-40. Biographical sketch of Ebenezer Porter
and review of his principles.

765 Jacob, C. F. Rhythm in Prose and Poetry. Qrt J Spch
Educ 13 (Nov.) 357-75. Rhythm as phenomenon of pitch,
duration, intensity, tone, and color in successive time
patterns.

766 Parrish, W. M. Interpretative Reading. Qrt J Spch Educ
13 (Apr.) 160-8. OI one of most difficult courses to or-
ganize: Offers suggestions on setting up objectives and
procedures for teaching such a course; reading not a science, but a skill.

1928

767 Baker, F. T. The Case for Oral Reading. Elem Engl Rev
5 (May) 131-4. Oral reading necessary for developing
reading skills.

768 Monroe, Harriet. Reading Aloud. Poetry 31 (Feb.) 271-4.
Poetry-recitation contest.

769 Parrish, W. M. Implications of Gestalt Psychology. Qrt J
Spch 14 (Feb.) 8-29. Teachings of new psychology of
Gestalt differ from those of the older theories currently
employed in texts on rhetoric and speech.

770 Wells, E. W. Methods of Memorization for the Speaker and
Reader. Qrt J Spch 14 (Feb.) 39-64. Theories from
experiments to improve efficiency of memory.

1929

771 Baker, G. P. Rhythm in Recent Dramatic Dialogue. Yale
Rev 19 (Sept.) 116-33. To develop a character one must

go beyond oaths, slang, and catch words to mirror the
emotions of characters presented.

772 Camp, Cordelia, & C. H. Allen. How Oral Reading Was
     Improved Through the Use of Gray's Check Tests. Elem
     Sch J 30 (Oct.) 132-5. Reducing difficulty with word
     recognition and pronunciation.

773 Craig, A. E. The Contents of a High School Course in
     Speech. Qrt J Spch 15 (June) 350-64. Believes OI best
     course for developing self-expression and platform skills.

774 Crocker, Lionel. The Refrain in Oratorical Prose. Qrt J
     Spch 15 (Feb.) 25-9. Believes there is such a thing as
     refrain in prose, distinct enough to be accorded separate
     treatment under general heading of repetition, found usu-
     ally in lyrical prose.

775 Gray, C. T. The Purposes and Values of Oral Reading in
     the Intermediate and Upper Grades of the Elementary
     School. Elem School J (Jan.) 335-43. There is a re-
     spectable body of scientific material on which any teacher
     interested in oral reading may base her/his procedures.

776 Hannah, Robert. The Oral Interpretation of Lyric Poetry.
     Qrt J Spch 15 (June) 374-80. Teaching methods for lyric
     poetry.

777 Simpson, I. J. Helping the Teacher Improve Oral Reading
     in the Grades. Elem Engl Rev 6 (Sept.) 167-70; (Oct.)
     201-3. Chief function of oral reading is to afford a means
     of transition from oral vocabulary to visual one.

778- Spaeth, J. D. On Standardizing Pronunciation. Qrt J Spch
9   15 (June) 323-30. Excessive emphasis on the normative
       approach breeds dogmatism. Communication without ex-
       pression is futile, but expression without communication
       is fatal.

1930

780 Baker, V. L. Old Books. Qrt J Spch 16 (Feb.) 133-7.
     Review of Kirkham's An Essay on Elocution (1833) and
     Mandeville's Elements of Reading and Oratory (1849).

781 Borchers, G. L. Outline of a Beginning High School Course.
     Qrt J Spch 16 (Apr.) 208-11. Function of OI and story
     telling.

782 Fritz, C. A. From Sheridan to Rush: The Beginnings of
     English Elocution. Qrt J Spch 16 (Feb.) 74-88. Under-
     standing early origins explains current methodologies.

782a Lahman, C. P. Speech Education in Teacher-Training Insti-
     tutions. Qrt J Spch 16 (Feb.) 42-61. Status of OI and
     suggested texts and terms.

783 Latham, A. J. Abandon: A Characteristic of Perfected
     Speech. Qrt J Spch 16 (Apr.) 171-5. Abandon defined
     as without artificial restraint, seen as key ingredient to
     successful performance. Cure for stage fright and in-
     fuses vigor to art.

784 Postle, A. S. Objectives of Teaching Drama. Qrt J Spch 16
     (Feb.) 69-73. High ranking and low ranking objectives for
     teaching drama.

785 Raubicheck, Letitia. Progress or Change? Qrt J Spch 16
     (Apr.) 149-55. Comments on reaction against elocution.

786 Simon, C. T. Appreciation in Reading. Qrt J Spch 16 (Apr.)
     185-93. Appreciation is response to meaning, significance,
     and beauty of lit.

787 Wichelns, H. A. The Undergraduate Reads from the Poets.
     Qrt J Spch 16 (Nov.) 454-8. Recollections of intercol-
     legiate poetry reading at Northampton.

1931

788 Hudson, H. H. The Tradition of Our Subject. Qrt J Spch
     17 (June) 320-9. Emphasizes import of knowing speech
     history.

789 Kaucher, Dorothy. The Verse Speaking Choir. Qrt J Spch
     17 (Feb.) 64-73. Performing choric speech; problem and
     solutions.

790 Poole, Irene. Speech Achievement in the Elementary School.
     Qrt J Spch 17 (Nov.) 478-92. Stresses expression and
     appreciation in OI.

791 Reynolds, G. F. Literature for an Audience. Studies in
     Philology 28 (1931) 810-19. Lit designed for an audience
     is valid classification; drama is most important form of
     such literature today.

792 Runchey, Geraldine. The Oral Approach to the Study of Lit-
     erature. Qrt J Spch 17 (Feb.) 89-95. Contrasts weak-
     nesses of silent reading to values of OI.

793 Saunders, M. E. The Oxford Verse Speaking Contest. Qrt
     J Spch 17 (June) 395-400. Encounter with chanting and
     conversational manners of reading.

1932

794 Bahn, Eugene. Interpretative Reading in Ancient Greece. Qrt J Spch 18 (June) 432-40. Development of Greek OI from art forms.

795 Bassett, L. E. Adapting Courses in Interpretation to the Academic Mind. Qrt J Spch 18 (Apr.) 175-87. Academic scholarship, judgment, taste, and motives of OI.

796 Bryan, E. C. Speech Training in Texas Colleges. Qrt J Spch 18 (Apr.) 261-70. Survey results on texts, titles and status of OI.

797 Camp, Cordelia. An Oral Reading Program in the Elementary Grades. Elem Schl J 32 (Feb.) 435-41. Students acquired dictionary habit, received some voice training and improved generally in their oral reading after an experimental class in interpretation for 4th-7th graders.

798 Daggy, M. L. Old Books. Qrt J Spch 18 (Feb.) 123-9. Review of Enfield's The Speaker.

799 Dalzell, C. D. New Settings for Old Stories. Qrt J Spch 18 (June) 422-32. Illustrations of performing methods.

800 Editorial. The Beginning Course. Qrt J Spch 18 (June) 453-5. Report of undergraduate communication condemning contents of fundamental speech course including OI.

801 Editorial. Interpretative Reading: Art or Tool? Qrt J Spch 18 (June) 455-6. Answers argument and insists that OI is no end in itself but means to end.

802 Farndale, W. G. A Lost Art. Lib J 57 (Sept. 1) 691-4. A plea to restore the art of reading aloud.

803 Jones, E. B. A Comparison of Comprehension Results in Oral and Silent Reading. Peabody J of Educ 9 (Mar.) 292-6. Comprehension with oral and silent reading.

804 Judson, L. S. Old Books. Qrt J Spch 18 (Apr.) 300. Review of Bronson's book--Elocution (1845).

805 Judson, L. S. Old Books. Qrt J Spch 18 (Apr.) 301. Review of J. W. Shoemaker's Advanced Elocution of 1896.

806 Loar, Grace. A Verse Speaking Choir in High School. Engl J 21 (Nov.) 710-15. Group speaking pleasant, constructive, worthwhile way to interest and direct large number of students.

807 Moore, A. E. Some Aspects of Oral Reading in Primary Grades. Elem Engl Rev 9 (Apr.) 83-5, 98. Two pro-

cesses--oral and silent reading--which have many elements in common but which should be used for different purposes have been compared as if they were almost totally different in nature.

808 Paul, V. A. Present Trends of Thought on Oral Reading. U Iowa Extension Bull, Coll of Educ Series 31 (Sept.).

809 Reynolds, G. F. Concerted Reading. Qrt J Spch 18 (Nov.) 659-61. Report of choral reading production at University of Colorado.

810 Sanderson, Virginia. The Speech Curriculum in Teachers Colleges. Qrt J Spch 18 (Apr.) 207-16. Discusses OI and storytelling.

811 Weaver, J. C. A Survey of Speech Curricula. Qrt J Spch 18 (Nov.) 607-12. OI emerges as individual item in speech curriculum.

1933

812 Baker, V. L. Old Books. Qrt J Spch 19 (Feb.) 108-110. Review of Russell's The American Elocutionist (1844), Pulpit Elocution (1846), and Orthophony (1870).

813 Debanke, Cecile. Speech Training in South Africa. Qrt J Spch 19 (Feb.) 77-9. Success of education and resultant public support.

814 Dennis, R. B. The Progressive Teacher. Qrt J Spch 19 (Apr.) 242-7. Teacher as molder of skills and attitudes within the student based on teacher's devotion to his/her work.

815 Little, Theodore. A Unit in Interpretation for High Schools. Qrt J Spch 19 (Nov.) 540-4. Method for guiding class discussions.

816 McLane, L. N. Sound Values in "The Cloud." Qrt J Spch 19 (Apr.) 224-7. Analysis of sound in Shelley's poem.

817 Rasmussen, Carrie. Choral Speaking in the Grades. Qrt J Spch 19 (Feb.) 43-51. Revitalizing poetry through choral speaking.

818 Sanderson, Virginia. Speech in the Schools. Qrt J Spch 19 (June) 421-7. Brief section on reading and OI.

819 Thonssen, Lester. Old Books. Qrt J Spch 19 (Feb.) 105-8. Review of A. Comstock's A System of Elocution (1844) and comment by V. L. Baker on Andrew Comstock's Phonetic Speaker.

1934

820 Allen, A. H. The Impersonation of Plays. Qrt J Spch 20
(Feb.) 57-72. Impersonation as expressive technique.

821 Beck, Warren. The Real Language of Men. Engl J 23
(Nov.) 731-9. Semantic change in lit toward simplicity.

822 Buddy, M. V. Books to Read Aloud. Pub Weekly 125 (June
30) 2334-5. Reading aloud as indoor sport.

823 Crocker, Lionel. Old Books. Qrt J Spch 20 (Feb.) 143-4.
Review of A. Crocker's The Art of Reading.

824 Crocker, Lionel. Old Books. Qrt J Spch 20 (June) 458.
Review of J. W. Shoemaker's Practical Elocution.

825 Heaps, W. A. Choosing Literature for Reading Contests.
Qrt J Spch 20 (June) 410-4. Suggests raising standards.

826 Henderson, E. C. Some Principles of Oral Reading. Qrt J
Spch 20 (Apr.) 287-99. Defense of conversational delivery
in OI.

827 Loughram, J. M. Oral English in Secondary Schools. Qrt
J Spch 20 (Feb.) 72-80. Inadequacy of curricular time
for oral English in high school.

828 MacGregor, V. C. Personal Development in Beginning Speech
Training. Qrt J Spch 20 (Feb.) 47-57. Role of OI in
developing expression and power.

829 Morris, A. R. A Note on the Inflection of Julia Marlow.
Qrt J Spch 20 (Apr.) 200-2. Example of dominant pitch
cadence in the English sentence.

830 Paul, V. A. Suggestions for Teaching Oral Reading. Qrt J
Spch 20 (Apr.) 299-306. Literary, social, personal, and
language development in elementary school through OI.

831 Rasmussen, Carrie. Creative Dramatization in the Auditori-
um. Qrt J Spch 20 (Apr.) 279-82. Elements of creative
drama help students adjust to all situations in life.

832 Rasmussen, Carrie. Verse Speaking and Bodily Activity.
Qrt J Spch 20 (Apr.) 282-6. To like a poem children
must live it.

833 Tiffin, Joseph. Scientific Apparatus and Lab Methods:
Simultaneous Records of Eye Movements and the Voice in
Oral Reading. Science 80 (Nov.) 430-1. Relation between
poor silent readers and inferior oral readers to sensory
processes in reading.

1935

834 Crocker, Lionel. Old Books. Qrt J Spch 21 (Nov.) 618-9. Review of J. W. Anderson's The Manner ... in Which the Common Prayer Was Read ... by Garrick (1797).

835 Darby, O. N. An Experiment in Teaching Oral Reading. NEA J 24 (Jan.) 11-2. Skeleton outline of procedure followed in conducting an oral reading lesson which was used with much success in an experimental class.

836 Edwards, David. Interpretation. Qrt J Spch 21 (Nov.) 561-4. Call for increased recognition of values of OI of lit.

837 Emsley, Bert. Old Books. Qrt J Spch 21 (Nov.) 616-7. Reviews John Mason's Essays on Poetical and Prosaic Numbers and Elocution (1761).

838 Harris, M. L. Story Telling in the Elementary School. Qrt J Spch 21 (June) 385-8. Story telling encourages relating personal experience and extemporaneous retelling of stories.

839 Henrikson, E. H. Declamation in the High Schools. Qrt J Spch 21 (June) 379-82. Necessary steps in producing effective speech course.

840 Howes, Margaret. Story Telling. Qrt J Spch 21 (June) 382-4. Focus of course working with different types of stories.

841 Hudson, H. H. Old Books. Qrt J Spch 21 (Feb.) 126-7. Review of P. A. Fitzgerald's The Exhibition Speaker (1886).

842 Jones, J. B. Oral Reading in the Mirey Pit. Qrt J Spch 21 (Nov.) 524-34. Calls for reinstatement of OI in elementary curriculum and defends it against charge for retarding silent reading rate.

843 Lutz, M. E. Choral Reading: Its Application to the Teaching of Speech. Sthn Spch Bull 1 (Oct.) 26-8. Choral reading as effective teaching aid.

844 Osband, Helen. Making Stories Live for Children. Qrt J Spch 21 (Apr.) 252-5. Focus of lab course on storytelling through dramatization pantomime and pageantry.

845 Pearson, Frances. The Storyteller and His Treasure Chest. Qrt J Spch 21 (Nov.) 543-7. Selects stories for different age groups and classifications.

846 Skinner, E. R. A Calibrated Recording and Analysis of the Pitch, Force and Quality of Vocal Tones Expressing

Happiness and Sadness. Spch Mono 2 (Oct.) 81-137. Effect of emotional states on voice examined.

847 Sonke, D. E. Speech Teaching in the Elementary Grades. Qrt J Spch 21 (Nov.) 534-8. Lay foundation for good speech by teaching its fundamental principles.

848 Thonssen, Lester. Old Books. Qrt J Spch 21 (Nov.) 612. Review of Jonathan Barber's Exercises in Reading and Recitation (1828), Grammar of Elocution (1830), and Practical Treatise of Gesture (1831).

849 Thonssen, Lester. Old Books. Qrt J Spch 21 (Nov.) 613-5. Review of Sargent's The Standard Speaker (1856).

850 Walsh, Rose. Whither the Verse Speaking Choir? Qrt J Spch 21 (Nov.) 461-66. Claims popular support for elocution in the name of verse speaking choir.

1936

851 Alden, D. H. The First Pronouncing Dictionary. Qrt J Spch 22 (Feb.) 12-8. Conception and execution of Sheridan's Dictionary.

852 Arbuthnot, M. H. Telling Stories and Reading Aloud to Young Children. Childhood Educ 12 (May) 347-51. Story selection and values of reading aloud.

853 Babcock, M. M. The National Association. Sthn Spch Bull 2 (Oct.) 34. Need for OI.

854 Booth, M. B. Interpretative Reading in the Secondary Schools. Qrt J Spch 22 (Apr.) 270-77. Argues oral intent of lit for grades 7-12.

855 Borchers, Gladys. An Approach to the Problem of Oral Style. Qrt J Spch 22 (Feb.) 114-7. Drawing the line between speech and English in language presentation.

856 Carnes, O. H. Declamation in the Small School. Qrt J Spch 22 (Feb.) 107-14. Aids to small town teacher in preparing students for declamation.

857 Crocker, Lionel. Old Books. Qrt J Spch 22 (Dec.) 675-6. Review of Thomas Sheridan's Lectures on Elocution (1787).

858 Dennis, R. B. Declamation Contests. Qrt J Spch 22 (Apr.) 305-6. Suggestions for improvement.

859 Downs, S. W. Speech Chorus Work in the Elementary Schools of Germany. Qrt J Spch 22 (Dec.) 669-70.

Choral speaking had inception in new social ideal of community cooperation after the world war. Chorus work affords child opportunity to be aware of beauties of poetry.

860 Editorial. A Course of Study in Speech for Secondary Schools. Qrt J Spch 22 (Apr.) 250-66. Report of Commission for the Advancement of Speech Education in Secondary Schools.

861 Galbraith, E. A. A Note on Three Choral Readings. Qrt J Spch 22 (Dec.) 648-51. Production notes of three high school productions.

862 Gray, W. S. The Place of Oral Reading in an Improved Program of Reading. Elem School J 36 (Mar.) 517-26. Place and value of oral reading study.

863 Hayes, J. J. The Rhythm of Prose. Engl J 25 (Dec.) 868-77. Prose rhythm integral part of lit.

864 Henning, J. H. The Development of Literary Appreciation Through Speech. Qrt J Spch 22 (Apr.) 278-83. Opening student's eyes to broader and richer experience through good lit.

865 Jones, M. E. The Case for Standard English. Qrt J Spch 22 (Oct.) 449-54. Questions and answers directed at salience of standard English.

866 Meader, E. G. Choral Speaking and Its Values. Qrt J Spch 22 (Apr.) 235-45. History definitions directing choral speaking.

867 Morris, A. R. Liddell's Laws of English Rhythm. Mich Acad of Science, Arts & Letters 22 (1936) 485-91. Using poetry of Coleridge as primary example, Morris describes how Liddell's system of phrasing and emphasis could apply to oral reading of other English works.

868 Parrish, W. M. Objective Literary Standards in Interpretation. Qrt J Spch 22 (Oct.) 368-79. Discovering poet's meaning and conveying it to audience.

869 Pearson, Frances. Speech Training Through Children's Plays. Qrt J Spch 22 (Dec.) 660-8. Plays as motivating factors in speech work.

870 Quiz, Quintus. Reading Aloud. Christian Century 53 (Apr. 29) 626. Values of reading aloud.

871 Rasmussen, Carrie. Rhythm in Bodily Action and Creative Dramatics. Qrt J Spch 22 (Apr.) 291-4. Conveying meaning and function of rhythm to children.

872 Sheperdson, Nadine. The Oral Interpretation of Literature. Sthn Spch Bull 1 (Mar.) 18-21. OI more sharing than performing.

873 Van Wye, B. C. The Efficient Voice in Speech. Qrt J Spch 22 (Dec.) 642-8. Voice improvement characteristics and techniques.

1937

874 Arbuthnot, M. H. What, Reading Aloud! Childhood Educ 14 (Nov.) 118-24. Oral reading helps children's speech habits and growth.

875 Bahn, Eugene. Interpretative Reading in Classical Rome. Qrt J Spch 23 (Apr.) 202-13. Reasons for rise and fall of OI in Rome.

876 Crawford, M. M. Speech Choirs in Europe. Qrt J Spch 23 (Oct.) 444-9. Choral speaking in England, Germany, Austria, France, and Switzerland.

877 Hevner, Kate. Experimental Study of Affective Value of Sounds in Poetry. Amer J of Psych 49 (1937) 419-34. Studies meter, voice inflection, vowel and consonant sounds.

878 Johnson, G. E. Backgrounds for Interpretation. Sthn Spch Bull 3 (Nov.) 11-5. OI need past experiences of science, art, philosophy, music, and lit.

879 Lewis, R. B., & II. D. Roberts. The Director's Part in the Verse Speaking Choir. Qrt J Spch 23 (Feb.) 63-6. Emphasizes meaning and purpose over choir.

880 Lyne, D. J. The Choral Verse Speaking Choir. Qrt J Spch 23 (Oct.) 449-51. Explanation of first production in high school.

881 Marsh, T. H. Some Problems of Oral Bible Reading. Qrt J Spch 23 (Oct.) 396-402. Presents rules and advice for the performer.

882 Ortleb, Ruth, & Joseph Tiffin. An Objective Study of Emphasis in Oral Reading of Emotional and Unemotional Material. Spch Mono 4 (1937) 56-68. Tests relationship of emphasis to pitch, time, and intensity.

883 Pellegrini, A. M. The Aim and Educational Content of Oral Reading. Qrt J Spch 23 (Dec.) 643-7. Purpose of OI lies in audience's understanding of lit's worth.

884 Rogers, M. V. Comprehension in Oral and Silent Reading.
J of Gen Psych 17 (Oct.) 394-7. Comprehension between
oral and silent reading for poor and good readers.

885 Stone, G. W. Garrick's Presentation of Antony and Cleopatra. Rev of Engl Stud 13 (Jan.) 20-38. Garrick's style
and presentation of the play.

1938

886 Adams, H. M. Listening. Qrt J Spch 24 (Apr.) 209-11.
Listening skill to be taught as well as speaking.

887 Anderson, H. R. A New First Course in Speech and English.
Qrt J Spch 24 (Feb.) 70-7. Basic speech course should
be first course in oral and written composition in colleges
and universities.

888 Armstrong, M. H. Certain Aspects of Choral Speech. Qrt
J Spch 24 (Feb.) 117-9. Marjorie Gullan and her work
with choric speech.

889 Beckey, R. E. Selecting Passages for Oral Reading. Engl J
27 (Mar.) 260-5. Use of OI to meet English course objectives.

890 Bradford, A. L. When Oral Interpretation Comes of Age.
Qrt J Spch 24 (Oct.) 444-52. OI not speech course but
course in lit.

891 Bryngelson, Bryng. The Interpretative Symbol. Qrt J Spch
24 (Dec.) 569-73. Nonverbals and teachers.

892 Cohen, Morris. A Transfer in Learning. Qrt J Spch 24
(Oct.) 443-4. Eliminating end stops in poetry transfers
to other poems.

893 Daw, S. E. The Persistence of Errors in Oral Reading in
Grades Four and Five. J Educ Research 32 (Oct.) 81-90.
What extent reading difficulties of the primary grades per-
sist in grades four and five and to suggest corrective
measures.

894 Dusenbury, Delwin, & F. H. Knower. Experimental Studies
of the Symbolism of Action and Voice I: A Study of the
Specificity of Meaning in Facial Expression. Qrt J Spch
(Oct.) 424-36. Facial expression communicates meaning
and variety of emotions.

895 Hinks, H. S. Choric Speaking. Sthn Spch Bull 3 (Mar.) 16-
8. Choric speaking justified.

896 Kalp, E. S. A Summary of the Des Moines High School
Speech Course of Study. Qrt J Spch 24 (Feb.) 90-5.
Section on OI.

897 Marsh, T. H. The Bible as a Source Material for Public
Speaking and Oral Reading. Qrt J Spch 24 (Apr.) 199-204.
Role of Bible as lit.

898 Marshman, J. T. The Mystery of Oral Interpretation. Qrt
J Spch 24 (Dec.) 596-603. Spiritual element in lit as
manifested by articulation and action.

899 Marshman, J. T. The Use of Narrative in Speaking. Sthn
Spch Bull 4 (Sept.) 1-6. Discusses handling narrative in
a speech.

900 Moore, C. E. A Preliminary Study of the Emotional Effects
of Letter Sounds. Qrt J Spch 24 (Feb.) 134-49. Survey
of opinions and results of experiments.

901 Robbins, R. H. A Further Justification of Choral Speaking.
Qrt J Spch 24 (Oct.) 437-42. Some poetry requires
choral speaking for effect.

902 Rodigan, M. V. New Approaches to Aims in Interpretative
Reading in Teachers Colleges. Qrt J Spch 24 (Apr.) 205-
8. Individual professional and social purposes of OI.

1939

903 Barnard, R. H. A Course in Characterization. Sthn Spch
Bull 4 (Jan.) 3-7. Fundamentals needed to precede the
work in dramatic art or acting.

904 Brees, P. R. The Teacher of Interpretation as a Reader.
Qrt J Spch 25 (Feb.) 62-6. Advantages and disadvantages
of OI teacher reading to students.

905 Dow, C. W. A Literary Interpretation Analysis Blank. Qrt J
Spch 25 (Apr.) 285-8. Presents a rating blank to impress
students with factors basic to artistic OI.

906 Dusenbury, Delwin, & F. H. Knower. Experimental Studies
of the Symbolism of Action and Voice II: A Study of the
Specificity of Meaning in Abstract Tonal Symbols. Qrt J
Spch 25 (Feb.) 67-75. Focus on ability to communicate
meaning in abstract tone symbols.

907 Eich, L. M. The Relation of Content, Form and Style to
Interpretative Reading. Qrt J Spch (Apr.) 281-5. Indicates pedagogical emphasis to maintain OI academic respectability.

908 Fairbanks, Grant, & Wilbert Pronovost. An Experimental Study of the Pitch Characteristics of the Voice During the Expression of Emotion. Spch Mono 6 (Dec.) 87-104. Relationship of pitch to contempt, anger, fear, grief, and indifference.

909 Hamm, A. C. Choral Speaking: A Word of Warning. Qrt J Spch 25 (Apr.) 225-7. Future of choral speaking in danger of unqualified practitioners.

910 Kibbe, D. E. Oral Reading. Improving the Reading Program in Wisconsin Schools 2 (Jan.) 42-7. Techniques for improving reading.

911 Parks, M. R. An Answer to the Administrators. Qrt J Spch 25 (Feb.) 13-6. Case for subbing speech course for English in public high schools.

912 Robbins, R. H. Choral Speaking at the Oxford Festivals. Qrt J Spch 25 (Apr.) 227-35. History, trends, practices, and list of produced poems.

913 Weniger, C. E. Old Books. Qrt J Spch 25 (Oct.) 484. Review of Albert Bacon's A Manual of Gesture (1870).

1940

914 Allensworth, Josephine. The Effectiveness of the One-Act Play. Qrt J Spch 26 (Apr.) 269-74. Effect of one-act play for developing effective oral reading, clear thinking, and speaking voice.

915 Baker, L. B. Aids in Teaching Interpretation in High School. Sthn Spch Bull 6 (Sept.) 6-9. Teacher recitations aid development of students.

916 Braden, W. W. The Interpretative Reading Festival. Qrt J Spch 26 (Feb.) 101-4. Suggested methods to eliminate problems with declamatory speaking programs.

917 Buchan, A. M. The Teacher of English in Speech. Qrt J Spch 26 (Dec.) 637-43. Understanding stylistic differences between English teacher and speech teacher.

918 Cunningham, C. C. Aims and Techniques of Oral Interpretation. Wstn Spch 4 (May) 1-5. OI as art.

919 Eisenson, Jon; S. G. Souther; & Jerome Fisher. The Affective Value of English Speech Sounds. Qrt J Spch 26 (Dec.) 589-94. Study to determine pleasant or unpleasant speech sounds.

920 Foster, F. M. A Read Aloud Baby Bookshelf. Elem Engl
Rev 17 (Jan.) 9-10. Bibliography.

921 Ginsberg, Walter. How Helpful Are Shakespeare Recordings?
Engl J 29 (Apr.) 289-300. Mercury recordings proved
valuable aid to appreciation of Shakespeare in classroom.

922 Ginsberg, Walter. Recordings for High School English.
Engl J 29 (Feb.) 134-40. Index of noteworthy records
for use in English class and information about radio programs, sources and distribution services.

923 Ginsberg, Walter. Sound Recording in the English Class.
Engl J 29 (Mar.) 230-2. How to use recording instrument
in English classroom.

924 Graham, D. F. A Program of Poet's Recordings. Engl J
29 (Jan.) 60. Bibliography.

925 Lee, C. I. Choric Reading and Kinetic Projection. Qrt J
Spch 26 (Dec.) 545-50. A look at presentation of poetry
with rhythmic movement.

926 Norvelle, Lee, & R. G. Smith. Testing for Improvement in
Oral Interpretation. Qrt J Spch 26 (Dec.) 540-5. Using
recording machines to measure improvement in pausing, in-
flecting, using force and emphasis in oral reading classes.

927 Passons, T. A. Present Trends in Oral Reading in Elementary Schools. Sthn Spch Bull 6 (Sept.) 10-3. Reading
fluently and intelligently as criteria for successful elementary education.

928 Rarig, F. M. Some Elementary Contributions of Aesthetics
to Interpretative Speech. Qrt J Spch 26 (Dec.) 527-39.
Importance of preparation and attitude of reader.

929 Robbins, R. H. A Checklist of Poems for Boys' Choirs.
Wstn Spch 4 (Jan.) 12-3. Choric poems for reading
aloud.

930 Seigfred, E. C. Analysis of Programs of Study and Demands
of Teaching Positions of MA Graduates in Speech. Spch
Mono 7 (Dec.) 93-100. Report of survey investigating
educational preparation of candidates who became teachers.

1941

931 Allen, Willadel. Teaching Interpretative Reading in the High
School. Qrt J Spch 27 (Feb.) 115-9. Justification for OI
classes by asking does any course justify existence? Who

judges? To whom are we to justify--School Board, children or the future?

932 Benson, A. R. Rhythmical Figures on the Metrical Frame. Engl J 30 (Jan.) 53-6. Discussion of metrical verse.

933 Brand, R. C. Radio Drama in the Small College. Sthn Spch Bull 7 (Sept.) 18-9. Radio drama as outlet for dramatic expression.

934 Clark, R. D. Reading Aloud and the Appreciation of Poetry. Wstn Spch 5 (Jan.) 18-21. Values of OI.

935 Crofton, G. E. Verse-Speaking and Poetry Appreciation. Engl J 30 (Nov.) 729-34. Teaching verse through choral reading.

936 Dow, C. W. Intelligence and Ability in Public Performance. Qrt J Spch 27 (Feb.) 110-5. Little relationship between ability in speaking and intelligence: great relationship between ability in literary interpretation and intelligence.

937 Editors. Drama as an Intramural Sport. Senior Scholastic 38 (Mar. 31) 42. Values of drama, with attention to group play reading.

938 Fairbanks, Grant, & L. W. Hoaglin. An Experimental Study of the Durational Characteristics of the Voice During the Expression of Emotion. Spch Mono 8 (Dec.) 85-90. Relationship of vocal duration to contempt anger, fear, grief, and indifference.

939 Hale, L. L. Principles of James Rush as Applied to Interpretation. Sthn Spch Bull 7 (Nov.) 43-5. Rush's observation method as criticism.

940 Hanna, Mark. College Speech and the Grapes of Wrath. Qrt J Spch 27 (Apr.) 223-7. To increase student's interest, read from classics.

941 Hollister, R. D. Application of Aesthetic Criteria to the Oral Presentation of Literature. Qrt J Spch 27 (Apr.) 281-9. Aesthetic test to evaluate OI.

942 Irwin, R. L. Declamation--A Cultural Lag. Qrt J Spch 27 (Apr.) 289-91. Students in declamation contests read respectable literature, perform with books, use incipient gestures and share student responses in literature.

943 Kirby, B. C. The Return of Oral Reading. J of Educ 124 (Feb.) 58-60. Argues importance of oral reading through views and poll results.

944 Lynch, G. E. Oral Interpretation: A Test of Literary Appreciation. Sthn Spch Bull 7 (Mar.) 112-5. OI as a test of critical appreciation.

945 Mescall, Gertrude. A Radio Reading Project. Engl J 30 (Mar.) 236-8. A group of grade 9 students perform The Seeing Eye Dog and become more self-reliant through performance.

946 Peeler, A. L. The Development of Voice Through Choral Speech. Sthn Spch Bull 7 (Sept.) 12-4. Choric speech in sixth grade.

947 Rasmussen, Carrie. Rhythm in Bodily Language and Creative Dramatics. Sthn Spch Bull 6 (Mar.) 84-5. Body is instrument of expression.

948 Staples, Grace. Don'ts and Do's in Choral Speaking. Wstn Spch 6 (Nov.) 22-3. Suggestions for selecting and presenting choral performances.

949 Stuurman, K. A. Staged Reading of Plays. Players Mag 18 (Oct.) 18-9. Group play reading as genesis of today's Readers' Theatre.

950 Trueblood, T. C. Pioneering in Speech. Qrt J Spch 27 (Dec.) 503-11. Recreation through personal narratives of the evolution of speech since 1870.

1942

951 Abrams, M. H. Unconscious Expectations in the Reading of Poetry. Engl Lit Hist 9 (Dec.) 235-44. How skills of experienced reader may come to limit range of his/her appreciation by citing certain elements in criticism of Johnson.

952 Andreini, C. B. In Defense of Collective Speech. Wstn Spch J 6 (Jan.) 22-4. Verse choir as method of group remedial work in voice and diction in beginning class.

953 Bacon, W. A. Source of Robert Daborne's The Poor Man's Comfort. Mod Lang Notes 57 (May) 345-8. Connects William Warner's Syrinx with Daborn's plot.

954 Clark, R. D. An Approach to Meaning in Teaching Poetry Appreciation. Wstn Spch 6 (Nov.) 16-20. Teaching appreciation.

955 Cunningham, C. C. The Sepia School of Interpretative Reading. Qrt J Spch 28 (Feb.) 37-41. Noncommittal OI is rejected in favor of artistic obligations.

956 Duff, Annis. Family Affair. Horn Book 18 (Jan.) 57-62. Reading aloud with reading list for children.

957 Flaccus, Kimball. An Adventure in Poetry. Qrt J Spch 28 (Oct.) 315-23. Phonographic library of contemporary poets.

958 Griggs, E. L. On Reading Poetry Aloud. U Penn Bulletin 42 (June) 221-9. Values of reading aloud.

959 Lindeman, E. C. Dum Placem Peream. Lib J 67 (Feb. 15) 157-9. How old fashioned reading circles can contribute to revitalizing of adult education and democracy.

960 McClusky, F. D. Oral Reading. Nation's Schools 30 (Oct.) 14-5. Values of oral reading.

961 Marshman, J. T. The Paradox of Oral Interpretation. Qrt J Spch 28 (Feb.) 31-6. Extended definition of OI focusing on reader's subservience to lit.

962 Plugge, D. E. Voice Qualities in Oral Interpretation. Qrt J Spch 28 (Dec.) 442-4. Formal classifications are rejected as teaching techniques.

963 Robb, M. M. Looking Backward. Qrt J Spch 28 (Oct.) 323-7. Brief summary of OI history.

964 Shaver, C. L. Studies on Delsarte. Sthn Spch J 8 (Sept.) 17. Study on papers, documents, and student notebooks of Delsarte.

965 Swain, L. H. Actors, Speakers or Equestrians? Sthn Spch J 7 (Mar.) 111. Problems with studying acting and public speaking together.

966 Williams, H. D. You Might Like the Verse Speaking Choir. Qrt J Spch 28 (Feb.) 41-5. Verse speaking can overcome dislike for poetry.

967 Winters, Roberta. Reading to the Eye. Sthn Spch J 8 (Sept.) 14-7. Pantomime and physical activity as stimulus to eye in performance.

1943

968 Chenoweth, E. C., & E. C. Mabie. Training and Occupations of Iowa Bachelor Graduates in Speech and Dramatic Art, 1931-40. Spch Mono 10 (Dec.) 103-7. Academic programs to nature of teaching positions.

969 Cohler, M. J. The Uses and Abuses of Oral Reading. Elem
Engl Rev 20 (Dec.) 327-9. Problems of oral reading in
classroom.

970 Davidson, Margaret. Reading Aloud. Pittsburgh Schls 17
(May) 153-7.

971 Davis, L. R. Mother Knows Least. Horn Book 19 (Jan.)
45-9. Rewards of reading aloud and how to please individual tastes.

972 Dodsen, Owen. Everybody Join Hands: Choral Drama.
Theatre Arts 27 (Sept.) 555-65. Choral play about Chinese and their fight for freedom.

973 Gray, G. W. The Voice Qualities in the History of Elocution. Qrt J Spch 29 (Dec.) 475-80. Expands Plugge and
traces history of voice from Rush (1827) to Woolbert
(1927).

974 Gray, G. W., & L. L. Hale. James Rush, Dramatist. Qrt
J Spch 29 (Feb.) 55-61. View of Rush and his play Hamlet, a dramatic prelude in five acts.

975 Morris, Charles. The Teaching of Oral and Written Communication as a Unified Program of Language Instruction.
Qrt J Spch 29 (Apr.) 209-12. Pedagogical method explained.

976 O'Hara, Vera. We Broadcast the Sohrab-Rustum Fight.
Engl J 32 (Jan.) 41-2. Students get involved in poetry
reading by relating to modern activities.

977 Paul, V. A. The Relation of Oral Reading to Remedial
Reading in Elementary and Secondary Schools. Qrt J Spch
29 (Apr.) 217-22. Aims, plans, successes, and failures of
projects in remedial reading.

978 Rarig, F. M. & Ralph Dennis. Qrt J Spch 29 (Apr.) 234-40.
Tribute.

979 Rice, John, & C. A. Fritz. An Introduction to the Art of
Reading with Energy and Propriety. Qrt J Spch 29 (Oct.)
380. Statement of principles.

980 Snidecor, J. C. Comparative Study of the Pitch and Duration
Characteristics of Impromptu Speaking and Oral Reading.
Spch Mono 10 (1943) 50-6. Difference between impromptu
and oral reading styles.

981 Wells, H. W. Literature and the Phonograph. Qrt J Spch
29 (Feb.) 68-73. Criteria for use of recorded oral reading: short list of appropriate recordings to 1943.

982 Winans, J. A. The Sense of Communication. Sthn Spch J
9 (Sept.) 3-11. Distinctions between declamation and OI.

1944

983 Drake, Christine. A Critique on the Curry Method. Sthn
Spch J 9 (Mar.) 112-7. Curry's greatness not in philosophy but inspiration as a teacher.

984 Hance, K. G. The American Lecture Platform Before 1930.
Qrt J Spch 30 (Oct.) 273-9. Three stages of lecture circuit as it developed from Civil War to 1900, and 1900-
1930.

985 Lowrey, Sara. Teaching Interpretative Reading as an Art.
Sthn Spch J 9 (Jan.) 70-4. OI as way of understanding
meaning and expressing that meaning.

986 McKelvey, D. P. A Survey of the Opinions of Speech Graduates Concerning Selected Aspects of Their Undergraduate
Speech Training. Spch Mono 11 (Oct.) 28-52. OI made a
greater impression on students than other speech activities.

987 Robinson, K. F. Getting Started in the High School Fundamentals Class. Qrt J Spch 30 (Oct.) 343-7. Sections on
reading aloud, memorization, and choral speaking.

988 Snidecor, J. C. An Objective Study of Phrasing in Impromptu
Speaking and Oral Reading. Spch Mono 11 (1944) 97-104.
Extension of previous study.

989 White, R. F. A Biographical Sketch of James Edward Murdoch. Sthn Spch J 9 (Mar.) 95-101. Focus on the
man.

1945

990 Burklund, C. E. On the Oral Reading of Poetry. Qrt J
Spch 31 (Oct.) 344-50. How to read poetry with understanding of metrical pattern and genius of poetry.

991 Casteel, J. L. College Speech Training and the Ministry.
Qrt J Spch 31 (Feb.) 73-7. OI neglected in undergraduate
ministry.

992 Compere, M. S. Speech: Science and/or Art? Qrt J Spch
31 (Dec.) 465-70. Attributes of OI in increasing eye
span, vocabulary, intellectual discrimination. Suggest
using reading hour and special reading clinics.

993 Cunningham, C. C. Stress Variations in Oral Interpretation. Qrt J Spch 31 (Feb.) 55-62. Two-year study explained.

994 Editorial. Digest of Report on Speech in Teacher Education. Qrt J Spch 31 (Apr.) 242-3. Summarizes offerings
and activities of state teachers colleges accredited by
American Association of Teachers Colleges.

995 Hunt, Everett. Hoyt Hopewell Hudson. Qrt J Spch 31 (Oct.)
272-4. Hudson's intellectual and educational pursuits.

996 Kaucher, Dorothy. Try It Again. Qrt J Spch 31 (Feb.) 47-
54. Guides for new teacher.

997 Lowrey, Sara. Interpretative Reading as an Aid to Speech
Correction, Acting, and Radio. Qrt J Spch 31 (Dec.) 459-
64. Many uses of OI.

998- Mosso, A. M. The Relationship of Oral Communication to
9 Other Aspects of the Oral Program. Engl J 34 (Oct.)
440-2. Tone of voice, manner and use of language take
on a meaning as useful tools of living and oral English
becomes an art rather than a chore.

1000 Palmer, Herbert. Some Notes on Verse Speaking and
Phonetics. Comp Lit Studies 17 (1945) 1-2. Seven hints
for verse speakers.

1001 Price, Helen, & J. B. Stroud. A Note on Oral Reading.
Qrt J Spch 31 (Oct.) 340-3. As OI declines in schools
the influence of silent reading on OI is more apparent.

1002 Sandberg, R. A. The Teacher as an Interpreter. Wstn
Spch 9 (Nov.) 3-5. Teacher should serve as role model
for students.

1003 Sawyer, R. On Reading the Bible Aloud. Horn Book 21
(Mar.) 99-107. Bible comes alive when read aloud.

1004 Seedorf, E. H. Shall We Have Expression? Sthn Spch J 11
(Nov.) 42-3. OI justified because it teaches intellectual
and emotional expression.

1005 Seip, H. S. A Study in Listener Reaction to Voice Quality.
Sthn Spch J 11 (Nov.) 44-52. Recommendations to make
student more voice conscious in everyday life.

1005a Urwin, J. T. Do You Know How to Read Aloud? Parents
26 (Sept.) 769. Importance of using stress modulation
and tempo in reading aloud.

1006 Winans, J. A. Whately on Elocution. Qrt J Spch 31 (Feb.)
1-8. Critical view of Whately's view of delivery as

springing from thought and feeling rather than rules and imitation.

1946

1007 Andrews, J. W. Poetry and the Radio. Poet-Lore 52 (Autumn) 261-7. Because words are main means of communication over radio it is well suited for poetry.

1008 Armour, R. W., & R. E. Howes. Addenda to Coleridge the Talker. Qrt J Spch 32 (Oct.) 298-303. John Clare, Sir Henry Taylor and Richard M. Milnes provide more information on Coleridge.

1009 Bolinger, D. L. The Intonation of Quoted Questions. Qrt J Spch 32 (Apr.) 197-202. Limitations in intonation of quoted questions.

1010 Burklund, C. E. Hyacinths and Bisquits--on a Rationale for the Oral Reading of Poetry. Qrt J Spch 32 (Dec.) 469-74. Best presentation of poetry inseparable fusion of art and conversation.

1011 Committee on Teacher Education. Speech in Teacher Education. Qrt J Spch 32 (Feb.) 80-102. Statistical summary of OI in teachers colleges.

1012 Cunningham, C. C. The Rhythm of Robinson Jeffers' Poetry as Revealed by Oral Reading. Qrt J Spch 32 (Oct.) 351-7. Oral reading can solve prosodic problems.

1013 Duncan, M. H. Localizing Individual Problems in Oral Interpretation. Qrt J Spch 32 (Apr.) 213-6. Difficulties in OI are probed by personality inventories, questionnaires, and test of expressiveness.

1014 Editors. Poetry Reading. Senior Scholastic 48 (Apr. 1) Suppl. 6. Values of reading aloud.

1015 Hamm, A. C. I Hate Poetry. Sthn Spch J 11 (Jan.) 76-7. Choral speaking and OI in elementary schools.

1016 Howell, W. S. De Quincey on Science, Rhetoric and Poetry. Spch Mono 13 (Jan.) 1-13. If criticism is to provide accurate description of difference between rhetoric/poetic, Aristotle would seem to establish better foundation than De Quincey.

1017 Kletzing, Evelyn. Choral Reading in the English Classroom. Engl J 35 (Feb.) 100-1. Effects of choral reading in English classes.

1018   Landry, K. E.   Enriching Oral Reading Through Better
       Speech.   Sthn Spch J 12 (Nov.) 25-7.   Skills in speech
       in elementary school.

1019   Lowrey, Sara.   Gesture Through Empathy.   Sthn Spch J 11
       (Jan.) 59-62.   Purpose and value of gesture in commun-
       icating lit.

1020   Lowrey, Sara.   As We Like It.   Sthn Spch J 12 (Nov.) 32-3.
       Effects of posture in voice training.

1021   Robinson, M. P.   Diary of a Problem Child.   Qrt J Spch
       32 (Oct.) 357-67.   Evolution of oral expression in form
       of diary: 600 B. C. to A. D. 1945.

1022   Runte, A. F.   Drama Reading: Key to Discussion.   Lib J
       71 (Mar. 15) 391-3.   Librarian's responsibility to create
       opportunities to study lit.

1023   Tousey, G. J.   A Preliminary Study of Underlying Causes
       of Poor Reading.   Sthn Spch J 11 (Mar.) 90-4.   Possible
       causes for reading problems in children.

1024   Wise, C. M.   Lanier's Theories as to the Relation of Music
       and Verse.   Sthn Spch J 11 (Mar.) 97-100.   Lanier's the-
       ory holds that sound relations which constitute music are
       identical with those which constitute verse.

                                 1947

1025   Bacon, W. A.   Note on The Tempest IV I.   Notes & Queries
       192 (Aug.) 343-4.   Brief discussion of Prospero.

1026   Brown, J. M.   Between the Dark and the Daylight.   Sat Rev
       30 (May 10) 26-9.   Father reads aloud to family.

1027   Carrighar, Sally.   San Francisco's Festival of Modern Po-
       etry: Some Problems of Verse Reading.   Poetry 70 (Sept.)
       344-7.   Common problems facing all people reading verse.

1028   Donner, S. T.   Mark Twain as a Reader.   Qrt J Spch 33
       (Oct.) 308-11.   Twain's preparation and abilities as reader.

1029   Editors.   Industry Gets a New Educational Idea.   America
       96 (Jan.) 410.   Reading aloud to workers.

1030   Edwards, Davis.   The Real Source of Vachel Lindsay's
       Poetic Techniques.   Qrt J Spch 33 (Apr.) 182-95.   Influ-
       ence of S. H. Clark on Lindsay's poetic techniques.

1031   Finlan, Leonard.   The Relation Between Training and
       Teaching Activities of College Teachers of Speech.   Qrt

J Spch 33 (Feb.) 72-9. Survey of teaching demands and qualifications.

1032 Friedman, I. R. Speaking of Choral Reading. Engl J 36 (Feb.) 95-6. Choral speech has use aside from poetry.

1033 Ghiselin, Brewster. Reading Sprung Rhythms. Poetry 70 (May) 86-93. Argues against Whitehall's view of G. M. Hopkins' works.

1034 Griffin, Leland. Letter to the Press--1778. Qrt J Spch 33 (Apr.) 143-50. Tribute to Crito as advocate of natural delivery.

1035 Haberman, F. W. John Thelwall: His Life, His School and His Theory of Elocution. Qrt J Spch 33 (Oct.) 292-8. Thelwall as part of elocutionary movement.

1036 Howell, W. S. Literature as an Enterprise in Communication. Qrt J Spch 33 (Dec.) 417-26. Relation of rhetoric and poetry as chief modes of communication and persuasion.

1037 Irwin, R. L. Taste in Declamation. Schl Act 19 (Sept.) 5-6. Plea for raising stand for lit and performance in declamation contests.

1038 Lembke, R. W. Relativist Esthetics and Dramatic Criticism. Spch Mono 14 (1947) 148-58. Discussion of standards and analysis of relativist esthetics and dramatic criticism.

1039 Lowrey, Sara. Impersonation as a Style of Interpretation. Sthn Spch J 13 (Nov.) 65-9. Erudition and adjustment as objectives of impersonation.

1040 MacKenzie, C. Reading Aloud at Home. NY Times Mag (June 15) 32. Values of reading aloud.

1041 McCoard, W. B. Oral Interpretation Speaks. Wstn Spch 11 (Oct.) 10 & 26. Fable of OI history.

1042 McLeod, Archibald. The Actor's Elocution. Sthn Spch J 12 (Mar.) 97-9. Elocution and Stanislavsky needed.

1043 Murphy, Theresa, & Richard Murphy. Charles Dickens as Professional Reader. Qrt J Spch 33 (Oct.) 299-303. Dickens' motives, preparation and reading success.

1044 Nauss, Lorraine. Reading the Language of Literature. Qrt J Spch 33 (Dec.) 474-9. Language of lit is primitive in usage and must be lived for it cannot be paraphrased.

1045 Paul, V. A. Choral Speaking as a Phase of Oral Interpretation. Sthn Spch J 13 (Nov.) 62-4. Choral speaking values.

1046 Shapiro, Karl. English Prosody and Modern Poetry. Engl Lit History 14 (June) 77-92. Discussion of meter in verse.

1948

1047 Bacon, W. A. Literary Reputation of John Ford. Huntington Lib Qrtly 11 (Feb.) 181-99. Discussion of Ford's place in English drama.

1048 Bowyer, Frances. A Ballad Should Be Heard, Not Seen. Engl J 37 (Mar.) 152-3. Emphasis on aural not visual enjoyment of poetry.

1049 Burklund, C. E. Notes for an Imagined Anthology. Qrt J Spch 34 (Dec.) 477-82. Character and contour necessary for good anthology.

1050 Chambers, R. F. The Fun of Reading Aloud. Horn Book 24 (June) 177-80. Values of reading to children.

1051 Cochran, Peggy. Let's Read Aloud. Parents Mag 23 (Nov.) 166. Advantages of reading aloud to child.

1052 Cunningham, C. C. Trying to Pos the Impossible. Wstn Spch 12 (Apr.) 11-3. Dangers of impersonation.

1053 Flanagan, J. T. Three Allied Arts. Qrt J Spch 34 (Feb.) 30-5. History, lit and public address form a coalition when studied according to climate which produces them and aesthetic qualities that each possesses.

1054 Herrick, M. T. The Place of Rhetoric in Poetic Theory. Qrt J Spch 34 (Feb.) 1-22. A look at the canons and exordium, narratio, proof and conclusion in oratory and poetry.

1055 Lowrey, Sara. Freedom Through Interpretative Reading and Educational Theatre. Sthn Spch J 14 (Nov.) 74-81. OI as medium of freedom.

1056 McCoard, W. B. Report on the Reading of Hiroshima. Qrt J Spch 34 (Apr.) 174-6. Reports preparation for reading.

1057 Nichols, R. G., & J. I. Brown. A Communication Program in a Technical College. Qrt J Spch 34 (Dec.) 494-8. Listening, reading, speaking and writing as basic skills for successful communication.

1058 Tousey, G. J. McGuffey's Elocutionary Teachings. Qrt J Spch 34 (Feb.) 80-7. Synopsis of McGuffey's contribution to general education; includes list of elements of elocution.

1059 Weiss, Harold. Needed: New Signals for Effective Oral Reading. Sthn Spch J 14 (Nov.) 119-23. Stresses punctuation marks effective for silent readers but not for OIers.

1949

1060 Anderson, Aurilla. Developing a Junior High Reading Program. Wstn Spch 13 (May) 17-8. Principles for developing junior high school reading program: recognizing individual differences, involvement with all learning, pupil interest, enjoyment, and reading seen as part of developmental process.

1061 Bacon, W. A. Graduate Studies in Interpretation. Qrt J Spch 35 (Oct.) 316-9. Research areas for OI for balance of scholarship and oral skill.

1062 Bassett, L. E. Speech in the West, 1949: Elocution Then, Oral Interpretation Now. Wstn Spch 13 (Mar.) 3-8. Elocutionists as readers.

1063 Benét, W. R. Phoenix West: Reading Poetry Aloud. Sat Rev 32 (June 25) 43. Need for poets to read their own poetry aloud.

1064 Cable, W. A. Have We Abandoned Training in Action? Wstn Spch 13 (Mar.) 21-2. Laments performance which ignores training in visible aspects of speech code. Urges strong physical participation in speaking and reading.

1065 Caffrey, John. Analysis of Sound Repetition. Word Study 25 (Dec.) 3-4. Reaction to S. L. Moody's new devices in sound repetition.

1066 Ciardi, John. Letter from Harvard: Poetry Readings. Poetry 74 (May) 112-3. Use of written copy of poems as interpreter reads.

1067 Clark, D. L. Some Values of Roman Declamatio. Qrt J Spch 34 (Oct.) 280-3. Discussion of controversia, a school exercise in judicial oratory of the law courts.

1068 Clark, R. D. Research Possibilities in Interpretative Speech. Wstn Spch 13 (Oct.) 16-19. Materials, techniques, and history as research potential.

1069 Dolman, John, Jr. On Graduate Study and Interpretation. Qrt J Spch 35 (Dec.) 510-1. Response to Bacon in QJS 35 (Oct. 1949) 316-9.

1070 Finkel, W. L. Robert Ingersoll's Oratory and Walt Whitman's Poetry. Spch Mono 16 (Aug.) 41-56. Comparison of rhetoric/poetic.

1071 Fleischman, E. E. Let's Take Another Look at Interpretation. Qrt J Spch 35 (Dec.) 477-84. Compares OI to public address and reveals faults in OI.

1072 Gray, G. W. Research in the History of Speech Education. Qrt J Spch 35 (Apr.) 156-63. Contributions and need for research.

1073 Green, C. P. Graduate Study in Oral Interpretation. Sthn Spch J 15 (Dec.) 128-37. Survey of higher education offerings in OI.

1074 Haberman, F. W. The Bell Family: A Dynasty in Speech. Sthn Spch Comm J 15 (Dec.) 112-6. Contributions of Bell family.

1075 Hale, L. L. Dr. James Rush: Psychologist and Voice Scientist. Qrt J Spch 35 (Dec.) 448-55. Summary of Rush's methods, philosophy, postulates, and contributions.

1076 Herrick, M. T. The Theory of the Laughable in the Sixteenth Century. Qrt J Spch 35 (Feb.) 1-16. Theories of laughable based on Greek and Roman writings.

1077 Kernodle, G. R. Basic Problems in Reading Shakespeare. Qrt J Spch 35 (Feb.) 36-42. Problems categorized by form, grammar, rhetoric, and coloring.

1078 McCoard, W. B. An Interpretation of the Times: A Report of the Oral Interpretation of W. H. Auden's "Age of Anxiety." Qrt J Spch 35 (Dec.) 489-95. Aids to understanding and analysis of poem "Age of Anxiety."

1079 Mouat, L. H. The Question Method for Teaching Emphasis in Oral Reading. Qrt J Spch 35 (Dec.) 485-8. Problem of emphasis solved by using question method so listeners can grasp meaning.

1080 Pardoe, T. E. Speech in the West, 1949: An Historical Overview. Wstn Spch 13 (Jan.) 5-11. OI in the West.

1081 Parrish, W. M. More About an Imagined Anthology. Qrt J Spch 35 (Feb.) 81-2. Comments on Burklund's essay in QJS 34 (Dec. 1948) 477-82.

1082 Robb, M. M. Ebenezer Porter, Early American Teacher. Wstn Spch 13 (May) 9-14. Theories and methods.

1083 Robb, M. M. Improving Declamation Contests. Engl J 38 (Sept.) 397-8. Declamation contests have lost usefulness; replace with OI.

1950

1084 Abbot, K. M. Rhetoric and Latin Literary Forms. Qrt J Spch 36 (Dec.) 457-61. Implications of rhetoric and Latin lit forms in early Rome.

1085 Ashbaugh, K. I. Mark Twain as a Public Speaker. Wstn Spch 14 (Jan.) 10-4. Twain seen as effective public speaker, even in old age. Quotes from his contemporaries regarding his public speaking skills.

1086 Bacon, W. A. On the Teaching of Interpretation. College Engl 11 (Apr.) 397-400. Values of OI and relationship to English.

1087 Ballet, A. H. Oral Interpretation in the English Class. Engl J 39 (Dec.) 560-7. Steps to good OI.

1088 Barclay, Dorothy. Fun for the First Readers. NY Times Mag (Nov. 12) 42. Relaxed approach in childhood aids later readers.

1089 Barzun, Jacques, et al. More on Sound Repetitions. Word Study 25 (Apr.) 2-3. Response to S. L. Mooney: New Devices in Sound Repetition.

1090 Black, J. W. Some Effects Upon Voice of Hearing Tones of Varying Intensity and Frequency While Reading. Spch Mono 17 (Mar.) 95-9. Effects of varying tones on reading aloud; includes graph and chart of frequencies.

1091 Bryant, D. C. Aspects of the Rhetorical Tradition: The Intellectual Foundation. Qrt J Spch 36 (Apr.) 169-76. Rhetoric as scholarly study, body of principle and precept.

1092 Dresden, K. W. Overcoming the Phobia of Poetry. Engl J 39 (June) 336-8. Le Seur's theory of teaching OI in high school English.

1093 Eckelmann, D. A., & Margaret Parret. Source Materials for Speech in the Elementary Schools. Qrt J Spch 36 (Apr.) 251-9. Concentrates on choral speaking.

1094 Editors. Spotlight on the Bible. Coronet 28 (Aug.) 28-9. Values of reading Bible aloud.

1095 Eich, L. M.   A Note on L. H. Mouat's Article.   Qrt J
Spch 36 (Apr.) 237.   Support of Mouat proposing emphasis
in oral reading.

1096 Froeschels, Emil.   A Note on Dr. James Rush.   Qrt J Spch
36 (Apr.) 242-3.   Modern phonetics should pay more attention to Rush.

1097 Geiger, Don.   Oral Interpretation and the New Criticism.
Qrt J Spch 36 (Dec.) 508-13.   OI verifies a basic insight
of new criticism into nature of lit structure and shows
how to enlarge this insight.

1098 Gordon, E. G.   Teaching Students to Read Verse.   Engl J
39 (Mar.) 149-54.   Focus on skills of OI.

1099 Hardin, E. R.   Fundamental Needs for Interpretative Attain-
ment.   Sthn Spch J 16 (Dec.) 141-4.   Thought, language,
voice, and action in effective OI.

1100 Hargis, D. E.   The General Speech Major.   Qrt J Spch 36
(Feb.) 71-7.   Survey results include academic status of
OI.

1101 Hodge, Francis.   Charles Matthews Reports on America.
Qrt J Spch 36 (Dec.) 492-9.   Matthews, a comedian, and
his observations as a tourist from England.

1102 Irwin, R. L.   Words and Music.   Qrt J Spch 36 (Apr.) 238-
40.   Importance of choosing poem to complement music
and vice-versa.

1103 Jackson, J. L.   A Use of Special Rhetoric in Elizabethan
Play.   Qrt J Spch 36 (Dec.) 540-1.   Speech taken from
Damon and Pithias as possible model oration.

1104 Jones, M. V.   Choral Reading and Speech Improvement.
Wstn Spch 14 (Jan.) 19-21.   Choric and speech defects.

1105 Kilbane, Evelyn.   The Sixth Grade Tries Oral Reading.
Wstn Spch 14 (Oct.) 47-8.   Suggested procedure for those
interested in oral reading, provides reading checklist of
guidelines.

1106 Laughton, Charles.   Storytelling.   Atlantic Monthly 185
(June) 71-2.   Personal meaning of storytelling to
Laughton.

1107 Poley, I. C.   We Like What We Know: Value of a Masefield
Poetry Reading Contest for American Schools.   Engl J 39
(Feb.) 97-9.

1108 Pollack, T. C. A Note on Objective Meaning and Oral Interpretation. Qrt J Spch 36 (Apr.) 232-3. Review of H. L. Smith article.

1109 Putnam, Ivan. The Speech Teacher and Copyright. Qrt J Spch 36 (Dec.) 500-7. Investigation of copyright for speech teacher.

1110 Reynolds, G. F. Oral Interpretation as Graduate Work in English. Coll Engl 11 (Jan.) 204-10. Four values of OI.

1111 Reynolds, G. F. We Need Better Readers and Better Listeners. Qrt J Spch 36 (Apr.) 242. Review of Fleischman's "Let's Take Another Look at Interpretation."

1112 Robb, M. M. Interpretation Revisited. Qrt J Spch 36 (Apr.) 237-8. Rebut of Fleischman's "Let's Take Another Look at Interpretation."

1113 Robb, M. M. Trends in the Teaching of Oral Interpretation. Wstn Spch 14 (May) 8-11. 21 teachers and 50 catalogues examined.

1114 Seedorf, E. H. Evaluating Oral Interpretation. Wstn Spch 14 (Mar.) 28-30. Growth is the factor.

1115 Smith, H. L. Objective Meaning and Dramatic Interpretation. Qrt J Spch 36 (Feb.) 39-43. Application of T. C. Pollack's work to OI.

1116 Wilson, G. B. The Acting of Edwin Forrest. Qrt J Spch 36 (Dec.) 483-91. 19th-century elocutionary techniques.

1117 Wilson, Garff. Oral Interpretation and General Education. Wstn Spch 14 (Oct.) 27-9. OI seen as valid avenue to general education; demonstrates this concept by analyzing Dover Beach.

1951

1118 Anderson, M. P. Interpretation and the Department of Speech. Wstn Spch 15 (Mar.) 51-4. Evaluation of OI: strengths and weaknesses in college level.

1119 Bacon, W. A. Review of Helen Husted's Love Poems of Six Centuries. Qrt J Spch 37 (Apr.) 251.

1120 Bassett, L. E. From Doghouse to Doctorate. Wstn Spch 15 (Mar.) 11-18. A survey of Bassett's years in speech communication and elocution.

1121 Bolton, Janet. Thomas C. Trueblood--Edwin P. Trueblood. Qrt J Spch 37 (Oct.) 417. Tribute.

1122 Burklund, C. E. Poetry: A Symphonic Structure. Qrt J Spch 37 (Apr.) 179-84. Explanation of poetic structure through layout of claims and frames of reference, analysis of poetry and a survey of value and purpose of poetry.

1123 Burklund, C. E. A Letter from an English Teacher. Wstn Spch 15 (Jan.) 5-9. How useful a course in OI of poetry can and should be.

1124 Clark, D. L. Imitation: Theory and Practice in Roman Rhetoric. Qrt J Spch 37 (Feb.) 11-22. Value of imitation, whom to imitate and methods of imitation.

1125 Clurman, Harold. Theatre: Don Juan in Hell. New Republic 125 (Dec. 24) 22. Review of stage production.

1126 Crocker, Lionel. Charles Laughton on Oral Reading. Cent Sts Spch J 3 (Dec.) 21-6. Personal views of Laughton on OI.

1127 Dyrenforth, H. O. Narration--The Cinderella of Radio and Film. Wstn Spch 15 (Mar.) 46-50. Narration as vital part of radio, film, and TV.

1128 Editors. First Drama Quartette: Don Juan in Hell. Commonweal 55 (Nov. 9) 118. Review of RT production.

1129 Friermood, E. H. Let's Read Aloud. Recreation 44 (Jan.) 449-50. Need for reading aloud with family.

1130 Frye, R. M. Rhetoric and Poetry in Julius Caesar. Qrt J Spch 37 (Feb.) 41-8. Rhetoric/poetic dichotomy examined.

1131 Geiger, Don. Note for a Theory of Literature. Wstn Spch 15 (Oct.) 17-21. Study of OI is way of studying literature.

1132 Gibbs, Wolcott. Theatre: Don Juan in Hell. New Yorker 27 (Dec. 8) 64. Diction, style, humor, and discipline in RT production of Shaw's Don Juan in Hell.

1133 Guthrie, Warren. The Development of Rhetorical Theory in America: 1635-1850--The Elocution Movement in England. Spch Mono 18 (Mar.) 17-30. Reviews elocution from Robinson to Austin.

1134 Hile, F. W. Everybody Creates? Wstn Spch 15 (Jan.) 9. Brief discussion of OI as important part of communication.

1135 Houseman, John. Drama Quartette. Theatre Arts 35 (Aug.) 14-5. Review Don Juan in Hell as RT.

1136 Howell, W. S. Oratory and Poetry in Fenelon's Literary
Theory. Qrt J Spch 37 (Feb.) 1-10. Examines Fenelon's
literary contributions: notes Fenelon's claim that all art
acts to influence conduct of mankind.

1137 Irwin, R. L. Group Theatrical Reading. Schl Act 22
(Mar.) 221-2. Advantages and problems of group reading.

1138 Johnson, T. E. Convention Reports. Qrt J Spch 37 (Feb.)
129-38. Evaluates OI convention activities.

1139 Jones, M. V. Effect of Speech Training on Silent Reading
Achievement. Wstn Spch 15 (Oct.) 39-42. Evidence indicates improvement in speech facility; accelerates silent
reading achievement.

1140 Krutch, J. W. Drama: Don Juan in Hell. Nation 173 (Dec.
22) 553-4. Reviews Don Juan in Hell.

1141 Laughton, Charles. Read Aloud, It's Fun. Reader's Digest
58 (Jan.) 19-21. Reading aloud as entertainment and
shared experience.

1142 Lepage, R. B. The Dramatic Delivery of Shakespeare's
Verse. Engl Studies 32 (1951) 63-8. In short, speed of
delivery is an integral part of general interpretation.

1143 Longwell, Daniel. Four Hollywood Veterans Go to Hell on
Broadway. Life 31 (Nov. 5) 46-7. Review.

1144 Mace, D. T. The Doctrine of Sound and Sense in Augustine
Poetic Theory. Rev of Engl Studies 2 (Apr.) 129-39.
The problem of relating non-meaning to meaning as it ap-
peared to the Augustans; and our most celebrated source
for the principal doctrines on the subject is Pope's "Essay
on Criticism."

1144a MacKinnon, Elizabeth. Communicating the Playwright's
Idea. Wstn Spch J 15 (May) 38-40. Director's and
actor's responsibilities in interpreting playwright's ideas.

1145 Marshman, J. T. Art Approach to Reading Aloud. Qrt J
Spch 37 (Feb.) 35-40. OI more than perfection of technique.

1146 Marshman, J. T. Fulton of Fulton and Trueblood. Cent
Sts Spch J 2 (Mar.) 46-54. Characteristics, contributions, and achievements.

1147 Matthews, T. S. Don Juan in Hell: First Drama Quartet.
Time 58 (Nov. 5) 63-4. Review concerned with Shaw's
work as RT.

1148- McCoard, W. B., & S. N. Lecount. An Oral Reading
9 Evaluation of Good and Poor Silent Readers. Spch Mono
18 (Nov.) 288-91. Significant difference in OI ability between good and poor silent readers.

1150 Minnick, W. C. Matthew Arnold on Emerson. Qrt J Spch
37 (Oct.) 332-6. Arnold's views on Emerson as they
reveal insights into temper of early 19th-century America.

1151 Morrison, Jack. Speech and Theatre. Wstn Spch 15 (Jan.)
27-30. Best interests of theatre are to be served by
professional life apart from speech.

1152 Muir, Malcolm. Don Juan in Hell. Newsweek 38 (Dec. 10)
50. Review concerned with box office reception.

1153 Newman, J. B. The Phonetic Aspect of Joshua Steele's
System of Prosody. Spch Mono 18 (Nov.) 279-87. System
based upon the nature and process of speech.

1154 Okey, L. L. Trueblood of Fulton and Trueblood. Cent Sts
Spch J 3 (Dec.) 5-10. Tribute.

1155 Panter-Downs, Mollie. Letter from London: Emlyn Williams as Charles Dickens. New Yorker 27 (Dec. 22) 53.
Emlyn Williams as Dickens.

1156 Parrish, W. M. The Concept of Naturalness. Qrt J Spch
37 (Dec.) 448-54. Naturalness to be approved, not when
it feels natural to performer, but when it seems natural
to audience.

1157 Reed, E. C. Of Reading to My Children. Horn Book 27
(Jan.) 13-8. Values of reading aloud.

1158 Shepherd, Ruth. I Would Like a Course That.... Wstn Spch
15 (Oct.) 10-12. OI for teachers.

1159 Straub, E. A. Building a Ballad Opera. Engl J 40 (Mar.)
161-3. RT in high school assembly.

1160 Snidecor, J. C. Pitch and Duration Characteristics of the
Oral Reading of Superior Women Speakers. Wstn Spch 15
(May) 62-3. Comparative study between superior women/
men speakers. Relates vocal characteristics in oral reading.

1161 Winters, Yvor. The Audible Reading of Poetry. Hudson
Rev 4 (Autumn) 433-47. Reading aloud part of the
art.

1952

1162 Anderson, T. V. Shall We Tell Them How to Say It?
Wstn Spch 16 (Jan.) 25-8. Discussion of question method
and conversational norm.

1163 Beyer, W. H. State of the Theatre: Impersonating Dickens.
Scholar & Society 75 (Mar. 22) 184.

1164 Black, J. W., & W. B. Tomlinson. Loud Voice: Imme-
diate Effects Upon the Listener. Spch Mono 19 (Nov.)
299-302. Physiological study of effects of loud talking
by the speaker.

1165 Breen, R. S. Montage and the Interpretation of Literature.
Cent Sts Spch J 3 (Mar.) 15-7. OI ever in need of more
refined methods in analysis of texts.

1166 Brown, J. M. Mr. Dickens Reads Again. Sat Rev 35
(Feb. 23) 26-8. Dickens' theatrical style compared to
Emlyn Williams.

1167 Burke, Kenneth. A Dramatistic View of the Origins of
Language: Part I. Qrt J Spch 38 (Oct.) 251-64. Locat-
ing specific nature of language in ability to use the negative.

1168 Cardwell, G. A. George W. Cable Becomes a Professional
Reader. American Lit 23 (Jan.) 467-70. Novelist discovers his skills as a lecturer.

1169 Click, D. W. Humor and Comprehension. Engl J 41 (June)
321. Use of humorous oral readings to check comprehension.

1170 Cortez, E. A. Concerning "Naturalness." Qrt J Spch 38
(Apr.) 208-9. A critical analysis of W. M. Parrish's
article "The Concept of Naturalness." Finds concept
vague.

1171 Dearing, Bruce. Experiments with Audio Visual Arts in
Teaching Poetry. Coll Engl 13 (Mar.) 322-4. Phonograph and tape recorder as instructional aids in teaching
poetry.

1172 Editors. John Brown's Body as Presented at the University of Utah. Newsweek 40 (Nov. 24) 88. Review.

1173 Editors. Meet Mr. Dickens. Life 32 (Mar. 3) 77-8.
Emlyn Williams reading Dickens.

1174 Editors. Mr. Dickens. Time 59 (Feb. 18) 61. Emlyn
Williams as Charles Dickens.

1175 Editors. Reading While Cigarmakers Work. Business Week
(July 19) 128. S. Gompers reads labor theory and socialist works to cigarmakers.

1176 Editors. Stage: Williams and Dickens. Commonweal 55
(Feb. 29) 516. Emlyn Williams reading Dickens: critique.

1177 Fadiman, Clifton. Party of One: Emlyn Williams as
Charles Dickens. Holiday 2 (May) 14. Enthusiastic support for reading aloud.

1178 Fadiman, Clifton. Judy and Juan: Two High Moments.
Holiday 2 (Mar.) 6. Argues that theatre is founded on
words and people.

1179 Gainsburg, J. C. Play Reading with Dynamic Meaning.
Engl J 41 (Oct.) 403-10. Plays read aloud release dynamic energy.

1180 Geiger, Don. A Dramatic Approach to Interpretative Analysis. Qrt J Spch 38 (Apr.) 189-94. Since lit presents experience it should be studied by situation/attitude relationships.

1181 Gooch, F. K. Speech Education in the First Quarter of the
20th Century. Sthn Spch J 17 (Mar.) 192-9. Focus on
principles.

1182 Hargis, D. E. What Is Oral Interpretation? Wstn Spch 16
(May) 175-80. OI as communication and re-creation.

1183 Higdon, Barbara. John Neihardt and His Oral Interpretation
of Poetry. Sthn Spch J 18 (Dec.) 96-101. Poet-reader
reinforces canons of OI.

1184 Hochmuth, Marie. Kenneth Burke and the New Rhetoric.
Qrt J Spch 38 (Apr.) 133-44. An explication of Burke's
principles. General concept of rhetoric, and methods of
analysis to discover his application of principles to specific
literary works.

1185 Johnson, G. E. When Laughton Reads the Bible. Coronet
32 (Aug.) 92-5. Laughton as master of interpretation.

1186 Kaucher, Dorothy. Interpretation and the Etymon. Qrt J
Spch 38 (Oct.) 300-4. Interpreters should know history of
words.

1187 Kretsinger, E. A. An Experimental Study of Gross Bodily
Movement as an Index to Audience Interest. Spch Mono 19
(Nov.) 244-8. Physical movement of audiences as indi-
cator of reactions.

1188 Krutch, J. W. Drama: Readings from Dickens. Nation 174 (Feb. 23) 189-90. Emlyn Williams readings from Dickens as new literary art.

1189 Laughton, Charles. How Mr. Laughton Became the Devil. NY Times Mag (Mar. 23) 21. Account of unconventional reading of Don Juan in Hell.

1190 Lorch, F. W. Cable and His Reading Tour with Mark Twain in 1884-85. American Lit 23 (Jan.) 471-86. Cable's skill as reader.

1191 Luce, H. R. Don Juan in the Dough. Fortune 45 (Jan.) 142. Profits.

1192 Martin, A. T. The Oral Interpreter and the Phonograph. Qrt J Spch 38 (Apr.) 195-8. Potentialities of recorded lit.

1193 Matthews, T. S. Happy Ham. Time 59 (Mar. 31) 62-4. Charles Laughton's production of Don Juan in Hell.

1194 McCoard, W. B. How Conversational Is the Conversational Norm? Wstn Spch 16 (May) 199-200. Concept helpful as long as one recognizes that reading situation is not natural but must seem so.

1195 McCoard, W. B. Materials for the Teaching of Oral Interpretation. Qrt J Spch 38 (Apr.) 211-8. Help for beginning teacher of OI: textbooks, anthologies and other background aids.

1196 Neihardt, J. G. The Interpretation of Poetry. Qrt J Spch 38 (Feb.) 74-8. Poetry determines the manner of its presentation.

1197 Parrish, W. M. The Burglarizing of Burgh, or The Case of the Purloined Passions. Qrt J Spch 38 (Dec.) 431-4. Piracy and mislabeling of various works of speech, elocution, and rhetorical grammar by printers, editors, and teachers.

1198 Parrish, W. M. More About Naturalness. Qrt J Spch 38 (Apr.) 209. Rebuts Cortez in QJS 38 (Apr. 1952) 208-9.

1199 Popkin, Henry. Poets as Performers. Theatre Arts 36 (Feb.) 27-30. Frost, Sitwell, Eliot, and Dylan Thomas reading their own works.

1200 Stylites, Simeon. Hope for the Ear. Christ Cent 69 (Apr. 23) 488. Values of public speaking.

1201 Weisman, H. M. An Investigation of Methods and Techniques in the Dramatization of Fiction. Spch Mono 19

(Mar.) 48-59.   Purpose and scope, procedure, analysis of data and findings in producing quality fictional dramatizations.

1202   Wilson, G. B.   The Growth of Oral Interpretation at the University of California.   Spch Tchr 1 (Sept.) 187-92. Attributes UC's OI success with liberal arts approach.

1203   Wyatt, E. V.   Emlyn Williams as Charles Dickens.   Catholic World 174 (Mar.) 462.   Review Williams' impersonation of Dickens.

1204   Wyatt, E. V.   Theatre: Don Juan in Hell.   Catholic World 174 (Feb.) 390-1.   Review.

1953

1205   Bacon, W. A.   Scholarship and the Interpreter.   Qrt J Spch 39 (Apr.) 187-92.   Questions OI's knowledge of lit and history.

1206   Bahn, Eugene.   A New Goethe Discovery: The Weilburger Goethe-Funde.   Qrt J Spch 39 (Dec.) 485-7.   New material by Wolff to aid theatre and OI studies.

1207   Bartine, N. G.   Literary Programs.   Engl J 41 (Oct.) 420-3.   List of lit programs.

1208   Baskerville, Barnett.   The Place of Oratory in American Literature.   Qrt J Spch 39 (Dec.) 459-64.   Pre-revolutionary orators and 19th-century orators receive focus.

1209   Bentley, Eric.   On the Sublime: "John Brown's Body. " New Republic 128 (Mar. 2) 22-3.   Review RT performance of John Brown's Body.

1210   Bentley, Eric.   On Being Read To.   New Republic 128 (May 11) 11.   Emlyn Williams' performance of Dickens' works.

1211   Bigelow, G. E.   Distinguishing Rhetoric from Poetic Discourse.   Sthn Spch J 19 (Dec.) 83-97.   Poetic/rhetoric dichotomy.

1212   Bolton, Janet.   Azubah Latham.   Qrt J Spch 39 (Feb.) 134. Tribute.

1213   Brown, J. N.   Marching On: Laughton's Production of "John Brown's Body. "   Sat Rev 36 (Mar. 14) 34-5.   Compares Laughton's Don Juan in Hell and John Brown's Body.

1214   Brown, J. R.   On the Acting of Shakespeare's Plays.   Qrt J Spch 39 (Dec.) 477-84.   Elizabethan attitudes of acting and reading verse for modern actors.

1215 Bryant, D. C. Rhetoric: Its Functions and Its Scope. Qrt J Spch 39 (Dec.) 401-24. Functions and scope of rhetoric for any rhetorical system.

1216 Burke, Kenneth. A Dramatistic View of the Origins of Language: Part III. Qrt J Spch 39 (Feb.) 79-92. Essay on negative theology and dramatistic theory of definition. A concept.

1217 Burklund, C. E. Melody in Verse. Qrt J Spch 39 (Feb.) 57-60. Why melody affords us pleasure.

1218 Cunningham, C. C. Phoneme or Nucleus? Wstn Spch 17 (Jan.) 25-8. Speech as a linguistic phenomenon.

1219 Editors. John Brown's Body. Vogue 121 (Feb. 1) 186-7. Review.

1220 Editors. Poetic Platform Drama: John Brown's Body. Life 34 (Jan. 26) 85-6. Printed poem surrounded by captions about performance highlights.

1221 Editors. Re-enter Mr. Dickens. Time 61 (May 4) 84. Emlyn Williams as Dickens reading Bleak House.

1222 Farris, H. J. Let's Read to the Children. Nat Educ Assc J 42 (Dec.) 545. Read aloud to children.

1223 Freestone, N. W. Forum: Phoneme or Nucleus. Wstn Spch 17 (Mar.) 129. Critique of Cunningham's article; his overgeneralization.

1224 Geiger, Don. Modern Literary Thought: The Consciousness of Abstracting. Spch Mono 20 (Mar.) 1-22. Many of the most important emphases in modern criticism and poetry can be understood as expression of acute modern consciousness of abstracting; this consciousness prepares for understanding of nature of literature.

1225 Geiger, Don. New Perspectives in Oral Interpretation. College Engl 14 (Feb.) 281-6. Values of OI.

1226 Gibbs, Wolcott. Mr. Williams as Mr. Dickens. New Yorker 29 (May 2) 52-3. Review Emlyn Williams as Dickens in Bleak House.

1227 Granfield, Geraldine. The Integration of Speech with English in the High School Curriculum. Spch Tchr 2 (Mar.) 114-8. Values of proper speaking ability in contrast to writing ability aids in integration of speech and English.

1228 Hadley, D. S. Preparing the Student for an Oral Reading. Sthn Spch J 19 (Dec.) 123-32. Adapting student and selection.

1229 Hargis, C. N., & D. E. Hargis. High School Literature and Oral Interpretation. Spch Tchr 2 (Sept.) 205-8. Motivation and stimulation can result from combining lit and OI in classroom.

1230 Haun, R. R. Creative Listening. Today's Spch 1 (Oct.) 18-20. Listening and OI.

1231 Hayes, Richard. Bleak House, Read by Emlyn Williams. Commonweal 58 (May 15) 151-2. Review Emlyn Williams.

1232 Hayes, Richard. On Stage: John Brown's Body. Commonweal 57 (Mar. 13) 576-7. Review John Brown's Body" RT style.

1233 Hewes, Henry. Tale of Thirty Six Characters: Emlyn Williams' Performance as Charles Dickens. Sat Rev 36 (May 9) 27-8. Emlyn Williams' readings of Dickens.

1234 Hewes, Henry. Backward Town of Llarregub. Sat Rev 36 (June 6) 24-5. Under Milk Wood Our Town of Welsh.

1235 Hile, F. W., & Brown, S. R. The 49ers and Three Experiments in Oral Interpretation. Spch Tchr 2 (Mar.) 105-8. 49ers and a group oriented to guide, implement, and facilitate worthwhile aims of adult groups through OI.

1236 Hoffman, Theodore. Couple of Masters: Monodrama of Bleak House. Theatre Arts 37 (July) 15. Review of E. Williams reading Dickens' Bleak House plus.

1237 Hunter, Kermit. Oral Interpretation in the Outdoor Theatre. Sthn Spch J 19 (Dec.) 133-9. Problems inherent in using OI in outdoor drama.

1238 Johnson, A. E. Medieval Influences on Modern Stage Design. Sthn Spch J 18 (Mar.) 180-5. Unusual and revolutionary staging techniques for many of our most successful modern productions are fundamentally a return to stationary staging devices of medieval France and Elizabethan playhouse.

1239 Kaulhausen, Marie-Hed. Philological and Speech-Method Interpretation of Poetry. Qrt J Spch 39 (Oct.) 340-6. OI and philology can enrich each other.

1240 Lennon, E. J. Mark Twain Abroad. Qrt J Spch 39 (Apr.) 197-200. Lennon claims Twain did not read, but was a topical speaker.

1241 Loper, R. B. Shakespeare All of a Breath. Qrt J Spch 39 (Apr.) 193-6. Discussion of William Poel's proposal to banish scenery and adhere to the text.

1242 Lowrey, Sara. Speech: Science or Art? Spch Tchr 2 (Jan.) 12-6. Account of beneficial use of OI with victims of cerebral palsy. OI improves rhythm; increases interest in meaning of words to be communicated rather than emphasizing the act of speech.

1243 Marsh, Robert. Aristotle and the Modern Rhapsode. Qrt J Spch 39 (Dec.) 491-8. Rough outlines of certain principles derived from Aristotelean attitudes toward lit and OI.

1244 Masson, D. I. Word and Sound in Yeats' "Byzantium." Engl Lit History 20 (June) 136-60. Analysis of sound in Yeats' poem.

1245 McCall, R. C. Forum: Thoughts on Reading Phoneme or Nucleus? Wstn Spch 17 (May) 201. McCall takes Cunningham to task for noting imperfections of colleagues in related fields without giving credit for their virtues.

1246 Newman, J. B. Joshua Steele's Role in the Development of American Speech Education. Spch Mono 20 (Mar.) 65-73. Steele's contributions were analysis of oral readings, speech science, and prosody.

1247 Reed, Helen. Nuclear Preparation of a Poem for Oral Interpretation. Wstn Spch 17 (May) 187-93. Nuclear force is denotative and connotative as applied to patterns.

1248 Roach, Helen. Does History Repeat Itself for Us? Today's Spch 1 (Oct.) 22-4. Reasons for hiring elocutionist at Columbia in 1860.

1249 Robb, M. M. An Extension of Reference for Elocution. Cent Sts Spch J 4 (July) 14-8. History of elocution.

1250 Sandoe, James. A Note or Two About Playreading. Wstn Spch 17 (Oct.) 225-9. Utility of playreading.

1251 Scheff, Aimee. Adelphi Readers Theatre. Theatre Arts 37 (June) 79. New RT at Adelphi College, Long Island.

1252 Smith, C. D. Speechmaking in the Iliad and Odyssey. Cent Sts Spch J 4 (Mar.) 6-11. The art of speechmaking in the two classics.

1253 Thalheimer, M. R. Helping the High School Student to Read Aloud. Cent Sts Spch J 5 (Fall) 18-9. Causes and cures of poor reading.

1254 Vandraegan, D. E. Thomas Sheridan and the Natural School. Spch Mono 20 (Mar.) 58-64. Sheridan's theory of elocution places him in natural school in spite of some mechanical aspects.

1255 Wyatt, E. V. Theatre: John Brown's Body. Catholic
      World 177 (Apr.) 67. Review John Brown's Body.

1256 Young, J. D. An Experimental Comparison of Vocabulary
      Growth Through Oral Reading, Silent Reading and Listen-
      ing. Spch Mono 20 (Nov.) 273-6. OI aids vocabulary
      growth.

1954

1257 Braden, W. W. The Beginnings of the Lyceum: 1826-1840.
      Sthn Spch J 20 (Winter) 125-35. Focus on growth and na-
      ture.

1258 Brennan, J. G. The Role of Emotion in Aesthetic Experi-
      ence. Qrt J Spch 40 (Dec.) 422-8. Emotion viewed as
      wholesome outlet with probable social benefits in various
      art mediums.

1259 Casebier, Gabriella. Once Upon a Time. Spch Tchr 3
      (Mar.) 131-2. Methods for effective storytelling.

1260 Constans, H. P. Lew Sarett: 1888-1954. Sthn Spch J 20
      (Winter) 174. Tribute.

1261 Du Charme, L. W. Robert McLean Cumnock: The Man.
      Cent Sts Spch J 5 (Spring) 15. Sketch.

1262 Fleischman, E. E. Oral Interpretation and Growth of Per-
      sonality. Today's Spch 2 (Jan.) 4-8. OI and human
      growth.

1263 Garrison, Geraldine. Bibliography of Choral Speaking in the
      Elementary School. Spch Tchr 3 (Mar.) 107-11. Defines
      choral speaking and its values plus 70 items and bibliog-
      raphy.

1264 Geiger, Don. Oral Interpretation and the Liberal Arts Con-
      text. Qrt J Spch 40 (Apr.) 137-44. Examines four argu-
      ments against emphasizing OI as means of studying liter-
      ature.

1265 Geiger, Don. The Interpreter's Artistic Emphasis: Tech-
      nique and Meaning in Moby-Dick. Sthn Spch J 20 (Fall)
      16-27. Tests Mark Schorer's thesis that technique is
      writer's means of discovering, exploring, developing his
      object, of conveying its meaning.

1266 Geiger, Don. The Oral Interpreter as Creator. Spch Tchr
      3 (Nov.) 269-77. OI as creative art.

1267 Hicks, H. G. Three American Ladies of Poesy. Today's
      Spch 2 (Apr.) 20-4. Biographical sketches of A. Lowell,
      E. Dickinson, and E. White.

1268 Hopkins, B. C. English Teachers Need the Speech Choir.
      Sthn Spch J 19 (Mar.) 214-23. Techniques and values of
      choric speaking.

1269 Irwin, R. L. Readings on Records: A Challenge. Today's
      Spch 2 (Nov.) 31-2. Using good readers to record poetry.

1270 Marsh, G. E. An Interpretative Approach to Speech. Qrt
      J Spch 40 (Oct.) 269-71. Affirms OI's educational value.

1271 Mattingly, A. S. The Playing Time and Manner of Delivery
      of Shakespeare's Plays in the Elizabethan Theatre. Spch
      Mono 21 (Mar.) 29-38. Elaboration on playing time, in-
      clusive of cuts and physical conditions, and manner of
      delivery in Elizabethan theatre.

1272 Miller, J. E. How About a Play Reading Group? Recrea-
      tion 47 (Sept.) 437. Values of reading aloud.

1273 Moorehead, Agnes. Staging Don Juan in Hell. Wstn Spch
      18 (May) 163-6. Producing and staging Don Juan in Hell,
      first modern RT.

1274 Ostroff, Anthony. New Criticism and Oral Interpretation.
      Wstn Spch 18 (Jan.) 37-44. Application of new criticism
      to OI with workable definitions for each.

1275 Parrish, W. M. Interpreting Emotion in Poetry. Sthn Spch
      J 19 (Mar.) 205-13. Proper study of elements of poetry
      will create proper emotion.

1276 Quimby, R. W. Making the Green One Red. Spch Tchr 3
      (Jan.) 29-32. OI creative or re-creative art? Quimby
      proposes two factors to help resolve the controversy.

1277 Simonson, H. P. Music as an Approach to Poetry. Engl J
      43 (Jan.) 19-23. Music and OI as related.

1278 Trenaman, Joseph. Radio and Reading. J of Comm 4
      (Spring) 9-13. Influence of radio dramatization on silent
      reading.

1279 Wagner, Vern. The Lecture Lyceum and the Problem of
      Controversy. J of Hist of Ideas 15 (Jan.) 119-35. More
      than entertainment it was free platform of the age.

1280 Wallace, K. R. The Field of Speech, 1953: An Overview.
      Qrt J Spch 40 (Apr.) 117-29. Section on interpreter as
      mediator.

1955

1281 Beloof, R. L. Sound and Rhythm: Textual Analysis and the Oral Interpreter. Wstn Spch 19 (Oct.) 239-44. Sound and rhythm and the unparaphrasable.

1282 Birdwhistell, R. L. Background to Kinesics. Etc 13 (Autumn) 10-18. Kinesics vocabulary.

1283 Breen, R. S. Some Difficulties in Reading Modern Poetry Publicly. Wstn Spch 19 (Oct.) 245-9. Problems arise in poem and reader.

1284 Burklund, C. E. The Presentation of Figurative Language. Qrt J Spch 41 (Dec.) 383-90. Poet should never be removed from the student of OI: the student should be brought to the poet and introduced as a blood-brother.

1285 Cartier, F. A. Listenability and Human Interest. Spch Mono 22 (Mar.) 53-6. Quantitative study of applicability to spoken language to human interest formula of Flesch's new readability yardstick.

1286 Geiger, Don. Emotion in Poetry: Interpreter's Special Responsibility. Sthn Spch J 21 (Fall) 31-8. Emotional code carries bulk of meaning in poetry.

1287 Geiger, Don. Pluralism in the Interpreter's Search for Sanctions. Qrt J Spch 41 (Feb.) 43-56. All lit theories can aid OI and should be studied.

1288 Hannah, R. G., & M. B. Underwood. Navy Bibliotherapy. Lib J (May 15) 1171-6. Experiments in use of books carried out at the naval hospital, Portsmouth, Va. to aid patients in their readjustments.

1289 Harwood, Kenneth. I. Listenability and Readability. Spch Mono 22 (Mar.) 49-52. Experimental study of listenability, investigates some relationships between written and spoken language of varying levels of difficulty.

1290 Haugh, O. M. The English Teacher as Teacher of Speech. Engl J 44 (Apr.) 205-10. Strong argument for inclusion of oral communication in curriculum, especially in English classrooms.

1291 Herrick, M. T. The Teacher as Reader and Interpreter of Literature. Qrt J Spch 41 (Apr.) 110-3. Special remembrance of a student mesmerized by teacher who read aloud; also special praise for Parrish's book Reading Aloud.

1292 Hicks, H. G. Three British Ladies of Poesy. Today's Spch 3 (Apr.) 15-9. Biographical sketches of E. Browning, E. Brontë, and C. Rosetti.

1293 Hochmuth, Marie. Great Teachers of Speech: III. Wayland Maxfield Parrish: Teacher and Colleague. Spch Tchr 4 (Sept.) 159-60. Tribute given as speech on Parrish's retirement.

1294 Horan, Robert. The Uniquity of Poetic Language. Wstn Spch 19 (Oct.) 231-7. Enigma of modern poetry.

1295 Ikegami, Yoshihiko. A Linguistic Essay on Parody. Ling: Internatl Rev 55 (Dec.) 13-31. A different view of lit form.

1296 Lennon, E. J., and W. W. Hamilton. Charles Laughton's Interpretative Reading. Spch Tchr 4 (Mar.) 87-8. Laughton's technical theory with emphasis on communicative sharing.

1297 Lilly, E. K. Great Teachers of Speech I: The Young Lew Sarett. Spch Tchr 4 (Jan.) 22-3. Tribute.

1298 Marsh, G. E. Oral Interpretation and a Philosophy of Liberal Education. Today's Spch 3 (Jan.) 19-21. Humanities come alive with OI.

1299 McBride, M. R. Great Teachers of Speech IV: Frank M. Rarig. Spch Tchr 4 (Nov.) 231-2. Tribute.

1300 McCall, R. C. Taking Literature Out of Cold Storage. Engl J 44 (Jan.) 30-3. Lit teaching is poor because teachers cannot read aloud effectively.

1301 Murphy, Richard. Great Teachers of Speech III: Wayland Maxfield Parrish--Colleague and Counselor. Spch Tchr 4 (Sept.) 161-2. Tribute.

1302 Murphy, Theresa. Interpretation in the Dickens Period. Qrt J Spch 41 (Oct.) 243-9. Elocution from 1850-75.

1303 Nelson, S. E. Great Teachers of Speech II: Charles Henry Woolbert. Spch Tchr 4 (Mar.) 113-7. Tribute.

1304 Sirois, L. M. Expression: A Trinity. Today's Spch 3 (Apr.) 7-9, 22. Delsarte's values of action.

1305 Smith, C. D. From the Discipline of Literary Criticism. Today's Spch 3 (Nov.) 33-4. Lit criticism as persuasion.

1306 Smith, J. F. Maud May Babcock. Qrt J Spch 41 (Apr.) 211-2. Tribute.

1307 Snidecor, J. C. Temporal Aspects of Breathing in Superior Reading and Speaking Performances. Spch Mono 22 (Nov.) 284-9. Measured differences in central tendency and variability.

1308 Stylites, Simeon. King of Indoor Sports. Christ Cent 72 (Dec. 28) 1520. Reading aloud and book choice.

1309 Woods, David. Is Radio Drama a Dying Art? Today's Spch 3 (Sept.) 17-20. Current survey.

1956

1310 Bacon, W. A. Magnetic Field: The Structure of Jonson's Comedies. Huntington Lib Qrtly 19 (Feb.) 121-53. Comparison of Jonson's and Shakespeare's structures.

1311 Baker, W. E. Listening: A Functional Part of Composition. J of Comm 6 (Winter) 174-7. Reading aloud aids composition.

1312 Beloof, R. L. About New Books. Wstn Spch 20 (Winter) 51-4. Review/essay on word, gesture, movement in OI, based on book Every Little Movement.

1313 Bennet, D. N. Auden's "Sept. 1, 1939": An Interpreter's Analysis. Qrt J Spch 42 (Feb.) 1-13. Lit criticism deepens OI's appreciation of aesthetics and poetry.

1314 Chapman, G. W. Experiment in Reading. Harpers 213 (Dec.) 73-5. Tennessee factory encourages reading aloud to workers.

1315 Cook, R. L. Notes on Frost the Lecturer. Qrt J Spch 42 (Apr.) 127-32. Frost's early lectures more for financial security: later lectures have been more extemporaneous and nonsystematic.

1316 Crocker, Lionel. Poetry in the Pulpit. Cent Sts Spch J 8 (Fall) 33-5. Interpreting life from contemporary poetry.

1317 Crocker, Lionel. Techniques in Teaching Interpretation. Sthn Spch J 22 (Winter) 95-101. Nine instructors share techniques.

1318 Geiger, Don. Recent Literary Criticism. Qrt J Spch 42 (Oct.) 298-304. Recent lit criticism has damaged audience for poetry.

1319 Gilbert, Edna. Oral Interpretation at Speech Festivals. Spch Tchr 5 (Mar.) 117-20. Advice for competitors under the headings of objectives, teaching, material, cutting, minimum essentials for students, and criteria for judges and teachers.

1320 Gray, G. W. A Bibliography of Studies in the History of Speech Education from 1925. Spch Tchr 5 (Jan.) 8-20. Includes OI items.

1321 Grimes, W. H. Paperbacks: The Teacher's Friends: III. Oral Interpretation of Literature. Spch Tchr 5 (Jan.) 34-6. List of paperbacks rich in possibilities for use in OI class and contests.

1322 Grimes, W. H. Choosing Literature for Oral Reading: Psychological Basis. Qrt J Spch 42 (Apr.) 133-8. Audience should dictate choice of literature.

1323 Grube, G. M. Rhetoric and Literary Criticism. Qrt J Spch 42 (Dec.) 339-44. Offers contrast between rhetoric and lit criticism based on classical models.

1324 Hadden, Jane. Developing Creativity Through Dramatization. Cent Sts Spch J 7 (Spring) 28-32. Creative drama one type of experience through which children can come to their growth and learning potential.

1325 Hewes, Henry. O'Casey Unbound. Sat Rev 39 (Apr. 7) 22. Reviews O'Casey.

1326 Hewes, Henry. Broadway Postscript: Pictures in the Hallway. Sat Rev 39 (June 16) 32. Review of I Knock at the Door by O'Casey.

1327 Jacobs, L. B. What Shall We Read to Our Children? Nat Parent Teachers 51 (Nov.) 34-7. Suggestion for selections for reading to youth.

1328 Levinson, H. J. Choral Speaking for the Severely Handicapped. Spch Tchr 5 (Sept.) 226-30. Remedial effects of choral speaking.

1328a Mansuy, Frank. Spot That Demagogue: The Rhetoric of Ralph Waldo Emerson. Today's Spch 4 (Apr.) 6-9. Emerson's views on importance of ethos/integrity to effective communication.

1329 Martin, R. G. Family Reading in the Living Room. House Beautiful 98 (Sept.) 92-3. Values of reading aloud.

1330 Maynard, Norma. Poor Reading: Handmaiden of Poor Speech. Spch Tchr 5 (Jan.) 40-46. Relationship of reading difficulty and speaking difficulty.

1331- Miller, M. H. Chautauqua in Lansing. Mich Hist 40 (Sept.)
2   257-74. Traces the traveling Chautauqua from 1909.

1333 Ness, O. G. The Value of Oral Interpretation to the Students in General Speech. Spch Tchr 5 (Sept.) 209-13. OI part of liberal arts tradition.

1334 Ostroff, Anthony. The Moral Vision in Dubliners. Wstn Spch 20 (Fall) 196-209. Unity of structure in the Dubliners.

1335 Peachy, Frederick. Pound's Cantos: A Greek Approach. Wstn Spch 20 (Fall) 210-7. Greek influence on Pound.

1336 Pooley, R. C. The English Teacher's Preparation in Speech. Spch Tchr (Sept.) 186-93. Emphasis on teacher's competence in spoken language, in speech awareness, in OI and other areas before entering teaching field.

1337 Ransom, J. C. The Strange Music of English Verse. Kenyon Review 18 (1956) 460-77. Study of musical elements in poetry.

1338 Robb, M. M. Oral Interpretation and the Book Review. Spch Tchr 5 (Nov.) 285-9. OI teachers should accept some responsibility for training book reviewers.

1339 Roth, L. M. Integrating English Literature with Radio. Spch Tchr 5 (Jan.) 47-50. Explains adaptational and presentational techniques.

1340 Shepard, J. R., & T. M. Scheidel. A Study of the Personality Configuration of Effective Oral Readers. Spch Mono 23 (Nov.) 298-304. Effective oral readers are individualistic, aesthetic, motivated, and somewhat self-centered and ego-involved.

1341 Thompson, D. W. Interpretative Reading as Symbolic Action. Qrt J Spch 42 (Dec.) 389-97. The OI'er features the unique experience of the lit work as center or goal of entire social act. Considers the audience first.

1957

1342 Aly, L. F. The Word-Sender: John G. Neihardt and His Audience. Qrt J Spch 43 (Apr.) 151-54. Neihardt's growing affection for his audience leads him to share poetic experience with them.

1343 Bacon, W. A. Review of Grover Smith's T. S. Eliot's Poetry and Plays. Qrt J Spch 43 (Apr.) 211-2.

1344 Bacon, W. A. Review of A. J. Sarett's Covenant with Earth. Qrt J Spch 43 (Oct.) 328.

1345 Bacon, W. A. Recent Criticism of Shakespeare and the Elizabethans. Qrt J Spch 43 (Oct.) 307-11. Reviews six books of Shakespeare and the Elizabethans.

1346 Decker, R. G. Introducing Poems. Engl J 46 (Mar.) 145-7. Poetry aloud in grade school.

1347 Bedell, W. M. Reading a Poem Together. Engl J 46 (Mar.) 159-61. Choral speaking and lit.

1348 Chatman, Seymour. Linguistics, Poetics and Interpretation: The Phonemic Dimension. Qrt J Spch 43 (Oct.) 248-56. System of suprasegmental notations for lit analysis.

1349 Clark, R. D. Lesson from the Literary Critics. Wstn Spch 21 (Spring) 83-9. Rhetorical criticism discussed as separate entity from lit and historical criticism yet rhetoricians draw upon lit criticism for form and structure.

1350 Coger, L. I. Let's Have a Readers Theatre. Oral Interp Nat Thesp Soc (57-8) 25-7. Emphasizes methods and values of RT in secondary schools.

1351 Corbin, Richard. Three Days to a Greater Interest in Poems. Engl J 46 (Mar.) 163-4. Values of oral poetry.

1352 Creed, R. P. The Andswarode-System in Old English Poetry. Speculum 32 (July) 523-8. Parry's sound method applied.

1353 Downer, A. S. Ghosts, Graves and Miracles: Broadway 1956-57. Qrt J Spch 43 (Oct.) 235-47. Reviews of year on B'way which produced View from the Bridge, Cat on a Hot Tin Roof, Bus Stop, Hatful of Rain, Separate Tables, Clearing in the Woods, plus many others.

1354 Editors. Poetry Spoken and Recorded. Lib J 82 (Dec. 15) 3228. Hearing the voice of poetry.

1355 Friedman, Norman. Diction Voice Tone: The Poetic Language of Cummings. PMLA 72 (Dec.) 1036-59. In-depth study of Cummings' prosody.

1356 Geiger, Don. The Conservatism of Modern Poetry. Today's Spch 5 (Apr.) 10-12. Modern poet has no respect for tradition, reader, or humanity.

1357 Geiger, Don. Tragic Order in Moby Dick: The Ishmael-Queequeg Relationship. Cent Sts Spch J 9 (Fall) 32-6. Meaning in Moby Dick may be derived from relationship between Ishmael and Queequeg.

1358 Hargis, D. E. James Burgh and the Art of Speaking.
Spch Mono 24 (Nov.) 275-84. Motivation outline, theories,
and teachings discussed.

1359 Haun, R. R. What About the Queen's English? Today's
Spch 5 (Nov.) 34. Fate of poetry and nobility of speech.

1360 Hayes, Francis. Gestures: A Working Bibliography.
Sthn Folklore Qrt 21 (Dec.) 218-317. Important bibliography for study of gesture.

1361 Hochmuth, Marie. Burkeian Criticism. Wstn Spch 21
(Spring) 89-95. Explanation of Burkeian dramatistic
criticism.

1362 Hollis, C. C. Whitman and the American Idiom. Qrt J
Spch 43 (Dec.) 408-20. New evidence on slang and idio-
matic language in Whitman. Manuscript reveals Whitman
as conscious artist of democratic America.

1363 Kramer, Magdalene. Oral Interpretation of Literature.
Today's Spch 5 (Jan.) 4-5. Values of OI.

1364 Krider, Ruby. A High School Course in Oral Interpretation.
Sthn Spch J 22 (Spring) 170-7. Outline of eight units.

1365 Lamson, M. V. Finding the Right Poem. Engl J 46 (Mar.)
148-53. Selecting poems for OI in grade school.

1366 Lee, R. F. Emerson Through Kierkegaard: Toward a
Definition of Emerson's Theory of Communication. Engl
Lit Hist 24 (1957) 229-48. There is a consistent rationale
for Emerson's understanding of the relation between himself and his audience to be found in his work and can be
expounded by reference to Kierkegaard.

1367 Lipton, Lawrence. Have You Heard Any Good Poems
Lately? A Study of the Functions of Sight and Sound in
Modern Poetry. Arizona Qtrly 13 (Summer) 133-43.
Oral intent of poetry.

1368 Lorch, F. W. Mark Twain's Public Lectures in England in
1873. American Lit 29 (Nov.) 297-304. Twain's reception in England.

1369 MacDonald, M. B. Let's Read to Our Children. Wilson
Lib Bulletin 32 (Oct.) 129-31. Values of oral reading
outloud.

1370 Montgomery, Ray. Elite Standard vs. Democracy. Qrt J
Spch 43 (Oct.) 303-4. Takes issue with belief that there
is one correct way to say something; favors a pluralistic
approach.

1371 Nilsen, T. R. Interpretative Function of the Critic. Wstn Spch 21 (Spring) 70-6. Function of critic is to reveal the way of acting and believing fostered by the speech and the possible consequences thereof.

1372 Oyer, H. J. A Comparison of Aesthetic Judgments Made by Sixteen Viewer-Auditors and Sixteen Auditors. Sthn Spch J 22 (Spring) 164-9. No significant difference between viewer-auditor and auditor group judgments of acceptability or non-acceptability of words spoken by college students with severe articulation defects.

1373 Parrish, W. M. Elocution: A Definition and a Challenge. Qrt J Spch 43 (Feb.) 1-11. Definition legitimizes elocution as useful tool; emphasizes analyzing meaning of words and their effect upon utterance.

1374 Penrod, J. H. Two Aspects of Folk Speech in Southwestern Humor. Kentucky Folklore Record 3 (Oct.) 145-52. Contributions of southwestern folk tellers.

1375 Redding, W. C. Extrinsic and Intrinsic Criticism. Wstn Spch 21 (Spring) 96-102. Proposal for scrutiny of current methods of rhetorical criticism focused upon certain issues that may be as relevant for public address as for lit.

1376 Schmidt, R. N. Cooperation Between High School and College in the Teaching of Oral Interpretation. Spch Tchr 6 (Jan.) 48-54. Suggestions for promoting OI through cooperative time and activity scheduling between high school and college.

1377 Seedorf, E. H. The Phonetic Approach to Choral Reading. Spch Tchr 6 (Mar.) 117-22. Teaching method based on automatic kinesthetic responses.

1378 Sherwin, J. S. Literature and Communication: A Search for a Unifying Principle. J of Comm 7 (Summer) 74-82. Values of lit.

1379 Simley, Anne. Hints for the Student Reader. Spch Tchr 6 (Sept.) 233-6. 18 principles for effective oral performance as well as other guidelines for considering text, audience and performance.

1380 Sloan, T. O. Public Recitation in Japan. Qrt J Spch 43 (Dec.) 394-8. Historical sketch of evolution and development of public recitation in Japan.

1381 Stang, Mary. Stories at Christmas Time. Recreation 50 (Nov.) 326-7. Values of and selections for reading aloud at Christmas.

1958

1382   Bacon, W. A.   Review of T. S. Eliot's The Use of Poetry
        and the Use of Criticism.   Qrt J Spch 44 (Oct.) 335.

1383   Behl, W. A.   Speech in the Universities of West Germany.
        Spch Tchr 7 (Jan.) 25-30.   Explains status and approaches
        to OI.

1384   Bowen, E. R.   Promoting Dynamic Interpretative Reading.
        Spch Tchr 7 (Mar.) 118-20.   Five procedures for promot-
        ing dynamic reading with students.

1385   Bowen, E. R.   The General Education Approach to Inter-
        pretative Reading.   Cent Sts Spch J 10 (Autumn) 33-6.
        Values of OI and leisure dilemma in America.

1386   Burnshaw, Stanley.   Speaking Versus Writing.   Today's Spch
        6 (Sept.) 16-9.   Function, appropriateness and suitability
        of two different modes of communication to specific tasks.

1387   Ciardi, John.   Dialogue with the Audience.   Sat Rev 41
        (Nov. 22) 10-12.   Theory and purpose of poetry, espe-
        cially good poetry.

1388   Cobin, M. T.   An Oral Interpreter's Index to Quintilian.
        Qrt J Spch 44 (Feb.) 61-6.   Index of Institutio Oratoria.

1389   Crocker, Lionel.   The Comprehensive Examination in Speech
        at Denison University.   Spch Tchr 7 (Mar.) 127-9.   Sam-
        ple OI questions.

1390   Crocker, Lionel.   The Break with Elocution: The Origins
        of James A. Winans' Public Speaking.   Today's Spch 6
        (Apr.) 23-6.   How Winans brought speech profession back
        to common sense of Greeks.

1391   Deer, Irving.   Interpretation--Chant or Rant?   Qrt J Spch
        44 (Oct.) 307-8.   Difference between acting interpretation;
        OI'ers goal more intimate than actor's.

1392   Dickenson, Hugh.   Time and Interpretation.   Cent Sts Spch J
        10 (Autumn) 7-14.   Problems and nature of time in nar-
        rative fiction.

1393   Eastman, R. M.   Drama as Psychological Argument.   Coll
        Engl 19 (May) 327-32.   Serious amateur holds key in his/
        her emotional response.

1394   Gibson, Walker.   Sound and Sense in Gerard Manley Hopkins.
        Mod Lang Notes 73 (Feb.) 95-100.   Study of prosody re-
        leases meaning and understanding.

1395 Grimes, W. H. Oral Interpretation and Criticism: A Bibliography. Wstn Spch 22 (Spring) 69-74. Eighty articles
relevant to OI and criticism.

1396 Grimes, W. H. Oral Reading Activities in Colleges and
Universities. Spch Tchr 7 (Nov.) 332-5. Oral reading as
extra-curricular activity.

1397 Hulme, Hilda. The English Language as a Medium of Literary Expression. Essays in Crit 8 (Jan.) 68-76. The
predilections of a Shakespearean linguist in the field of
language-lit relations.

1398 Hunsinger, Paul. Festivals and Changing Patterns. Spch
Tchr 7 (Mar.) 93-8. Festivals de-emphasize winning
which pleases some, but not others; contrasts with speech
contests which promote winning.

1399 Hynes, Sam. Poetry, Poetic, Poem. Coll Engl 19 (Mar.)
263-7. Explores relationship of three terms.

1400 Irwin, R. L. A Further Note on Yvor Winters' Theory of
Oral Reading. Qrt J Spch 44 (Dec.) 432-3. A performer's advocacy of method is worthy of serious attention
only if he is natively endowed with or acquires by training
certain minimal skills. Winters does not have these skills.

1401 Konigsberg, Evelyn. Can Speech Be Taught Effectively in
English Courses? Spch Tchr 7 (Nov.) 306-8. Knowledge
of speech essential; also ability to make necessary adjustments on part of teacher.

1402 Lowenthal, Leo. An Author Objects. Qrt J Spch 44 (Apr.)
179-80. Response to McCollum's review of Literature and
the Image of Man.

1403 Lowrey, Sara. Preparing Students in Oral Interpretation for
Contests. Sthn Spch J 23 (Summer) 204-10. Choosing lit,
and winning and losing contests.

1404 Matlaw, Myron. Discovery, Probability and Mimetic Art.
Qrt J Spch 44 (Feb.) 70-1. How to reveal through imitation the spiritual or inward life of characters.

1405 McCoard, W. B. Contemporary Textbooks in Oral Interpretation. Wstn Spch 22 (Winter) 46-51. Critical review
of major texts including Aggertt and Bowen's Communicative Reading, Dolman's Art of Reading Aloud, and Henneke's Reading Aloud Effectively.

1406 McCollum, W. G. The Reviewer Explains. Qrt J Spch 44
(Apr.) 180-1. Response to Lowenthal's objections in QJS
44 (Apr. 1958) 179-80.

1407 McLaughlin, J. C. Linguistics and Literary Analysis. Qrt J Spch 44 (Apr.) 175-8. Response to Chatman's article in QJS, October 1957.

1408 Murphy, Richard. The Speech as Literary Genre. Qrt J Spch 44 (Apr.) 117-27. The speech as literary form is redefined, some difficulties which prevent appreciation of the form are discussed, and a mild plea is made for a return to the appreciation of speech as a literary genre.

1409 Newman, J. B. The Meanings of Poetry. Today's Spch 6 (Sept.) 28-30. Multi-dimensional analysis of meaning in totality of meanings.

1410 Ogilvie, Mardel. Creative Speech Experiences in the Elementary Schools. Spch Tchr 7 (Jan.) 6-10. OI, creative dramatics and puppetry seen as valuable mediums for children. They enhance perception, group interaction and role playing.

1411 Ostroff, Anthony. Notes Toward a Theory of Diction. Qrt J Spch 44 (Apr.) 166-74. Essentials for arriving at a theory of diction. Theory must include nature and function of denotation, connotation and context as control on meaning.

1412 Parrish, W. M. The Roots of the Matter. Cent Sts Spch J 10 (Autumn) 43-5. Language, pronunciation, and spelling.

1413 Rossky, William. Imagination in English Renaissance Psychology and Poetic. Studies in the Renaissance 5 (1958) 49-73. Examines psychological operation of poet's imagination as justification of poet's imagination.

1414 Schuelke, G. L. Slipping in Indirect Discourse. American Spch 33 (May) 90-8. Discussion slips from indirect to direct discourse and compares modern English to old Icelandic.

1415 Sutherland, Ronald. Structural Linguistics and English Prosody. Coll Engl 20 (Oct.) 12-7. Science of linguistics has good deal to offer English prosody and thus English lit criticism.

1416 Utley, F. L. The Study of Folk Literature: Its Scope and Use. J Amer Folklore 71 (Apr.) 139-48. Response to the many questions from students and colleagues who wish quick orientation and some sense of judgment in the vast field of published work on folklore.

1417 Woodall, Robert. The Dickens Readings. Contemp Rev 1109 (May) 248-51. Dickens' story-telling style.

1418 Wright, B. A. Stressing of the Preposition "Without" in the Verse of Paradise Lost. Notes and Queries 5 (May) 202-3. Unaccountable poetic value found in the common word when first syllable is accented.

1959

1419 Adams, H. M. Poetry Should Be Heard. Engl J 48 (Apr.) 206-7. Oral intent and listening.

1420 Baker, Virgil. Reading in Action: Production of New Plays. Players Mag 35 (Feb.) 102-3. Using scripts in otherwise full-scale productions permits many new plays each season to be produced at a university theatre.

1421 Balcer, C. L. The Vocal Aspect of Delivery Traced Through Representative Works in Rhetoric and Public Speaking: Aristotle to Rush. Cents Sts Spch J 11 (Autumn) 27-34. Chronological discussion of vocal delivery.

1422 Barclay, Dorothy. Whatever Became of Reading Aloud? NY Times Mag (Dec. 20) 41. Ease and advantages of reading aloud.

1423 Baskerville, Barnett. The Dramatic Criticism of Oratory. Qrt J Spch 45 (Feb.) 39-45. Need for distinction between oratory and drama.

1424 Brandon, J. R. Addendum of Public Recitation in Japan. Qrt J Spch 45 (Feb.) 71. Clarification of Sloan's essay in QJS 43 (Dec. 1957) 394-8.

1425 Brentlinger, W. B. William Russell: Educator and Elocutionist. Cent Sts Spch J 10 (Winter) 38-45. Russell's efforts to counteract mechanical school while keeping rules.

1426 Brick, A. R. Wuthering Heights: Narrators, Audience and Message. College Engl 21 (Oct.) 80-6. Function of individual narrators in Wuthering Heights.

1427 Broadbent, J. B. Milton's Rhetoric. Mod Phil 56 (May) 224-42. Analysis of Milton's rhetorical devices.

1428 Carey, Marjorie. Children's Literature--Creative Speech Practice. Today's Spch 7 (Nov.) 26-9. Children's lit good for stimulating physical movement and reticent speech in children.

1429 Clark, D. L. Rhetoric and the Literature of the English Middle Ages. Qrt J Spch 45 (Feb.) 19-28. Discussion of some allegories of rhetoric and lit of Middle Ages suggests that rhetoric has taught poets as well as prose writers to find arguments and use embellished and copious style.

1430 Cleary, J. W. John Bulwer: Renaissance Communicationist. Qrt J Spch 45 (Dec.) 391-8. Career and work of first man to systemize study of gesture and to design a hand alphabet for the deaf.

1431 Clevenger, Theodore, Jr., & M. T. Cobin. An Experiment in Open Circuit Television Instruction in the Basic Course in Oral Interpretation. Spch Mono 26 (June) 149-54. Effectiveness of TV instruction as option to inexperienced teachers and TA's.

1432 Cobin, M. T. Utilizing Television in the Interpretation Program. Spch Tchr 8 (Jan.) 31-6. Instructional and presentational aspects of curricular and extra curricular OI activities.

1433 Cope, J. I. Rhetorical Genres in Davenant's First Day's Entertainment at Rutland House. Qrt J Spch 45 (Apr.) 191-4. Inaccurate to describe entertainment as simply a debate, or rather two monologues padded out. Davenant's speakers seen as propagandists and his play more than propaganda. Play gives us character in full richness of its literary development returning to its spoken origins.

1434 Curley, T. F. The Imagination at Bay. Commonweal 70 (Aug. 14) 422-4. Claims modern novelists and poets are indeed creating art.

1435 Curry, Haskell. Memories of S. S. Curry. Today's Spch 7 (Nov.) 7-8. Tribute from his son.

1436 Dahl, Torsten. Alliteration in English Prose: Gleanings and Comments. Engl Studies 40 (Oct.) 449-54. Use of alliteration during Elizabethan age and 20th century.

1437 Deer, Irving. Teaching Oral Interpretation. Wstn Spch 23 (Winter) 32-6. Find a definite characteristic of lit which OI can aim at expressing.

1438 Dickinson, Hugh. Readers or Rhapsodes? Qrt J Spch 45 (Oct.) 258-63. Three male established actors have implanted in public mind conception of OI that may come to serve both in competency and technique as standard of performance.

1439 Fleischman, E. E. Choral Reading Can Be Fun. Today's Spch 7 (Sept.) 16-18. To enjoy, participate.

1440 Gagliardo, Ruth. Our Teacher Reads to Us. Nat Educ Assc J 48 (Feb.) 55. Values of reading aloud to children.

1441 Ginsberg, Allen. Notes Written on Finally Recording "Howl."
Evergreen Rev 3 (Nov.) 132-5. Personal recollections of
Ginsberg.

1442 Haun, R. R. Communicative Reading. Today's Spch 7
(Apr.) 31-2. Go beyond verbalism to recreate art.

1443 Haun, R. R. Creed or Quality. Today's Spch 7 (Nov.) 9-
10. Sharing the quality of life in lit.

1444 Hillbruner, Anthony. Interpretation, Aesthetics and the
Speech Curriculum. Spch Tchr 8 (Jan.) 22-6. OI and
aesthetics help scholar develop spirit of inquiry and power
of individualism.

1445 Hollander, John. The Metrical Emblem. Kenyon Rev 21
(Spring) 279-96. Notion of a poem seems to demand linguistic analysis.

1446 Howell, W. S. Sources of the Elocutionary Movement in
England: 1700-1748. Qrt J Spch 45 (Feb.) 1-18. Elocutionary role in revitalizing classical rhetoric.

1447 Loesch, K. T. Dangerous Criminal Still at Large. Notes
& Queries New Series 6 (Jan.) 8-9. Reincarnation of
Professor Moriarty in T. S. Eliot's "MacAvity."

1448 Marshman, J. T. Speaking the Speech. Cent Sts Spch J
10 (Winter) 64-6. Fears we have given up speaking skills
as unworthy of scholarship.

1449 Mattingly, A. S. The Teacher as Critic in Interpretation
Performance. Spch Tchr 8 (Nov.) 321-4. Critical and
historical inquiry for objective judgmental standards.

1450 Nitchie, Elizabeth. The Language of Men. Centennial Rev
3 (Spring) 189-205. Poetic language: the poet is the
choreographer who makes words dance together.

1451 Pomeroy, Ralph. Modern Poetry and a Kat Called Krazy.
Today's Spch 7 (Sept.) 14-5. Modern poet's world reflected in poetry.

1452 Sharp, W. L. Meter and Oral Interpretation. Wstn Spch
23 (Winter) 26-31. Meter primary in poetry.

1453 Smith, R. G. Development of a Semantic Differential for
Use with Speech Related Concepts. Spch Mono 26 (Nov.)
263-72. Development and standardization of scale to
measure response, especially in speech-related situations.

1454 Utley, F. L. Structural Linguistics and the Literary Critic.
J Aesthetics Art Crit 18 (June) 319-28. Linguistics is a

discipline that can help us see light in tangled jungle of lit.

1455 Wimsatt, W. K., & M. C. Beardsley. The Concept of Meter: An Exercise in Abstraction. PMLA 74 (Dec.) 585-98. Considers two influential current schools of thought about scanning and examines critically a fundamental mistake made by both of them.

1960

1456 Abernethy, R. L. The Role of Storytelling--A Preliminary Report of an Investigation in the United States. Spch Tchr 9 (Nov.) 283-6. Survey of storytelling taught at college level. Emphasis on storytelling's values.

1457 Bacon, W. A. Review of Norman Friedman's E. E. Cummings. Qrt J Spch 46 (Feb.) 102.

1458 Bacon, W. A. Review of John Unterecker's A Reader's Guide to W. B. Yeats. Qrt J Spch 46 (Feb.) 102.

1459 Bacon, W. A. Review of Leslie Hotson's Shakespeare's Wooden O. Yale Rev 50 (Autumn) 107-10.

1460 Bacon, W. A. Review of Eliseo Vivas's D. H. Lawrence: The Failure & the Triumph of Art. Christ Cent 77 (Nov.) 1380-1.

1461 Bacon, W. A. The Dangerous Shores: From Elocution to Interpretation. Qrt J Spch 46 (Apr.) 148-52. OI balance between lit, criticism, and performance techniques.

1462 Boyd, Lorenz. Chamber Drama: Versatile Language Arts Tool. Scholastic Tchr 2 (Nov.) 14-5. Chamber theater as stimulus for language arts in primary and secondary school activities.

1463 Brooks, Keith. Oral Interpretation in American Universities. Wstn Spch 24 (Summer) 142-7. Survey of OI courses in U.S. universities between 1946 and 1957. Includes percentages and other variables.

1464 Cannon, Garland. Linguistics and Literature. College Engl 21 (Feb.) 255-60. Future relations of linguistics and lit.

1465 Denues, Celia. Lee Emerson Bassett. Spch Tchr 9 (Sept.) 265-6. Tribute.

1466 Denues, Celia. Lee Emerson Bassett: 1872-1959. Wstn Spch 24 (Spring) 110-11. Tribute.

1467 Glenn, Stanley. Echo to the Sense. Wstn Spch 24 (Spring)
88-93. Emphasis on student's understanding of playwright's intent in literary work.

1468 Gray, G. W. What Was Elocution? Qrt J Spch 46 (Feb.)
1-7. Elocution as it has changed in focus and been under-
served by early theories and their originators.

1469 Hamm, A. C. Why the Professional Cold Shoulder? Qrt
J Spch 46 (Feb.) 80-1. Questions inactivity in choral
speaking.

1470 Hargis, D. E. Interpretation as Oral Communication. Cent
Sts Spch J 11 (Spring) 168-73. Importance of oral aspects of OI.

1471 Herbert, T. W. Tunes of Poetry: Experiments in Recognition. Emory Univ Qtrly 16 (Fall) 164-73. Demonstrates
music in poetry.

1472 Hopkins, M. F. Interpretative Reading at State Contests.
Sthn Spch J 25 (Summer) 298-304. How judges score OI.

1473 Jarvis, J. B. A Note on Oral Interpretation. Wstn Spch
24 (Winter) 29-32. Values of OI.

1474 Johnson, D. M. Emotion and the Fiction Writer. Discourse 3 (Apr.) 113-8. Central role of emotions in creative writing.

1475 Jones, L. S. The Notebook: Letters to the Editor. Wstn
Spch 24 (Spring) 115-6. Editorial stressing that OI teacher must possess wide acquaintance with good lit of all
genres.

1476 Kirk, G. S. Homer and Modern Oral Poetry: Some Con-
fusions. Classical Qrtly 10 (Nov.) 271-81. Homeric
studies, from time to time, tend to crystallize and tend
to become orthodoxy. This is to be avoided.

1477 Knox, George. An Epitaphic Note on Sincerity. Wstn Spch
24 (Winter) 12-7. Meaning and implications of sincerity.

1478 Lewis, C. S. Metre. Rev Engl Lit 1 (Jan.) 45-50. Brief
discussion of meter in poetry.

1479 McLuhan, Marshall. Myth: Oral and Written. Commentary
30 (July) 90-1. Critique of Richard Dorson's American
Folklore.

1480 McMahon, F. R. Speech and the Critics. Wstn Spch 24
(Spring) 101-5. All high school classes should provide
some instruction in oral communication.

1481 Mooney, S. L. Hopkins and Counterpoint. Victorian Newsl
18 (Fall) 21-2. Comparative study of Hopkins and other
Victorian poets.

1482 Rarig, F. M. Reflections While Retiring--and Afterward.
Cent Sts Spch J 11 (Winter) 123-5. Reflections on state
of the art.

1483 Robertson, Roderick. Producing Playreadings. Educ Theat
J 12 (Mar.) 20-3. Playreadings second best to full production but do have certain audience appeal and can produce stimulating imaginative experience.

1484 Roethke, Theodore. Some Remarks on Rhythm. Poetry 97
(Oct.) 35-46. English language is essentially iambic but
most memorable passages are strongly stressed, even
sprung.

1485 Ryan, J. J. Poetry and Communication Once Again.
Renascence 12 (Spring) 143-8. Response to article by
Rooney. Rooney has dealt with issue of poetry in a way
that seems confusing and misleading.

1486 Sansom, Clive. Choral Speaking. Qrt J Spch 46 (Oct.)
306-7. Response to Hamm's essay in QJS 46 (Feb.) 80-1.

1487 Smith, W. J. Rhythm of the Night. Horn Book 36 (Dec.)
495-500. Need to read aloud to children.

1488 Spender, Stephen. Poetry vs. Language Engineering. New
Rep 143 (Aug. 15) 17-18. Need for creative element in
poetry keeps it human.

1489 Tallman, Warren. Kerouac's Sound. Evergreen Rev 4
(Jan.-Feb.) 153-69. Analysis of use of sound in Kerouac's
novels.

1490 Thornley, Gwendella. Come to Our Festival. Wstn Spch
24 (Winter) 43-4. Activities purpose and participation at
the annual poetry festival in Utah.

1491 Trauernicht, M. M. Woolbert as a Teacher. Spch Tchr 9
(Sept.) 200-6. Tribute and explanation.

1492 Viguers, R. H. More Thoughts on Reading to Children.
Horn Book 36 (Dec.) 501-3. Reading aloud helps children
understand books.

1493 Warfel, H. R. Syntax Makes Literature. Coll Engl 21
(Feb.) 251-5. Syntax is inner dynamic that makes lit
work.

1961

1494 Bessinger, J. B. The Oral Text of Ezra Pound's "The Seafarer." Qrt J Spch 47 (Apr.) 173-7. Pound's reading of the poem appraised emphasizing rhythm.

1495 Black, J. W. Aural Reception of Sentences of Different Lengths. Qrt J Spch 47 (Feb.) 51-3. Attempts to answer question of whether length of sentence affects listener's identification of words as well as auditory reception.

1496 Blattner, Helene. Lee Emerson Bassett. Wstn Spch 25 (Spring) 101-2. Sketch and tribute.

1497 Brewer, J. M. North Carolina Negro Oral Narratives. N C Folklore 9 (July) 21-33. Current theories and origins of oral narrative with collection of narratives.

1498 Campbell, P. N. Poetry, Non-Poetry, Prose and Verse. Wstn Spch 25 (Winter) 20-4. Definitions and characteristics that differentiate prose-non-prose-poetry-verse.

1499 Carson, H. L. Theatre Language: A Dictionary of Terms in English from Medieval to Modern Times. Qrt J Spch 47 (Dec.) 439-40. Review of Bowman and Ball Theatre Language.

1500 Cobin, M. T., & Theodore Clevenger, Jr. Television Instruction, Course Content, and Teaching Experience Level: An Experimental Study in the Basic Course in Oral Interpretation. Spch Mono 28 (Mar.) 16-20. Measured relationship of TV instruction to conventional experience.

1501 Crocker, Lionel. How to Multiply the Side Values of Oral Interpretation. Spch Tchr 10 (Jan.) 63-4. Guides OI to non-fiction lit.

1502 Davis, W. R. A Note on Accent and Quantity in A Booke of Ayers. Mod Lang Qrtly 22 (Mar.) 32-6. Rhythmical and metrical problems in Booke of Ayers.

1503 Detweiler, A. G. Music and Poetry. Brit J of Aesthetics 1 (June) 134-43. Oral intent of poetry.

1504 Donaghue, Denis. Poetry and the Behavior of Speech. Hudson Rev 14 (Winter) 537-49. Review of Paul Valery.

1505 Fonagy, Ivan. Communication in Poetry. Word 17 (Aug.) 194-218. The predictability of sounds.

1506 Forrest, W. C. Teaching Poetry as a Mode of Speech. Engl Record 11 (Spring) 2-5. Oral performance yields portion of poetic meaning.

1507 Geiger, Don. Essay on a Poem's Being Meaning Something. Wstn Spch 25 (Fall) 242-9. Structure, form, and meaning.

1508 Hargis, D. E. Enfield and Elocution. Wstn Spch 25 (Fall) 222-31. Essay on elocution based on eight specific canons through which the art of elocution can be learned.

1509 Haun, R. R. Poetry Reading and the American Idea. Today's Spch 9 (Nov.) 12-3. Values of OI.

1510 Hoopes, N. E. What Literature Should Be Used in Oral Interpretation? Spch Tchr 10 (Sept.) 206-10. Responses of 15 specialists in OI.

1511 Johnson, E. W. Teaching Poetry to an Unpoetical Age: A Junior High School Unit. Engl J 50 (Nov.) 546-50. Values of OI.

1512 Jones, J. H. Commonplace and Memorization in the Oral Tradition of the English and Scottish Popular Ballads. J of Amer Folklore 74 (Jan.) 97-112. Development of quatrain ballad from couplet ballad form.

1513 Lanbert, J. W. Recorded Literature and Drama. J Brit Institute of Recorded Sound 1 (Summer) 63-70. Bibliography of recorded lit.

1514 Marinello, L. J. Robert Frost's Inaugural Dedication: The Poet in Public Ceremony. Today's Spch 9 (Nov.) 22-3. Frost's poetic instinct.

1515 Marlor, C. S. Reader's Theatre Bibliography. Cent Sts Spch J 12 (Winter) 134-7. Plays, poems, and prose used in RT productions.

1516 Miller, M. H. Charles Dickens at the English Charity Dinner. Qrt J Spch 47 (Apr.) 143-9. Dickens as best after dinner speaker in England.

1517 Nist, John. Gerard Manley Hopkins and Textual Intensity: A Linguistic Analysis. Coll Engl 22 (Apr.) 497-500. From the basic level of sound patterning to the acme of philosophical content, Hopkins a master of textual intensity.

1518 Okey, L. L. Ways of Speaking Managed Ideas. Communication Techniques for the Mass Media, TV Radio & Film Commission, Indiana area, Methodist Church, 1961, pp. 47-52.

1519 Okey, L. L. Improving Your Oral Reading of the Bible. Communication Techniques for the Mass Media, TV Radio & Film Commission, Indiana area, Methodist Church, 1961, pp. 31-9.

1520 Okey, L. L. Improving Your Delivery of the Manuscript
Speech. Communication Techniques for the Mass Media,
TV Radio & Film Commission, Indiana area, Methodist
Church, 1961, pp. 40-6.

1521 Plummer, Gail. Maud May Babcock. Wstn Spch 25 (Spring)
99-101. Sketch and tribute.

1522 Rasmus, Ward. Voice and Diction: Historical Perspective.
Qrt J Spch 47 (Oct.) 253-61. Examination of history of
voice and diction to understand and interpret the present
and possibly predict trends.

1523 Reynolds, N. J. A Lively Art. Today's Spch 9 (Apr.) 15-
7. OI very prevalent in first quarter of century and professional reading traced to present time.

1524 Reynolds, N. J. It Wasn't Elocution: Five Professional
Oral Interpreters. Qrt J Spch 47 (Oct.) 244-52. Theory
and practice from performers of the Chautauqua circuit.

1525 Wellwarth, G. E. Nigel Dennis: The Return of Intellectual
Satire. Sthn Spch J 27 (Fall) 56-61. In praise of N.
Dennis.

1526 Wise, C. M. A Shakespeare Cipher in the Bible. Sthn
Spch J 26 (Summer) 261-70. As title states.

1527 Yarbrough, R. C. The Preacher and His Vocal Equipment.
Today's Spch 9 (Sept.) 22-4, 29. Desirable speech goals
for preachers.

1962

1528 Bacon, W. A. Review of W. P. Bowman & R. H. Ball
Theatre Language. Shakespeare Qrtly 13 (Fall) 576.
Says use of book is frustrating.

1529 Bahn, Eugene. Interpretative Reading in Contemporary
Greece. Qrt J Spch 47 (Oct.) 271-6. Modern purpose of
OI similar to past's.

1530 Batson, E. J. George Bernard Shaw: The Orator and the
Man. Engl 14 (Autumn) 97-100. Praises Shaw for hu-
manitarian acts and dexterity as orator.

1531 Blankenship, Jane. A Linguistic Analysis of Oral and Written Style. Qrt J Spch 48 (Dec.) 419-22. Problem of
making useful and distinct discrimination between oral and
written style.

1532 Brooks, Keith. Readers Theatre: Some Questions and Answers. Dramatics 24 (Dec.) 14, 27. Definition of RT,

suggests methods of preparing RT productions and urges
RT as form of communication.

1533 Brown, C. T., & P. W. Keller. A Modest Proposal for
Listening Training. Qrt J Spch 48 (Dec.) 395-9. Value
of listening; more training in listening skills needed.

1534 Carlson, E. W. Robert Frost on Vocal Imagination, The
Merger of Form and Content. American Lit 33 (Jan.)
519-22. Vocal imagination and dramatic tone.

1535 Ciardi, John. The Silences of Poetry. Mich Alumnus Qtrly
Rev 44 (1962) 298-307.

1536 Cobin, M. T. Response to Eye Contact. Qrt J Spch 48
(Dec.) 415-8. Eye contact important for audience response in face-to-face situation.

1537 Cohen, Herman. The Mirror Image: 18th Century Elocutio
and the New Philosophy. Wstn Spch 26 (Winter) 22-8.
Elocutio as defined by 18th-century theorists, with influence of new philosophy on theories of elocutio.

1538 Creed, R. P. The Singer Looks at His Sources. Comp
Lit 14 (Winter) 44-52. Comparison between Beowulf and
The Odyssey.

1539 Deen, L. W. The Rhetoric of Newman's Apologia. Engl
Lit History 29 (Mar.) 224-38. Key to Apologia is the life
of thought.

1540 Donner, S. T. Ralph Dennis: A Great Teacher. Spch Tchr
11 (Sept.) 214-20. Tribute.

1541 Geiger, Don. Oral Interpretation and the Teaching of Literature. Spch Tchr 11 (Sept.) 202-7. Reviews Curry and
emphasizes balance between text and physical and vocal
approach.

1542 Gilbert, Edna. Ralph Dennis. Spch Tchr 11 (Nov.) 294-7.
Tribute.

1543 Gray, J. W. The Public Reading of Edgar Allan Poe.
Sthn Spch J 28 (Winter) 109-15. Response to Poe's readings and lectures.

1544 Hope, John. Reading Aloud in the Family Circle. Engl
Stud in Africa 5 (Mar.) 78-80. OI in the family setting.

1545 Kershner, A. G. John Dolman, Jr. Spch Tchr 11 (Nov.)
290-2. Tribute.

1546 Kildahl, E. E. Jacob Engstrand's Use of Persuasive Devices in Ibsen's Ghosts. Cent Sts Spch J 13 (Winter) 106-

11. How Engstrand achieves three goals using varied persuasive methods: deductive reasoning, cause and effect reasoning, logical use of evidence, etc.

1547 Klyn, M. S. The Serio-Comic Tension: A Study in Response. Wstn Spch 27 (Summer) 146-52. Audience response to paradox.

1548 Larusso, Dominic. Elocutio: A Story of Action and Reaction. Wstn Spch 26 (Winter 62) 6-13. Ciceronianism, a literary development of renaissance is critiqued for its influence on rhetoric.

1549 Lee, C. I. Cornelius Carmen Cunningham. Spch Tchr 11 (Nov.) 297-9. Tribute to Cunningham's intuitive approach to OI.

1550 Levin, S. R. Suprasegmentals and the Performance of Poetry. Qrt J Spch 48 (Dec.) 366-72. Suprasegmental analysis demonstrates that OI nullifies poem's syntactic ambiguity.

1551 Lewis, Robert. Emotional Memory. Tulane Dr Rev 6 (June) 54-60. It is important for the actor in his daily living to store up emotional fuel for subsequent use in performance.

1552 Loney, G. E. Classic Drama Revivals in Greece. Qrt J Spch 48 (Dec.) 379-87. Revival represents desire for authenticity and preservation of ancient art form.

1553 Mays, W. A. Wayne C. Booth: The Rhetoric of Fiction. Critique 5 (Fall/Winter) 84-90. Finds Booth confusing and vague and not really usable.

1554 McCormack, Robert. Unspeakable Verse. Canadian Lit 12 (Spring) 28-36. Importance of discovering and recognizing personality of speaker that guides and controls work.

1555 McHugh, Vincent. Man to Read the Meter. The Nation 194 (May 26) 476-9. The dilemma that some poetry should be seen and not heard and some should be heard and not seen.

1556 McMahon, F. R. Jacobean Elocutio. Wstn Spch 26 (Winter) 13-22. Discusses Cicero's influence and characterizes Jacobean elocutio.

1557 Miller, M. H. Charles Dickens and His Audience. Cent Sts Spch J 13 (Autumn) 283-8. Dickens' observation of other speakers and audience.

1558 Mouat, L. H. Lee Emerson Bassett. Spch Tchr 11 (Nov.) 299-302. Tribute.

1559 Murphy, Richard. Wayland Maxwell Parrish. <u>Spch Tchr</u> 11 (Nov.) 307-10. Tribute.

1560 Nathan, L. E. Reading to a Friend Whose Work Has Come to Nothing. <u>Wstn Spch</u> 26 (Fall) 307-10. The voice of the poem is examined; OI depends for its validity on the voicing.

1561 Nelson, S. E. Charles Henry Woolbert. <u>Spch Tchr</u> 11 (Nov.) 302-4. Tribute: known for bringing to OI concept of empathy.

1562 Nielsen, M. A. Have You Tried Readers Theatre? <u>Sec Schl Theat Conf News</u> 1 (Winter) 10-12.

1563 Nist, John. Sound and Sense: Some Structures of Poetry. <u>College Engl</u> 23 (Jan.) 291-5. Mechanics of sound in poetry.

1564 Okey, L. L. Thomas Clarkson Trueblood: Pioneer, 1856-1951. <u>Spch Tchr</u> 11 (Jan.) 10-4. Focus on Trueblood and Fulton.

1565 Perrine, Laurence. The Nature of Proof in the Interpretation of Poetry. <u>Engl J</u> 51 (Sept.) 393-8. Is there such a thing as an incorrect reading of poetry? Perrine offers some illustrated answers.

1566 Phillips, G. M. Rhetorical Gleanings from the Wisdom Literature. <u>Wstn Spch</u> 26 (Summer) 157-63. Wisdom lit in five books of the Bible.

1567 Ready, William. The Sound of Poetry. <u>Bull Amer Lib Assc</u> 56 (Feb.) 153-4. Importance of listening to artist on recordings before purchasing books; value of literary recordings.

1568 Reclam, Herta. Choric Speaking in Greek Tragedies Performed by Students. <u>Spch Tchr</u> 11 (Nov.) 283-9. Discusses productions in German, French, Italian, and Portuguese, as well as voice and movement.

1569 Sloan, T. O. Review of <u>Symmetry & Sense: The Poetry of Sir Phillip Sidney</u> by R. L. Montgomery, Jr. <u>Qrtly J Spch</u> 48 (Apr.) 210-19.

1570 Sloan, T. O. A Rhetorical Analysis of John Donne's "The Prohibition." <u>Qrt J Spch</u> 48 (Feb.) 38-45. Poem analyzed by Ramist system of logic and rhetoric.

1571 Sloan, T. O. Review of <u>Age of the Splendid Machine</u> by Don Geiger. <u>Qrt J Spch</u> 48 (Oct.) 324.

1572 Sloan, T. O. A Note on Invention & Judgement in John
      Donne's Poetry. Cent Sts Spch J 13 (Winter) 116-7.
      Study of Donne's use of words, invention, and judgment.

1573 Smith, J. F. Maud May Babcock. Spch Tchr 11 (Nov.)
      304-7. Tribute.

1574 Solem, D. E. A Course in Symbolic Expression: Coor-
      dinating the Arts. Sthn Spch J 27 (Spring) 195-201. Co-
      ordination of the arts as a unit through concept of sym-
      bolic action.

1575 Thompson, D. W. Frank M. Rarig. Spch Tchr 11 (Nov.)
      292-4. Tribute.

1576 Weevers, Theodoor. On the Origins of an Accentual Verse
      Form Used by William Morris and Henriette Roland Holst.
      Neophilologus 46 (July) 210-26. Metrical patterns de-
      veloped by Morris and adopted by Roland Holst.

1963

1577 Bateson, F. W. Literary Artifact. J Gen Educ 15 (July)
      79-92. Relation of spelling and punctuation to sound.
      Argues for oral study of lit.

1578 Bierbaum, M. L. Individualized Approach to Enrichment
      Reading. Grade Tchr 81 (Nov.) 85-113. Mentions oral
      reading.

1579 Bode, Carl. Sound of American Literature a Century Ago.
      J Gen Educ 15 (Apr.) 1-17. History and various per-
      formances of American lyceum.

1580 Brooke-Rose, Christine. Notes on the Metre of Auden's
      "The Age of Anxiety." Essays in Crit 13 (July) 253-64.
      Prosodic analysis of Auden's metre.

1581 Brown, J. R. Shakespeare's Subtext: I. Tul Dr Rev 8
      (Fall) 72-94. Points to importance of not overlooking
      subtextual investigation of Shakespeare's plays.

1582 Brown, J. R. Shakespeare's Subtext: II. Tul Dr Rev 8
      (Winter) 85-102. Continuation of study in previous issue.

1583 Cain, E. R. Elocution in German Rhetorical Theory:
      1750-1850. Wstn Spch 27 (Fall) 222-6. Winkler's theory
      of elocution.

1584 Coger, L. I. Theatre for Oral Interpreters. Spch Tchr 12
      (Nov.) 322-30. Interpreters theatre a device for creative
      programming using whole width of lit.

1585 Coger, L. I. Interpreters Theatre: Theatre of the Mind. Qrt J Spch 49 (Apr.) 157-64. Definition and discussion of RT.

1586 Coger, L. I. Let It Be a Challenge: A Production of Up the Down Staircase. Drama Mag 40 (Feb.) 11-4. Adapting book for performance.

1587 Dace, Wallace. The Concept of Rasa in Sanskrit Dramatic Theory. Educ Theat J 15 (Oct.) 249-54. Need for equivalent English term to distinguish between experience as theatre audience and real-life of pity and fear.

1588 Dahle, T. L. Speech: What Is It? Today's Spch 11 (Sept.) 17-8, 31. OI defined for layperson.

1589 Dane, Chase. For Reading Out Loud. PTA Mag 58 (Nov.) 13. Family reads together.

1590 Davis, O. B. Samuel Silas Curry: 1847-1921. Spch Tchr 12 (Nov.) 304-7. Summary of Curry's theories.

1591 Ebbit, P. F. Drama for Slow Learners. Engl J 52 (Nov.) 624-6. Reading aloud best suggestion for poorer students.

1592 Edgerton, Kathleen. The Lecturing of Edgar Allan Poe. Sthn Spch J 28 (Summer) 268-73. Poe as lecturer-reader.

1593 Faries, Elizabeth. Defense of Elocution. Sthn Spch J 29 (Winter) 133-40. Influence of elocutionary theory transmitted to present day speech education.

1594 Fearing, Franklin. Problem of Metaphor. Sthn Spch J 29 (Fall) 47-55. Metaphors in cognitive-perceptual functioning.

1595 Force, W. M. Plays Should Be Heard in the Classroom. Engl J 52 (Mar.) 206-8. Reading plays aloud adds meaning.

1596 Garforth, John. Poetry and All That Jazz. Encore 10 (Oct.) 45-51. Close relation of poetry to music.

1597 Genet, Jean. Note on Theatre. Tul Dr Rev 7 (Spring) 37-41. Genet prefers communion over diversion.

1598 Griffin, Christine. Choral Reading: A New Use. Today's Spch 11 (Sept.) 14. Uses of choric speaking.

1599 Gunkle, George. Empathy: Implications for Theatre Research. Educ Theat J 15 (Mar.) 15-23. Treats consequences of imprecise and narrow definition of the term and its effect on research.

1600 Henderhan, R. C.; Alan Billings; & Keith Brooks. A Philosophy of Readers Theatre. Spch Tchr 12 (Sept.) 229-32. Stresses retention of basic principles of OI in RT. Suggests possible use of selected theatrical devices to enhance experience of the lit.

1601 Hopkins, Richard. Oral Interpretation Versus Silent Reading. Qrt J Spch 49 (Dec.) 446-7. Response to suprasegmentals: (QJS, Dec. 1962). Interpreters can work with ambiguity.

1602 Irwin, R. L. Review of New World Writing. Qrt J Spch 49 (Feb.) 89-90.

1603 Jewkes, W. T. Physicists' Poetry. J Gen Educ 15 (Oct.) 202-11. Investigates total structure of poem as source of meanings; encourages intuitive responses.

1604 Kirk, G. S. Oral Poetry. Class Rev 13 (Mar.) 19-21. Review of Singer of Tales by A. B. Lord, which discusses Yugoslav oral singers and their value for understanding Homer.

1605 Koe, Winefride. Thoughts Arising Out of a Verse Speaking Festival. Spch & Dram (Jan.) 21. Reactions to British Festival.

1606 Kramer, Magdalene. Azubah J. Latham: Creative Teacher. Spch Tchr 12 (Sept.) 187-90. Tribute to Latham and method.

1607 Krempel, Daniel. Imaginary Forces: Minority Report. Qrt J Spch 49 (Dec.) 383-8. Audience creative participation after theatrical experiences.

1608 Lee, C. I. The Line as a Rhythmic Unit in the Poetry of Theodore Roethke. Spch Mono 30 (Mar.) 15-22. Poetic line integral to poem's intended sound pattern and meaning.

1609 Levine, George. Madame Bovary and the Disappearing Author. Mod Fict Stud 9 (Summer) 103-19. Flaubert's and James' attempts to make narrator objective.

1610 Littledale, H. A. How to Read a Bedtime Story. Parents Mag 38 (Nov.) 69, 154. Reading to induce pleasant sleep.

1611 Maher, A. C. Poetry for Children. Grade Tchr 80 (Mar.) 60, 115-7. Mentions oral reading of verse.

1612 Miles, Josephine. Reading Poems. Engl J 52 (Mar.) 157-64. How to read poetry and understand it.

1613 Nichols, J. W. Shakespeare as a Character in Drama. Educ Theatre J 15 (Mar.) 24-32. Dramatists' use of

Shakespeare to criticize contemporary theatre scene and comment on playwright himself, man, and dramatist.

1614 Perrine, Laurence. The Importance of Tone in the Interpretation of Literature. College Engl 24 (Feb.) 389-95. Tone is located in no specific element in the poem. It arises from diction, images, structure, rhymes, meter-- in short, from the whole. If we miss the tone, we miss the meaning.

1615 Phillipson, Jane. Verse Speaking Festival at RBTC. Spch & Dram 12 (Jan.) 20-1. Describes verse speaking at Rose Burford Training College.

1616 Post, R. M. Achievement of Empathic Response in Oral Reading. Sthn Spch J 28 (Spring) 236-40. Mental, emotional, physical aspects of empathy and how to use these to achieve empathic response.

1617 Pugliese, R. E. The Tape Recorder for Dramatic Critiques. Educ Theatre J 15 (Mar.) 62-5. Advantages of recorder for critical reactions as basis for discussions in performance feedback.

1618 Rennie, Christine. Place of Speech and Drama in Teaching of English. Spch & Dram 13 (July) 13-4. Relationship of speech and English in Britain.

1619 Robb, M. M. Growing a Taste for Poetry. Spch Tchr 12 (Nov.) 317-21. Value of the development of aesthetic appreciation of poetry.

1620 Robertson, Roderick. Interpreters Theatre. Qrt J Spch 49 (Oct.) 321-2. Response to Coger's articles in QJS (Apr. 1963) 157-64. Points out that in RT there is a visual channel as well as aural one and this leads to problems in translation.

1621 Rosenberg, Marvin. The Language of Drama. Educ Theat J 15 (Mar.) 1-16. Nonverbal language, gesture and sound, and their powers to communicate experience.

1622 Schmidt, R. N. Speaking a Written Speech. Today's Spch 11 (Feb.) 4-5. One aid to speech making is training in OI.

1623 Shawcross, J. T. Milton's Decision to Become a Poet. Mod Lang Qrt 24 (Mar.) 21-30. Interprets Milton's poetry after 1637.

1624 Sloan, T. O. The Rhetoric in the Poetry of John Donne. Studies in Engl Lit 3 (Winter) 31-44. Examines Donne's rhetoric strategies and views poem as argument.

1625 Sloan, T. O. Review of John Donne's Lyrics: The Eloquence of Action by Arnold Stein. Qrt J Spch 49 (Oct.)
333-4.

1626 Stambusky, Alan. Speech in the Theatre: The Importance
of Voice Science to Director and Actor. Spch Tchr 12
(Nov.) 289-98. Voice science imperative to director and
actor.

1627 Tolch, C. J. The Problem of Language and Accuracy in
Identification of Facial Expression. Cent Sts Spch J 14
(Feb.) 12-16. Low percentage of correct judgments of
facial expression and false notions about naming facial
expressions due to choosing descriptive terms for the
expression and methods of recording terms.

1628 Wilcox, L. L. Stories to Read Aloud at Christmas Time.
House Beautiful 105 (Dec.) 24. Stories for Christmas.

1964

1629 Bacon, W. A. The Elocutionary Career of Thomas Sheridan: 1719-1788. Spch Mono 31 (Mar.) 1-53. Lengthy
review of Sheridan's lifelong interest in arts of reading
and speaking. Includes bibliography of his works from
1743-1786.

1630 Bevan, Angela. Festival of Poetry at Royal Court Theatre.
Spch & Dram 13 (Jan.) 15-6. Review of spoken verse in
Britain.

1630a Bolton, Janet. The Garnishing of the Manner of Utterance.
Wstn Spch 28 (Spring) 83-91. Nature, style, and status
of delivery.

1631 Broderick, J. C., et al. Articles on American Literature
Appearing in Current Periodicals. Amer Lit 36 (Mar.-
Jan.) 131-51; 260-69; 412-29; 559-71.

1632 Brooks, Keith, & J. E. Bielenberg. Readers Theatre as
Defined by New York Critics. Sthn Spch J 29 (Summer)
288-302. Literature readers' techniques, staging, and
criticism of New York RT.

1633- Brooks, Keith, & I. M. Wulftange. Listener Response to
4 Oral Interpretation. Spch Mono 31 (Mar.) 73-9. Response
to TV, audio tape, and live presentation are compared.

1635 Casmir, F. L. Tell It Again. Today's Spch 12 (Sept.) 8-9.
Storytelling as an art.

1636 Cobin, M. T.   Criticism in Teaching: Oral Interpretation and Drama. Wstn Spch 28 (Winter) 27-34. Evaluation and guidance in critiquing OI and theatre.

1637 Coger, L. I.   Stanislavski Changes His Mind.   Tulane Dr Rev 9 (Fall) 63-8. Stanislavski's later methods.

1638 Collins, R. E.   A Study of Oral and Silent Reading Comprehension. Wstn Spch 28 (Fall) 217-21. Difference between scores significantly higher for oral readers than for silent readers.

1639 Crowell, Laura. Wilma H. Grimes. Qrt J Spch 50 (Feb.) 102-3. Tribute.

1640 Editors. Symposium: The Measurement of Creativity. J Educ Measurement 1 (Dec.) 91-114. Phases and problems in measuring creativity.

1641 Geiger, Don. Prosody as Functional Criticism for the Oral Interpreter. Wstn Spch 28 (Summer) 134-45. Understanding prosody is key to understanding poem.

1642 Gerber, J. C.   Preparation of High School English Teachers. J Gen Educ 16 (July) 121-35. Makes passing reference to failure of college English programs to teach students to read aloud well.

1643 Hargis, D. E.   A French Elocutionist: 1877. Sthn Spch J 30 (Fall) 24-35. Ernest Legouve in natural school.

1644 Haun, R. R.   Communicative Reading. Today's Spch 12 (Nov.) 30-1. OI as experience and communication.

1645 Hunter, E. F.   Peace of Great Books. Horn Book 40 (Dec.) 651-9. Reading aloud keeps doors of communication open between parents and children.

1646 Klyn, M. S.   Symposium: Standpoints in Oral Interpretation. Wstn Spch 28 (Summer) 133. A few words of explanation about editing the symposium presented in this issue.

1647 Klyn, M. S.   The Problem of Evil: A Further Study in Response. Wstn Spch 28 (Winter) 22-7. Reader audience response to evil.

1648 Klyn, M. S.   The Terms of Feeling. Wstn Spch 28 (Summer) 159-66. OI as way of reducing alienation.

1649 MacArthur, D. E.   Readers Theatre: Variations on a Theme. Spch Tchr 13 (Jan.) 47-51. Notes variety of presentations, that RT programs tend to fall into three categories: traditional OI of prose/poetry, semi-dramatic interpretation of generic lit and dramatic interpretation.

1650 Malone, Kemp. The Next Decade. College Engl 25 (Mar.)
458-61. Values of OI in English.

1651 Mattingly, A. S. Follow Nature: A Synthesis of 18th Century Views. Spch Mono 31 (Mar.) 80-4. Provides meaning of nature, understanding of mechanical natural dichotomy and aesthetic insights.

1652 Mattingly, A. S. The Listener and the Interpreter's Style.
Wstn Spch 28 (Summer) 154-9. Speaker-listener in essay, lyric, narrative, and drama.

1653 McMahon, F. R. Elocutio in Mid-Seventeenth Century England. Wstn Spch 28 (Spring) 92-7. Some of the changes
of the language influenced by four stylistic modes of the
17th-century.

1654 Mohrmann, G. P. Children's Literature and the Beginning
Class in Oral Interpretation. Spch Tchr 13 (Mar.) 128-32.
Dramatists' use of Shakespeare to criticize contemporary
introductory course in OI.

1655 Mohrmann, G. P. , & A. W. Staub. Rhetoric and Poetic:
A New Critique Applied I. Sthn Spch J 30 (Fall) 36-45.
Ethical stress in early 19th-century American poetry.

1656 Monroe, E. A. The Group Reading: Expression for Drama
of Mental Action. Central States Spch J 15 (Aug.) 170-6.
The Cocktail Party as covert action.

1657 Morse, Ben. Three Ballads. Players Mag 40 (Feb.) 138.
Review of New York theatre scene; three productions
leaning toward RT.

1658 Painter, H. W. Trends in the Language Arts. Grade Tchr
81 (Apr.) 49, 78. Includes reference to oral reading.

1659 Parks, G. B. Turn to Romantic in Travel Literature of
18th Century. Mod Lang Qrt 25 (Mar.) 22-33. Survey
of lit with emotional responses to nature in 18th century.

1660 Perry, J. O. Action, Vision or Voice: The Moral Dilem-
mas in Conrad's Tale-Telling. Mod Fict Stud 10 (Spring)
3-14. Analyzes Conrad's use of Marlow as oral story
teller.

1661 Pierson, R. M. The Meter of the Listeners. Engl Stud 45
(Oct.) 373-81. Metrical analysis.

1662 Post, R. M. Everyday Reading Aloud. Today's Spch 12
(Apr.) 22-3. Hints about OI for laypersons.

1663 Sampson, Olive. A Linguistic Study of the Written Composition of Ten-Year-Old Children. Lang & Spch 7 (July)

176-82. In oral and written language, sentence length and complexity indicate maturity.

1664 Schwartz, Elias. Rhythm and Meaning in English Verse. Crit 6 (Summer) 246-55. Relation between rhythmic effects of poetry and meaning.

1665 Senneff, S. F. Song and Music in Beckett's Watt. Mod Fict Stud 10 (Summer) 137-49. Nonprint oral elements are key to understanding this novel.

1666 Sloan, T. O. Review of Poetry & The Physical Voice by Francis Berry. Qrt J Spch 50 (Feb.) 92.

1667 Sloan, T. O. Argument and Character in Wyatt's "They Flee from Me." Wstn Spch 28 (Summer) 145-53. Rhetorical analysis of the poem.

1668 Stiles, L. J. What Shall We Do About Poetry in the Schools? Elem Schl J 65 (Dec.) 175-8. Plea for greater emphasis on poetry--reading aloud and listening to it.

1669 Thompson, D. W. Frank M. Rarig: 1880-1963. Qrt J Spch 50 (Oct.) 348-9. Tribute.

1670 Wamboldt, H. J. Haiku as a Tool in Teaching Oral Interpretation. Spch Tchr 13 (Sept.) 171-5. Study and writing of Haiku verse to overcome student prejudice against poetry in basic OI course.

1671 Whitaker, B. J. John Ciardi on Poets' Recorded Readings. Sthn Spch J 29 (Spring) 209-13. Ciardi favors readings as valuable because of informative content, special authenticity and preservation of metrical value of language.

1965

1672 Appel, Alfred, Jr. "Powerhouse's Blues." Stud Short Fict 2 (Spring) 221-34. Eudora Welty's story as jazz, folklore, and oral performance.

1673 Bailliet, C. A. The History and Rhetoric of the Triplet. PMLA 80 (Dec.) 528-34. Appendix-summary of occurrence of triplet in pentameter couplet verse.

1674 Ballew, L. M. The Absurdity of the Absurd. Sthn Spch J 31 (Winter) 147-52. Interpretation of absurd lit.

1675 Barba, Eugenio. Theatre Laboratory 13 Rzedow. Drama Rev 9 (Spring) 153-71. Brief explanation of Grotowski theory of acting.

1676 Barba, Eugenio, & Ludwik Flaszen. A Theatre of Magic
      and Sacrilege. Drama Rev 9 (Spring) 172-89. The Jerzy
      Grotowski modern secular ritual of archetypal symbols,
      myths, and images.

1677 Bass, Eden. Verbal Failure of Lord Jim. College Engl 26
      (Mar.) 438-44. Language of Jim and other characters re-
      flect personal trials and surrounding social conditions.

1678 Breneman, Bren, & Lucille Breneman. Once Upon a Time.
      Spch Tchr 14 (Sept.) 216-23. Characteristics and themes
      in Gaelic story telling.

1679 Bronstein, A. J., & E. M. Bronstein. A Phonetic-Lin-
      guistic View of the Reading Controversy. Spch Mono 32
      (Mar.) 25-35. Review of contributions in methods of
      teaching reading.

1680 Brown, C. T. 3 Studies of the Listening of Children.
      Spch Mono 32 (June) 129-38. Listener abilities analyzed.

1681 Brown, Calvin. Can Musical Notation Help English Scan-
      sion? J Aesth Art Crit 23 (Spring) 329-34. Musical
      notation as means of establishing poetic meter, rhythm,
      etc.

1682 Cannon, Garland. Linguistics and the Performance of Po-
      etry. Coll Comp & Comm 16 (Feb.) 20-6. Application
      of general grammar to clarify poem's ambiguities.

1683 Carmichael, C. W., and Gary Cronkhite. Frustration and
      Language Intensity. Spch Mono 32 (June) 107-11. Intensity
      related to auditory reception of lit.

1684 Carr, Elizabeth. Joseph Fielding Smith, 1899-1964. Qrt
      J Spch 51 (Feb.) 118-9. Tribute.

1685 Chevigny, B. G. Instress and Devotion in Poetry of G. M.
      Hopkins. Vict Stud 9 (Dec.) 141-53. Hopkins' concepts
      analyzed through life, theology and works.

1686 Cogswell, Fred. Imprisoned Galaxies. Canad Lit 23 (Win-
      ter) 65-7. Folklore in Phyllis Gotheb's book, Within the
      Zodiac.

1687 Culp, R. B. Drama and Theatre in the American Revolu-
      tion. Spch Mono 32 (Mar.) 79-86. Related to poetic/
      rhetoric controversy.

1688 DeVito, J. A. Comprehension Factors in Oral and Written
      Discourse of Skilled Communicators. Spch Mono 32 (June)
      124-8. Differences in comprehension of lit predictable.

1689 Emblen, D. L.   A Comment on Structural Patterns in the
      Poetry of Emily Dickinson.   Amer Lit 37 (Mar.) 64-5.
      Author denies findings of Suzanne Wilson's work in this
      area.

1690 Gorman, T. R.   Dos Passos and the Drama.   Spch Mono
      32 (Nov.) 420-6.   Dos Passos' career with theatre.

1691 Grover, D. H.   Elocution at Harvard: The Saga of Jonathan
      Barber.   Qrt J Spch 51 (Feb.) 62-7.   By linking oral and
      physical tradition, Barber encouraged more comprehensive
      approaches to elocution.

1692 Gruner, C. R.   Is Wit to Humor What Rhetoric Is to Po-
      etic?   Cent Sts Spch J 16 (Feb.) 17-22.   Differences be-
      tween rhetoric and poetic.

1693 Hadley, D. S.   A Readers Theatre Performance.   Dramatics
      36 (Apr.) 13, 29.   Staging procedures used in production
      of Spoon River Anthology.

1694 Hansen, B. K.; G. M. Phillips; & W. E. Arnold.   Measur-
      ing the Message Delivered by a Dramatic Production.
      Spch Mono 32 (Nov.) 461-4.   Audience measure of diffi-
      culties.

1695 Hardwig, L. A.   Folk Language in Haliburton's Humor.
      Canad Lit 24 (Spring) 37-46.   Discusses homily, simile,
      and equine metaphor in Haliburton's works.

1696 Hargis, D. E.   Hiram Corson and Oral Interpretation.
      Wstn Spch 29 (Winter) 37.   Historical evaluation of Cor-
      son's contributions.

1697 Hoffman, F. J.   The Scholar-Critic: Trends in Contempo-
      rary British and American Literary Study.   Mod Lang Qrt
      26 (Mar.) 1-15.   Notes changing trends in criticism over-
      view.

1698 Holloway, John.   The Critical Theory of Yvor Winters.
      Crit Qrt 7 (Spring) 54-68.   Questions cogency of poet's
      arguments as a critic-theorist.

1699 Hornby, Richard.   Books and Theatre: A Bibliography.
      Dram Rev 9 (Summer) 179-207.   Theatre and related
      books published in U.S.

1700 Huck, C. S.   Literature's Role in Language Development.
      Childhood Educ 42 (Nov.) 147-50.   Stresses reading aloud
      to children.

1701 Hutchings, P. A.   Organic Unity Revindicated.   J Aest Art
      Crit 23 (Spring) 323-7.   Unity of structure in poetry and
      other works of art.

1702 Jones, A. R. Necessity and Freedom: The Poetry of
Robert Lowell, Sylvia Plath and Anne Sexton. Crit Qrt 7
(Spring) 11-30. Analyzes content and tone in poems as
poets' private response to unbearable suffering and de-
privation.

1703 Kafka, F. I. What's All This About Readers Theatre?
Encore 4 (Mar. -Apr.) 5. RT at Eastern Montana College.

1704 Kilmer, Rosamund. Books My Father Read to Me. Horn
Book 41 (June) 319-20. Ordinary household chores are
brightened up when books are read aloud.

1705 Kleinau, Marion, & M. D. Kleinau. Scene Location in
Readers Theatre: Static or Dynamic? Spch Tchr 14
(Sept.) 193-9. Rules, guides, techniques, and focus in
RT.

1706 Kleinau, Marion; J. R. Rockey; & K. D. Frandsen.
Changes in the Factorial Composition of a Semantic Differential as a Function of Difference in Readers Theatre
Production. Spch Mono 32 (June) 112-8. Response to RT
can be quantified with semantic differential.

1707 Klyn, M. S. Potentials for Research in Oral Interpretation.
Wstn Spch 29 (Spring) 108-13. Potential areas of OI
for study and a rationale for research.

1708 Knowlson, J. R. The Idea of Gesture as a Universal Language in the 17th and 18th Centuries. J of Hist of Ideas
26 (Oct.) 495-508. Gesture as universal form of communication.

1709 Lamb, J. H. John Walker and Joshua Steele. Spch Mono
32 (Nov.) 411-19. Doubts validity of claim Walker
plagiarized Steele.

1710 Lazier, Gil. Burke, Behavior and Oral Interpretation.
Sthn Spch J 31 (Fall) 10-14. Ideal OI situation exists
when experiences of performance are identical to author
of lit and audience.

1711 Leonardo, Manuel, & W. R. Tiffany. A Study of Six Machine Programs in Oral Reading Improvement. Spch Mono
32 (June) 192-7. Quantitative data concerning the feasibil-
ity of using machine approach in teaching selected speech
skills.

1712 Loesch, K. T. Literary Ambiguity and Oral Performance.
Qrt J Spch 51 (Oct.) 258-67. Oral performance demands
more than understanding of normal intonations and syntactic ambiguities.

1713 MacLow, Jackson. Verdurous Sanguinaria: Act 1. Tulane
Dr Rev 10 (Winter) 119-22. Examination of improvisational RT based on dictionary entries selected by chance.

1714 Marshall, T. A. Klein's Poetic Universe. Canad Lit 25
(Summer) 43-52. Jewish upbringing as influence on
Klein's work.

1715 Matlon, R. J. Jonathan Barber and the Elocutionary Movement. Spch Tchr 14 (Jan.) 38-43. Barber's theories and
teaching of Steele and Austin analyzed.

1716 McCarthy, R. D. Gertrude Johnson, 1877-1965. Qrt J
Spch 51 (Dec.) 489-90. Tribute.

1716a Millis, G. H. Let's Use Oral Reading Right. Grade Tchr
83 (Sept.) 103. Oral reading as method of teaching children to read.

1717 Mills, J. A. Language and Laughter in Shavian Comedy.
Qrt J Spch 51 (Dec.) 433-41. Linguistic components of
Shaw's comic style.

1718 Mohrmann, G. P. Kames and Elocution. Spch Mono 32
(June) 198-206. Demonstrates Kame's treatise as significant contribution to elocution.

1719 Moore, Sonia. The Method of Physical Actions. Dram Rev
9 (Summer) 91-4. Stanislavski method of physical action.

1720 Morgan, H. C. Gertrude E. Johnson, 1887-1965. Players
Mag 41 (May) 196. Eulogy outlining Johnson's accomplishments as founder of PLM and scholarship in OI.

1721 Mowrer, O. H. Stage Fright and Self-Regard. Wstn Spch
29 (Fall) 197-200. Treating stage fright.

1722 Ong, W. J. Oral Residue in Tudor Prose Style. PMLA
80 (June) 145-54. Influence of oral cast of mind on
Tudor prose.

1723 Ostriker, Alicia. Song and Speech in the Metrics of George
Herbert. PMLA 80 (Mar.) 62-8. Derivation of both elements in Herbert's works and his utilization and treatment
of borrowings.

1724 Paller, Ruth. Choral Reading in Junior High School. Engl
J 54 (Feb.) 121-3. Choric appreciation.

1725 Patterson, S. W. Setting as Character in Lorca. Sthn
Spch Comm J 30 (Spring) 215-22. Problems in translating
Lorca.

1726 Reed, D. W. A Theory of Language, Speech and Writing. Elem Engl 42 (Dec.) 845-51. Attacks theory of primacy of speech over writing.

1727 Salper, D. R. The Imaginative Component of Rhetoric. Qrt J Spch 51 (Oct.) 307-10. Rhetorical abstracting may slight imaginative element and scope of poetic function in lit.

1728 Schechner, Richard. Reality Is Not Enough. Dram Rev 9 (Spring) 118-52. Interview with Alan Schneider.

1729 Scully, D. W. Alfred Ayres, Drama Critic, as Compiler of a Pronouncing Dictionary. Qrt J Spch 51 (Feb.) 45-51. Ayres' effort to chart effective course between excesses of both overly precise and slurred pronunciation.

1730 Skelton, Robin. The House That Frye Built. Canad Lit 24 (Spring) 63-6. Review of Northrop Frye's book Fables of Identity: Studies in Poetic Mythology.

1731 Skinner, E. R. Gertrude Johnson: Pioneer in the Oral Interpretation of Literature. Spch Tchr 14 (Mar.) 226-9. Johnson's theories and accomplishments.

1732 Sloan, T. O. Persona as Rhetor: An Interpretation of Donne's Satyre III. Qrt J Spch 51 (Feb.) 14-27. Rhetorical dimension is added to dramatic approach.

1733 Steinberg, M. W. Poet of a Living Past. Canad Lit 25 (Summer) 5-20. Jewish tradition and heritage in poetry of A. M. Klein.

1734 Stelzner, H. G. Analysis by Metaphor. Qrt J Spch 51 (Feb.) 52-61. Examines figurative language in contemporary discussion of oral communication, emphasizing power that has been demonstrated by mechanical, evolutionary or biological, and military concepts.

1735 Stelzner, H. G., & Danio Baro. Oracle of the Tobacco Bench. Sthn Spch Comm J 31 (Winter) 124-31. History of oral reader to tobacco factory workers.

1736 Stevens, P. B. Acting and Interpretation: The Reader Faces the Contest. Spch Tchr 14 (Mar.) 116-22. Lit not roles important in performance.

1737 Tallman, Warren. Poet in Progress: Notes on Frank Davey. Canad Lit 24 (Spring) 23-7. Mention made of development of articulation and development of the poet.

1738 Thorpe, James. The Aesthetics of Textual Criticism. PMLA 80 (Dec.) 465-82. Need for textual critic to work both extrinsically/intrinsically to most fully interpret linguistic intent of author.

1739 Van Ness, M. D. The Bell Rings--Then What? Grade Tchr 83 (Sept.) 72-3; 138. Oral reading as way of getting school day started.

1740 Waddington, Miriam. Signs on a White Field: Klein's Second Scroll. Canad Lit 25 (Summer) 21-32. Analyzes diction of A. M. Klein.

1741 Wagner, Guy, & Max Hosier. Helping Them Hear and See What They Read. Grade Tchr 82 (Mar.) 96-100. Reading aloud as way to teach understanding of lit in elementary school.

1742 Wees, W. C. Ezra Pound as a Vorticist. Cont Lit 6 (Winter-Spring) 56-72. Effect of the vortex on Pound's poetry.

1743 Weidig, P. D. Why Not Schedule a Pause in the Day's Activities? Grade Tchr 82 (Feb.) 57; 92-3. Oral reading as activity to vary elementary day.

1744 Weiss, Aureliu. The Interpretation of Dramatic Works. J Aesth Art Crit 23 (Spring) 305-21. Differences in authors' and actors' interpretation of a play.

1745- Williams, Frederick; R. A. Clark; & Barbara Sundene.
6   Effects of a Speech Training Program Upon Semantic Compatibility. Spch Mono 32 (June) 119-23. Related to group reading sessions, audience analysis and reader studies.

1966

1747 Aurbach, Joseph, & R. B. Kaplan. Teaching Language Rhythm: Unstressed Function Words. Spch Tchr 15 (Jan.) 77-81. Teaching foreign student intonation analogous to teaching poor readers to read.

1748 Bahn, Eugene. Epochs in the History of the Oral Interpretation of Literature. Chapter in The Communicative Arts & Sciences of Speech, edited by Keith Brooks. Indianapolis: Bobbs-Merrill.

1749 Benson, L. D. The Literary Character of Anglo-Saxon Formulaic Poetry. PMLA 81 (Oct.) 334-41. Dangers of assuming oral origins and composition of all old English poetry or seeing it as explanation for the style.

1750 Bevill, R. L. Stir with the Beat of a Drum. Childhood Educ 43 (Dec.) 197-9. Choral speaking included in PTA program.

1751 Booth, W. C. Dramatic Aspects of Aztec Rituals. Educ Theat J 18 (Dec.) 421-8. Dramatic elements in festivals, sacrifices and impersonations.

1752 Bowen, E. R. A Baker's Dozen for the Oral Interpreter. Spch Tchr 15 (Nov.) 276-8. Selection, consideration, investigation, introduction, familiarization, visualization, phonation, diction, projection, animation, attention, suggestion, communication as key elements of OI.

1753 Braden, W. W. Three Southern Readers and Southern Oratory. Sthn Spch J 32 (Fall) 31-40. Analyzes southern readers and southern oratory.

1754 Broderick, J. C., et al. Articles on American Literature Appearing in Current Periodicals. Amer Lit 38 (Mar. - Jan.) 150-59; 277-84; 437-53; 605-23.

1755 Chambers, Dewey. Storytelling: The Neglected Art. Elem Engl 43 (Nov.) 715-9. Cause for neglect and good bibliography.

1756 Chatman, Seymour. On the Intonational Fallacy. Qrt J Spch 52 (Oct.) 283-6. Response to Loesch in QJS 51 (Oct.) 258-67.

1757 Compain, Rita. Let the Students Be Storytellers. Grade Tchr 84 (Nov.) 122-4. Older pupils read to younger.

1758 Conger, Lesley. Notes from a Happy Second Childhood. Writer 79 (Apr.) 7-8. Reading aloud to children is better than recordings.

1759 Conger, Lesley. For Writing Out Loud. Writer 79 (Aug.) 7-8. Reading aloud should be understood from author's experience.

1760 Cook, A. S. Language & Action in the Drama. Coll Engl 28 (Oct.) 15-25. Importance of language in plays from Greeks to present.

1761 Crocker, Lionel. An Elocutionist Saves Matthew Arnold's Tour: Or the Ungrateful Matthew Arnold. Wstn Spch 30 (Summer) 189-94. Delivery saves Arnold.

1762 Deboer, K. B. The Rhymes of Phillip Freneau: A Reflection of 18th-Century American Pronunciation. Spch Mono 33 (Mar.) 50-6. Changing pronunciation trends noted.

1763 Delawter, Jayne, & Maurice Eash. Focus on Oral Communication. Elem Engl 40 (Dec.) 880-91, 901+. Approach to oral language instruction in elementary school.

1764 DeVito, J. A. Psychogrammatical Factors in Oral and
Written Discourse by Skilled Communicators. Spch Mono
33 (Mar.) 73-6. Analysis of lit for audience comprehension.

1765 Dunning, R. W. Tales of an Indian People. Canad Lit 29
(Summer) 75-6. Review of Norval Morriseau's Legends
of My People the Great Ojibway.

1766 Early, Margaret. Helping Children Identify ... Through
the Literary Experience. Childhood Educ 42 (Jan.) 287-9.
Including children's listening to lit.

1767 Ebemaeu, M. B. Style and Meaning in Oral Literature.
Lang 42 (Apr.-Jun.) 323-45. Stylistic analysis of the
songs of today.

1768 Emerick, L. L. Bibliotherapy for Stutterers: Four Case
Histories. Qrt J Spch 52 (Feb.) 74-9. Cases may be
useful in working with adolescent and adult stutterers.

1769 Farrell, E. J. Listen My Children and You Shall Read.
Engl J 55 (Jan.) 39-45. Listening to words as an aid to
reading.

1770 Fischler, Alexander. Theatrical Techniques in Thomas
Hardy's Short Stories. Stud in Short Fict 3 (Summer)
435-45. Hardy's experiences with forms foreshadow CT
and RT.

1771 Friedrich, Gerhard. The English Teacher and the Process
of Communication. Engl J 55 (Jan.) 19-27. Major emphases in teaching English.

1772 Friend, J. H. Teaching Grammar of Poetry. Coll Engl 27
(Feb.) 361-8. How to make the student of poetry aware
of symmetry, proportion and semantic patterns.

1773 Gibson, J. W.; C. R. Gruner; R. J. Kibler; & F. J. Kelly.
Quantitative Examination of Differences and Similarities in
Written and Spoken Messages. Spch Mono 33 (Nov.) 444-
51. Formal lit analysis of spoken style.

1774 Greet, A. H. Negation and Affirmation in Jacques Prevert's
Word Games. Cont Lit 7 (Summer) 131-41. Poet's use
of language as game and elimination of all but necessary
words.

1775 Gross, Beverly. Narrative Time and the Open Ended Novel.
Criticism 8 (Feb.) 362-75. Insignificance of present time
in plot structures.

1776 Gunter, Richard. On the Placement of Accent in Dialogue:
A Feature of Context Grammar. J Ling 2 (Oct.) 159-79.
Accent properly placed can make dialogue intelligible.

1777 Hall, J. L. Opportunity in Children's Theatre. Educ Theat
J 18 (Oct.) 259-63. Opportunity writers of child plays.

1778 Halle, M., & S. J. Keyser. Chaucer and Study of Prosody.
Coll Engl 28 (Dec.) 187-220. Describes and analyzes
Chaucer's use of iambic pentameter.

1779 Hartman, Geoffrey. Beyond Formalism. Mod Lang Notes
81 (Dec.) 542-56. Isolating aesthetic fact from human
content as method.

1780 Henley, E. F. Charles Dickens on Aesthetic Distance & A
Possible Dickens' Influence. Lang Qrt 5 (Fall) 2-3. Explores paragraph in Bleak House as indicator of awareness
of aesthetic distance and suggests influence on Ortega y
Gasset.

1781 Hester, M. B. Metaphor and Aspect Seeing. J Aesth Art
Crit 25 (Winter) 205-12. Image-exhibiting function of poetic language, specifically poetic metaphor.

1782 Hornby, Richard. Books & Theatre: A Bibliography.
Dram Rev 10 (Summer) 239-64. Theatre-related books
published in U. S. 1965-66.

1783 Irwin, R. L. The Bases of Criticism in Oral Interpretation. Today's Speech 14 (Feb.) 5-6. Discussion of youth's
normative judgment of art.

1784 Jensen, James. Construction of Seven Types of Ambiguity.
Mod Lang Qrt 27 (Sept.) 243-59. Empson's critical review
by Richards and Graves.

1785 Jisha, H. J. Development of Imagery as an Integral Element of Interpretative Reading 1933-1960. Spch Mono 33
(Aug.) 258. Review of Jisha's dissertation.

1786 Jones, S. E. Attitude Change of Public Speakers During the
Investigative & Expressive Stages of Advocacy. Spch Mono
33 (June) 137-46. Reading speeches aloud caused attitude
change in subjects.

1787 Le Pere, J. M. Living Literature. Childhood Educ 43
(Dec.) 204-7. Importance of child's listening to lit read
aloud.

1788 Lewis, Claudia. Pleasant Land of Counterpane. Horn Book
42 (Oct.) 542-7. When a child listens to a story, he/she
is an intensified life spread out in new dimensions of time

and place. The adult must make himself responsible to find works suitable to the child's mastery.

1789 Livesay, Dorothy. The Sculpture of Poetry: On Louis Dudek. Canad Lit 30 (Fall) 26-35. Shape, form, sound, Dudek's syntax, and origins of rhythm in poetry.

1790 Loesch, K. T. A Reply to Mr. Chatman. Qrt J Spch 52 (Oct.) 286-9. Rebut to Chatman in QJS 52 (Oct. 1966) 283-6.

1791 Mahan, M. H. Reading Aloud and Story Telling. Scholastic Life 42 (Mar.) 24-5. Values of reading aloud.

1792 Marcoux, J. P. Current Trends in Literary Analysis for Oral Interpretation: An Overview. Spch Tchr 15 (Nov.) 324-7. Seven trends well-documented.

1793 Marlow, C. S. Readers Theatre Bibliography: 1960-64. Cent Sts Spch J 17 (Feb.) 33-9.

1794 McCurdy, F. L. Reading Symbols of Poetry. Spch Tchr 15 (Jan.) 42-8. Poetic symbols as organic parts of the poem serving to reveal its experience and attitudes.

1795 Mills, J. A. Comic in Words: Shaw's Cockneys. Dram Survey 5 (Summer) 137-50. Shaw's use of dialect and other linguistic devices to produce comic effects.

1796 Mohrmann, G. P. The Language of Nature and Elocutionary Theory. Qrt J Spch 52 (Apr.) 116-24. Survey of assessments of elocutionary movements, sketch of elocution rationale, and a consideration of parallel doctrines in Scottish common sense philosophy.

1797 Murphy, Richard. Teaching Rhetorical Appreciation of Literature. Engl J 55 (May) 578-82. Rhetorical analysis leads to understanding and appreciation of poetry and lit.

1798 Nichols, A. C. Audience Ratings of the Naturalness of Spoken and Written Sentences. Spch Mono 33 (June) 156-9. Listener response to literary messages.

1799 Pooley, R. C. Oral Communication in the English Curriculum. Spch Tchr 15 (Jan.) 26-9. Response to oral lit at all levels.

1800 Rahlf, A. W. Let's Sing-Read. Spch Tchr 15 (Sept.) 229-31. Program of songs and poems described.

1801- Reitz, Mathias. The Application of Selected Dramatic The-
2 ories of Stanislavsky as a Solution to Disunity in Readers Theatre. Spch Tchr 15 (Sept.) 191-6. Stanislavsky's

concepts of super-objective, character objective, spine, through-line-of-action, scene objective, score, inner monologue, and given circumstances applicable to RT performer.

1803 Rubin, J. B.   The Arts in Action.   Childhood Educ 43 (Dec.) 195-6.   OI included as one of elementary school arts.

1804 Schechner, Richard.   Approaches to Theory/Criticism.   Tul Dr Rev 10 (Summer) 20-53.   Comparisons between theatre and related performance activities including play, games, sport, and ritual.

1805 Smith, R. G.   Semantic Differential Dimensions and Form.   Spch Mono 33 (Mar.) 17-22.   A means of measuring connotative meaning, especially theatre.

1806 Stassen, Marilyn.   Creating Dynamic Choral Reading.   Pac Spch Qrt 1 (Oct.).   Inspiring and practical suggestions for making choral reading interesting to modern youth.

1807 Stead, C. K.   Poetry and the Criticism of Poetry.   Crit Qrt 8 (Winter) 323-7.   Takes to task critic's approach which dissects rather than providing critic's own view and understanding of work.

1808 Takenfuta, Yukio, & J. W. Black.   Perception of Foreign Accent in American, British and Japanese English by Listeners.   Spch Mono 33 (Aug.) 372-6.   Example of listener response measurement.

1809 Triesch, Manfred.   Men and Animals: James Thurber and the Conversion of a Literary Genre.   Stud Short Fict 3 (Spring) 307-13.   Thurber's fables compared with oral tradition of fable, proverb, and fairy tale.

1809a Waal, Carla, & Don Richardson.   Increasing the Reliability of Judgements of Acting Performance.   Qrt J Spch 52 (Dec.) 378-82.   Ranking scale used to evaluate performance.

1810 Witt, Daniel.   Audience Response to Acting, Readers Theatre and Silent Reading of Realistic and Anti-Realistic Drama.   Wstn Spch 30 (Spring) 123-9.   Differences in audience response to RT and acting.

1967

1811 Alter, Robert.   Fielding & the Uses of Style.   Novel: Forum on Fict 1 (Fall) 53-63.   Creative language use is Fielding's contribution to novel.

1812 Anderson, R. G. James Rush: His Legacy to Interpretation. Sthn Spch J 33 (Fall) 20-8. Rush's principles aid
to delivery.

1813 Bacon, W. A. Review of J. W. Bennett's Measure for
Measure as Royal Entertainment. Qrt J Spch 59 (Apr.)
165.

1814 Bacon, W. A. Review of Kenneth Burke's Language as
Symbolic Action. Qrt J Spch 53 (Oct.) 295.

1815 Bacon, W. A. Review of Marion Smith's Dualities in
Shakespeare. Qrt J Spch 53 (Feb.) 82.

1816 Berry, Ralph. The Frontier of Metaphor and Symbol.
Brit J of Aesth 7 (Jan.) 76-83. Metaphor and symbol as
complementary aspects of perceptive act.

1817 Brandes, P. D., & Marie Shepardson. The Effect of the
Introduction on a Literary Communication. Qrt J Spch 52
(Apr.) 152-5. Introduction does influence audience re-
ception.

1818 Brecht, Bertolt. Tul Dram Rev 12 (Fall). Entire issue on
Brecht useful for seeing parallels in Brecht and RT.

1819 Broderick, J. C., et al. Articles on American Literature
Appearing in Current Periodicals. Amer Lit 39 (1967)
137-43; 270-77; 451-65; 597-609. Amer Lit 40 (1968)
117-31; 273-77; 444-58; 602-14. Amer Lit 43 (1971) 157-
64; 319-22; 513-24; 688-98. Bibliography by date; subjects noted.

1820 Brown, Ivor. The High Froth. Dramatics 38 (Winter) 32-
4. Comments on flowing eloquent dialogue as enhancement
of conflict in drama.

1821 Burwick, Frederick. Associationist Rhetoric and Scottish
Prose Style. Spch Mono 34 (Mar.) 21-34. Objective summary of associationist criteria of style plus examination
of stylistic techniques of various Scottish authors in terms
of these criteria.

1822 Butterfield, Rita. Canadian Literature. Can Lit 32 (Spring
1967) 83-104. Can Lit 36 (Spring 1968) 101-209. Can Lit
48 (Spring 1971) 95-119. Checklist of Canadian literature
published in indicated year.

1823 Campbell, Brenton. Linguistic Meaning. Lint: Intl Rev 33
(July) 5-23. Attempt at clarification of theories explaining
nature of meaning in language.

1824   Carson, A. L.   Sources for Research.   Chapter in Steps in Successful Speaking, edited by H. L. Carson.   Princeton: Van Nostrand.

1825   Crannell, K. C.   Review of Reading Aloud by Wayland Maxfield Parrish.   Spch Tchr 16 (Sept.) 236.   Emphasis on voice and speech.

1826   Criscuolo, N. P.   Getting the Most from Oral Reading.   Grade Tchr 84 (Mar.) 146.   Hints for teaching reading aloud, especially in primary grades.

1827   DeVito, J. A.   Style and Stylistics: An Attempt at Definition.   Qrt J Spch 53 (Oct.) 248-55.   Demands appreciation of methods and theories of linguistic science; also includes definition of style and characterization of the field.

1828   DeVito, J. A.   Oral & Written Style: Directions for Research.   Sthn Spch J 33 (Fall) 37-43.   Discusses research to clarify oral and written style.

1829   DeVito, J. A.   A Linguistic Analysis of Spoken and Written Language.   Cent Sts Spch J 18 (May) 81-5.   Analysis of sample of spoken and written language.

1830   DeVito, J. A.   Levels of Abstraction in Spoken & Written Language.   J Comm 17 (Dec.) 354-61.   Oral language is less abstract.

1831   Dobie, A. B.   Attempts to Unsettle an Audience: The Epic Theatre of Bertolt Brecht.   Dramatics 38 (Jan.) 24 & 38.   Brief summary of Brecht's theatre for those unfamiliar.

1832   Donato, Eugenio.   Of Structuralism and Literature.   Mod Lang Notes 82 (Dec.) 549-74.   Development and popularity of structuralism.

1833   Farrell, E. J.   English Education and the Electronic Revolution.   Spch Tcher 91 (Sept.) 12-3.   Excerpts from NCTE's 77-page booklet, English Education & the Electronic Revolution.

1834   Fowler, Roger.   Linguistics & the Analysis of Poetry.   Crit Survey 2 (Summer) 78-89.   Linguistic analysis of Cummings' "Anyone Lived in a Pretty How Town."

1835   Franks, J. R.   Determining Habitual Pitch by Means of Increased Reading Rate.   Wstn Spch 31 (Fall) 281-7.   Investigates a study of method of determining habitual pitch to see whether or not reading aloud at a rapid rate might be valid method of facilitating judgment of habitual pitch in clinical situation.

1836   Friedman, A. W.   A Key to Lawrence Durrell.   Cont Lit 8
       (1967) 31-42.   Key to Durrell is in his book: Key to
       Modern British Poetry.

1837   Gately, Gardner.   Does Training in Oral Interpretation Help
       Speech Therapists?   Sthn Spch J 33 (Winter) 140-2.   OI
       does aid.

1838   Graff, G. E.   The Later Richards & the New Criticism.
       Crit 9 (Summer) 229-42.   Contends that same theory is
       found in both early and late Richards.

1839   Grimm, Reinhold.   Brecht's Beginnings.   Tulane Dr Rev 12
       (Fall) 22-35.   Brecht subject of entire issue: includes
       articles by Esslin, Roland Barthes, and Brecht.

1840   Grotowski, Jerzy.   Towards the Poor Theatre.   Tul Dr Rev
       11 (Spring) 60-5.   Discussion by Grotowski of approach to
       theatre through spiritual and scenic techniques of the actor.

1841   Gustafson, Ralph.   New Wave in Canadian Poetry.   Can Lit
       32 (Spring) 6-14.   Critical examination of new wave po-
       etry: distinguishing factor is said to be methodology.

1842   Harbage, Mary.   We Consider Reading.   Childhood Educ 44
       (Sept.) 37-43.   Teacher's oral reading as stimulus for
       student activity.

1843   Heston, L. A.   Review of A. P. Kerman's The Plot of
       Satire.   Qrt J Spch 53 (Apr.) 197.

1844   Heston, L. A.   Review of John Casey's The Language of
       Criticism.   Qrt J Spch 53 (Dec.) 389-90.

1845   Hobsbaum, Philip.   Current Aesthetic Fallacies.   Brit J
       Aesth 7 (Apr.) 107-26.   Calls fallacious current aesthetic
       theories.   For example: argues theory of empathy deletes
       possibility of art extending personal experience.   Believes
       aesthetics should give place to critical theory of a specific
       art.

1846   Hungerland, Helmut.   Selective Current Bibliography for
       Aesthetics & Related Fields.   J Aest & Art Crit 25 (Sum-
       mer) 497-523.   1966: lists 1966 publications for philos-
       ophy, scientific or theoretical study of arts and related
       phenomena.

1847   Kingston, A. J., & W. F. White.   The Relationship of
       Reader's Self-Concepts and Personality Components to
       Semantic Meanings Perceived in the Protagonist of a Read-
       ing Selection.   Read Res Qrt 2 (Spring) 107-16.   Studies
       revealing that semantic meaning of main character in story
       is significantly influenced by reader's personality and self-
       concept variables.

1848 Koch, Walter. A Linguistic Analysis of a Satire. Ling: Intl Rev 33 (July) 68-81. Basis for linguistic approach to lit.

1849 Langman, F. H. The Idea of the Reader in Literary Criticism. Brit J Aest 7 (Jan.) 84-94. Role of reader opposed to professional critic in lit explored.

1850 Le Brun, Philip. T. S. Eliot and Henri Bergson. Rev Engl Stud 18 (May) 149-61. Plus 18 (Aug.) 274-86. Two-part discussion of influence of Bergson on Eliot.

1851 Lightfoot, M. J. Prosody and Performance. Qrt J Spch 53 (Feb.) 61-6. Challenges assumption regarding form and ambiguity.

1852 Loesch, K. T. Review of Interpretation: The Poetry of Meaning, edited by Stanley Hopper and David Miller. Qrt J Spch 53 (Oct.) 315. Says interpretation is the language of being.

1853 Long, C. C. The Poem's Text as a Technique of Performance in Public Group Readings of Poetry. Wstn Spch 31 (Winter) 16-29. Traditional concepts of poetry, especially lyric poetry, are not adequately developed to voice the inventiveness of poets.

1854 Myline, Vivienne. Reading & Rereading Novels. Brit J Aesth 7 (Jan.) 67-75. Aesthetic purposes for reading and rereading novels.

1855 Neuman, Ilene. Special Language. Horn Book 43 (Aug.) 498-500. Need to teach poetry at young age.

1856 Oppenheim, Helen. Coppin: How Great? Alec Bogot's Father of the Australian Theatre. Aust Lit Stud 3 (Oct.). History of Australian theatre.

1857 Pleydell-Pearce, A. G. Sense, Reference and Fiction. Brit J Aest 7 (July) 225-36. Contends fiction has not only sense but presentation--aesthetic analogue to reference.

1858 Post, R. M. Albee's Alice. Wstn Spch 31 (Fall) 260-5. Analysis of Albee's Tiny Alice.

1859 Post, R. M. Oral Interpretation and the Stanislavsky Method. Sthn Spch J 32 (Spring) 180-7. Applying Stanislavsky system to performance in OI.

1860 Rauch, Irmengard. Dimensions of Sound Change in Relation to an Early Holderlin Poem. Ling: Intl Rev 34 (Aug.) 46-54. Linguistics as relevant to poetry analysis.

1861 Rodway, Allan. Life, Time & the Art of Fiction. Brit J
      Aesth 7 (Oct.) 374-84. Complex effect of audience, at
      once involved and contemplative, achieved by exploitation
      of certain character of style and time.

1862 Ryder, Frank. Vowels & Consonants as Features of Style.
      Ling: Intl Rev 37 (Dec.) 89-110. Sound effects created
      by vowels and consonants in poems of Goethe and Klopstock
      serving as springboard for examining phenomenon in other
      poems.

1863 Shelton, Richard. The Poem in Context: Aiken's "Morning
      Song." Spch Tchr 16 (Jan.) 28-32. Poem seen as Aiken's
      struggle to gain and express self-awareness. Also call
      for knowledge of form of poem as revelatory of meaning.

1864 Sloan, T. O. Review of the Shakespeare Inset: Work &
      Picture by Francis Berry. Qrt J Spch 53 (Feb.) 81.

1865 Sloan, T. O. Review of Interpreting Literature by K. C.
      Hill. Qrt J Spch 53 (Oct.) 296.

1866 Sloan, T. O. Restoration of Rhetoric to Literary Study.
      Spch Tchr 16 (Mar.) 91-7. Rhetoric helps OI in articulat-
      ing critical and educational goals.

1867 Stephan, Eric. Sheridan's and Walker's Use of the Pause.
      Sthn Spch J 33 (Winter) 119-23. Examination of two the-
      orists' use of pause sheds light on mechanical/natural
      dichotomy.

1868 Torrach, Dean. Scenery for the Touring Company. Drama-
      tics 33 (Mar.) 20-1; 31. Usefulness of cardboard scenery.

1869 Tulip, James. Three Women Poets. Poet Austr 19 (Dec.)
      35-40. Critical review of Sylvia Plath's The Colossus;
      Anne Sexton's To Bedlam and Part Way Back & Other
      Poems; and Grace Perry's Frozen Section.

1870 Van Egmond, Peter. Walt Whitman and the Platform.
      Sthn Spch J 32 (Spring) 215-24. Whitman's delivery and
      merits as a speaker.

1871 Veilleux, Jere. The Concept of Action in Oral Interpreta-
      tion. Qrt J Spch 53 (Oct.) 281-4. Symbolic action of lit
      needs to be transformed into creative action by performer.
      Individual interpreter must re-create the gestures of the
      spoken act inherent in the written text, not through stage
      movement but through imaginative use of aural space.

1872 Veilleux, Jere. The Interpreter: His Role, Language and
      Audience. Spch Tchr 16 (Mar.) 124-33. Two contribu-
      tions of OI: 1) performance of lit which existed first of

all as oral; 2) performance of unpublished avant-garde works. OI is speech art which can communicate values and philosophies.

1873 Venezky, R. L. English Orthography: Its Graphical Structure & Its Relation to Sound. Read Res Qrt 2 (Spring) 75-105. Relates orthograph patterns, phonemic and morphemic, to sound patterns in the English language.

1874 Wagner, Arthur. Transactional Analysis and Acting. Tul Dr Rev 11 (Summer) 81-8. Eric Berne's principles applied to acting.

1875 Warland, S. G.; M. M. Trauernicht; & C. R. Gruner. Audience Response to Visual Stimuli in Oral Interpretation. Sthn Spch J 32 (Summer) 289-95. Physical presence of performer adds to aesthetic enjoyment.

1876 White, M. R. The Current Scene and Readers Theatre. Today's Spch 15 (Feb.) 22-3. Discussion of materials for RT including newspapers.

1877 White-Price, Jacquelyn. Teaching Poetry to EMR Students. Ill Schls J 47 (Winter) 268-70. Reading aloud plays important part of process of teaching poetry.

1878 Wild, P. H. Hearing Poetry: W. S. Merwin's "Leviathon." Engl J 56 (Oct.) 954-7. Analysis of poem using aural and oral techniques.

1879 Work, William. Employment Opportunities in Speech: Fact and Prophecy. Cent Sts Spch J 18 (Feb.) 19-23. Positions in OI discussed.

1880 Worrell, Elizabeth. Oral Interpretation. NEA J 56 (Mar.) 37-9. Influence of Don Juan in Hell on OI.

1881 Yeomans, G. A. Southern Oratory and the Art of Story Telling: A Case Study. Sthn Spch J 32 (Summer) 251-60. Devices used by Tom Heflin to master art of storytelling.

1968

1882 Adamov, Arthur. Mod Intl Drama 2 (Sept.) 57-75. Translation of four absurdist plays usable in RT.

1883 Adams, Hazard. Yeats: Dialectic and Criticism. Crit 10 (Summer) 185-99. Yeatsian dialectic and comments on critic's function.

1884 Barclay, M. T. Alfred Ayres: Maverick Elocutionist. Qrt J Spch 54 (Oct.) 226-31. Biographical sketch of Ayres and contributions to elocution in 19th century.

1885 Bateson, F. W. T. S. Eliot: The Poetry of Pseudo-Learning. J Gen Educ 20 (Apr.) 13-27. Influences on Eliot and his critical essays.

1886 Benson, A. W. The Dramatic Director & Readers Theatre: Blessing or Curse? Spch Tchr 17 (Nov.) 328-30. RT a valuable development in speech area, but not to be seen as adequate substitute for real theatre experience.

1887 Berger, Harry, Jr. Poetry as Revision: Interpreting Robert Frost. Criticism 10 (Winter) 1-22. Frost's poetry as everlasting renewal of words.

1888 Booth, W. C. The Rhetoric of Fiction & the Poetic of Fiction. Novel: Forum on Fict 1 (Winter) 105-17. Booth's defense of his position.

1889 Boxell, P. J. P. T. Barnum's Lectures for Londoners. Qrt J Spch 54 (Apr.) 140-6. Highlights controversy of his lectures on money making.

1890 Carlisle, F. E. Walt Whitman: The Drama of Identity. Criticism 10 (Fall) 259-76. Approach to interpreting Whitman through philosophy of unity.

1891 Chamberlin, W. H. Pleasures of Reading Aloud. Sat Rev 51 (Mar.) 107-8.

1892 Cochrane, Kirsty. Orpheus Applied: Some Instances of the Importance of the Humanist View of Language. Rev Engl Stud 19 (Feb.) 1-13. Support of thesis that humanist learning up to 17th century applied orphic eloquence to ethical values.

1893 Cormenzana, J. M. Train to H.... Mod Intl Drama 1 (Mar.) 217-8. Short play usable in RT, about an important journey.

1894 Cullen, W. H. The First Thirty Minutes of Choral Reading. Engl J 57 (Mar.) 395-9, 419. Teaching choric speaking on high school level.

1895 DeVito, J. A. Morphology and Style. Qrt J Spch 54 (Apr.) 159-61. Offers explanation for use of term "choice" and how one exercises choice at the phonological and morphological levels of language.

1896 Dillard, R. L. Readers Theatre: Some Beginning Suggestions. Pac Spch Qrt Part I 2 (Dec.), Part II 3 (Mar.). Practical approach to RT, including adaptation for performance, staging, movement, focus, physical contact, and script use.

1897 Dumais, A. J. Readers Theatre: A Neglected Tool of the
      Speech and Drama Teacher. Express 5 (Jan.) 14-7. RT
      overlooked as effective teaching device.

1898 Fernandez, T. L. Oral Interpretation and Secondary Teach-
      ers of English. Spch Tchr 17 (Jan.) 30-3. Evidence
      pertinent to the criteria for competent professional prepar-
      ation in oral reading.

1899 Forrest, W. C. Kinesthetic Feel of Literature. Bucknell
      Rev 16 (Dec.) 91-106. Physical and symbolic dimensions
      of kinesthesia.

1900 Frye, Northrop. On Value Judgments. Cont Lit 9 (1968)
      311-8. Value judgments while interesting, should not be
      mistaken or substituted for knowledge.

1901 Grannis, C. B. Books, Gifts and Reading Out Loud. Pub
      Weekly 194 (Nov. 11) 29. Reading aloud for family and
      making it enjoyable.

1902 Gunkle, George. An Experimental Study of Some Vocal
      Characteristics of Spontaneity in Acting. Spch Mono 35
      (June) 159-65. Study on rehearsed performances.

1903 Hess, J. B. There's More Than Talk to Choral Reading.
      Grade Tchr 85 (Feb.) 107-9. Choral reading of poetry
      in elementary classroom.

1904 Heston, L. A. Review of Ronald Paulson's The Fictions of
      Satire. Qrt J Spch 54 (Oct.) 305. Review.

1905 Hirsch, E. D., Jr. Literary Evaluation as Knowledge.
      Cont Lit 9 (1968) 319-31. Lit evaluation depends on
      demonstrable knowledge.

1906 Hopkins, L. B. Negro Poets: Through the Music of Their
      Words. Elem Engl 45 (Feb.) 206-8. Developing new
      image of Negro via Negro poetry.

1907 Howe, J. H., ed. AFA Calendar for 68-69. Am Forensics
      Assc 5 (Spring) 64-78. College forensics tournaments from 9-
      68 through 5-69. Includes OI festivals, and workshops.

1908 Howell, W. S. Aristotle and Horace on Rhetoric and Po-
      etics. Qrt J Spch 54 (Dec.) 325-39. Distinction between
      two terms seen as persuasive and aesthetic is drawn from
      the philosophies of Aristotle and Horace.

1909 Kirk, J. W. Kenneth Burke's Dramatistic Criticism Applied
      to the Theatre. Sthn Spch J 33 (Spring) 161-77. Explica-
      tion of Burke's critical philosophy as applied to analysis of
      plays.

1910 Kreuger, John. Language and Techniques of Communication as Theme or Tool in Science Fiction. Ling: Intl Rev 39 (May) 68-86. Survey authors handle problem of language and communication in Sci-Fi.

1911 Lawton, C. W. Thoreau and the Rhetoric of Dissent. Today's Spch 16 (Apr.) 23-5. Thoreau seen as effective rhetorician with considerable influence today.

1912 Levin, Saul. Traditional Chironomy of the Hebrew Scriptures. J of Biblical Lit 87 (1968) 59-70. Chironomy is the art of moving the hand to regulate the voice. It was practiced because visual guidance helped in the right phrasing of words. Records of chironomy exist making possible analysis of its tradition in detail.

1913 Lodge, David. Toward a Poetics of Fiction: An Approach Through Language. Novel: Forum Fict 1 (Winter) 158-69. All criticism equals response to language.

1914 Loesch, K. T. The Shape and Sound Configurational Rime in the Poetry of Dylan Thomas. Spch Mono 35 (Nov.) 407-24. Stylistic devices in Thomas' poetry.

1915 Loesch, K. T. Phonology and Style. Qrt J Spch 54 (Feb.) 70. Critique of DeVito's article in QJS 54 (Apr. 1968) 159-61.

1916 Loveless, R. L. Interrelating the Arts in the High School. Schl Arts 67 (Jan.) 34-7. Experiment in interrelating poetry/painting/dance/music.

1917 Macksoud, S. J. Anyone's How Town: Interpretation as Rhetorical Discipline. Spch Mono 35 (Mar.) 70-6. Analytical approach as rhetorical.

1918 Martin, Sue. Techniques for the Creative Reading or Telling of Stories to Children. Elem Engl 45 (May) 611-18. How-to plus bibliography.

1919 Miller, M. H. Grass Roots Chautauqua in Michigan. Mich Hist 52 (Winter) 299-309. Discussion of small community reactions to Chautauqua.

1920 Miller, Terry. The Prosodies of Robert Lowell. Spch Mono 35 (Nov.) 425-34. Change in Lowell's prosodic styles.

1921 Mohrmann, G. P. The Real Chironomia. Sthn Spch J 34 (Fall) 17-27. Chironomia as introduction to study of entire elocutionary movement. Includes discussion of purposes, scope and analysis of gesture in chironomia.

1922 Molette, Carlton. Aristotle's Union of Rhetoric and Dramatic Theory. Sthn Spch J 34 (Fall) 47-54. Concludes that
Aristotle envisioned a union of rhetoric and dramatic poetry (theatre).

1923 Neal, Larry. The Black Arts Movement. Drama Rev 12
(Summer) 29-39. Relation of black arts movement to black
power.

1924 Parrish, W. M. Getting the Meaning in Interpretation.
Sthn Spch J 33 (Spring) 178-86. Factual, emotional, contextual, attitudinal aspects of analysis.

1925 Post, R. M. Oral Approach to the Teaching of High School
Literature. Spch Tchr 17 (Mar.) 156-9. High school lit
becomes living experience.

1926 Prosser, M. H. A Rhetoric of Alienation as Reflected in
the Works of Nathaniel Hawthorne. Qrt J Spch 54 (Feb.)
22-8. Rhetoric of alienation clearly revealed in Hawthorne: factors leading to alienation are similar to earlier
established rhetorical concepts.

1927 Rahskopf, H. G. The Curry Tradition. Spch Tchr 17
(Nov.) 273-80. Curry's tradition lives in spite of scientific "objectivity."

1928 Seaberg, D. I. Can the Ancient Art of Storytelling Be Re-
vived? Spch Tchr 17 (Sept.) 246-9. Values of storytelling.

1929 Shumaker, Wayne. A Modest Proposal for Critics. Cont
Lit 9 (Summer) 332-48. Authority of critics depends not
on oracular utterance but on demonstrated soundness of
views.

1930 Smith, A. J. The Canadian Poet: Part I to Confederation.
Can Lit 37 (Summer) 6-14. Concise historical study of
development of movements, topics, and poets.

1931 Smith, A. J. The Canadian Poet: Part II--After Confederation. Can Lit 38 (Fall) 41-9. Continuation of entry 1930.

1932 Sosnoski, J. J. Craft & Intention in James Agee's A Death
in the Family. J Gen Educ 20 (Oct.) 170-83. Interpretation of novel as a composition for voices.

1933 Speede, S. A. African Americans Understanding Their Poetry. J Blk Poet 1 (Fall) 78. Short insight into interpretation of black poetry and its language as projection of
mores of black nation.

1934 Thompkins, P. K. The Rhetoric of James Joyce. Qrt J
Spch 54 (Apr.) 107-14. Biographical sketch of Joyce.
Cites contributions in rhetorical criticism.

1935 Tulip, James. Robert Lowell & James Dickey. Poet Austr
24 (Oct.) 39-47. Discussion of Lowell/Dickey as repre-
sentatives of distinctive achievement in American poetry
in 60's.

1936 Van Allen, R. Let Not Young Souls Be Smothered Out.
Childhood Educ 44 (Feb.) 354-7. Creative language experiences include oral reading.

1937 Weber, Rose-Marie. The Study of Oral Reading Errors: A
Survey of the Literature. Read Res Qrt 4 (Fall) 96-119.
Reviews study of oral reading errors for insight into nature of reading process. High correlation found between errors made by one subject in both oral and silent reading.

1938 Whitaker, B. J. Edward Bullough on Psychical Distance.
Qrt J Spch 54 (Dec.) 373-82. Bullough's concept of aesthetic distance. Claims Bullough a seminal source and
fullest explanation of concept essential to understanding of
aesthetic experiences of OI and theatre.

1939 Ziskind, Sylvia. Children's Literature with Emphasis on Oral
Interpretation. Elem Engl 45 (Dec.) 1051-2. Suggestions
on oral reading for children's librarians.

1969

1940 Anonymous. Hippolytus Hippopotamus. Grade Teacher 87
(Sept.) 42-5. Activities associated with story poem include reading aloud for elementary students.

1941 Becker, S. L. Symposium: Empirical and Experimental
Studies in Oral Interpretation--A Critique. Wstn Spch
33 (Fall) 269-75. Critiques of various papers dealing with
empirical studies in OI.

1942 Beloof, R. L. The Oral Reader and the Future of Literary
Studies. Spch Tchr 18 (Jan.) 9-12. Interpretive criticism
and teaching used for understanding poetic-rhetoric.

1943 Boden, Anneke-Jan. Readers Theatre: An Integrated Student
Enterprise. Spch Tchr 18 (Sept.) 245-6. RT at Eastern
Montana College.

1944 Bogard, M. R., & Nancy Coffin. The Year-Round Program.
Dramatics 41 (Nov.) 24-9. Emphasizes advantages of RT
and CT as forms of production.

1945 Boyd, J. D. T. S. Eliot as Critic and Rhetorician. Criticism 11 (Spring) 167-82. Discusses rhetoric of lit criticism as related to Eliot.

1946 Bruns, G. L. The Story-Teller and the Problem of Language in Beckett's Fiction. Mod Lang Qrt 30 (June) 265-81. Detailed discussion of resemblances between writer and persona.

1947 Collins, Philip. Dickens' Public Readings: The Performer and the Novelist. Stud in the Novel 1 (Summer) 118-30. Relevance of Dickens' readings to nature of his art.

1948 Colton, E. V. Art as a Language. Schl Arts 69 (Sept.) 14-5. Advocates inter-relationship of painting, sculpture, poetry, and music as means of communication in elementary grades.

1949 Crane, August. Responsibility for Reading Education. Ill Educ J 49 (Winter) 285-92. Relationship between silent and oral reading with emphasis on silent reading.

1950 Cronkhite, Gary. Samuel Beckett: En Attendant Fin de l'Univers. Qrt J Spch 55 (Feb.) 45-53. Problems in projecting lack of action not resulting in audience boredom in Waiting for Godot and Endgame.

1951 DeVito, J. A. Some Psycholinguistic Aspects of Active & Passive Sentences. Qrt J Spch 55 (Dec.) 401-6. A study on differential responses to sentences.

1952 Durant, J. D. R. B. Sheridan's "Verses to the Memory of Garrick." Sthn Spch J 35 (Winter) 120-31. Sheridan's verses added to English stage history a fresh concept of poetry reading as theatrical entertainment.

1953 Forrest, W. C. The Poem as a Summons to Performance. Brit J Aesth 9 (July) 298-305. Performance as aspect of poetic creativity.

1954 Forrest, W. C. Literature as Aesthetic Object: The Kinesthetic Stratum. J Aesthetics & Art Crit 27 (Summer) 455-59. Discussion of the sensuousness in kinesthetic percept.

1955 Goodman, K. S. Let's Dump the Uptight Model in English. Elem Schl J 70 (Oct.) 1-13. Make language supple, fully flexible tool of thought, learning, and communication.

1956 Gray, P. H. The Romantic as Reader: S. S. Curry and Expressive Aesthetics. Qrt J Spch 55 (Dec.) 364-71. Curry's theories of expression as influenced by romantics; focuses on reader audience and lit.

1957 Grover, D. H. John Walker: The Mechanical Man Revisited. Sthn Spch J (Summer) 288-97. Views Walker as synthesizer rather than originator of elocutionary theory, raising doubts about labels "mechanical" and "natural."

1958 Gunderson, D. V. Reading Problems: Glossary of Terminology. Read Res Qrt 4 (Summer) 534-49. Compiled by interdisciplinary committee on reading problems including meanings of terms used in various disciplines concerned with reading. Useful for OI in critique of performance problems.

1959 Hargis, D. E. The Shortest Treatise on the Art of Reading. Wstn Spch 33 (Winter) 25-39. Ayres' treatise seen as extended essay attempting to provide new attitude toward elocution and an outline of revolutionary practices. Ayres influenced transition from elocution to oral interpretation.

1960 Harris, W. V. A Reading of Rosetti's Lyrics. Vict Poetry 7 (Winter) 299-308. Justification of Rosetti's different styles present in his lyrics; focuses on challenge of reader.

1961 Heston, L. A. Richard II: A Study in Movement. Ill Spch & Theat J 23 (Fall) n. p.

1962 Hopkins, M. F. Linguistic Analysis as a Tool for the Oral Interpreter. Spch Tchr 18 (Sept.) 200-3. Sound structure and phonemic analysis key to understanding poetry.

1963 Hurford, J. R. The Judgement of Voice Quality. Lang & Spch 12 (Oct.) 220-37. Discusses cockney dialect: valuable for reader with phonetic background.

1964 Kleinau, Marion. Symposium: Experimental and Empirical Studies in Oral Interpretation--The Interpreter. Wstn Spch 33 (Fall) 227-40. Sets up general areas of investigation pertaining to OI as performer of texts. Also see pages 275-7 for Kleinau's rebut to Becker critique in same issue.

1965 Kleinau, Marion; J. D. Reynolds; & K. T. Loesch. Responses to Professor Becker's Critique. Wstn Spch 33 (Fall) 275-82. Rejoinders to Becker's original critique.

1966 Kushauri, Kupa. The Poets and Performers at the New Heritage Theatre. Black Theatre 4 (Apr.) 41. Review of performance purposes of black poetry.

1967 Lachenmeyer, Charles. The Feeling of the Language of Literature: A Conceptual Analysis. Ling: Intl Rev 55 (Dec.) 32-47. Behaviorist analysis of response to literature.

1968 Leathers, D. G. Whately's Logically Derived Rhetoric: A Stranger in Its Time. Wstn Spch 33 (Winter) 48-58. Whately's assumptions quite foreign to his time. Focuses on Whately's logical rather than rhetorical assumptions.

1969 Lessac, Arthur. A New Definition of Dramatic Training. Qrt J Spch 55 (Apr.) 116-25. Dramatic training suggests fusion of technical style with emotional memory style.

1970 Livingston, M. L. The Natural Art of The Winters Tale. Mod Lang Qrt 30 (Sept.) 340-55. Finds Perdita a symbol of the ideal which cannot be improved by further art.

1971 Loesch, K. T. Responses to Professor Becker's Critique. Wstn Spch 33 (Fall) 279-82. Response regarding experimental studies in OI.

1972 Loesch, K. T. Empirical Studies in Oral Interpretation-- The Text. Wstn Spch 33 (Fall) 250-68. Establishment of new texts through linguistic and associated techniques. Includes both written texts and performances as bases.

1973 Loesch, K. T. Review of George Herbert's Lyrics by Arnold Stein. Qrt J Spch 55 (Feb.) 93-4. Stein's sensitivity to aural values.

1974 Long, C. C. Symposium: Empirical and Experimental Studies in Oral Interpretation: Introduction. Wstn Spch 33 (Fall) 222-6. Suggestions for research in OI.

1975 Maclay, J. H. The Aesthetics of Time in Narrative Fiction. Spch Tchr 18 (Sept.) 194-6. Managing time as writer and performer.

1976 Mayhew, S. H. This Sixth Grade Loves Poetry. Grade Teacher 86 (Apr.) 146-52. Teaching appreciation of poetry to 6th graders, emphasizing poetry is to be read aloud.

1977 Merritt, Francine. Concrete Poetry: Verbivocovisual. Spch Tchr 18 (Mar.) 109-14. Concrete poetry blend of word/sight/sound.

1978 Merritt, Francine. Eyear: Shape/Sound of Concrete Poetry. Sthn Spch J 34 (Spring) 213-24. Background and introduction to concretism, graphic, and experimental verse forms in participation.

1979 Miller, W. H. A Reading Program for Disadvantaged Children. Ill Educ J 49 (Summer) 111-18. Language experience approach and technique for oral exercises as method of teaching reading skills to disadvantaged primary school children.

1980   Murphy, M. W.   Violent Imagery in the Poetry of Gerard
        Manley Hopkins.   Vict Poetry 7 (Spring) 1-16.   Discussion
        of violent imagery in terrible sonnets and popular Hopkins'
        poems.

1981   Newton, Robert.   Voweled Undersong.   Mod Lang Notes 84
        (Apr.) 387-414.   In-depth discussion of musical patterns
        and verse melody.

1982   Nichols, N. S.   Poetry in the 2nd Grade.   Grade Teacher
        87 (Sept.) 176-82.   Second graders read poetry aloud and
        silently, then write their own poetry.

1983   Page, Norman.   Eccentric Speech in Dickens.   Crit Survy 4
        (Summer) 96-100.   Dialogue in Dickens' novels; also
        Dickens as performer of own works.

1984   Parker, David.   Verbal Moods in Shakespeare's Sonnets.
        Mod Lang Qrt 30 (Sept.) 331-40.   Views sonnets as dis-
        guises of imperative mood, not as mere statements but
        live revelations of states of mind.

1985   Perrine, Laurence.   Browning's Too Late: A Reinterpreta-
        tion.   Vict Poetry 7 (Winter) 339-45.   Analysis of drama-
        tic monologue with emphasis on building scene.

1986   Post, R. H.   Cognitive Dissonance in the Plays of Edward
        Albee.   Qrt J Spch 55 (Feb.) 54-60.   Examination of sev-
        eral Albee plays in terms of Festinger's theory of cogni-
        tive dissonance.   Albee's characters often retreat into
        world of illusion rather than resolving dissonance.   Ironi-
        cally illusory world intensifies conflict.

1987   Rago, Henry.   The Poet in His Poem.   Poetry Mag 113
        (Mar.) 413-20.   Symbol and emblem as indicators of poet's
        voice in poem.

1988   Reynolds, J. D.   Empirical Studies in Oral Interpretation:
        The Audience.   Wstn Spch 33 (Fall) 241-9.   The OI must
        always return to refocus on the configuration of author,
        reader and listener no matter how much that process has
        been atomized.

1989   Reynolds, J. D.   Responses to Professor Becker's Critique.
        Wstn Spch 33 (Fall) 277-9.   Rebut of Becker's critique.

1990   Rolfe, Bari.   The Actor's World of Silence.   Qrt J Spch 55
        (Dec.) 394-400.   Nonverbal exercises included to free
        actor/interpreter physically.

1991   Schmitt, Natalie.   Impassioned Art: An Interpretation of
        Tonight We Improvise by Luigi Pirandello.   Wstn Spch 33
        (Summer) 184-91.   Analysis of play; play demonstrates

variety of techniques which may be used to bring life to theatre art.

1992 Schwartz, Elizabeth. Slow Readers Can Enjoy Oral Reading. Educ Digest 34 (Jan.) 36-7. Tapes by junior high school slow readers improve oral skills and help elementary readers.

1993 Shapiro, P. P. The Language of Poetry. Elem Schl J 70 (Dec.) 130-34. Oral reading as well as the writing of poetry should be kept in mind.

1994 Sloan, T. O. The Oral Interpreter and Poetry as Speech. Spch Tchr 17 (Sept.) 187-90. Use of rhetoric in current lit studies.

1995 Sloan, T. O. A Renaissance Controversialist on Rhetoric: Thomas Wright's Passions of the Minde in Generall. Spch Mono 36 (Mar.) 38-54. Discussion of Wright's theories.

1996 Slote, Bernice. Willa Cather Reports Chautauqua 1894. Prairie Schooner 43 (Spring) 117-28. Discussion of atmosphere.

1997 Smith, L. E. English in a College of Education. Crit Survey 4 (Summer) 141-4. Teacher training in England: mentions poets reading own works.

1998 Tomlinson, Charles. Poetry and Physiology. Poetry Mag 114 (June) 193-5. Review of Poemas Humanos by C. Vallego (tr. Clayton Eshleman) containing references to muscularity in much 20th-century writing.

1999 Veilleux, Jere. Toward a Theory of Interpretation. Qrt J Spch 55 (Apr.) 105-15. OI viewed as celebrative event.

2000 Veilleux, Jere. Convention and Style in Interpretation, Approaches to Oral Interpretation: A Symposium, IV. Spch Tchr 18 (Sept.) 197-99. Examination of conventions in OI such as stools, stands scripts.

2001 Whitaker, B. J. Critical Reason and Literature in Performance. Spch Tchr 18 (Sept.) 191-3. Kinds of reasons that may be cited to support critical judgments of lit in performance.

2002 Williamson, George. A Reader's Guide to the Metaphysical Poets. London: Thames and Hudson, 1968. Reviewed by C. G. Williamson in Rev Engl Stud 20 (Nov. 1969) 527-8.

2003 Yoder, R. A. Emerson's Dialectic. Crit 11 (Fall) 313-28. Discusses Emerson's methods of using dialectic as structure device.

1970

2004 Anonymous. Literature and Psychology 20 (1970). Entire
issue. Annotated bibliography dealing with lit and psychology of 100+ journals.

2005 Bacon, W. A. Review of J. L. Styan's Shakespeare's Stage-
craft. Shakespeare Qrtly 21 (Spring) 187-8.

2006 Bahn, Eugene, & John Cambus. Speech Education in
Greece. Chapters in International Studies of National Speech
Education Systems, edited by Fred Casmer & L. S.
Harms. Minneapolis: Burgess.

2007 Blanchard, Margaret. Rhetoric of Communion: Voice in
The Sound and the Fury. Amer Lit 41 (Jan.) 555-65.
Detailed study of the language forms pointing to a narrator who adopts reader's perspective but not his tone and
whose style is persuasive.

2008 Chapman, M. C. Mezza Theatre: A New Venture.
Dramatics 41 (Feb.) 11-3, 18. Staging techniques for RT
and CT as practiced at Florida State University and More-
head State University. Described as combination of reading and acting on stage.

2009 Clark, Philip, & Herbert Mirels. Fluency as a Persuasive
Element in the Measurement of Creativity. J of Educ
Measure 7 (Summer) 83-6. Failure to correct for fluency
raises correlation between measures of creativity and
causes errors.

2010 Cronkhite, Gary. The Place of Aesthetics and Perception in
a Paradigm of Interpretation. Wstn Spch 34 (Fall) 274-87.
Theoretical framework which may clarify some ways that
we may find empirical methods helpful.

2011 Davies, Don. The Ecology of Teacher Education. Ill Educ
J 50 (Spring) 5-12. Place and form of OI in future education.

2012 Eaton, Trevor. The Foundation of Literary Semantics.
Ling: Intl Rev 62 (Oct.) 5-19. Contends that any work of
lit may be explained in terms of linguistic theory.

2013 Editors. A Conversation with Geoffrey Grigson. Rev:
Mag of Poetry & Crit 22 (June) 15-26. Interesting reminiscences of former editor of magazine New Verse.

2014 Freeman, William. Whately and Stanislavski: Complementary Paradigms of Naturalness. Qrt J Spch 56 (Feb.) 61-6.
Complementary elements of delivery an actor prepares and
elements of rhetoric.

2015 Gardner, D. P. Do Your Own Thing. Alpha Psi Omega Playbill (1970) 13-4.

2016 Haas, Richard. Elocutionary Oratory in 1893. Qrt J Spch 56 (Oct.) 314. Editorial presenting some of the comments made by elocution critics following S. H. Clark's presentation in 1893 which analyzes Antony's funeral oration according to the literary canon of unity.

2017 Hadwiger, Ken. Some Effects of Voice Quality on Retention. J of Broadcast 14 (Fall) 139-43. Research indicated certain voice qualities acted as deterrent to retention of factual material.

2018 Hancher, Michael. The Science of Interpretation and the Art of Interpretation. Mod Lang Notes 85 (Dec.) 791-802. Relation between interpretations and actual meaning.

2019 Hargis, D. E. Bibliography of American Elocution. Bibliographic Annual in Speech Communication 1 (1970) 241-56. About 300 entries; headnote lists bibliographies preceding this one.

2020 Hargis, D. E. The Rhapsode. Qrt J Spch 56 (Dec.) 388-98. Historical discussion of rhapsode as educator and entertainer.

2021 Helms, Randel. Orc: The Id in Blake and Tolkien. Lit & Psych (Jan.) 31-5. Orc as radical element vs. orc as conservative element in Tolkien and Blake.

2022 Hill, P. G. A Reading of The Firebugs. Mod Drama (Sept.) 184-93. Discusses difficulty of producing play and demands on audience's imagination.

2023 Hopf, T. S. Reticence and the Oral Interpretation Teacher. Spch Tchr 19 (Nov.) 268-71. Case study and definition of reticence with descriptive tools for identifying the reticent; how OI can help.

2024 James, Clive. The Tin Pan Alley Extension. Rev: Mag Poetry & Crit 22 (June) 3-13. Contemporary music-poets as continuation of early songwriters.

2025 Kukendall, R. B. Oral Interpretation and Readers Theatre. Bull of Nat Assc Sec Schl Principals 54 (Dec.) 86-93.

2026 La Branche, Anthony. Imitation: Getting in Touch. Mod Lang Qrt 31 (Sept.) 308-29. Questions role of imitatio in writing poetry, especially Drayton, Daniel, and Wyatt.

2027 MacKenzie, N. H. Gerard Manley Hopkins' The Dragon's Treasure Horde Unlocked. Mod Lang Qrt 31 (June) 236-

44. Reviews five books about poetry; good source for students.

2028 McCormick, Bernard. A John O'Hara Geography. J Mod Lit 1 (Apr. 1970-71) 151-68. Discusses influence of Pottsville, Pa. as setting for much of O'Hara writing.

2029 McDowell, R. E. Mothers and Sons. Prairie Schooner 43 (Winter) 356-68. Discussion of black lit from So. Africa, West Indies, and America; theme of young man growing up in matriarchal family.

2030 McGuckin, Henry. Forensics in the Liberal Education. West Spch 34 (Spring) 133-8. Plea for expanding forensic format to include rhetorical and perhaps aesthetic events relevant to liberal education.

2031 Meersman, Roger. A 17th-Century View of Delivery. Sthn Spch J 36 (Spring) 204-14. Rapin's theories of empathy, audience relationships, nature and art, delivery and meaning, as precursors of English elocutionary school.

2032 Mihailescu-Urechia, Venera. Are Novelists Free to Choose Their Own Style? Ling: Intl Rev 59 (July) 37-61. Process of building sentences is question of mathematical laws and not act of independence.

2033 Nelson, Max. Abstracts of Doctoral Dissertations in the Field of Speech Communication, 1969. Bibliographic Annual in Speech Communication 1 (1970) 23-6. Individual dissertations listed by author.

2034 Odland, Norine. Discovering What Children Have Learned About Literature. Elem Engl 47 (Dec.) 1072-6. How children choose books and how to determine their reaction to what they read.

2035 Orringer, Nelson. Ortega y Gasset's Sportive Theories of Communication. Mod Lang Notes 85 (Mar.) 207-34.

2036 Parker, Elizabeth. The Author's Voice in Story. Elem Engl 47 (Apr.) 483-5. Author's voice directs reader through story.

2037 Perloff, Marjorie. Angst and Animism in the Poetry of Sylvia Plath. J Mod Lit 1 (Jan.) 57-74. Discusses elements of angst and animism in Plath imagery and emotional tones.

2038 Post, R. M. Auditory Imagination, Mythic Consciousness and the Oral Interpreter. Wstn Spch 34 (Summer) 203-11. T. S. Eliot's concept of auditory imagination as aid to OI in performing and analyzing lit for performance.

2039 Post, R. M. Perception Through Performance of Literature. Spch Tchr 19 (Sept.) 168-72. Relates perception to OI and offers suggestions for sharpening student's perceptions of lit through performance.

2040 Rang, Jack. The Play's the Thing. Alpha Psi Omega Playbill (1970) 12-3. Text must be featured. Also notes dangers in multimedia productions.

2041 Russo, J. P. Love in Lawrence Durrell. Prairie Schooner 43 (Winter) 396-407. Explores complexity of various attitudes of love in Alexandria Quartet.

2042 Sackman, L. H. Backstage: The Challenge of Readers Theatre. Dramatics 41 (Feb.) 32. Discussion of RT and conflicting philosophies.

2043 Said, Edward. Notes on the Characterization of a Literary Text. Mod Lang Notes 85 (Dec.) 765-90. Piaget's structuralism as related to textual analysis.

2044 Simonson, H. P. Writing Through Literature. Coll Comp & Comm (May) 139-43. Includes principles relevant to OI regarding the human voice in lit.

2045 Smith, R. S. Jerome S. Bruner: The Basis for a Solution. Ill Educ J 50 (Spring) 28-37. Explication of Bruner's theories of natural relationship between man and environment, intellectual development and knowledge; implications for analysis of OI as cognitive act.

2046 Stoll, J. E. Psychological Dissociation in the Victorian Novel. Lit & Psych 20 (1970) 63-73. Discusses search for form in Victorian novel in terms of socio-psychological climate of times.

2047 Teeply, H. M. The Oral Tradition That Never Existed. J Biblic Lit 89 (Mar.) 56-67. Rejects idea of oral tradition originating with Jesus, flowing to disciples then to apostles in church.

2048 Thompson, Phyllis. The Teacher Bemused: The Use of the Other Arts in the Teaching of Poetry. Elem Engl 47 (Jan.) 130-34. Use pictures, music, and oral reading in teaching poetry to children.

2049 Usmiani, Renate. The Invisible Theatre: The Rise of Radio Drama in Germany After 1945. Mod Drama (Dec.) 259-69. Why was radio drama ignored on this continent?

2050 Watkins, Brian. Drama in the Classroom. New Theat Mag 10 (Spring) 4-6. Function and qualities of drama teacher in secondary education.

2051 Wright, W. F. Hardy Transcribed. Prairie Schooner 44 (Winter) 363-4. Reviews Bailey's The Poetry of Thomas Hardy: A Handbook and Commentary.

2052 Young, J. D. Evaluating a Readers Theatre Production. Spch Tchr 19 (Jan.) 37-42. Suggestions for evaluating effectiveness of RT production in an OI course.

1971

2053 Ashmore, John. Interdisciplinary Roots of the Theatre of the Absurd. Mod Drama (May) 72-83. Scope and variety of absurd drama.

2054 Barish, J. A. Yvor Winters and the Antimimetic Performance. New Lit Hist 2 (Spring) 419-44. Extensive examination of Winters' theories, primarily applied to drama.

2055 Beckerman, Bernard. Dramatic Analysis and Literary Interpretation: The Cherry Orchard as Exemplum. New Lit Hist 2 (Spring) 391-406. Examination of differences between dramatic analysis and various forms of other literary interpretation.

2056 Brack, H. A. New Priorities in Oral Interpretation. Spch Tchr 20 (Jan.) 71-3. Concentrate more on audience's understanding and appreciation than on how student perceives himself orally functioning.

2057 Broderick, J. C., et al. Articles on American Literature Appearing in Current Periodicals. Amer Lit 43 (Mar.-Jan.) 157-64; 319-22; 513-24; 688-93.

2058 Browne, R. M. The Shropshire Lad as Funeral Orator. Qrt J Spch 57 (Apr.) 134-9. Rhetorical analysis used for consideration of Housman's poem, "To an Athlete Dying Young." Poem should be analyzed based on poet's biography and historical context.

2059 Campbell, P. N. Communication Aesthetics. Today's Spch 19 (Summer) 7-18. Proposal for establishing communication aesthetics as new area in field of communication. Need exists in communication as a discipline.

2060 Campbell, P. N. Performance: The Pursuit of Folly. Spch Tchr 20 (Nov.) 263-74. The process of pursuit, of following determinedly the implications of our arguments, no matter where they lead, is crucial.

2061 Carson, H. L. Living Theatre: U.S.A. and Experimental Theatre: From Stanislavsky to Today. Qrt J Spch 57 (Feb.) 112-4. Review.

2062 Coger, L. I. Staging Literature with Minimal Props for
Maximal Meaning. Scholastic Tchr 51 (Oct. 11) 24-5+.
RT is theatre of the mind and suggestion can convey
images and meaning to audience.

2063 Coger, L. I. Put Drama in Your Life: Try Readers Theatre. Scholastic Voice 51 (Oct. 11) 2-3. RT can be
used to increase interest in lit and performance.

2064 Crannell, K. C. Voice & Articulation in Oral Interpretation
in Proceedings: Mini-Course in Spch Comm, Ed. by R.
C. Jeffrey. SCA (1971) 72-7.

2065 Cronkhite, Gary. Cronkhite on Fletcher. Wstn Spch 35
(Fall) 273. Response to Fletcher on pages 271-2.

2066 Dalan, N. C. Audience Response to Use of Offstage Focus
and Onstage Focus in Readers Theatre. Spch Mono 38
(Mar.) 74-7. Onstage focus did not affect comprehension
of content, though some effect on connotative meaning.

2067 De Spain, J. L. A Rhetorical View of J. R. R. Tolkien's
The Lord of the Rings Trilogy. Wstn Spch 35 (Spring) 88-
95. Critical examination/analysis of Tolkien's fiction, intent, characteristics of book and audience reaction to it.

2068 Dollerup, Cay. On Reading Short Stories. J Reading 14
(Apr.) 445-54. Analysis of readers' responses to intensity, tension, suspense in short stories.

2069 Donato, Eugenio. The Shape of Fiction: Notes Towards a
Possible Classification of Narrative Discourse. Mod Lang
Notes 86 (Dec.) 807-22. Nature of language of fiction.

2070 Editors. Titles of Graduate Theses & Dissertations, An
Index of Graduate Research in Speech Communication, 1970.
Bibliographic Annual in Speech Communication 2 (1971)
144-209. Dissertations and theses by institution for 1970.

2071 Editors. Abstracts of Doctoral Dissertation in the Field of
Speech Communication, 1970. Bibliographic Annual in
Communication 2 (1971) 55-9. Ten OI dissertations listed
by author.

2072 Editors. A Conversation with Stephen Spender. Rev: Mag
of Poetry & Crit 23 (Sept.-Nov.) 20-32. Comments on
craft and contemporaries.

2073 Fennimore, Flora. Choral Reading as Spontaneous Experience. Elem Engl 48 (Nov.) 870-76. Choral reading as
outlet for children.

2074 Finder, Morris. Teaching to Comprehend Literary Texts: Poetry. J of Reading 14 (Mar.) 353-8. Special ways to help students read imaginative lit.

2075 Fleming, Susan. The Demise of the Reluctant Reader. Schl Tchr 42 (Jan.) 12-3, 22. Report of motivation through production of TV programs in teaching reading in elementary school.

2076 Fletcher, J. F. Fletcher on Cronkhite. Wstn Spch 35 (Fall) 271-2. The role of empirical investigation in study of OI based on Cronkhite's sequential perceptual interface program.

2077 Forrest-Thomson, Veronica. Irrationality and Artifice: A Problem in Recent Poetics. Brit J of Aesthet 11 (Spring) 123-33. Attempt to bring to conscious formulation systems of organization inescapably present in reading and writing poetry.

2078 Gerber, P. L. Dreiser's Financier: A Genesis. J Mod Lit 1 (Mar.) 354-74. Discusses influence of life of multi-millionaire C. T. Yerkes upon birth and shape of the financier character in Dreiser's Trilogy of Desire.

2079 Gossman, Lionel. Literary Education & Democracy. Mod Lang Notes 86 (Dec.) 761-89. Effects of oral and textual lit on culture.

2080 Haight, M. R. Nonsense. Brit J of Aesth 11 (Summer) 247-56. Description of way nonsense and absurdity work in literature.

2081 Harrison, A. C. Basic Lore of the Lecture Recital. Spch Tchr 20 (Jan.) 10-5. Return to lecture recital as sound homebase for teaching OI principles.

2082 Haslam, Gerald. American Oral Literature: Our Forgotten Heritage. Engl J 60 (Sept.) 709-23. Call for concern with oral lit.

2083 Heckman, John. From Telling Stories to Writing. Mod Lang Notes 86 (Dec.) 858-72. Structural character of forerunners of novel.

2084 Hopkins, M. F. Russian Poetry into English: Linguistic Analysis and Poetry in Translation. Spch Mono 38 (Mar.) 56-64. Method for using linguistic analysis to study both original and translated poem and to indicate the information to be gained from such a method.

2085 Howe, J. H., ed. AFA Calendar for 71-72. Am For Assc 7 (Spring) 288-301. Calendar of college forensic tournaments from 10-71 to 5-72. Includes OI festivals/workshops.

2086 Howe, J. H. , ed.   AFA Calendar for 70-71 Supplement.
      Am For Assc 8 (Fall) 105-8.   Calendar of college forensic
      tournament 10-70 to 5-71.   Includes OI festivals and work-
      shops.

2087 Howell, W. S.   The British Elocutionary Movement: 1702-
      1806.   Chapter in 18th Century British Logic & Rhetoric.
      Princeton, NJ: Princeton Univ. , 1971.   pp. 143-256.

2088 Hynes, Sam.   The 30's as a Literary Period.   Cont Lit 12
      (1971) 122-7.   Case for 30's being distinct lit period.

2089 Johnson, Josephine.   Yeats: What Method? An Approach
      to the Performance of the Plays.   Qrt J Spch 57 (Feb.)
      68-74.   Yeats' work as so-called indefiniteness of char-
      acterization or inconsistency in dramatic development.

2090 Jones, Peter.   Works of Art and Their Availability for Use.
      Brit J Aest 11 (Spring) 115-22.   Problems of interpretation
      of lit including constructed interpretation.

2091 Kaster, Barbara.   Massaging the Message: Marshall Mc-
      Luhan and Oral Interpretation.   Sthn Spch Comm J 37
      (Winter) 195-9.   McLuhan claims we are returning to the
      oral tradition.   Kaster examines the oral tradition and
      compares it with what McLuhan describes.

2092 Kennedy, A. J.   Directory of Universities and Colleges Con-
      ducting Summer High School Speech Communication Insti-
      tutes: 1971.   Am for Assc J 7 (Winter) 224-33.   Includes
      OI programs.

2093 Killham, John.   A Novel's Relevance to Life.   Brit J
      Aesth 11 (Winter) 63-73.   Judging lit, especially the
      novel, as rendering human experience which has per-
      manent value.

2094 Larrick, Nancy.   Pop-Rock Lyrics: Poetry and Reading.
      J of Reading 15 (Dec.) 184-90.   Rich possibilities offered
      by pop-rock lyrics for teaching reading, poetry, and lan-
      guage appreciation.

2095 Lightfoot, M. J.   Numerical, Sequential and Temporal Pat-
      terns in English Verse.   Qrt J Spch 57 (Apr.) 193-203.
      Prosody in poetry, particular emphasis patterns of metri-
      cal stress.

2096 Makay, J. J.   John Milton's Rhetoric.   Cent Sts Spch J 22
      (Fall) 186-95.   Three foci: review of Miltonic research,
      examination of his persuasive intentions and suggestion
      about what effect Milton had if his purpose in writing was
      persuasive.

2097 Maling, J. M. Sentence Stress in Old English. Ling Inq 2
(Summer) 379-99. Examines sentence stress in Beowulf.

2098 Meersman, Roger. Père Rene Rapin's Eloquence des
Belles-Lettres. Spch Mono 38 (Nov.) 290-301. Study
views Rapin's entire work and extracts from eleven of his
critical works, and the major elements of his Belletristic
theory.

2099 Mercer, Peter. The Rhetoric of Giles Goat-Boy. Novel:
Forum Fict 4 (Winter) 147-58. Highlights heroic diction.

2100 Mew, Peter. Metaphor & Truth. Brit J Aesth 11 (Spring)
189-95. Grasping meaning of metaphor depends on knowledge of non-semantic truths or common beliefs not about
literal meanings of words.

2101 Parrella, Gilda. Projection and Adoption: Toward a Clarification of the Concept of Empathy. Qrt J Spch 57 (Apr.)
204-13. Historical origins and types of empathy.

2102 Perreault, John. Oedipus, A New Work. Drama Rev 15
(Summer) 141-7. A script/description of work's first
performance; bears some resemblance to current forms
of RT.

2103 Post, R. M. An Oral Interpreter's Approach to the Teaching of Elementary School Literature. Spch Tchr 20 (Sept.)
167-73. Applying principles to elementary classroom.

2104 Ramsey, Paul. W. C. Williams as Metrist: Theory and
Practice. J Mod Lit 1 (May) 578-90. Williams poor
prosodist in theory but excellent one in verse.

2105 Replogle, Justin. Marianne Moore & the Art of Intonation.
Cont Lit 12 (1971) 1-17. Linguistic examination of
Moore's "making tunes out of printed words."

2106 Rissover, Frederic. Beat Poetry, The American Dream
and the Alienation Effect. Spch Tchr 20 (Jan.) 36-43.
Using alienation devices in plays jolts audience out of
periods of amusement or emotion to greater awareness of
real life roles in the world.

2107 Rogers, H. L. Review of The Lyre and the Harp: A Comparative Reconsideration of Oral Tradition in Homer & Old
English Epic Poetry by Ann Chalmers Watts. Rev Engl
Stud 22 (Nov.) 465-6. Question about oral formulaic tradition is useless; concentration should be on texts.

2108 Salper, D. R. The Sounding of a Poem. Qrt J Spch 57
(Apr.) 129-33. Deals with the dominance of the print-
visual mode of perception and modern emphasis in criticism on poetic technique.

2109 Sandifer, C. M. From Print to Rehearsal: A Study of Principles for Adapting Literature to Readers Theatre. Spch Tchr 20 (Mar.) 115-20. Principles most agreed on are: lit must be significant; benefit from RT performance; have strong characters, conflict, action and variety; and have audience appeal.

2110 Schechner, Richard. Audience Participation. Drama Rev 15 (Summer) 73-89. Theatre as event in space shared by audience and performers, with audience playing the bass line and performers playing melody line.

2111 Sharpham, J. R.; G. A. Matter; & Wayne Brockriede. The Interpretative Experience as a Rhetorical Transaction. Cent Sts Spch J 22 (Fall) 143-50. The necessary elements in OI experience, how these elements interact in process of constituting an experience, and how the rhetorical nature of the experience affects aesthetic response.

2112 Sloan, T. O. Oral Interpretation in the Ages Before Sheridan and Walker. Wstn Spch 35 (Summer) 147-54. New means exist for interpreting history of OI before the 18th century.

2113 Sloan, T. O. Rhetoric & Meditation: Three Case Studies. J Medieval & Renais Studies 1 (Fall) 45-58. Argues that art of meditation adds to 17th-century rhetoric.

2114 Sloan, T. O. Hermeneutics: The Interpreter's House Revisited. Qrt J Spch 57 (Feb.) 102-7. Reviews and compares Palmer's hermeneutics.

2115 Talbot, Norman. The Stranger Songs: Pop Lyrics of the 60's. Poet Austr 38 (1971) 52-60. Lyrics of pop songs are more craftsmanlike and interesting than much so called serious poetry.

2116 Tulip, James. The Poetic Voices of Robert Lowell. Poet Austr 39 (Apr.) 49-57. From early references to Lowell's reading of his own poetry moves to duality of poetic voices in Lowell's works.

2117 Weintraub, Samuel, et al. Summary of Investigations Relating to Reading: July 1, 1969 to June 30, 1970. Read Res Qrt 6 (Winter) 135-9. See 188-90 for discussion of studies of oral reading: sex differences, errors, variables.

2118 White, M. R. Story-Readers Theatre. Dramatics 42 (Jan.) 12, 13, 24. Yale's Story Theatre viewed as RT in context of principles of RT.

2119 Williams, D. A. The Reader-Audience Paradox. Interface (Sept.) 6-10. Relationship of reader/listener in modern OI.

1972

2120 Abimbola, W. Y. Oral Tradition: Introduction to Nigerian Literature, B. A. King, ed. Africana Publishing Co., 1972, pp. 12-23. Oral traditions in Nigerian lit.

2121 Allen, G. D. The Location of Rhythmic Stress Beats in English: An Experimental Study I. Lang & Spch 15 (Jan.) 72-99. Correlation of lexico-grammatical stress and rhythmic stress.

2122 Allen, G. D. The Location of Rhythmic Stress Beats in English: An Experimental Study II. Lang & Spch 15 (Apr.) 179-95.

2123 Atkinson, Michael. A Precise Phenomenology for the General Scholar. J Gen Educ 23 (Jan.) 261-97. Overview of major aspects of phenomenology.

2124 Bacon, W. A. Oral Interpretation and the Teaching of Literature. Ill Spch & Theat J 26 (Fall.)

2125 Bacon, W. A. The Performing Arts and the Humanities. Texas Spch Assc Newsltr (Winter).

2126 Barba, Eugenio. Words or Presence. Drama Rev 16 (Mar.) 47-54. Body training and voice as prolongation of body.

2127 Barclay, Martha. The Genesis of Modern Oral Interpretation: 1915-1930. Spch Tchr 21 (Jan.) 39-45. From elocution to literary components.

2128 Baron, F. X. Visual Presentation in Beroul's "Tristan." Mod Lang Qrt 33 (June) 99-112. Narrative technique and irony in "Tristan."

2129 Birch, Cyril. Language of Chinese Literature. New Lit Hist 4 (Autumn) 141-50. Syntax diction and vocabulary in 8th-century Chinese lit.

2130 Bormann, D. R. The Willing Suspension of Disbelief: Kames as a Forerunner of Coleridge. Cent Sts Spch J 23 (Spring) 56-60. Discusses two theories to explain tragic pleasure and explicates Lord Kame's theory of dramatic illusion as forerunner of Coleridge's doctrine of poetic faith.

2131 Breen, R. S. Chamber Theatre. Ill Spch & Theat J 26 (Fall) 22-3.

2132 Brodwin, Stanley. The Humor of the Absurd: Mark Twain's Adamic Diaries. Criticism 14 (Winter) 49-64. Twain's humor related to theological determinism.

2133 Brown, K. L. Speech Communication and the Language Arts. Today's Spch 20 (Fall) 25-31. Student's personal and intellectual development and suggests expanded role of speech communication in the secondary curriculum through blending of both movements.

2134 Buell, L. J. Reading Emerson for the Structures: The Coherence of the Essays. Qrt J Spch 58 (Feb.) 58-69. Attempt to pin down extent to which Emerson's essays have continuity, taking their genesis into account, and disregarding the metaphysical implications of Emersonian structure.

2135 Carson, H. L. Playreader's Repertory. Qrt J Spch 58 (Apr.) 239. Textbook and anthology of drama.

2136 Caruso, Thelma. High School Speech and English: A Communication Department. Today's Spch 20 (Fall) 33-7. Call for merger of speech and English into a communication department. Basic goal would be to encompass oracy-speaking and listening and literacy-reading and writing.

2137 Casmir, F. L. Goethe and His Search for a Rhetorical Standard. Cent Sts Spch J 23 (Winter) 237-40. Goethe's distrust of formalized expression of ideas and its resolution through need to provide formal instruction for actors.

2138 Cavalieri, Grace. Playwriting: The Organic Art. Dramatics 44 (Oct.) 22-3, 38. Interview with playwright growing out of a group experiment; illustrated by examination of devices for student involvement.

2139 Coger, L. I. Interpreters Theatre in the Secondary Curriculum. Ill Spch & Theatre J 26 (Fall) 17-9. Defines RT.

2140 Crowley, J. W. Visual-aural Poetry: The Typography of E. E. Cummings. Concerning Poet 5 (Fall) 51-3. Argues Cummings exploited through imaginative use of typography centuries old shift in poetry from oral-aural to visual-aural.

2141 Durant, J. D. Laughter and Hubris in She Stoops to Conquer: The Role of Young Marlow. Sthn Spch Comm J 37 (Spring) 269-80. By examining directorial prerogatives in the interpretation of young Marlow, this essay suggests that Goldsmith's She Stoops can be performed as high and critical comedy.

2142 Editors. Antic Yevtushenko. Time 99 (Feb. 14) 65. Soviet poet prepares U. S. tour.

2143 Editors. Titles of Graduate Theses & Dissertations, An Index of Graduate Research in Speech Communication, 1971.

Bibliographic Annual in Speech Communication 3 (1972) 160-219. Dissertations and theses listed by institution and author.

2144 Editors. Abstracts of Doctoral Dissertations in the Field of Speech Communication, 1971. Bibliographic Annual in Speech Communication 3 (1972) 73-8. Twelve dissertations in OI.

2145 Eldridge, G. G. Creativity in Playwriting. Dramatics 43 (Oct.) 14-7. Exploration of principles of playwrighting and scripting.

2146 Elliott, E. B., Jr. Persona and Parody in Donne's "The Anniversaries." Qrt J Spch 58 (Feb.) 48-57. Donne's use of persona allows one to appreciate better the dramatic power through which Donne persuasively presents his arguments for middle way of Anglicanism.

2147 Espinola, J. C., & K. C. Crannell. Status of Graduate Degree Programs in Oral Interpretation. Spch Tchr 21 (Mar.) 123-6. Survey of geographical areas, objectives and newness.

2148 Evans, W. O. Le Morte d'Arthur. Lang & Style 5 (Winter) 67-73. Oral style in Malory, Chaucer and Sir Gawain and the Green Knight.

2149 Fagerlie, Anna. An Afternoon at the Vachel Lindsay Home. Elem Engl 49 (Dec.) 1187-1189. Brief summary of Lindsay's life and work.

2150 Franklin, W. G. An Experimental Study of the Acoustic Characteristics of Simulated Emotions. Sthn Spch Comm J 38 (Winter) 168-80. Study to determine whether subjects vocally simulating emotional states employ an underlying breath-group pattern, and whether pitch levels were varied during such utterances.

2151 Friedenberg, Robert. America's Most Widely Read Speech Teachers: The Brothers McGuffey. Spch Tchr 21 (Mar.) 79-85. Contributions of McGuffey Brothers to speech education.

2152 Galvin, Michael. Loose Ends. Poet Australia 44 (1972) 53-60. Poetry of Ted Berrigan, Anselm Hollo, and Gael Turnbull as poets of disparate thoughts, impressions and observations requiring readers' participation in putting impressions together.

2153 Genette, Gerard. Valery et la Poetique du Langage. Mod Lang Notes 87 (May) 600-15. Poetic language significance.

2154 Gillespie, P. P. Plays: Well-Constructed and Well-Made. Qrt J Spch 58 (Oct.) 313-21. "Denotation," "connotation," and implications of the terms when they refer to plays.

2155 Goldsmith, V. G. Help Stamp Out Round Robin! Grade Tchr 89 (Mar.) 35-6. Oral reading alternative to Round-Robin reading.

2156 Goss, Blaine. Effect of Sentence Context on Associations to Ambiguous, Vague, & Clear Nouns. Spch Mono 39 (Nov.) 286-9. Study and results on word association.

2157 Gronbeck, B. E. Gorgias on Rhetoric and Poetic: A Rehabilitation. Sthn Spch Comm J 38 (Fall) 27-38. Review of constructive aspects of Gorgias' thinking, epistemology, views of rhetoric and poetic as theories of discourse.

2158 Gronbeck, B. E. Thomas Sprat's Quest for a Philosophy of Language. Cent Sts Spch J 23 (Fall) 158-64. The 17th-century stylistic revolt. Emphasis on movement toward plain style.

2159 Hatch, J. V. A White Folks Guide to 200 Years of Black & White Drama. Dram Rev 16 (Dec.) 5-24. Issue devoted primarily to black theatre history in America.

2160 Haynes, D. T. The Narrative Unity of "A Boy's Will." PMLA 87 (May) 452-64. Narrative structure reveals discrepancy between historical and mythical Frost.

2161 Howard, A. B. The World as Emblem: Language & Vision in the Poetry of Edward Taylor. Amer Lit 44 (Nov.) 359-84. Use of language and metaphor to produce emblems in Taylor's poetry.

2162 Hunsinger, Paul. Public Reading of Poetry in Britain. Speech & Drama 22 (Summer) 6-11. Survey with description of form and style of public reading.

2163 Jeffrey, P. R. Resurrecting the Past: Historical Documents as Materials for Readers Theatre. Spch Tchr 21 (Nov.) 310-14. Adaptation of documentary for OI with methods noted.

2164 Johnson, Albert, & Bertha Johnson. Plays for Readers Theatre. Dramatics 43 (Oct.) 8. Description of six pop classics adapted for RT.

2165 Kaufman, M. W. O'Casey's Structural Design in Juno and the Paycock. Qrt J Spch 58 (Apr.) 191-8. Analysis of the play with emphasis on contradictory moods and incongruous actions within the play.

2166 Kim, M. W. Dance and Rhythm: Their Meaning in Yeats and Noh. Mod Dram 15 (Sept.) 195-208. Dance and rhythm as a single poetic image.

2167 King, J. Y. Chamber Theatre by Any Other Name...? Spch Tchr 21 (Sept.) 193-6. Fictional presentation and demands.

2168 Kirby, E. T. The Delsarte Method: Three Frontiers of Actor Training. Drama Rev 16 (Mar.) 55-69. Three methods: rhythmic gesture, kinesics, and semiology.

2169 Kirby, E. T. The Mask: Abstract Theatre, Primitive & Modern. Drama Rev 16 (Sept.) 5-21. Examples relate to oral traditions and RT.

2170 Kirby, Michael. On Acting and Non-Acting. Dram Rev 16 (Mar.) 3-15. Examination of acting/non-acting continuum for purpose of developing methods for analysis of performance.

2171 Kleinau, Marion, & J. L. McHughes. The Actor and the Interpreter: Suggestions for Comparison. Ill Spch & Theat J 26 (Fall) 24-9. Examines actor/interpreter dichotomy.

2172 Korg, Jacob. Language Change and Experimental Magazines: 1910-30. Cont Lit 13 (Spring) 144-61. Imagist, futurist, and other movements and their use of language.

2173 Lake, M. L. Whom Do They Write For? Grade Tchr 89 (Feb.) 84-5. Reading aloud stories written by children helps direct them to write for each other.

2174 Lambert, R. M. Poetry Readings in the Classroom. Engl J 61 (May) 677-9, 714. Values of reading aloud.

2175 Lane, P. K., & M. S. Miller. Listening: Learning for Underachieving Adolescents. J of Reading 15 (Apr.) 488-91. Training in listening skills moved underachieving students toward better critical reading, enjoyment, and appreciation.

2176 Lewis, G. L. Creative Dramatics: Problems and Processes. Cent Sts Spch J 23 (Spring) 18-27. Materials, methods, techniques for stimulating creative behavior in secondary school students in performing.

2177 Lieberman, M. R. Some Day My Prince Will Come: Female Acculturation Through the Fairy Tale. Coll Engl 34 (Dec.) 383-95. Fairy tales portray females in typical social role of woman.

2178 Lieberman, Marcia, & Philip Lieberman. Olson's Projective
Verse & The Use of Breath Control as a Structural Element. Lang & Style 5 (Fall) 287-98. Experimental examination of breath groups as prosodic element.

2179 Lindfors, B. O. Oral Tradition and the Individual Literary
Talent. Stud in Novel 4 (Summer) 200-17. Modern African novelists echo traditional oral art.

2180 Magliola, Robert. The Phenomenological Approach to Literature: Its Theory & Methodology. Lang & Style 5
(Spring) 79-99. Examines origins and characteristics of
phenomenological approach to lit criticism.

2181 Marlor, C. S. Readers Theatre Bibliography. Bibliographic
Annual in Speech Communication 3 (1972) 21-35. Lists
articles, books, dissertations, theses, plays, poetry, and
selected programs related to RT.

2182 McDonough, John. Technicalities: The Use of Recorded
Music for the Stage. Dramatics 44 (Nov.) 35-7. Practical suggestions for using recorded music.

2183 McGuckin, Henry. Better Forensics: An Impossible
Dream? Am for Assc 8 (Spring) 182-5. Need oral criticism of interpretation performance in tournaments.

2184 Messenger, A. P. John Arden's Essential Vision: Tragic-
Historical-Political. Qrt J Spch 58 (Oct.) 307-12. Examination of private and public elements of plays helps
reveal his coherent vision and conflict which underlie all
of his plays.

2185 Miller, L. M. Multi-Media Motivational Technique. Dramatics 43 (Jan.) 18-9, 22. Director's experience using multi-
media techniques.

2186 Mowe, Gregory, & W. S. Nobles. James Baldwin's Message
for White America. Qrt J Spch 58 (Apr.) 142-51. The
rhetorical strategies used by Baldwin to white America.

2187 Murphy, R. P. Nonverbal Communication and the Overlooked Action in Pinter's The Caretaker. Qrt J Spch 58
(Feb.) 41-7. Is the play tragic, and if so, why and for
whom? Also considers whether there is some recognizable
point in the play which informs the play and makes it
cease to be funny.

2188 Ortolani, Benito. Zeami's Aesthetics of the No and Audience Participation. Educ Theat J (May) 109-17. Main
principles in the No drama.

2189 Parrella, Gilda. Image and Mirror: Empathy in Language
Devices. Wstn Spch 36 (Fall) 251-60. Certain language
devices are embodiments of the empathic processes and
can awaken responses to experiences in the printed text
as well as performance of that text.

2190 Parret, Margaret. Teaching Oral Interpretation to Children
Through Readers Theatre. Ill Spch & Theat J 26 (Fall)
5-8.

2191 Porter, D. T., & G. W. King. Use of Video Tape Equipment in Improving Oral Interpretation Performance. Spch
Tchr 21 (Mar.) 99-106. Effects of feedback on OI performance.

2192 Rabinowitz, Isaac. Word & Literature in Ancient Israel.
New Lit Hist 4 (Autumn) 119-39. Ancient Israeli belief
in power and properties of words.

2193 Ramsey, B. A. An Interdisciplinary Course in the Rhetoric
of Literature. Spch Tchr 21 (Nov.) 319-21. Three hy-
potheses for designing and teaching course in applied literature.

2194 Reader, W. D. Dramatic Structure and Prosodic Form in
Milton's Sonnet on His Deceased Wife. Lang Qrt 11 (Fall-
Win.) 21-58, 28. Analysis with some of the viewpoint of
OI.

2195 Rhodes, Jack. The Selection of Materials for Contest in
Oral Interpretation. Am For Assc 8 (Winter) 135-8.
Protest choice of inferior lit for interpretation performance
in contests; attacks requirement of a clearly defined theme
in readings; suggests that focus be on "how" rather than
"what."

2196 Sanderson, S. E. Establishing Objectives for Course in
Reading Aloud. Spch Tchr 21 (Sept.) 169-76. Problems
and assignments for behavioral objectives.

2197 Seaberg, D. T., & W. M. Zinsmaster. What Can Teachers
Learn from Directors in the Performing Arts? Elem Schl
J 72 (Jan.) 167-75. Aesthetics and problems common to
all performing artists, directors and teachers.

2198 Sloan, T. O. Review of Classical Rhetoric in English Poetry
by Brian Vickers. Qrt J Spch 58 (Oct.) 351.

2199 Sloan, T. O. Review of the Imagery of John Donne's "Sermons by Winfried Schleiner." Style 6 (Spring) 203-6.
Discussion of analysis method has serious oversights.

2200 Sloan, T. O. Review of Rhetoric/Ritual by P. N. Campbell.
Qrt J Spch 58 (Oct.) 364-5.

2201 Smith, C. R. The Coming of Transcendent Rhetoric. Today's Spch 20 (Summer) 19-24. Seeks to answer question
of why sophisticated rhetoric dominated so long. Examines
contemporary tendencies in rhetoric education and politics.

2202 Speer, J. H. The Rhetoric of Ibsenism: A Study of the
Poet as Persuader. Sthn Spch Comm J 38 (Fall) 13-26.
Study of poetry from rhetorical perspective.

2203 Stewig, J. W. Creative Drama & Language Growth. Elem
Schl J 72 (Jan.) 176-88. OI as logical first step in development of creative drama techniques and achieving language growth.

2204 Strine, M. S. Ethics and Action in Conrad's Heart of Darkness. Wstn Spch 36 (Spring) 103-8. Heart of Darkness
as act in response to its social context.

2205 Swigger, R. T. Reflections on Language in Queneau's Novels. Cont Lit 13 (Fall) 491-506. Realization by Queneau's
characters of the importance of language.

2206 Thomas, D. P. Goodbye to Berlin: Refocusing on Isher-
wood's Camera. Cont Lit 13 (Winter) 44-52. Author's
narrative point of view is camera-like.

2207 Valdes, M. J. Toward a Structure of Criticism. New Lit
Hist 3 (Winter) 263-78. Diction, syntax, symbol, metaphor, and their importance to lit criticism.

2208 Veilleux, Jere. Some Aphorisms for Readers Theatre.
Spch Tchr 21 (Jan.) 64-6. Series of aphorisms puncturing
set principles. For example, costumes interpretation:
as in life, the readers are always in costume. The question is: which ones?

2209 Voznesensky, Andrei. Ice-69. Poet Austr 43 (1972) 40-55.
Part I of triptych, author says, planned as warning of
danger threatening nature.

2210 Vulcan, W. A. Narration in Readers Theatre. Dramatics
44 (Oct.) 36-7. Steps and principles of performance in RT.

2211 Waal, Carla. Rhetoric in Action: Orators in the Plays of
Henrik Ibsen. Sthn Spch Comm J 37 (Spring) 249-58.
Six plays of Ibsen illustrate his knowledge of dynamics of
rhetoric and social impact of public speaking.

2212 Wiebe, Rudy. Songs of the Canadian Eskimo. Canad Lit 52
(Spring) 57-69. Brief introduction to classic Eskimo song
and poetry. Classic because unaffected by western rhymes
and images.

2213 Winterowd, W. R. The Uses of Grammar. Today's Spch 20 (Winter) 3-10. Explores three ways in which generative grammar has been or can be used in rhetorical study.

2214 Young, J. D. Environmental Everyman. Dramatics 44 (Dec.) 34-5+. Way one group developed environmental theatre from three constant elements: script, actors, and space.

2215 Young, M. J. The Unity of the English Mystery Cycles. Qrt J Spch 58 (Oct.) 327-37. Examination of unifying nature of the cycles from three vantage points: the scope of the plays, the protagonists, and depth of central action.

1973

2216 Abel, L. G. , & R. M. Post. Towards a Poor Readers Theatre. Qrt J Spch 59 (Dec.) 436-42. Grotowski's theory applied to RT makes it rich.

2217 Abraham, Werner, & Kurt Braunmuller. Toward a Theory of Style and Metaphor. Poet: Intl Rev Theory Lit 7 (1973) 103-48. Style is function of two pragmatic variables: speaker and spoken to.

2218 Aeschbacher, Jill. Kenneth Burke, Samuel Beckett and Form. Today's Spch 21 (Summer) 43-7. Beckett rejects conventional forms and uses techniques that invite the observer to participate in the making of his plays. Burke's style different.

2219 Anapol, M. M. , & H. T. Hurt. Graduate Study in Speech 1966-1971. Spch Tchr 22 (Jan.) 18-26. Changing trends in graduate and post-graduate curriculum.

2220 Angotti, V. L. Return to Man: Jacques Copeau and the Actor. Cent Sts Spch J 24 (Fall) 151-7. Through community of actor-directors and teachers, Copeau laid basis for modern approach to acting as influential as that of Stanislavski.

2221 Bacon, W. A. The Margery Bailey Memorial Lectures. Spch Mono 40 (June) 75-100. Discussion of diseased state in Henry IV, Part II, and reason and will in the disordered world of Troilus and Cressida.

2222 Bacon, W. A. Problems in the Interpretation of Shakespeare. Spch Tchr 22 (Nov.) 273-81. Plea for primacy of language in performance.

2223 Barker, Robert. Contemporary Fairy Tales. Dramatics 44 (Feb.) 12-3. Account of series of fairy tales at La Canada, California High School, similar to story theatre.

2224 Barranger, M. S. Ibsen's New Armor: Structural Patterns in the Late Plays. Sthn Spch Comm J 39 (Winter) 123-33. Structural patterns in Ibsen's late plays; and sets forth new approach to Ibsen's last work, When We Dead Awaken.

2225 Berleant, Arnold. The Verbal Presence: An Aesthetics of Literary Performance. J Aesth Art Crit 31 (Spring) 339-46. Philosopher talks of speech, language and OI.

2226 Braudy, Leo. Form of the Sentimental Novel. Novel: Forum Fict 7 (Fall) 5-13. Early 18th-century novel as preparing way for much pre-romantic poetry by exploring new forms.

2227 Briggs, N. E. Rhetorical Dimensions of the Nursery Rhyme. Spch Tchr 22 (Sept.) 215-9. Nursery rhyme as form of persuasive discourse and way nursery rhyme may move child from powerlessness to power in his cognitive environment.

2228 Brown, W. R. A Function of Metaphor in Poetry. Spch Tchr 22 (Jan.) 32-7. Significance of disparity, stressing function of metaphor to total poetic meaning and experience.

2229 Bruneau, Thomas. Communicative Silences: Forms and Functions. J Comm 23 (Mar.) 17-46. Nature of silence in relation to speech, signs, sensations, perceptions, and metaphorical movement.

2230 Callan, Edward. Huddon and Duddon in Yeats' "A Vision": The Folk Tale as Gateway to the Universal Mind. Mich Acad 6 (Summer) 5-16. Yeats regarded folklore as manifestation of racial or universal consciousness.

2231 Campbell, P. N. A Rhetorical View of Locutionary, Illocutionary, and Perlocutionary Acts. Qrt J Spch 59 (Oct.) 284-96. Attempts to show why Austin's work How to Do Things with Words has not had effect on study of communication, and also why to the extent Austin is representative of ordinary language philosophy, that the philosophy movement has had little impact on speech communication.

2232 Carlsen, J. W. Bibliography of Studies in Oral Interpretation, 1972. Bibliographic Annual in Speech Communication 4 (1973) 69-73. Surveys over 100 journals related to OI.

2233 Carson, H. L. Modern World Drama: An Encyclopedia. Qrt J Spch 59 (Apr.) 247-8. Review of Myron Matlaw's Modern World Drama.

2234 Coffin, Lawrence. Liquefaction in Herrick's "Upon Julia's Clothes." Concerning Poetry 6 (Fall) 56-9. Historical, scientific, and contextual use of liquefaction in poem.

2235 Courtney, Richard. Theatre and Spontaneity. J of Aesthetics & Art Crit 32 (1973) 79-88. Relationship of spontaneity in art to objectivity in form.

2236 Dickie, George. Psychical Distance: In a Fog at Sea. Brit J Aesth 13 (Winter) 17-29. Edward Bullough's theory of aesthetic distance examined.

2237 Dorter, Kenneth. Ion: Plato's Characterization of Art. J Aesth Art Crit 32 (Fall) 65-78. Section by section explanation of Ion.

2238 Editors. Graduate Theses & Dissertations in the Field of Speech Communication, 1972. Bibliographic Annual in Speech Communication 4 (1973) 208-62. Dissertations and theses listed by institution and author.

2239 Emenyonu, E. N. Igbo Literary Backgrounds. Conch 5 (1973) 43-60. Oral narratives, proverbs, sayings, and songs are source of Igbo lit.

2240 Fish, R. S. A Review of Two Oral Interpretation Text Books. Qrt J Spch 59 (Feb.) 118-9. Reviews W. A. Bacon's Art of Interpretation and O. J. Aggert & E. R. Bowen's Communicative Reading.

2241 Frank, Ted. Strindberg's Damascus Plays: The Pilgrimage of an Uneasy Rider. Sthn Spch Comm J 39 (Winter) 185-9. Relationship between Strindberg's real life and fictive life as apparent in his Damascus Trilogy and attempts to construct a dominant motif of character and setting which is characterized as a pilgrimage theme.

2242 Frisby, P. T. Endorsing Readers Theatre. Dramatics 44 (Apr.) 35-7. Positive experience of director with RT: examination of methods used to solve problems of transitions, entrances, casting.

2243 Gamble, T. K., & M. W. Gamble. The Theatre of Creative Involvement: An Introduction to Drama for Children. Spch Tchr 22 (Jan.) 41-3. Theatre of creative involvement as innovative method of furthering growth of this type of drama and growth of child.

2244 Geiger, Don. Poetic Realizing as Knowing. Qrt J Spch 59 (Oct.) 311-8. Documents poetic participation as experience.

2245 Goldhamer, A. D. Everyman: A Dramatization of Death. Qrt J Spch 59 (Feb.) 87-98. Indicates author's departure

from relevant medieval death literature and discusses the
hero's attitude.

2246 Gray, P. H. The Evolution of Expression: S. S. Curry's
Debt to Elocution. Spch Tchr 22 (Nov.) 322-7. Examination of expressionist and elocutionist approaches to teaching oral reading.

2247 Hartshorn, Edwina, & John Brantley. Effects of Dramatic
Play on Classroom Problem Solving Ability. J Educ Research 66 (Feb.) 243-46. Study using "spontaneous play"
as training in problem solving.

2248 Hendricks, B. L. Mythmaking with Children Through Improvisation. Spch Tchr 22 (Sept.) 226-30. Emphasis on
exploring children's personal myths before traditional
public myths are examined.

2249 Heston, L. A. An Exploration of the Narrator in Robbe-
Grillet's Jealousy. Cent Sts Spch J 24 (Fall) 178-82.
Explores roles and problems of narrator in the work and
those facing OI in performance of lit.

2250 Heston, L. A. Note on Prose Fiction: Performance of
Dialogue Tags. Spch Tchr 22 (Jan.) 69-72. Opposes
blanket cutting tags; sees them as revelatory of nature of
narrator, character, and situation.

2251 Hollander, John. Poem in the Ear. Yale Rev 62 (June)
486-506. It is the aspects of poetic language that are
most like the resources of speech, rather than those of
song, which come to the aid of poetic resonance.

2252 Hoover, R. M. Prose Rhythm: A Theory of Proportional
Distribution. Coll Comp & Comm 24 (Dec.) 366-74.
Prose rhythm indicates we are creatures of balance.

2253 Hopkins, M. F. Interpreting Anglican Allusions in English
Literature. Spch Tchr 22 (Mar.) 153-5. Study of religious implications in English lit.

2254 Hudson, Lee. Oral Interpretation as Metaphorical Expression. Spch Tchr 22 (Jan.) 27-31. Argues for metaphorical framework as structural definition of OI.

2255 Hunsinger, Paul. Using Stories in Messages. Comm Assc
Pacific 2 (Jan.) 41-9. Storytelling in public speaking.

2256 Hutchings, Geoffrey. Discourse in Context: A Stylistic
Analysis. Lingua 32 (1973) 83-94. Focuses at syntactic
level on forms used in indirect discourse.

2257 Jentoft, C. W. Surrey's Four Orations and the Influence of
Rhetoric on Dramatic Effect. Papers in Lang & Lit 9

(Summer) 250-62. Surrey's poetry as modeled after Greek and Latin orations.

2258 Jones, J. B. Impersonation and Authenticity: The Theatre as Metaphor in Kopit's Indians. Qrt J Spch 59 (Dec.) 443-51. A study of Indians reveals acute, perceptive and precise understanding of his work.

2259 Jurak, Mirdo. Dramaturgic Concepts of the English Group Theatre: The Totality of Artistic Involvement. Mod Drama 16 (June) 81-7. Provides lineage for contemporary theatre, including RT.

2260 Kell, Richard. Great Repression. Brit J Aesth 13 (Winter) 41-6. Role of control and repression in expression of art forms in performance.

2261 Kellogg, Robert. Oral Literature. New Lit Hist 5 (Fall) 55-66. Ways in which lit can be said to incorporate the oral, stressing oral narrative.

2262 Klammer, T. P. Foundations for a Theory of Dialogue Structure. Poet: Intl Rev Theory Lit 9 (1973) 27-64. Studies give and take between speaker/hearer as collection of tagmemic units.

2263 Klinzing, D. R. A Study of the Personality Differences Between Effective and Ineffective Student Actors. Today's Spch 21 (Spring) 47-50. Effective student actors are more aesthetically oriented, less economically and politically oriented and less sociable than ineffective student actors.

2264 Larson, Valentine. Improving English Through Choral Speaking. Comm Assc Pacific 2 (Nov.) 61-74. Values types of choral speaking procedures with specific illustrations.

2265 Lentricchia, Frank. Robert Frost: The Aesthetics of Voice and the Theory of Poetry. Crit 15 (Winter) 28-42. Discusses Frost's ideas of aural element in his poetic theory.

2266 Loesch, K. T. Review of Music for a King: George Herbert's Style & the Metrical Psalms by Coburn Freer. Qrt J Spch 59 (Apr.) 245-6.

2267 Logue, C. M. Abstracts of Doctoral Dissertations in the Field of Speech Communication, 1972. Bibliographic Annual in Speech Communication 4 (1973) 95-207. Fourteen dissertations on OI on pp. 113-17.

2267a Long, B. W. Research Directions in the Performance of Literature. Spch Mono 40 (Aug.) 238-42. Affirms need for and suggestions for research in OI.

2268 Loveland, G. G., & Robert Michielutte. Correlates of Aesthetic Interest. Spch Tchr 22 (Mar.) 125-32. Attempt to identify some factors which may help to explain why certain individuals value aesthetic experience more highly than others.

2269 Lyon, T. E. Borges and the (Somewhat) Personal Narrator. Mod Fict Stud 19 (Autumn) 363-72. All of Borges' lit creates intimate narrators.

2270 Marceau, Felicien. Liberty Begins with the Comic. Mod Drama 16 (Dec.) 369-72. Discusses differences between comedy/tragedy from contemporary point of view.

2271 Matlack, C. S. Metaphor and Dramatic Structure in the Chalk Garden. Qrt J Spch 59 (Oct.) 304-10. Linguistic techniques of play based on dialogue and sequence. Evidence places play in tradition of high comedy.

2272 McGregor, Marjorie. Cognitive Development Through Creative Dramatics. Spch Tchr 22 (Sept.) 220-5. Several less obvious but equally significant concepts which further the cognitive development of child through creative drama situation.

2273 Obiechina, E. N. Problem of Language in African Writing: The Example of the Novel. Conch 5 (1973) 11-28. English language unable to express fully African oral heritage.

2274 Overstreet, Robert. Speaking of Poetry in Charles Williams' Descent into Hell. Sthn Spch Comm J 38 (Summer) 385-90. What Williams has to say to interpreter in this novel.

2275 Pavel, Thomas. Some Remarks on Narrative Grammars. Poetics: Intl Rev Theory of Lit 8 (1973) 5-30. Linguistic analysis of theory of narrative structures.

2276 Post, R. M. The Outsider in the Plays of John Osborne. Sthn Spch Comm J 39 (Fall) 63-74. Examination of six Osborne plays; sees Osborne as outsider who dramatizes weaknesses in the bourgeoisie.

2277 Rickert, W. E. Communication Models for Teaching Oral Interpretation. Spch Tchr 22 (Mar.) 133-9. Possibilities for use of models as pedagogical instruments; four models proposed.

2278 Robbins, K. R. John McCullough: Pigmy Giant of the American Stage 1832-1885. Sthn Spch Comm J 38 (Spring) 244-54. Finding McCullough's place in American theatrical history as well as reasons for his slip into oblivion.

2279 Robinson, M. P. Notes from the Classroom of Gertrude
Johnson. Spch Tchr 22 (Nov.) 328-33. Basic tenets of
Johnson's philosophy and approach to OI.

2280 Roloff, L. H. The Roles of the Interpreter and the Actor.
Spch Tchr 22 (Mar.) 144-7. Argues that interpreter may
and perhaps should "act."

2281 Salper, D. R. Some Rhetorical and Poetic Crossroads in
the Interpretation of Literature. Wstn Spch 37 (Fall) 264-
72. What is neglected in both Aristotle's brief treatment
of epic fiction and several modern accounts of poetry is a
rhetorical outlook; there follows a brief look at Aristotle
on narration, a Hemingway narrative, a Purdy narrative,
the lyric voice and a Wilbur poem--"The Juggler."

2282 Schechner, Richard. On Kinesic Analysis: A Discussion
with Daniel Stern. Dram Rev 17 (Sept.) 115-26. Using
kinesic analysis in rehearsal.

2283 Schechner, Richard, & Cynthia Mintz. Kinesics and Performance. Dram Rev 17 (Sept.) 102-8. Review of lit and
implications for rehearsal and performance.

2284 Schmidt, Siegfried. On the Foundation and the Research
Strategies of a Science of Literary Communication. Poetics: Intl Rev Theory of Lit 7 (1973) 7-35. Devises a
metatheoretical program for lit studies.

2285 Sloan, T. O. On Showing What Literature Does Rather
Than Telling What It Says. Qrt J Spch 59 (Dec.) 477-80.
Review of S. E. Fish's Self Consuming Artifacts: The Ex-
perience of 17th Century Literature.

2286 Spiegel, Alan. Flaubert to Joyce: Evolution of a Cinema-
tographic Form. Novel: Forum Fict 6 (Spring) 229-43.
Word action that evokes expressive visual images.

2287 Steyers, J. D. The Long Morning: A Re-evaluation of
Arthur Schnitzler's Anatol. Wstn Spch 37 (Winter) 34-46.
Analysis of structure and theme of Anatol; sees play as
process author knew well and may have undergone himself.

2288 Stock, Noel. Reflections on Eliot and the Art of Reading.
Poetry Austr 49 (1973) 50-6. Argues for evaluation of
Eliot's poetry by itself instead of constant scholarly ref-
erencing to sources.

2289 Thompson, D. W. Teaching the History of Interpretation.
Spch Tchr 22 (Jan.) 38-40. Strategy and suggestions for
development of such a course.

2290 Towns, Stuart, & C. L. Roberts. A Bibliography of Speech and Theatre in the South for the Year 1972. Sthn Spch Comm J 39 (Fall) 75-87.

2291 Trautmann, Frederick. Harriet Beecher Stowe: Public Readings in Central States. Cent Sts Spch J 24 (Spring) 22-8. Historical tracing of the successful rendering by author of her own works.

2292 Wallace, Robert. A Note on Simile and Metaphor. Concerning Poetry 6 (Fall) 64. Argues against old saw that metaphor is more powerful than simile.

2293- West, Carole, & Allen Williams. Awareness: Teaching
4 Black Literature in Secondary School. J Black Stud 3 (June) 455-71. Black lit should be singled out and taught as black lit.

2295 Williams, D. A., & D. C. Alexander. Effects of Audience Responses on the Performances of Oral Interpreters. Wstn Spch 37 (Fall) 273-80. Study of positive and negative feedback on performance.

2296 Winterowd, W. R. Richard M. Weaver: Modern Poetry and the Limits of Conservative Criticism. Wstn Spch 37 (Spring) 129-38. Critique of Weaver's conservatism as short-sighted under subtitles, "Weaver on Modern Poetry," "Modern Egocentricity," and "The Use of Egocentricity."

1974

2297 Beebe, S. A. Eye Contact: Nonverbal Determinant of Speaker Credibility. Spch Tchr 23 (Jan.) 21-5. Effects of eye contact on credibility in public speaking situation.

2298 Breneman, Lucille & Bren. Storytelling Handbook, An Approach to the Art of Storytelling. Comm Assc Pacific 3 (Oct.) 1-86. Portions of book include system for preparing stories and annotating bibliographies.

2299 Brooks, Keith, & Joshua Crane. Semantic Agreement in Readers Theatre. Wstn Spch 38 (Spring) 124-32. Inquiry into use of semantic agreement as way of measuring RT cast and audience agreement on perceived meaning of lit as performed. 1) Semantic agreement can indicate degree of consensus; 2) when lit is appropriately communicative, agreement between cast and audience increases; 3) agreement affected by such variables as education, training, experience, and familiarity with lit.

2300 Brown, William; Joseph Epolito; & Nancy Stump. Genre Theory and the Practice of Readers Theatre. Spch Tchr

23 (Jan.) 1-8. Given the interaction of synedoche and methnomy as its formal principle, RT will not only continue as most portable of all forms of theatre, but will become more and more a moveable feast.

2301 Carlsen, J. W. Bibliography of Studies in Oral Interpretation, 1973. Bibliographic Annual in Speech Communication 5 (1974) 103-12. Over 200 articles from over 100 selected journals.

2302 Carlsen, J. W.; Ladonna McMurray; & Judith Wells. Oral Interpretation in Undergraduate Education: A Survey. Spch Tchr 23 (Mar.) 156-8. Investigation of role of OI in undergraduate program.

2303 Cohen, Edwin. The Role of the Interpreter in Identifying the Concept of Folk. Wstn Spch 38 (Summer) 170-5. Defined characteristics of folk songs, folkness is demonstrated by performer, not composer.

2304 Cook, Mary; Jacqueline Smith; & M. G. Lalljee. Filled Pauses and Syntactic Complexity. Lang & Spch 17 (Jan.) 11-6. Two studies of syntactic complexity in relation to filled pause rates are described.

2305 Editors. Graduate Theses & Dissertations in the Field of Speech Communication, 1973. Bibliographic Annual in Speech Communication 5 (1974) 246-98. Dissertations and theses in OI, see pp. 254-6.

2306 Espinola, J. C. The Nature, Function & Performance of Indirect Discourse in Prose Fiction. Spch Mono 41 (Aug.) 193-204. Nature functions and effects of two basic types of indirect discourse (indirect speech and free indirect speech) during performance of text. Suggests ways OI can reflect characteristics of indirect discourse during solo and group performance.

2307 Frentz, T. S. Toward a Resolution of the Generative Semantics/Classical Theory Controversy: A Psycholinguistic Analysis of Metaphor. Qrt J Spch 60 (Apr.) 125-33. Psycholinguistic approach to puzzling controversy.

2308 Gledhill, P. R. The National Theatre Program in Mexico. Wstn Spch 38 (Summer) 176-81. Description of individual programs within system.

2309 Gorelik, Mordecai. On Brechtian Acting. Qrt J Spch 60 (Oct.) 265-78. Lengthy discussion of Brechtian concepts.

2310 Gura, T. J. The Accepted Intruder: Shakespeare's Use of the Publicized Privacy. Ill Spch & Theat J 28 (Spring) 6-9.

2311 Lazier, Gil; Douglas Zahn; & Joseph Bellinghiere. Empirical Analysis of Dramatic Structure. Spch Mono 41 (Nov.) 381-90. Found similar perceptions of dramatic structure with those who only read play, only saw it and those who read it, then saw it.

2312 Lee, R. R. The Modified Tutorial Approach in Teaching Psychomotor Skills for Oral Interpretation. Spch Tchr 23 (Jan.) 60-4. Suggestions for improvement in beginning OI class.

2313 Lee, R. R. Behavioral Analysis in Oral Interpretation. Sthn Spch Comm J 39 (Summer) 379-88. Differences in verbal behavior between typical entering student in OI and experienced OI-er.

2314 Logue, C. M. Abstracts of Doctoral Dissertation in the Field of Speech Communication 1973. Interpretation. Bibliographic Annual in Speech Communication 5 (1974) SCA 139-245. 16 dissertations listed. Individual entries for each dissertation are listed under name of author.

2314a Long, B. W. Cognition and Audience in a Performance Class. Spch Tchr 23 (Jan.) 63-6. Difference in roles and preparation of audience members will influence the quality of text produced and experience of class members.

2315 Longman, S. V. Mussolini and the Theatre. Qrt J Spch 60 (Apr.) 212-24. Mussolini as man of theatre; looks at concept of fascism as it was profoundly theatrical in nature, then sees how Mussolini fits into this scheme.

2316 Miller, M. J. Pinter as a Radio Dramatist. Mod Drama 17 (Dec.) 403-11. Effect of reading Pinter's plays over radio.

2317 Nichols, H. J. The Prejudice Against Native American Drama from 1778 to 1830. Qrt J Spch 60 (Oct.) 279-88. Examines attitudes toward native American drama from Revolutionary War to 1830.

2318 Overstreet, Robert. The Accentual Fallacy in Interpretation. Spch Tchr 23 (Sept.) 257-9. In dealing with accents, one can master the accent of the story, avoid performing it, or using hints of accent while emphasizing the depth of the story in own sound.

2319 Parrella, Gilda. Through the I of the Beholder: A Rationale for Physicalization in the Performance of Narratives. Cent Sts Spch J 25 (Winter) 296-302. Rational for physicalization in performance based on considerations of form and structure in narrative prose.

2320 Pehrsson, R. S. The Effects of Teacher Interference During the Process of Reading. J of Reading 17 (May) 617-21. Determines whether teacher helps student to make fewer errors in word recognition by correcting student during oral reading.

2321 Post, R. M. Ensemble Oral Interpretation. Spch Tchr 23 (Mar.) 151-5. Ensemble OI as means of studying lit, especially multi-voiced lit.

2322 Post, R. M. Readers Theatre as a Method of Teaching Literature. Engl J 63 (Sept.) 69-72. By orally and physically performing a literary work, students come into vital, active contact with the selection.

2323 Powlick, Leonard. A Phenomenological Approach to Harold Pinter's A Slight Ache. Qrt J Spch 60 (Feb.) 25-32. Phenomenological implications in Pinter's play.

2324 Rinear, D. L. The Day the Whores Came Out to Play Tennis: Kopit's Debt to Chekhov. Today's Spch 22 (Spring) 19-23. Kopit draws from Cherry Orchard, even same central idea.

2325 Schrero, E. M. Intonation in Nineteenth Century Fiction: The Voices of Paraphrase. Qrt J Spch 60 (Oct.) 289-95. Examines typical passages by Dickens and James for ways in which intonation patterns are made to serve the ends of a narrative.

2326 Seligman, K. L. Shakespeare's Use of Elizabethan Dress as a Comedic Device in The Taming of the Shrew: Something Mechanical Encrusted on the Living. Qrt J Spch 60 (Feb.) 39-44. Taming of the Shrew reveals comments on role of dress in Elizabethan society.

2327 Shepard, R. C. Oral Language Performance and Reading Instruction. Elem Engl 51 (Apr.) 544-6. Significant relationship exists between child's oral language performance and readiness for beginning reading.

2328 Sloan, T. O. Review of G. L. Bruns' Modern Poetry & the Idea of Language: A Critical & Historical Study. Qrt J Spch 60 (Oct.) 400-1.

2329- Towns, Stuart, & C. L. Roberts. A Bibliography of Speech,
30   Theatre and Broadcasting in the South for the Year 1973. Sthn Spch Comm J 40 (Fall) 81-93.

2331 Wilson, M. G. Charles Kean: Tragedian in Transition. Qrt J Spch 60 (Feb.) 45-57. Kean as important figure in history of English acting.

2332 Zanger, Jules. The Minstrel Show as Theatre of Misrule.
Qrt J Spch 60 (Feb.) 33-8. Themes of anarchy and anti-
authoritarianism seen in minstrel.

1975

2333 Adler, T. P. The Dialogue of Incompletion: Language in
Tennessee Williams' Later Plays. Qrt J Spch 61 (Feb.)
48-58. Analysis of verbal confusion in Williams.

2334 Arrington, R. M. Some American Indian Voices: Resources
in Intercultural Rhetoric and Interpretation. Spch Tchr 24
(Sept.) 191-4. Sources and resource materials for research and performance.

2335 Bacon, W. A. Practical Prosody. Ill Spch & Theat J 29
(Spring) 1-6.

2336 Bacon, W. A. Alone on the Moon: Our Stammering Society. Wstn Spch Comm 39 (Fall) 218-29. Growing diver-
sification in field of speech. Emphasizes focus on orality
as opposed to written word.

2337 Campbell, P. N. Metaphor and Linguistic Theory. Qrt J
Spch 61 (Feb.) 1-12. Discussion of metaphor and linguistic theory as dimensions of language.

2338 Carlsen, J. W. Bibliography of Studies in Oral Interpretation, 1974. Bibliographic Annual in Speech Communication
6 (1975) SCA 75-80. Over 200 articles from over 100 selected periodicals.

2339 Coger, L. I., & S. H. Pelham. Kinesics Applies to Interpreters Theatre. Spch Tchr 24 (Mar.) 91-9. Body movement and gestures and their application to RT production.

2340 Cohen, Edwin. A Genetic Interpretation of Tevye, the
Dairyman, and His Culture. Sthn Spch Comm J 40 (Summer) 419-28. Compares original story to modern adaptation of fiddler to aid interpreter with greater understanding
of its roots.

2341 Crane, Joshua. Genesis. Chapter in The Communicative
Act of Oral Interpretation by Brooks, Bahn and Okey.
Boston: Allyn & Bacon.

2342 Editors. SCA-ATA Joint Task Force: Guidelines for Speech
Communication and Theatre Programs in Teacher Education. Spch Tchr 24 (Nov.) 343-64. Guidelines for basic
programs, advanced programs, faculty, students, and
evaluations.

2343 Editors. Graduate Theses & Dissertations in the Field of Speech Communication, 1974. Bibliographic Annual in Speech Communication 6 (1975) 197-249. For dissertations and theses in OI see pp. 204-5.

2344 Gillespie, P. P. Plays: Well-Complicated. Spch Mono 42 (Mar.) 20-8. Examination of three of Eugene Scribe's construction techniques in order to define a well-made play.

2345 Gura, T. J. The Solo Performer and Drama. Spch Tchr 24 (Sept.) 278-81. Rationale for drama performance based on what audience expects from this performance, what it accepts and to what extent the drama depends on spectacle.

2346 Heston, L. A. The Solo Performance of Prose Fiction. Spch Tchr 24 (Sept.) 269-77. Limitations of and possibilities for solo vs. group performance of prose.

2347 Hobbs, Gary. The Influence of Counterattitudinal Acting on the Attitudes of Actors. Spch Tchr 24 (Nov.) 323-34. Significant attitude change in subjects who acted rather than read a counterattitudinal role.

2348 Hynes, S. S. Dramatic Propaganda: Mercy Otis Warren's The Defeat, 1773. Today's Spch 23 (Fall) 21-7. The Defeat portrays some heroes and villains in movement for colonial independence; demonstrates Warren's skill as propagandist early in 1770's.

2349 Kolin, P. C. Obstacles to Communication in Cat on a Hot Tin Roof. Wstn Spch Comm 39 (Spring) 74-80. Interpersonal communication viewed as most difficult things in play, as well as one of most important; examines barriers to communication.

2350 Lass, N. J., & D. R. Lutz. The Consistency of Temporal Speech Characteristics in a Repetitive Oral Reading Task. Lang & Spch 18 (July-Sept.) 227-35. To explore consistency of secondary school temporal speech character in a repetitive oral reading task.

2351 Lee, R. R., & D. E. Hewes. Reliability and Validity of Two Empirical Measures of Oral Interpretation. J Amer Forensics Assc 12 (Fall) 61-9. Both behavioral and impressionistic measures of OI produce acceptable estimates of reliability and validity.

2352 Logue, C. M. Abstracts of Doctoral Dissertations in the Field of Speech Communication, 1974. Bibliographic Annual in Speech Communication 6 (1975) 109-96. Eleven dissertations in OI, pp. 130-4.

2353 Maher, M. Z. What Should Be the Role for Drama in Oral Interpretation? A Response. ISS in Interp 1 (Fall) 12-4. Drama and OI used together.

2354 Maher, M. Z. Internal Rhetorical Analysis and the Interpretation of Drama. Cent Sts Spch J 26 (Winter) 267-73. Viability of internal rhetoric from inside the realm of the play.

2355 Matlon, R. J. , & I. R. Matlon. Index to Journals in Communication Studies Through 1974. Falls Church, Va: SCA, 1975. Index to 13 speech-related journals with author and subject index.

2356 Matter, G. A. , & Lewis Davis. Response to a Reply to Metaphor and Linguistic Theory. Qrt J Spch 61 (Oct.) 322-5. Discusses metaphorical process theory and disclaims Campbell's article.

2357 McElroy, Hilda-Njoki. Problems in Developing and Teaching an Interpretation of Black Drama Course. Spch Tchr 24 (Sept.) 211-7. Academic considerations and techniques in coordinating black drama course.

2358 O'Brien, Jill. The Interpreter and Ethnic Texts: Jewish-American Literary Experience. Spch Tchr 24 (Sept.) 195-201. While OI may not have experience within domain of ethnic lit, he may expand understanding through textual experience and the experience organized, sharpened, and exposed by the literary creation.

2359 Overstreet, Robert. Sarah Bernhardt in Savannah. Wstn Spch Comm 39 (Winter) 20-5. Divine Sarah's performances in Savannah in 1892 and 1906.

2360 Overstreet, Robert. A Note on Public Reading in the Life of Emperor Claudius. Spch Tchr 24 (Mar.) 171-2. Clarifies some points of interest about oral reading in Claudius' life.

2361 Paden, F. F. Riddling in W. H. Auden's "The Wanderer. " Spch Mono 42 (Mar.) 42-6. In OI, first step is to unravel language which reflects Auden's view that all experience is a riddle. Analysis of this technique.

2362 Phillips, Jean. Flor y Canto: Chicano Literature and Performance. Spch Tchr 24 (Sept.) 202-8. Combination of English and Spanish is challenge to OI, but offers exciting possibilities.

2363 Schweik, R. C. Rhetorical Art and Literary Form in Mill's The Subjection of Women. Qrt J Spch 61 (Feb.) 23-30. Mill's work seen from different point of view.

2364 Skloot, Robert.   Putting Out the Light: Staging the Theme of Pinter's Old Times.   Qrt J Spch 61 (Oct.) 265-70. Focuses on Pinter's theatrical use of light to define his ideas concerning individual's existential obligation to create the self.

2365 Sloan, T. O.   Review of Speech in the English Novel by Norman Page.   Qrt J Spch 61 (Oct.) 369-70.

2366 Speer, J. H.   Folklore and Interpretation: Symbiosis. Sthn Spch Comm J 40 (Summer) 365-76.   Rationale for more productive relationship between folklore and IO.

2367 Speer, J. H.   Culture Contact Through Literature Performance.   Spch Tchr 24 (Sept.) 209-10.   Reading hours were based on lit of different cultures to enrich students.

2368 Sturges, C. A.   The Effect of a Narrator's Presence on Audience Response to Character in the Staging of Narrative Literature.   Spch Tchr 24 (Jan.) 46-52.   Narrator's presence affects audience perception and interpretation of character, relationships of distance and reliability.

2369 Towns, Stuart, & C. L. Roberts.   A Bibliography of Speech, Theatre and Broadcasting in the South for the Year 1974. Sthn Spch Comm J 41 (Fall) 82-92.

2370 Valentine, K. B.   The Appeal of William Morris' Artistic Philosophy.   Ky J Comm Arts 6 (Spring) 10-1.   Arts as psychological necessity.

2371 Valentine, K. B.   Interpretation of Prose.   Ky J Comm Arts 6 (Fall) 7-8.   Guidelines for high school interpreters for contest work.

2372 Valentine, K. B.   Motifs from Nature in the Design Work & Prose Romances of William Morris 1876-96.   Vict Poetry 13 (Fall-Winter) 83-9.   Discussion of Morris' nature motifs.

1976

2373 Angoff, Charles.   The Ethnic Aspects of American Literature.   Lit Review 19 (Summer) 357-65.   Intercultural domination of American lit.

2374 Atwood, Norman.   Cordelia and Kent: Their Fateful Choice of Style.   Lang & Style 9 (Winter) 42-54.   Critique of opening scene in King Lear which shows Cordelia's and Kent's attitudes of open honesty and conflict with courtly style which presages their eventual tragedies.

2375 Bacon, W. A. A Sense of Being: Interpretation and the Humanities. Sthn Spch Comm J 41 (Winter) 135-41. Embraces humanities as fundamentally vital to betterment of human lot using OI as vehicle.

2376 Bacon, W. A. Review of Sloan and Waddington's The Rhetoric of Renaissance Poetry. Qrt J Spch 62 (Feb.) 87-9.

2377 Bacon, W. A. Review of C. H. Shattuck's John Philip Kemble Promptbooks. Qrt J Spch 62 (Apr.) 208.

2378 Beale, W. H. Colloquy I. on Rhetoric and Poetry: John Donne's "The Prohibition Revisited." Qrt J Spch 62 (Dec.) 376-86. Response to T. O. Sloan's rhetorical analysis of "The Prohibition." Finds Sloan's approach short, both in Sloan's application of rhetorical theory and in general postulates.

2379 Bilan, R. P. The Basic Concepts and Criteria of F. R. Leavis' Novel Criticism. Novel: Forum on Fiction 9 (Spring) 197-216. Leavis' view of novel as affirmation and criticism of life.

2380 Bleich, David. Pedagogical Directions in Subjective Criticism. College Engl 37 (Jan.) 454-67. Argues that assumptions of critical objectivity should be curtailed and superseded by assumption that consequential knowledge is developed, created, or synthesized by subjective initiative of individuals and groups.

2381 Booth, M. W. The Art of Words in Songs. Qrt J Spch 62 (Oct.) 242-9. Songs as rhetoric: songs increase impact of meaning in the mind by offering a mood or experience, as opposed to increasing impact through discursive meaning.

2382 Bowen, E. R. A Quarter-Century of Collegiate Oral Interpretation Festival Going. Comm Educ 25 (Mar.) 127-31. Major advantages of the festival; festival going offers opportunity to learn by listening as well as by performing.

2383 Bozek, Philip. Hugh McDiarmid's Early Lyrics: A Syntactic Examination. Lang & Style 9 (Winter) 29-41. Shows his view of man's relationship to earth: physical boundaries but mental freedom.

2384 Burke, Kenneth. Colloquy I. The Party Line. Qrt J Spch 62 (Feb.) 62-8. Background of modern rhetoric theory selectively surveyed and criticized by Burke, who cites many of his earlier works here. He concentrates on the new rhetoric.

2385 Burns, Landon. The Second Supplement of a Cross-Referenced Index. Stud in Short Fiction 13 (Spring) 113-276.
Short fiction anthology with author and title listings.

2386 Carringer, R. L. Rosebud, Dead or Alive: Narrative and
Symbolic Structure in Citizen Kane. PMLA 91 (Mar.)
185-93. Views Rosebud as intentional device which intensi-
fies rather than diminishes film's ironic complexity.

2387 Carson, H. L. Review of Bernard Dukore's Dramatic Theory & Criticism: Greeks to Grotowski. Qrt J Spch 62
(Feb.) 103. Review.

2388 Chantland, Gloria. The Case of the Reluctant Readers.
Today's Ed 65 (Nov. /Dec.) 32-39. Mystery tales and
oral reading by teacher led below average high school
seniors to increased reading rates, better comprehension,
and improved listening skills.

2389 Crawford, Richard. Watts for Singing: Metrical Poetry in
American Sacred Tunebooks 1761-1785. Early Amer Lit
11 (Fall) 139-46. Metrical psalms and hymns as popular
poetry in American colonies.

2390 Crusius, Tim. In Praise of Pirsig's Zen and the Art of
Motorcycle Maintenance. Wstn Spch Comm 40 (Summer)
168-77. Examination of Zen's content and form: content
(symbolic acts surrounding term quality) is manifest in
form (as movement toward the whole person).

2391 Daly, J. A.; J. C. McCroskey; & V. P. Richmond. Judgments of Quality Listening and Understanding Based Upon
Vocal Activity. Sthn Spch Comm J 41 (Winter) 189-97.
Analyzes major role vocal activity plays in interpersonal
interactions.

2392 Davis, Diana, & Ronald Taft. A Measure of Preference for
Speaking Rather Than Writing & Its Relationship to Expressive Language Skills in Adolescents. Lang and Spch
19 (July/Sept.) 224-35. Correlated positively with sociabil-
ity and quality of oral expression.

2393 Devine, M. E. , & C. M. Clark. The Stanislavski System
as a Tool for Teaching Dramatic Literature. College Engl
38 (Sept.) 15-24. Term paper assignment: write Stanis-
lavskian analysis of one character of own sex presented
from character's perspective. Much Ado used as example.

2394 Dillon, G. L. Clause, Pause and Punctuation in Poetry.
Linguistics: Intl Rev 169 (Mar.) 5-20. Study proposing
strategy for pause.

2395 Ekman, Paul. Movements with Precise Meanings. J of
Communication 26 (Summer) 14-26. Gestures or emblems
distinguished from illustrators.

2396 Fertow, F. M. Strata and Structure: A Reading of Shakespeare's Sonnet 73. Concerning Poetry 9 (Fall) 23-5.
Structural considerations of focus, movement, and formal
balance of sonnet form.

2397 Fish, S. E. How to Do Things with Austin & Searle:
Speech Act Theory and Literary Criticism. Mod Lang Notes
91 (Oct.) 983-1025. Uses speech act theory to interpret
Shakespeare's Coriolanus stressing limit of theory for literary criticism purposes.

2398 Foster, D. W. Reiterative Formulas in García Lorca's
Poetry. Lang & Style 9 (Summer) 171-91. García Lorca's
use of imagery sustains emotional power.

2399 Fowler, Rowena. Metrics and the Transformational-Generative Model. Lingua 38 (Feb.) 21-36. Outlines historical
development and affiliations for generative metrics.

2400 Francis, Claude. Vincente Huidobro: Image as Magic.
Papers on Lang & Lit 12 (Summer) 311-20. Huidobro's
theory of creativism and unveiling of surreal.

2401 Frye, Northrop. The Responsibilities of the Critic. Mod
Lang Notes 91 (Oct.) 797-813. How words fit together
(structure) is primary to how they reflect world. Myth
is common origin of poetry, history, and philosophy.
Critic's role is to interpret structure.

2402 Genette, Gerard. Boundaries of Narrative. New Lit Hist 8
(Autumn) 1-13. Traces history of diegesis and mimesis.
Presents exclusions and restrictive conditions and how
modern lit becomes a contestation of the narrative term.

2403 Gerstenberger, Donna. Conceptions Literary & Otherwise:
Women Writers & the Modern Imagination. Novel: Forum
on Fiction 9 (Winter) 141-50. Problems contemporary
feminist writer faces when confronting myth and language.

2404 Gilbert, Connie, & Jill Dardig. Cut-Up Stories to Read
Aloud. Grade Tchr 93 (Mar.) 86-7. Group readings in
elementary school.

2405 Goldman, R. M., & W. D. Crano. Black Boy and Manchild
in the Promised Land: Content Analysis in the Study of
Value Change Over Time. J Black Stu 7 (Dec.) 169-80.
Comparative possibilities of content, analytic method in
personality assessment, and utility of social and psychological

theory as related to black experience in contemporary America.

2406 Gribben, Alan. It Is Unsatisfactory to Read to One's Self: Mark Twain's Informal Readings. Qrt J Spch 62 (Feb.) 49-56. Twain's interpretive reading, especially of Browning, Hay, Kipling, and others.

2407 Haberly, D. T. The Literature of an Invisible Nation. J Black Stud 7 (Dec.) 133-50. Finding a language for lit of invisible black nation in white America.

2408 Hatch, James. Speak to Me in Those Old Words, You Know, Those La-la Words, Those Tung-tung Sounds: Some African Influences on the Afro-American Theatre. Yale Theat 8 (Fall) 25-34. Recounts historical, conscious, and intuitive use of neo-Africanisms and Africanisms by American playwrights.

2409 Hiatt, Mary. The Sexology of Style. Lang & Style 9 (Spring) 98-107. Lexical survey of randomly selected books by male and female authors point to differences in writing styles and suggests that style may be culturally bound but changing American values may bring other differences.

2410 Hinz, E. J., & J. J. Teunissen. Savior and Cock: Allusion and Icon in Lawrence's The Man Who Died. J Mod Lit 5 (Apr.) 279-96. Lawrence derived story's central symbolism of risen Savior as escaped cock from Vatican's phallic icon Savior of the world.

2411 Hirschfield-Medalia, Adeline. Stylized Movement in Interpreters Theatre. Comm Educ 25 (Mar.) 111-20. Search for a rationale and system of training for combining movement and musical accompaniment with spoken word in variety of forms of OI.

2412 Hirst, D. J. A Distinctive Feature Analysis of English Intonation. Ling: Intl Rev 168 (Feb.) 27-42. Suggests that five intonation features account for all syntactic ambiguities that occur in language.

2413 Howell, W. S. Colloquy II. The Two Party Line: A Reply to Kenneth Burke. Qrt J Spch 62 (Feb.) 69-77. Howell examines dramatistic view of rhetoric by citing works such as Shakespeare's Julius Caesar and Dante's Divine Comedy, while contrasting his views of rhetoric and lit criticism with those articulated in Burke's Counterstatement.

2414 Hunt, S. A. Readers Theatre Bibliography: Supplement and Up-Date. Cent Sts Spch J 27 (Winter) 320-1. Supplement to other bibliographies.

2415 Irmscher, W. F. Analogy as an Approach to Rhetorical
Theory. College Comp Comm 27 (Dec.) 350-4. Adapts
Burke's Pentad into rhetorical model for all arts enabling
analogies between them to be drawn.

2416 Jeffrey, P. R., & Jane Work. ERIC Report: The Teaching
of Literature Through Performance. Comm Educ 25
(Mar.) 132-7. Focus on performance of lit to heighten
lit awareness and self-understanding.

2417 Jeffrey, R. C. Speech and the Humanities: Departmental
Philosophy. Sthn Spch Comm J 41 (Winter) 158-64. Emphasizes need to train future students' humanistic values.

2418 Johnson, Chris. Performance and Role-Playing in Soyinka's
Madmen & Specialists. J Commonwealth Lit 10 (Apr.)
27-33. Political play on Nigerian Civil War.

2419 Jones, Phyliss. Biblical Rhetoric and the Pulpit Literature
of New England. Early Amer Lit 11 (Winter) 245-58.
Sermon as principal pop literary form in early New England.

2420 Joost, Nicholas. A Handful of Dust: Evelyn Waugh and the
Novel of Manners. Papers on Lang and Lit 12 (Spring)
177-96. A Handful of Dust as work that fuses complex
allusiveness and violence within structured framework of
novel of manners.

2421 Jordan, W. J., & W. C. Adams. I. A. Richards' Concept
of Tenor-Vehicle Interaction. Cent Sts Spch J 27 (Summer) 136-43. To facilitate the study of metaphor, Richards
developed terms "tenor" and "vehicle" as labels for consistent elements of metaphor and initiated considerations
concerning interaction of tenor and vehicle in resolution of
metaphoric discourse.

2422 Kishler, T. C. Hobbes' Answer to Davenant: Some Aspects
of the Style. Lang & Style 9 (Spring) 130-8. Analysis of
Hobbes' work shows clarity of his thinking; uses language
to explain and to persuade.

2423 Kostelanetz, Richard. From An ABC of Contemporary Reading. Poetry Austr 59 (June) 33-40. Guide to perception
and reading new forms of lit.

2424 Lapidus, L. A. Lean Not Onto Thine Own Understanding:
Grammar as Theme in George Herbert's "Good Friday" and
"Prayer (I)." Qrt J. Spch 62 (Apr.) 167-78. Herbert's
works lift reader out of poet's mere words so that reader
feels a unity of God and Man as something understood.

2425 Lee, David. The Inheritors and Transformational Generative Grammar. Lang & Style 9 (Spring) 77-97. Study

of language shows how it affects perception of Lok's world.

2426 Leggett, B. J. The Poetry of Insight: Persona and Point of View in Housman. Vict Poetry 14 (Winter) 325-39. Restrictions imposed by persona relegate him to minor poet.

2427 Levi, A. W. Teaching Literature as a Humanity. J Gen Educ 28 (Spring) 283-7. Consideration of lit's relations to humanistic disciplines.

2428 Loesch, K. T. Review of The Study of Oral Interpretation: Theory and Comment, edited by Richard Haas and David Williams. J Aesthetics Art Crit 34 (Spring) 360-1. Basis in aesthetics and lit theory.

2429 Long, B. O. Recent Field Studies in Oral Literature and Their Bearing on Old Testament Criticism. Vetus Testamentum 26 (Apr.) 187-98. Attention drawn to recent anthropological lit on the oral tradition and some new implications for Old Testament studies are found, with special reference to form and traditio-historical research.

2430 Maher, M. Z. Literature as a Liberal Art: An Assessment. Comm Educ 25 (Mar.) 91-2, 131. Using oral study of lit as context, suggests a role for teacher, a professional who may function as a guide through fluctuating ethical climates.

2431 Malkin, Michael, & Pamela Malkin. Readers Theatre: A New Stage for Learning. Tchr 93 (Apr.) 70-2. Summarizes RT values, techniques and theory for school children.

2432 Martin, E. G. They're on the Air. Grade Tchr 93 (Feb.) 47-8. Students learn oral skills by broadcasting over own radio.

2433 Morrison, Blake. In Defence of Minimalism. Crit Quart 18 (Summer) 43-51. Affirmation of minimalism in modern British poetry.

2434 Murphy, M. C. Detection of the Burglarizing of Burgh: A Sequel. Comm Mono 43 (June) 140-1. Origins of Sheridan's rhetorical grammar; concludes that Sheridan himself, contrary to Parrish's earlier thesis, plagiarized Burgh's The Art of Speaking by publishing it with a rhetorical grammar in 1781.

2435 Naida, Patricia. Light and Enlightenment in Flannery O'Connor's Fiction. Stud in Short Fict 13 (Winter) 31-6. Recurring imagery of treelines, sun, and purple and their function in fiction.

2436 Nelson, Gary. Reading Criticism. PMLA 91 (Oct.) 801-15.
Examines manipulation of readers by writer/critic. Suggests more iconoclastic approach by critic.

2437 Nevo, Ruth. Again, "Byzantium." Lang & Style 9 (Fall)
247-59. Critique of Yeats' poem and its statement of author's view of visionary fancy: poet as prophet.

2438 Nnolim, C. E. The Journey Motif: Vehicle of Form,
Structure and Meaning in Mongo Beti's Mission to Kala. J
Black Stud 7 (Dec.) 181-94. Way in which journey motif
shapes novelistic form.

2439 Perrin, Norman. The Interpretation of the Gospel of Mark.
Interpretation: J Bible & Theol 30 (Apr.) 115-24. Literary criticism's concern for the text of Mark as a unity.

2440 Poyatos, Fernando. Language in the Context of Total Body
Communication. Ling: Intl Rev 168 (Feb.) 49-62.
Treats and suggests more broadly based investigation of
language as more than verbal constructs only.

2441 Pritner, C. L. The Theatrical Contract: An Alternative to
Theatrical Convention. Players Mag 51 (Summer) 142-5.
Director/actor/audience relationship.

2442 Reed, W. L. The Problem with a Poetics of the Novel.
Novel: Forum on Fiction 9 (Winter) 101-13. Problems
inherent in poetics of novel as lit form.

2443 Rickert, W. E. Structural Functions of Rhyme and the Performance of Poetry. Qrt J Spch 62 (Oct.) 250-5. Rhyme
affects formality, audience expectation and use of closure
in building the mood of poem. Performer cannot perceive
the total poem without considering rhyme and one cannot
consider rhyme without considering the total poem.

2444 Ross, Donald. Who's Talking? How Characters Become
Narrators in Fiction. Mod Lang Notes 91 (Dec.) 1222-42.
Discusses linguistic cues (such as tense and attribution)
which reveal point of view in third-person narrative.

2445 Schneider, R. J. The Visible Metaphor. Comm Educ 25
(Mar.) 121-6. The physical or nonverbal way to stage
metaphor to illustrate transformation and illumination of
text.

2446 Schoenberg, E. I. The Identity of the Cyclops Narrator in
James Joyce's Ulysses. J Mod Lit 5 (Sept.) 534-9.
Poses the identity of this narrator as Simon Dedalus.

2447 Shaughnessy, M. X. Black Writers and American Values.
Ill Schl J 56 (Fall) 51-63. Reviews three writers from

different periods (Baldwin, Ellison, Wright) to show change in attitudes of American blacks.

2448 Shuman, Richard. The Place of Drama in Today's High Schools. Ill Schls J 56 (Winter) 3-11. Sees drama as essential in school activities to develop individual student growth in experience and understanding.

2449 Sloan, T. O. Colloquy II. On Prohibition and Repeal. Qrt J Spch 62 (Dec.) 387-8. Succinct critical exploration of the application of new approaches to rhetoric.

2450 Smith, R. E. Student Literature Preferences in the Basic Oral Interpretation Course. Comm Educ 25 (Mar.) 93-102. Number and types of materials presented in 20 OI classes taught over five-year period.

2451 Somers, Bill. Relational Interaction: An Alternative to Developing a Character. Players Mag 51 (Dec./Jan.) 54-7. Relationship and attitudes determine character building.

2452 Spelman, J. L. Spring Smash. Grade Tchr 93 (Mar.) 78-80. Interpretation of poetry in third grade.

2453 Steele, Shelby. Ralph Ellison's Blues. J Black Stud 7 (Dec.) 151-68. Influence of blues on Ellison's existentialism.

2454 Swiss, Thom. Approaches to Teaching Concrete Poetry: An Annotated Bibliography. College Engl 38 (Sept.) 46-9. Visual, phonetic and kinetic poems briefly distinguished, with sources suggested for further exploration.

2455 Tammany, J. E. Readers Theatre Workshop 76. Spch & Dram 25 (Autumn) 29-31. Productions at London RT workshop described.

2456 Todorov, Tzvetan. The Origins of Genres. New Lit Hist 8 (Autumn) 159-70. Centers on transformations that certain speech acts undergo to produce lit genres. Both arise from codification of discursive properties.

2457 Walker, Warren. Bibliography. Stud in Short Fiction 13 (Summer) 395-419. List of short story explications, Apr. 1, 1975, to Mar. 31, 1976.

2458 Ward, J. W. N. J. Loftis' Black Anima: A Problem in Aesthetics. J Black Stud 7 (Dec.) 195-210. Exposure of black concerns through analysis of Loftis' work as problem in aesthetics.

2459 Weaver, R. L. Josiah Holbrook: Feeding the Passion for Self-Help. Crit Qrt 24 (Fall) 10-8. Role of Holbrook, father of the American lyceum, an adult self-help, self-education movement, 1830-1850.

2460 Wilcher, Robert. What's It Meant to Mean?: An Approach to Beckett's Theatre. Crit Quart 18 (Summer) 9-37. Impact of Beckett's plays in performance: symbolic without symbolism.

2461 Winterowd, W. R. The Rhetorical Transaction of Reading. College Comp Comm 27 (May) 185-91. Relates rhetorical concepts of invention (logos, ethos, and pathos), arrangement, and style to reading theory.

2462 Young, R. J., Jr. Unpredictable Features in the Style of Benavente's Los Intereses Creados. Lang & Style 9 (Spring) 108-17. Approach to language of main characters shows their drives and goals.

1977

2463 Bacon, W. A. Higher Education and Speech Communication: The Next Decade. Sthn Spch Comm J 43 (Fall) 9-15. Communication, as a humanistic discipline, should lead us outward.

2464 Bacon, W. A. Review of James Edie's Speaking & Meaning: The Phenomenology of Language. Qrt J Spch 63 (Apr.) 208.

2465 Barge, Laura. Colored Images in the Black Dark: Samuel Beckett's Later Fiction. PMLA 92 (Mar.) 273-84. Analyzes progression from earlier works to later ones tracing hero figure.

2466 Beicken, P. U. Kafka's Narrative Rhetoric. J Mod Lit 6 (Sept.) 398-409. Use of narrative rhetoric to influence reader to author's viewpoint.

2467 Bolton, G. M. Psychical Distance in Acting. Brit J Aesthetics 17 (Winter) 63-7. Physical, evoked, spatial, temporal contexts determine aesthetic distance.

2468 Bunge, N. L. Unreliable Artist-Narrators in Hawthorne's Short Stories. Studs in Short Fict 14 (Spring) 145-50. Focus on artist-narrators who do not possess brotherhood.

2469 Chisholm, David. Generative Prosody & English Verse. Poetics 6 (Sept.) 111-53. Rules of prosody in lyric iambic pentameter.

2470 Crouch, I. M. Robert Frost: Rhetoric and Correspondence. New Mex Comm 4 (Oct.) 32-40. Finds Frost intent on achieving communication with readers.

2471 Crouch, I. M. Rhetoric, Drama, and the Oral Interpreter. New Mex Comm 3 (Apr.) 11-20. Indicates rhetorical analysis advantageous for dramatic interpretation.

2472 Crowell, Laura. Three Sheers for Kenneth Burke. Qrt J Spch 63 (Apr.) 150-67. Burke uses word "sheer" seven times on single page in last two major works; author proposes to use Burke's method of indexing as basis for way into his eight major books.

2473 DeWolfe, A. S. The Many Faces & Facets of Empathy. NC J Spch Drama 11 (Fall) 5-22. Discussion of the concept of empathy and ways to test it.

2474 Espinola, J. C. Oral Interpretation Performance: An Act of Publication. Wstn J Spch Comm 41 (Spring) 90-7. Scholarly approach to OI performance.

2475 Fine, E. C., & J. H. Speer. A New Look at Performance. Comm Mono 44 (Nov.) 374-89. Discussion of importance of performance of interpretation.

2476 Forrest, W. C. Empathy, the Kinesthetic Feel of Language, & Shakespeare's Sonnet 65. NC J Spch Drama 11 (Fall) 37-49. Use of empathy in OI.

2477 Gibbs, L. W. Ritual Play and Transcendent Mystery. Bucknell Rev 23 (Spring) 127-39. Social, psychological, and theological ideals for play, drama, and ritual.

2478 Gourd, William. Cognitive Complexity and Theatrical Information Processing. Comm Mono 44 (June) 136-51. Experimental study of audience response to plays and characters based on processing abilities of audience members.

2479 Hays, Michael. Dramatic Literature as History: Some Suggestions About Theory and Method. Bucknell Rev 23 (Fall) 131-41. German theatre is example that drama, like history, provides structural and cultural information.

2480 Heller, J. R. Enjambment as a Metrical Force in Romantic Conversation Poems. Poetics 6 (Mar.) 15-25. Reading of run-on sentences in verse.

2481 Hopkins, M. F. An Evening with Reed Whittemore. Chapter in Group Performance of Literature, ed. by B. W. Long; Lee Hudson; & P. R. Jeffrey. Englewood Cliffs, NJ: Prentice-Hall.

2482 Hopkins, M. F. Structuralism: Its Implications for the Performance of Prose Fiction. Comm Mono 44 (June) 93-105. Structuralism and linguistic theatre with reference to Barthes and Virginia Woolf.

2483   Johnson, Irmgard. Senzo Sai No Performance: An Eye and
       Ear Witness Account. Sthn Spch Comm J 43 (Fall) 33-47.
       Description of special Japanese Noh drama performance.

2484   Kaplan, S. J. , & G. P. Mohrmann. Reader Text Audience:
       Oral Interpretation and Cognitive Tuning. Qrt J Spch 63
       (Feb.) 59-65. Question: would different communication
       roles in OI situations result in different perceptions of the
       lit?

2485   Loesch, K. T. Empathy with Unconscious Fantasy in Keats'
       Ode to Melancholy Literary Possibilities of an Adapted
       Psychoanalytic Technique. NC J Spch Drama 11 (Fall)
       50-67. Psychoanalytic concepts of empathy in OI.

2486   McAdams, Mona. A Study in the Oral Interpretation of the
       Laboratory. New Mex Comm 3 (Apr.) 20-8. Suggestion
       for teaching OI to high school students.

2487   McHughes, J. L. The Poesis of Space: Prosodic Structures
       in Concrete Poetry. Qrt J Spch 63 (Apr.) 169-79. Pros-
       ody of concrete poetry.

2488   Meserole, H. T. Shakespeare: Annotated World Bibliog-
       raphy for 1976. Shakespeare Qtrly 28 (Autumn) 389-512.
       Issue is bibliography and subject index.

2489   Meyer, J. J. Bartleby the Scrivener: Performing the Nar-
       rator's Inner Conflict in Chamber Theatre. Comm Educ
       26 (Nov.) 348-51. Conflicting reactions of narrative can
       best be revealed and highlighted by using two narrators.

2490   Mitchell, Sally. Sentiment and Suffering: Women's Recrea-
       tional Reading in the 1860's. Vict Studs 21 (Autumn) 29-
       46. Review and analysis of lit read by women of Victorian
       middle class.

2491   Morse, Jonathan. Dos Passos' U. S. A. and the Illusions
       of Memory. Mod Fiction Stud 23 (Winter) 543-56. His-
       torical figures used in U. S. A. blur boundary between
       history and aesthetics.

2492   Osborne, Michael. The Evolution of the Archetypal Sea in
       Rhetoric and Poetic. Qrt J Spch 63 (Dec.) 347-63.
       Traces process of sea symbol as transformed by dramatic
       changes in human circumstance; also investigates most in-
       teresting feature of this evolution, the gradual emergence
       of two separate patterns of meaning for sea symbol in
       poetry and public rhetoric.

2493   Parrella, Gilda. Empathy in the Works of Dylan Thomas.
       NC J Spch Drama 11 (Fall) 23-36. Thomas' writings il-
       lustrate empathy in poetic technique and attitude.

2494 Parssinen, T. M. Mesmeric Performers. Vict Studs 21 (Autumn) 87-104. Historical review and analysis of mesmerism in early Victorian England.

2495 Pazereskis, John. Multiple Casting in Publicly Performed Group Interpretation. Comm Educ 26 (Mar.) 169-71. Using several performers to portray several facets of one character may work where audience knows conventions of CT, but such may be confusing to other audiences.

2496 Petrosky, A. R. Response to Literature. Engl J 66 (Oct.) 96-8. Views roles of personality, culture, cognition, growth and development in influencing a reader's response to lit.

2497 Potts, M. L. Developing Creativity: Anaïs Nin a Model. Wstn J Spch Comm 41 (Spring) 83-9. Nin as model of newly emerging concepts of humanistic freedom; diary seen as aesthetic presentation of Rank's theory of creativity.

2498 Ramsey, J. W. "The Wife Who Goes Out Like a Man Comes Back as a Hero": The Art of Two Oregon Indian Narratives. PMLA 92 (Jan.) 9-18. Structural analysis of dramatic elements of two myth-narratives as appeal for reclamation of native Indian lit.

2499 Rickert, W. E. Winston Churchill's Archetypal Metaphors: A Mythopoetic Translation of World War II. Cent Sts Spch J 28 (Summer) 106-12. Churchill's metaphoric language used in WWII speeches transforms British public's view from literal reality into that of archetypal struggle of good over evil.

2500 Sattler, E. E. Narrative Stance in Kafka's "Josephine." J Mod Lit 6 (Sept.) 410-18. Interpretation of work through study of shifting narrative viewpoint.

2501 Shaver, C. L.; David Ritchey; & Gresdna Doty, eds. Southern Theatre History: A Bibliography of Theses and Dissertations. Sthn Spch Comm J 42 (Summer) 362-739. Arranged by southern states.

2502 Sloan, T. O. Readers Theatre Illusions and Classroom Realities. Engl J 66 (May) 73-8. Real magic of RT cannot be produced until all the pretense is dropped.

2503 Sheborn, D. R. Mythic Criticism and Interpretation. Comm Educ 26 (Mar.) 160-3. Mythic interpretations exist as options in performing lit and critics and performers should be flexible enough to utilize those options.

2504 Small, Christopher. Pitlochry Festival Theatre: Scotland's Theatre in the Hills. Perf Arts Rev 7 (1977) 383-452.

Reviews history and future of arts festival in Scotland which includes poetry readings, drama, music, and visual arts.

2505 Steirck, Philip. Naive Narration: Classic to Post-Modern. Mod Fiction Stud 23 (Winter) 531-42. Examples of novels where jumps in narrative voice dramatize naivete of writer in projecting younger self as opposed to mature self.

2506 Taubman, Joseph. Some Implications of Copyright to the Arts and Education. Performing Arts Rev 7 (1977) 296-327. Examines copyright law and performing arts.

2507 Towns, W. S. The Florida Chautauqua: A Case Study in American Education. Sthn Spch Comm J 42 (Spring) 228-45. Elocution at 19th-century Florida Chautauqua.

2508 Toyama, S. X., & A. I. Ohsawa. New Tendency in Japanese Reading: An Oral Style. J Reading 21 (Dec.) 253-7. Lit written in oral style credited with increasing appreciation.

2509 Valentine, K. B. Readers Theatre Productions of Combined Arts: The Pre-Raphaelite Paradigm. Wstn Spch Comm J 41 (Spring) 98-109. Discussion of paintings as mute poetry and poetry as spoken paintings.

2510 Van Metre, P. D. Oral Interpretation, A Path to Meaning. Lang Arts 54 (Mar.) 278-82. Selection adaptation staging of lit by and for children.

2511 Weiher, Carol. American History on Stage in the 1960's: Something Old, Something New. Qrt J Spch 63 (Dec.) 406-12. Commonplace historical illusions peddled over the years on the American stage were countered in the 60's by drama which used historical materials in original ways, and Americans were made to view their heritage in a new light.

2512 Wilson, D. K. Developing Skill in the Oral Reading of Informational Prose. Comm Educ 26 (Nov.) 352-4. Effective articulation is as necessary in reading informational prose as in reading poetry.

1978

2513 Adair, Suzanne; Margaret Davidson; & E. C. Fine. Behavioral Objectives for an Introductory Course in Oral Interpretation. Comm Educ 27 (Jan.) 68-71. Proposes system whereby student answers questions related to poems and later performs some of the poems to meet those objectives; shown as effective method of teaching OI.

2514 Banfield, Ann. Where Epistemology, Style and Grammar
Meet Literary History: The Development of Represented
Speech and Thought. New Lit History 9 (Spring) 415-54.
Consciousness may include that passive reception of speech
which is hearing (and interpreting) but it includes active
powers of expression and thought which find their equival-
ents in linguistic functions.

2515 Beckerman, Bernard. Explorations in Shakespeare's Drama.
Shakespeare Qrtly 29 (Spring) 133-45. Performance is
considered central approach to Shakespeare study.

2516 Benson, P. C., & Christine Hjelt. Listening Competence:
A Prerequisite to Communication. Mod Lang J 42 (Mar.)
85-90. Review of linear, verbal habit called listening.
Applied primarily for teachers of second language, but
also applicable to oral reading.

2517 Benson, T. W. The Senses of Rhetoric: A Topical System
for Critics. Cent Sts Spch J 29 (Winter) 237-50. After
classifying rhetorical critics according to genre of rhetoric
they criticize, Benson notes that his system is not concerned with mere form, but with action as well.

2518 Block, Ed, Jr. Lyric Voice and Reader Response: One
View of the Transaction to Modern Poetics. 20th Cent Lit
24 (Summer) 154-68. Suggests how four poems in differing
styles lend themselves to contrastive analysis of reader
response.

2519 Bogen, James. Metaphors as Theory Fragments. J of Aesthetics and Art Crit 37 (Winter) 177-88. Determining con-
vincing and unconvincing metaphors.

2520 Brown, Janet. Kenneth Burke and the Mod Donna: The
Dramatistic Method Applied to Feminist Criticism. Cent
Sts Spch J 29 (Summer) 138-46. Posits use of drama
theory as a criterion for identifying feminist impulse in
dramatic art.

2521 Brown, Merle. Poetic Listening. New Lit Hist 10 (Autumn)
125-39. Poems can be human creations and not just psy-
chic process.

2522 Burdick, N. R. "The Coatsville Address:" Crossroads of
Rhetoric and Poetry. Wstn J Spch Comm 42 (Spring) 73-
82. "The Coatsville Address" is marriage of poetic and
rhetorical structure that insures its survival.

2523 Burns, Edward. Introduction: To Tell It as So. 20th Cent
Lit 24 (Spring) 3-7. Introduction to special edition of
Gertrude Stein.

2524 Cain, M. A. Born to Read: Making a Reading Culture. Tchr 95 (Jan.) 64-6. Effective reading aloud part of literary culture.

2525 Cassata, M. B. Profiles of the Users and Usages of Afro-American Literature. J Black Stud 9 (Sept.) 45-66. Communications and library research strategies for studies in black experience.

2526 Clare, John. Form in Vers Libre. Eng 27 (Summer & Autumn) 150-70. Includes discussion of sounds of verse.

2527 Collard, Christopher. Greek Drama. Class Rev 92 (1978) 69-70. Reviews Peter Walcot: Greek Drama in Its Theatrical & Social Context (Cardiff: U of Wales Press, 1976), which stresses Greek drama as oral form.

2528 De Grazia, Margreta. Shakespeare's View of Language. Shakespeare Qrtly 29 (Summer) 374-88. Shakespeare's own view of language differs from current language theory.

2529 Elgin, Suzette. Don't No Revolutions Hardly Ever Come by Here. College Engl 39 (Mar.) 791-9. Spoof of oral English and defense of transformational grammar.

2530 Elsea, J. G. Interpretation & Society. J Arizona Comm & Theatre Assoc 9 (Spring) 27-31. Question and answer form the argument for interpretation in social contexts.

2531 Enos, R. L. The Hellenic Rhapsode. Wstn J Spch Comm 42 (Spring) 134-43. Efforts of rhapsodes to preserve the oral nature of Homerick Greek, both in practice and also in theoretical development of notational systems, justifies their association with the history of rhetoric.

2532 Faller, B. A. The Basic Basic: Getting Kids to Read. Learning: Mag for Creative Tching 6 (Feb.) 100-1. Importance of reading aloud to children in classroom.

2533 Farwell, M. R. Feminist Criticism & the Concept of the Poetic Persona. Bucknell Rev 24 (Spring) 139-56. Critic must consider sexual identity.

2534 Feld, T. B. An Aide to Reading. Tchr 95 (Mar.) 89-91. Reading aloud as effective teaching method.

2535 Freeman, D. C. Keats's "To Autumn": Poetry as Process and Pattern. Lang and Style: An Internat'l J 11 (Winter) 3-17. How Keats' syntactic strategy functions to help create poetic form and statement in one of his richest short poems.

2536 Groff, Patrick. Readers Theatre by Children. Elem Schl J 79 (Sept.) 15-22. Its use for development in children of oral and critical reading skills and interest in lit.

2537 Hainsworth, J. B. Winged Word. Class Rev 92 (1978) 207-8. Review Berkeley Peabody's The Winged Word: A Study in the Technique of Ancient Greek Oral Composition as Seen Principally Through Hesiod's Works and Days (Albany: St. U. of N.Y. Press, 1975).

2538 Hoffer, S. P. Studying Small Group Communication & Interpreters Theatre. J Arizona Comm & Theatre Assoc 9 (Spring) 14-9. Application of Crowell & Scheidel categories for analysis of idea development to interpret theatre rehearsals.

2539 Honeyman, D. E. Attitude: A Holistic View for the Interpreter. Cent Sts Spch J 29 (Fall) 194-200. Analyze and synthesize what is meant by term, attitude, so as to gain a holistic understanding of its meaning and application to the interpretation of poetry.

2540 Kase, J. B.; S. M. Sikes; & C. D. Spielberger. Emotional Reactions to Frightening and Neutral Scenes in Story Theatre. Comm Mono 45 (June) 181-6. Experimental study of impact of dramatic scenes on emotional reactions of children.

2541 Khatchadourian, Haig. Movement and Action in the Performing Arts. J of Aesthetic and Art Crit 37 (Fall) 25-36. Relation of movement to action in dramatic work and reality.

2542 Kintgen, Eugene. Psycholinguistics and Literature. College Engl 39 (Mar.) 755-69. Cognitive approach to lit, specifying what happens to readers as they read.

2543 Madden, David. The Singer. Dramatics 50 (Sept./Oct. 78) 22-32. Text and discussion of widely performed OI and RT piece.

2544 Marder, Louis. Teaching Through Performance. Shakespeare Newslet 28 (Feb.) 1, 6. Workshop at Southern Illinois University. Focus: Shakespeare on film, oral interpretation and coaching.

2545 Marder, Louis. Wallace Bacon of Northwestern Stars in Interpreting Shakespeare Film. Shakespeare Newslet 28 (Feb.) 5. 33-minute color film, "A Sense of the Other." Bacon's abilities bring students to love text: scenes from Macbeth, Pericles, etc.

2546 Mazor, Rickey. Drama as Experience. Lang Arts 55 (Mar) 328-33. Improvisational drama for problem solving in intercultural schools.

2547 Merren, James. The Resolute Wife, or a Hazard of New Criticism. Short Fict 15 (Summer) 291-300. Argues for contextual as well as formal criticism.

2548 Meserole, H. T. Shakespeare: Annotated World Bibliography for 1977. Shakespeare Qrt 29 (Autumn) 456-619. Issue is bibliography and subject index.

2549 Morrison, Johanna. Your Voice Is a Musical Instrument-- Learn to Play It. Dramatics 49 (Mar./Apr.) 31-7. Offers ideas for vocal development and improvement.

2550 O'Neill, Terry, & William Paden, Jr. Toward the Performance of Troubadour Poetry: Speech and Voice in Pierre Vidal. Educ Theat J 30 (Dec.) 482-94. As title suggests.

2551 O'Shea, Catherine, & Margaret Egan. A Primer of Drama Techniques for Teaching Literature. Engl J 67 (Feb. 78) 51. Dramatic action stimulates students to share lit and improves writing skills.

2552 Paden, F. F. Theatre Games and the Teaching of English. Engl J 67 (Feb. 78) 46-50. Drama techniques used to teach methods lit criticism.

2553 Paley, Vivian. The Use of Dramatics in Kindergarten. Elem Schl J 78 (May) 319-23. Dramatization and narration of stories used to develop effective speech in children.

2554 Pfeil, Fred. Icons for Clowns: American Writers Now. College Engl 39 (Jan.) 525-40. Explores 39 writers and their appearance.

2555 Pollack, Seymour. English Prosodics: A Contrastive Approach. Mod Lang J 42 (Dec.) 410-4. Review of separate phonological, syntactic and semantic components for sound patterns in oral English compared with oral Spanish.

2556 Postlewait, Thomas. Self-Performing Voices: Mind, Memory and Time in Beckett's Drama. 20th Cent Lit 24 (Winter) 473-91. Action of Beckett's drama is located essentially in minds of characters who are listening to the voices of consciousness.

2557 Psaty, B. M. Cicero's Literal Metaphor and Propriety. Cent Sts Spch J 29 (Summer) 107-17. Specific use of metaphor in Cicero.

2558 Raphael, Bonnie. Class Acts. Dramatics 50 (Nov./Dec.)
38-9. Helpful physical and vocal warmups.

2559 Ravenscroft, A. X., ed. Index. J Commonwealth Lit 13
(Dec.) 1-180. Superb index of lit of 1977 in Africa,
Australia, Canada, India, Malaysia, Singapore, New Zea-
land, Sri Lanka, and West Indies.

2560 Read, M. K. Fernando De Rojas' Vision of the Birth and
Death of Language. Mod Lang Notes 93 (Mar.) 163-75.
Excellent discussion analysis of De Rojas' La Celestina
and a language crisis that results in catastrophes.

2561 Richardson, N. J. Homer and Oral Poetry. Class Rev 92
(1978) 1-2. Review of G. S. Kirk: Homer & the Oral
Tradition. Cambridge: U. Press, 1976.

2562 Rickert, W. E. Commercializing Elocution: Parlor Books
for Home Entertainments. Sthn Spch Comm J 43 (Summer) 384-94. Parlor books were not intended to deny
elocution. Instead they were a vestige of 19th-century
society without a performing discipline that had matured
into an academically reputable field of study.

2563 Rigg, Pat. Dialect and/in/for Reading. Lang Arts 55
(Mar.) 285-90. Oral reading of dialect lit by children.

2564 Roberts, T. J. Fiction Outside Literature. Lit Review 22
(Fall) 5-21. Fiction as source of knowledge about reality.

2565 Roedder, Kathleen. Books for Children. Childhood Educ
55 (Oct.) 37-44. List of books appropriate for designated
age groupings included in all issues.

2566 Rosenberg, Joe. Rehearsal Problems in Bilingual Theatre.
Lat American Theatre Rev 2 (Spring) 81-90. Proposes
organic approach to language as aspect of social environment.

2567 Roser, Nancy, & Julie Jensen. Real Communication--The
Key to Early Reading and Writing. Childhood Educ 55
(Nov./Dec.) 90-3. Operational look at teaching child to
read; important for OI scholars as well.

2568 Salem, Robin. Interpretation as a Method for Group Discussion of Feminist Literature. J Arizona Comm & Theatre Assoc 9 (Spring) 7-13. Experimental study shows
participants increased self-esteem as a result of interpretation and discussion.

2569 Sojka, G. S. The American Short Story into Film. Studs
in Short Fict 15 (Spring) 203-4. Review of NET American
Short Stories Film Series.

2570 Stewig, J. W. Storyteller: Endangered Species. Lang Arts 55 (Mar.) 339-45. Storytelling techniques and values for teachers and children.

2571 Strine, M. S. The Confessions of Nat Turner: Styron's Meditation on History as Rhetorical Act. Qrt J Spch 64 (Oct.) 246-66. Styron's work seen not only as performing piece, but as rhetorical counterstatement to the argument that the only way to achieve racial justice is through violence.

2572 Sturdivant, P. S. "Ode to a Nightingale": Analysis for Oral Performance. Sthn Spch Comm J 43 (Winter) 162-3. Analysis explores structural divisions of poem as well as interlocking areas of tension surrounding the persona and the siren.

2573 Tucker, G. M. Prophetic Speech. Interpretation: J of Bible & Theology 32 (Jan.) 31-45. Oral communication was essential feature of prophet's vocation and work.

2574 Valentine, K. B., & Maureen Donovan. Rationale for Communication Arts in Correctional Institutions. J Arizona Comm & Theatre Assoc 9 (Spring) 2-6. OI as part of rehabilitation activities in penal institutions.

2575 Versteeg, Robert. Rehearsing Creatively: Freeing the Natural Actor Within Us. Dramatics 50 (Nov./Dec.) 32-9. 52 rehearsal techniques helpful for RT.

2576 Vitz, E. B. La Vie de Saint Alexis: Narrative Analysis of the Quest for the Sacred Subject. PMLA 93 (May) 396-407. Examines various aspects of the subject-object relation in medieval narrative.

2577 Taylor, M. V. The Grammar of Conduct: Speech Act Theory and the Education of Emma Woodhouse. Style 12 (Fall) 357-71. Searle's speech act theory applied to Jane Austen's work.

2578 Wagner, B. J. The Use of Role. Lang Arts 55 (Mar.) 323-7. Role playing by teacher and student to expand language awareness.

2579 Walker, J. E. Holistic Interpretation in Worship & Liturgy. J Arizona Comm & Theatre Assoc 9 (Spring) 21-6. Historical framework of communication arts in worship and liturgy from which holistic interpretation can be viewed.

2580 Whitehouse, P. G. The Meaning of Emotion in Dewey's Art as Experience. J Aesthetics and Art Crit 37 (Winter) 149-56. Emotion as directing force of aesthetic experience.

2581 Widmann, V. F. Developing Oral Reading Ability in Teen-
agers Through the Presentation of Children's Stories. J
Reading 21 (Jan.) 329-34. As title suggests.

1979

2582 Arnold, P. J. Agency, Action and Meaning in Movement:
An Introduction to Three New Terms. J of Phil of Sport
6 (1979) 49-57. Three concepts of movement are described: "movistruct," which is the visualization of the
performer's possible movement patterns; "movicept," the
performer's sense of flow patterns; and "movisymbol,"
the importance a performer places on a movement.

2583 Backscheider, P. R. Woman's Influence. Studs in the
Novel 11 (Spring) 3-22. Means and limits of influence in
novels by women.

2584 Beatty, M. J.; R. R. Behnke; & F. H. Goodyear. Effects
of Speeded Speech Presentations on Confidence Weighted
and Traditional Comprehension Scores. Comm Mono 46
(June) 147-51. Presentation rate measured by comprehension rate in experimental study.

2585 Bellringer, Alan. The Wings of the Dove: The Main Image.
Mod Lang Rev 74 (Jan.) 12-25. James' indirect presentation of his main image in his novel.

2586 Borrus, Bruce. Bellow's Critique of the Intellect. Mod
Fict Stud 25 (Spring) 29-46. Intellectual heroes in Bellow's
stories alienated from rest of society, unable to find productive use of their thinking.

2587 Bradley, B. E. Speech Communication and Liberal Education. Sthn Spch Comm J 45 (Autumn) 1-11. Argues for
speech communication as part of liberal education.

2588 Braunmuller, A. R. A World of Words in Pinter's Old
Times. Mod Lang Qrt 40 (Mar.) 53-74. The play-within-
a-play of varying actors' reports of facts in Pinter's
plays; narration altered in dramatic dialogues.

2589 Champagne, R. A. The Dialectics of Style: Insights from
the Semiology of Roland Barthes. Style 13 (Summer) 279-
91. Style as manner of relating writer and reader in
dialectics of text.

2590 Clemmer, E. J.; D. C. O'Connell; & Wayne Loui. Rhetorical Pauses in Oral Reading. Lang and Spch 22 (Oct./
Dec.) 397-405. Comparative study of lectors. Beginning
and advanced drama students perform Paul (I Cor 13:1-13),
with information on audience and with some biographical
information on Paul.

2591 Comley, Nancy. From Narcissus to Tiresias: T. S.
Eliot's Use of Metamorphosis. Mod Lang Rev 74 (Apr.)
281-6. Analysis of fluctuations of identity so prevalent
in early poems of Eliot.

2592 Cummins, Walter. Inventing Memories: Apocalyptics and
Domestics. Lit Rev 23 (Fall) 127-33. Familiar reality
in American fiction (domestic authors: Irving, Woiwade,
Gardner, and Robertson) has displaced apocalyptic writers
(Pynchon, Coover, Vonnegut, and Barth).

2593 Dahlo, Rolf. Milton's Artis Logicae and Development of the
Idea of Definition in Milton's Works. Huntington Lib Qrt
43 (Winter) 25-36. Contributions for reconstructing the
process of Milton's intellectual development, unmapped
to now.

2594 Draine, Betsy. Changing Frames: Doris Lessing's Memories of a Survivor. Studs in the Novel (Spring) 51-62.
Evaluation of Lessing's manipulation of frame and other
techniques.

2595 Duchastel, Philippe. Learning Objectives and the Organization of Prose. J Educ Psy 71 (Feb.) 100-6. Study of
recall (ideational prominence) in two sources experimentally
manipulated.

2596 Editors. New Fiction by Garber, Lish, Shelnutt, et al.
Lit Rev 23 (Fall) 24-126. Contemporary short fiction.

2597 Edwards, W. F. Speech Acts in Guyana. J Black Stud 10
(Sept.) 20-39. Ritual games of insult are tantalism and
busin, both nonverbal and verbal play.

2598 Ferguson, Suzanne. The Face in the Mirror: Authorial
Presence in the Multiple Vision of the Third-Person Im-
pressionist Narrative. Crit 21 (Summer) 23-50. Seeing
author/narrator as one, examines how indirect free speech
creates irony and ambiguity, especially in Woolf's To the
Lighthouse.

2599 Field, Leslie. Saul Bellow and the Critics--After the Nobel
Award. Mod Fict Stud 25 (Spring) 3-14. Developing view
of Bellow up to the award.

2600 Firchow, P. E. Another Centenary: E. M. Forster.
Mod Fict Stud 25 (Winter) 559-61. A brief look at an
autobiographical thought of the great lit critic.

2601 Fowler, Roger. Anti-Language in Fiction. Style 13 (Summer) 259-78. Applied socio-linguistic theory to two novels.

2602 Gray, P. H. Strange Bedfellows: My Life and Hard Times
in a Speech Communication Department. Sthn Spch Comm

J 44 (Winter) 159-66. Relationships among theatre, interpretation and communication.

2603 Gross, R. V. Narrator as Demon in Grass and Alain-Fournier. Mod Fict Stud 25 (Winter) 625-39. Review of demonic heroes of myths, creating their complicated patterns of representations and misrepresentations, and thereby obscuring their own demonism.

2604 Guzlowski, Field. Criticism of Saul Bellow: A Selected Checklist. Mod Fict Stud 25 (Spring) 149-71. Bibliographical and biographical information.

2605 Hall, R. A. Once More--What Is Literature? Mod Lang J 63 (Mar.) 91-7. Review of critical approaches to defining lit, style, and message as important concepts about memorable discourse.

2606 Hughes, L. K. Dramatic and Private Personae: Ulysses Revisited. Vict Poetry 17 (Autumn) 192-203. Controversy about whether speaker in Ulysses is ironic or straightforward and if poem functions as dramatic monologue.

2607 Humble, M. E. Brecht and Posterity: The Poets' Response to the Poet. Mod Lang Rev 74 (Jan.) 97-116. Traces Brecht's influence by defining ways recent poets have responded to his works.

2608 Hyman, L. W. Moral Attitudes and the Literary Experience. J Aest and Art Crit 38 (Winter) 159-65. Dynamic interaction between real world and art world.

2609 Johnson, L. A. Ain'ts, Us'ens, and Mother-Dear. J Black Stud 10 (Dec.) 139-66. Lit language studies for LeRoi Jones, Ishmael Reed, and Haki Madhubutu to determine codes indicative of ideological or aesthetic predispositions.

2610 Kahane, Claire. Comic Vibrations and Self-Construction in Grotesque Literature. Lit and Psychology 29 (1979) 114-9. Oscillation between familiar and unfamiliar, comic and fearful frame of reference in creation of grotesque in O'Connor's Wise Blood and Faulkner's As I Lay Dying.

2611 Kreps, Barbara. Time and Harold Pinter's Possible Realities: Art as Life, and Vice Versa. Mod Drama 22 (Mar.) 47-60. Reality as an artifact and problem of perception.

2612 Lubienski, Bodenham. The Origins of the 15th Century View of Poetry as Seconde Rhetorique. Mod Lang Rev 74 (Jan.) 26-38. Historical study of debate over nature/purpose of poetry; nine viewpoints explored.

2613 Lund, Michael. Beyond the Text of Vanity Fair. Studs in
      the Novel 11 (Summer) 147-61. Reader-response and
      Vanity Fair.

2614 Marz, Charles. Dos Passos' Newsreels: The Noise of
      History. Studs in the Novel 11 (Summer) 194-200. News-
      reels chronicle voices of public sphere.

2615 McCaffery, Larry. The Gass-Gardner Debate: Showdown
      on Main Street. Lit Rev 23 (Fall) 134-44. Gardner as
      traditionalist vs. Gass as rebel: point/counterpoint con-
      frontation.

2616 McLean, A. M. Teaching Shakespeare. Shakespeare Newsl
      29 (Nov.) 39. Notes numerous recent articles in teaching
      Shakespeare through performance.

2617 Mellard, James. Consciousness Fills the Void: Herzog,
      History and the Hero in the Modern World. Mod Fict Stud
      25 (Spring) 75-92. Herzog becomes symbol of modern
      man in search of self and identity, reality and history.

2618 Melnick, Daniel. Fullness of Dissonance: Music and the
      Reader's Experience of Modern Fiction. Mod Fict Stud
      25 (Summer) 209-22. Dissonance, with its relation to
      disorder, enables reader to engage in vision of disinte-
      grating experience of meaning in lit, its spirit and inten-
      tions.

2619 Miall, D. S. Metaphor as a Thought-Process. J Aest and
      Art Crit 38 (Fall) 21-8. Metaphor as ongoing, dynamic
      process, able to reformulate itself and originate new con-
      cepts beyond awareness of thinker.

2620 Morson, G. S. Socialist Realism and Literary Theory. J
      Aest and Art Crit 38 (Winter) 121-33. Lit as dynamic
      system interacting with other dynamic systems--historical
      relativism.

2621 Natanson, Maurice. Phenomenology, Anonymity. and Alien-
      ation. New Lit History 10 (Spring) 533-46. Relates these
      three terms of tribute in one way or another to the com-
      munality of our lives.

2622 Nichols, John. Development of Perception of Own Attain-
      ment and Causal Attributions for Success and Failure in
      Reading. J Educ Psy 71 (Feb.) 94-99. Children's pre-
      dictions and explanations of success and failure, with
      cognitive maturity best indicator.

2623 Norton, R. W., & L. S. Pettegrew. Attentiveness as a
      Style of Communication: A Structural Analysis. Comm
      Mono 46 (Mar.) 13-26. Attentiveness is a function of
      posture, verbal behavior and eye contact.

2624 Opdahl, K. M. You'll Be Sorry When I'm Dead: Child-
Adult Relations in Huck Finn. Mod Fict Stud 25 (Winter)
613-25. The way various decades interpret Huck, as
hero.

2625 Post, J. F. Guenevere's Critical Performance. Vict Poetry (Winter) 317-28. In Morris' "The Defence of Guenevere." Queen's verbal abilities alert us to value of human utterance in Morris' poetry.

2626 Preston, John. The Silence of the Novel. Mod Lang Rev
74 (Apr.) 257-67. Examines novel as paradox in a form
of speech, existing in silence on printed page, as Culler
and other critics put it, a model by which society con-
ceives itself.

2627 Richards, I. A. Some Notes on Hardy's Verse Forms.
Vict Poetry 17 (Spring/Summer) 1-8. Strangeness of
Hardy's diction as means to and sources of poetic power.

2628 Rose, E. C. It's All a Joke: Science Fiction in Kurt
Vonnegut's The Sirens of Titan. Lit and Psychology 29
(1979) 160-8. Science fiction as a tool for humor that
smiles through tears.

2629 Ross, C. S., ed. Special Issue Vladimir Nabokov. Mod
Fict Stud 25 (Autumn) 400-61. Eight articles related to
Nabokov and his works.

2630 Ross, S. M. Voice in Narrative Texts: The Example of
As I Lay Dying. PMLA 94 (Mar.) 300-10. Ross pries
loose some cherished assumptions about fictional reality
by applying uses of the mimetic and textual voice to As
I Lay Dying.

2631 Ryan, Michael. A Talk on Wallace Stevens. Poetry 134
(Sept.) 353-8. Poetry as a way of knowing the world.

2632 Saldivar, Ramon. Review Essay: Readings and Systems of
Reading. Studs in the Novel 11 (Winter) 472-83. Review
of Iser, Sternberg, and Kestner on reading texts.

2633 Salomon, Gavriel. Media and Symbol Systems as Related
to Cognition and Learning. J Educ Psy 71 (Apr.) 131-48.
Rather than considering media as undifferentiated entities,
this article focuses on media language and symbol systems
by experimental approaches.

2634 Scott, Trudy. The Audience of One: Jamie Leo. Drama
Rev 23 (Dec.) 49-54. Description of performance of
Bye Bye Blacksheep--a piece written and directed for
actor Mark Bronnenberg. Performance translated technical elements into human performance terms.

2635 Shapiro, Karl. Creative Glut. Poetry 135 (Oct.) 36-50.
Deterioration of creative writing and general English skills.

2636 Sieburth, Richard. He Do the Enemy in Different Voices.
Poetry 134 (Aug.) 292-302. Review of Pound's radio
speeches.

2637 Snyder, Gary. Poetry, Community and Climax. Field:
Contemp Poetry and Poetics 20 (Spring) 21-36. Finds
fault with first person personal pronoun when used in
performance and on paper. Subjectivity can hide important aspects of text.

2638 Splitter, Randolph. Proust, Joyce, and the Theory of Metaphor. Lit and Psychology 29 (1979) 4-18. Proust and
Joyce as examples of Freudian theory of metaphor and
metaphorical semiological theory of Freud.

2639 Sprague, Claire. Dialectic and Counter-Dialectic in the
Martha Quest Novels. J Commonwealth Lit 14 (Aug.) 39-
52. Analysis of ironic dialectic and counter-dialectic in
Lessing's Martha/Anna novels.

2640 Tolliver-Weddington, Gloria. Ebonics (Black English): Implications for Education. J Black Stud 9 (June) 363-493.
Nine articles in special issue to examine black English--
linguistic and paralinguistic features.

2641 Zwillinger, Frank. Maharol. Mod Intl Drama 13 (Fall)
7-48. Contains German five-act drama, translated by
Granz Haberl.

2642 Zwillinger, Frank. Between Death and Life. Mod Intl
Drama 13 (Fall) 51-87. Contains German dramatic works
in seven phases, translated by Roger Clement.

1980

2643 Arkans, Norman. Vision and Experience in Hardy's Dream
Poems. Mod Lang Qrt 41 (June) 302-16. Dreams as
tensions between reality and private visions, or between
actual experience and dreams.

2644 Arnez, N. L. Black Poetry: A Necessary Ingredient of
Survival and Liberation. J Black Stud 11 (Sept.) 3-22.
Many poems used to analyze black ideas of survival and
liberation.

2645 Baltzer, J. A. Theory Construction and Model Building:
A New Approach to Oral Interpretation. J Ariz Comm
and Theat Assc 12 (Autumn) 34-43. Model of artistic
fusion of reader/text/audience.

2646 Barth, John. The Literature of Replenishment: Postmodernist Fiction. Atlantic 245 (Jan.) 65-71. Author asks
if postmodernist fiction is an art form to be taken seri-
ously but comes to no final conclusion.

2647 Bayer, J. G. Narrative Techniques and the Oral Tradition
in The Scarlet Letter. Amer Lit 52 (May) 250-63. Oral
dimensions of Hawthorne's writing.

2648 Ben-Zui, Linda. Harold Pinter's Betrayal: The Patterns
of Banality. Mod Drama 23 (Sept.) 227-37. Pinter's
work Betrayal as departure from familiar Pinter land-
marks, banal as menace in this play.

2649 Bizzel, Patricia, & Bruce Herzberg. Inherent Ideology,
Universal History, Empirical Evidence, and Context Free
Writing: Some Problems in E. D. Hirsch's The Philosophy of Composition. Mod Lang Notes 95 (Dec.) 1181-
1202. Arguements against Hirsch's work.

2650 Blanchard, Lydia. Women and Fiction: Literature as
Politics. Studs in the Novel 12 (Spring) 65-72. Argues
for feminist literary criticism.

2651 Bleich, David. Identity of Pedagogy and Research in Study
of Response to Literature. Coll Engl 42 (Dec.) 350-66.
Epistomological approach to classroom studies by respond-
ing to new information in lit but also by using new research approaches in understanding lit.

2652 Brantlinger, Patrick. The Gothic Origins of Science Fiction.
Novel: Forum on Fict 14 (Fall) 30-43. Science fiction's
movement toward increased realism and seriousness and
mainstream fiction.

2653 Breslin, Paul. Warpless and Woofless Subtleties. Poetry
137 (Oct.) 42-50. Review of poetry of John Ashbery and
his superb ear.

2654 Breslin, Paul. Black Mountain: A Critique of the Curriculum. Poetry 136 (July) 219-39. Critique of Black Mountain poets who treat poetry as process of consciousness
rather than readability.

2655 Brienza, S. D., & P. A. Knapp. Imagination Lost and
Found: Beckett's Fiction and Frye's Anatomy. Mod Lang
Notes 95 (May) 980-94. Beckett's fiction as test for
Frye's hypothesis about fictional modes. Comparison with
Robbe-Grillet, Pynchon, and Barth.

2656 Burnett, Archie. Compound Words in Milton's English Poetry. Mod Lang Rev 75 (July) 492-506. Perhaps most
clear link with Elizabethan poetic practice, use of compound words important literary device for Milton.

2657   Campbell, Gordon.   The Son of God in De Docrina Christiana
        and Paradise Lost.   Mod Lang Rev 75 (July) 507-14.
        Comparison/contrast study in two named works, stemming
        from look at Milton's Artis Logicae.

2658   Christensen, Paul.   The New American Romances.   Twenty
        Cent Lit 26 (Fall) 269-77.   Look at Pound, Olson, Eliot,
        and Williams as belonging to the tradition of European
        verse-romance, especially in their longer poems.

2659   Church, Margaret, & W. T. Stafford, eds.   Doris Lessing:
        Special Issue.   Mod Fict Studies 26 (Spring).   Criticism
        and explication directed at Lessing's work.

2660   Cooke, John, & Jeanie Thompson.   Three Poets on the
        Teaching of Poetry.   Coll Engl 42 (Oct.) 43-52.   Tess
        Gallegher, Sandra McPherson and Galway Kinnell share
        views on teaching poetry, especially at university level.

2661   Daw, C. P.   Swift's Favorite Books of the Bible.   Huntington
        Lib Qrt 43 (Summer) 201-12.   Swift's formula for writers
        --proper words in proper places, makes the true definition
        of style--is observed from accounts from the Book of
        Matthew.

2662   Dean, J. S.   If Music Be the Actor's Food.   Shakespeare
        Newsl 20 (May) 28.   Abstract of author's contention in a
        lingering act: Elizabethan music and acting.   Suggests
        Elizabethan acting style parallels Elizabethan musical style.

2663   Deboer, K. B.   Protecting the Voice.   Comm Educ 29
        (July) 256-9.   Voice and articulation training helps stu-
        dents select, sift, structure, and support their ideas for
        more effective communication.

2664   Donnell-Kotrozo, Carol.   The Intentional Fallacy: An Ap-
        plied Reappraisal.   British J Aesthetics 20 (Autumn) 356-
        65.   Author's intention is relevant.

2665   Dupuis, M. M.   The Cloze Procedure as a Predictor of
        Comprehension in Literature.   J of Educ Research 74
        (Sept./Oct.) 27-33.   Matching student reading levels to
        appropriate lit is analyzed and support offered for use of
        cloze procedure as predictor for short stories.

2666   Durrani, Osman.   Here Comes Everybody: An Appraisal of
        Narrative Technique in Gunter Grass' Der Butt.   Mod
        Lang Rev 75 (Oct.) 810-22.   Complex narrative structure
        in Der Butt and lengthy time-spans cause reader difficulty
        in following relationship between narrator and plot.

2667   Eckman, Barbara.   Quantitative Metrical Analysis of the
        Philippians Hymn.   New Testament Studs 26 (Jan.) 258-66.
        Scanning the Greek text of Philippians 2:6-11.

2668 Editors. New Work from 34 Poets. Lit Rev 23 (Spring)
339-60 & 378-412. New poems by contemporary American
poets: Blasing, Das, De Foe, Delaney, Kretz, Lanier,
Pratt, et al.

2669 Editors. Contemporary Theatre in the German-Speaking
World. Mod Drama 23 (Jan.) 327-514. Special issue
with Peter Handke, Thomas Bernhard, Heiner Miler,
Bertolt Brecht, F. X. Kroetz, emancipation of dance,
youth plays of grips, and bibliography of major critical
studies of East German playwrights.

2670 Edwards, Duane. D. H. Lawrence: Tragedy in the Modern
Age. Lit Rev 24 (Fall) 71-88. Lawrence's concept of
tragedy and its application to modern world.

2671 Eichmann, Raymond. The Artistry of Economy in the Fab-
liaux. Stud in Short Fict 17 (Winter) 67-73. Economy in
oral narratives.

2672 Eisenstein, E. L. The Emergence of Print Culture in the
West. J of Comm 30 (Winter) 99-106. The impact of
printing, experienced first by literary groups in early
modern Europe, changed the character of the Italian
Renaissance and ought to be considered among the causes
of both the Protestant Reformation and the rise of modern
science.

2673 Espriu, Salvador. Death Around Sinera. Mod Intl Drama
14 (Fall) 5-60. Contemporary Spanish play in two parts
with interlude by Ricard Salvat. Based on narrative,
poetic and dramatic texts by Salvador Espriu.

2674 Exum, C. J. Promise and Fulfillment: Narrative Art in
Judges 13. J Biblical Lit 99 (Mar.) 43-59. Relationship
between literary structure and meaning.

2675 Fein, R. J. The Life of Life Studies. Lit Rev 23 (Spring)
326-38. Analysis of Lowell's work: "Skunk Hour."

2676 Glenn, C. G. Relationship Between Story Content and
Structure. J Ed Psych 72 (Aug.) 550-60. Prose processing is the center of experimental study. Episodic
structure of the lit helps listener to process and remember the story, as opposed to the content relationship with
the real world.

2677 Glover, J. A., et al. Nobody Knows How to Remember
That Prose. J Educ Research 73 (July/Aug.) 340-3.
Two experimental studies are reported using effect of ob-
jectives on reader comprehension of prose.

2678 Gohlke, M. S. Re-Reading The Secret Garden. Coll Engl
41 (Apr.) 184-92. Examines way reading calls into being

our past as well as present selves, ways we may be
moved through memory by lit.

2679 Gordon, Mel. Laurie Anderson: Performance Artist.
Drama Rev 24 (June) 51-64. How the performer or author can bring raw, unmeditated materials from his life
and structure them to strike a balance between his own
needs and that of the author. A description of some of
Laurie Anderson's work.

2680 Gornall, J. F. The Poetry of Wit: Gongora Reconsidered.
Mod Lang Rev 75 (Apr.) 311-21. Donne's contemporary,
Gongora excelled among late Renaissance European verse
poets, though the aesthetic appeal is not recognized by
most 20th-century critics.

2681 Graham, Keith. Discussion: The Recovery of Illocutionary
Force. Phil Qrt 30 (Apr.) 141-8. People are generally
capable of correctly construing the illocutionary force of
utterances they encounter, but there is still no complete
account of how it is that such a decoding can take place.

2682 Halperin, John. Leslie Stephen, Thomas Hardy, and a
Pair of Blue Eyes. Mod Lang Rev 75 (Oct.) 738-45.
Examination of source of ideas for Hardy's famous scene
in which knight slips over a cliff and remembers thousands
of years of world history while dangling over deep chasm.

2683 Hart, J. T.; J. T. Guthrie; & Linda Winfield. Black English Phonology and Learning to Read. J Ed Psych 72
(Oct.) 636-46. Experimental study dealing with difficulties
young students have in correlating black spoken English
with standard written English.

2684 Hartley, James, et al. Underlining Can Make a Difference.
J Educ Research 73 (Mar./Apr.) 218-24. Underlined
words are definitely more accurately recalled than words
not underlined.

2685 Havelock, E. A. The Coming of Literary Communication to
Western Culture. J of Comm 30 (Winter) 91-8. Invention
of alphabet created a tension between arts and ways of
oral and written communication

2686 Hocking, J. E., & D. G. Leathers. Nonverbal Indicators
of Deception: A New Theoretical Perspective. Comm
Mono 47 (June) 119-31. Studies monitoring and controlling
nonverbal behaviors; difference in liars and truthtellers examined.

2687 Hughson, Lois. Dos Passos' World War: Narrative Technique and History. Studs in the Novel 12 (Spring) 46-61.
Closes gap between storyteller and reader and maintains
moral stance.

2688   Hurst, B. M.   An Integrated Approach to the Hierarchical
       Order of the Cognitive and Affective Domains.   J Educ
       Psych 72 (June) 293-303.   Hierarchical relationships exist
       between behaviors in cognitive and affective domains, us-
       ing linear and nonlinear tasks.

2689   James, L. B.   The Influence of Black Orality on Contempo-
       rary Black Poetry and Its Implications for Performance.
       Sthn Spch Comm J 45 (Spring) 249-67.   Black oral tradi-
       tion, poetry and performance.

2690   Johnson, G. B.   The Gullah Dialect Revisited.   J Black Stud
       10 (June) 417-24.   Linguistic study of acculturation of
       blacks on St. Helens Island, South Carolina.

2691   Johnson, N. S. , & J. M. Mandler.   A Tale of Two Struc-
       tures: Underlying and Surface Forms in Stories.   Poet:
       Intl Rev Theory Lit 9 (June) 51-86.   Relates to oral
       tradition.

2692   Jones, Janet.   Learning and Movement: Great Dance Part-
       ners.   Learning: Mag for Creative Teachers 9 (Nov.) 14.
       14 dancelike exercises to help youth learn about animals
       and plant life.

2693   Katz, J. J.   Chomsky on Meaning.   Lang 56 (Mar.) 1-41.
       Urges rejection of Chomsky's position on meaning.

2694   Keaveney, M. M.   Oral History and Oral Interpretation.   J
       Ariz Comm & Theat Assc 12 (Autumn) 31-3.   Dramatized
       oral history.

2695   Khatchadourian, Haig.   Movement and Action in Film.
       British J Aesthetics 20 (Autumn) 349-55.   Relation of
       movement to text.

2696   King, Noel.   Pinter's Progress.   Mod Drama 23 (Sept.)
       246-57.   Importance of noticing Pinter's use of various
       media in various capacities and plays in context of overall
       body of work.

2697   Kintgen, Eugene.   The Perception of Poetry.   Style 14 (Win-
       ter) 22-40.   Perceptual style study using tape-recorded
       thoughts of readers as they interpret poems.

2698   Kobler, J. F.   The Sexless Narrator of Mansfield's "The
       Young Girl. "   Stud in Short Fict 17 (Summer) 269-74.
       Explicates unusual narrator of Mansfield's story.

2699   Labeille, Daniel.   The Formless Hunch: An Interview with
       Peter Brooks.   Mod Drama 23 (Sept.) 219-26.   Brooke's
       ideas on directing.

2700 Little, B. B. Enter Teacher (Sleuth, Witch, and Mad Scientist). Learning: Mag for Creative Teaching 9 (Nov.) 70-1. Props, costumes, and some creative teacher shenanigans awaken students to joys of writing.

2701 Malin, Irving. Portrait of the Artist in Slapstick: Malamud's Pictures of Fidelman. Lit Rev 24 (Fall) 121-38. Malamud's concern with relationship of art and life in his fiction.

2702 Martin, H. A. Ordinary Story Telling and the Experience of Literature. J Ariz Comm & Theat Assc 12 (Autumn) 23-30. Storytelling teaches performance techniques.

2703 Martin, T. P. Henry James and Percy Lubbock: From Mimesis to Formalism. Novel: Forum on Fict 14 (Fall) 20-9. Artist's task is to present ordered world in contrast to imitation of world experience.

2704 McFarlin, A. S. Hallie Quinn Brown: Black Woman Elocutionist. Sthn Spch Comm J 46 (Autumn) 72-82. Importance of Brown's speaking, performing, writing, and political involvement.

2705 McGill, W. J. Voices in the Cathedral: The Chorus in Eliot's Murder in the Cathedral. Mod Drama 23 (Sept.) 292-6. Reading of choral odes which identifies principal thematic and dramatic voices.

2706 Meringoff, L. K. Influence of the Medium on Children's Story Apprehension. J Educ Psych 72 (Apr.) 261-80. Children's apprehension through unfamiliar story read to them or presented as TV film.

2707 Millinger, D. M. Legal Rights of the Fine Artist. J Commonwealth Lit 30 (Autumn) 10-22. Inadequacy of 1976 revision of U.S. Copyright Act and new proposals.

2708 Mohrmann, G. P., & S. J. Kaplan. The Effect of Training on the Oral Interpreter's Reception of a Text. Cent Sts Spch J 31 (Summer) 137-42. Argues for use of dramatistic appraisal to analysis of lit.

2709 Nickolas, Brian. Is Tartuffe a Comic Character? Mod Lang Rev 75 (Oct.) 755-65. Comic nature of play tends to overshadow philosophical, satirical and subjective elements which are very evident in the play.

2710 Nisly, P. W. The Prison of the Self: Isolation in Flannery O'Connor's Fiction. Stud in Short Fict 17 (Winter) 49-54. Isolation of characters in O'Connor's stories.

2711 Novitz, David. Fiction, Imagination and Emotion. J Aest and Art Crit 38 (Spring) 279-88. Necessity of emotional involvement for proper understanding of fiction.

2712 O'Hanlon, Redmond. Meta-Tragedy in Anouilh's Antigone. Mod Lang Rev 75 (July) 534-46. Inner play vs. outer play clarified by prologue and chorus is key to understanding Antigone the play and thus Antigone the character.

2713 Ong, W. S. Literacy and Orality in Our Times. J of Comm 30 (Winter) 197-204. Understanding the history and functions of oral communication sheds new light on problems of literacy in media world.

2714 Osborne, Harold. Aesthetic Implications of Conceptual Art, Happenings, etc. British J Aesthetics 20 (Winter) 6-22. Happenings are socially reputable, artistically wrong.

2715 Overstreet, Robert. Preservation of Line Shape in the Performance of a Poem. Sthn Spch Comm J 45 (Spring) 268-81. Suggestions for preserving line shape in poetry performance.

2716 Paolucci, Anne. Pirandello and the Waiting Stage of the Absurd (With Some Observations on a New Critical Language). Mod Drama 23 (June) 102-11. Pirandello's influence on theatre of the absurd, poetry of concrete and objectified images of stage itself.

2717 Pearce, H. D. A Phenomenological Approach to the Theatrum Mundi Metaphor. PMLA 95 (Jan.) 42-57. Pertinent characteristics that make the theatrum mundi metaphor available at anytime.

2718 Pearse, J. A. Beyond the Narrational Frame: Interpretation and Metafiction. Qrt J Spch 66 (Feb.) 73-84. Performing metafiction.

2719 Pflaum, S. W., & T. H. Bryan. Oral Reading Behaviors in the Learning Disabled. J Educ Research 73 (May/June) 252-8. Linguistic cue use by normal group and by learning disabled in experiment studied.

2720 Phillips, K. J. The Double Trap of Robbe-Grillet: A Reading of Le Voyeur. Twenty Cent Lit 26 (Fall) 323-32. R-G's works reveal their own devices as art, in contrast to objective or subjective author.

2721 Prenshaw, P. W. Persephone in Eudora Welty's "Livvie." Stud in Short Fict 17 (Spring) 149-56. Welty's fusion of reality with myth.

2722 Prigozy, Ruth, et al. F. Scott Fitzgerald: Special Issue.
      Twenty Cent Lit 26 (Summer). Six critical articles on
      Fitzgerald.

2723 Rabinowitz, Nancy & Peter. The Critical Balance: Reader,
      Text and Meaning. Coll Engl 41 (Apr.) 924-32. Balance
      between subjective and objective criticism is not easy to
      find, but unless it is sought, the whole enterprise of cri-
      ticism is passionless and pointless.

2724 Raffel, Burton. Robert Lowell's Life Studies. Lit Rev 23
      (Spring) 293-325. Examination of Lowell's poems.

2725 Raval, Suresh. Intention and Contemporary Literary The-
      ory. J Aest and Art Crit 38 (Spring) 261-77. Discussion
      of crucial features that characterize controversy on con-
      cept of intention in criticism.

2726 Ray, P. C. Meaning and Textuality: A Surrealist Example.
      Twenty Cent Lit 26 (Fall) 306-23. Review of possible
      procedures for reading a poem, especially surrealistic
      poems by means of dialectical indirection.

2727 Roedder, K. R. Books for Children. Childhood Educ 57
      (Sept. /Dec.) 42-46, 110-4. Brief annotated list of books
      appropriate to various ages.

2728 Sadoff, D. F. Storytelling and the Figure of the Fathers in
      Little Dorrit. PMLA 95 (Mar.) 234-45. Work as double
      story which identifies yet questions genealogy and the
      patriarchal family as metaphors for narrative structure.

2729 Sauro, D. A. Oral Interpretation as a Survival Skill. J
      Ariz Comm & Theat Assc 12 (Spring) 23-8. OI aids in
      learning what it means to be human.

2730 Schlueter, June. Goats and Monkeys and the Idiocy of Lan-
      guage: Handke's Kaspar and Shakespeare's Othello. Mod
      Drama 23 (Mar.) 25-32. Construction and destructive
      capacities of language in Othello and possibilities and
      limitations in Kaspar.

2731 Schultz, S. C. Principles of Interpretation. Shakespeare
      Newsl 29 (Feb.) 10. Abstract of author's Poel, Barker,
      and Richard II which traces Poel's influence on Granville-
      Barker's theories of Shakespeare interpretation.

2732 Shattuck, Roger. How to Rescue Literature. New York Rev
      of Books 27 (Apr. 17) 29-35. There is a constant need to
      reconsider theories of lit and ways of approaching it.
      Much can be gained from attention to the trials and rewards
      of oral interpretation.

2733 Shaw, D. W.   The Optical Metaphor: Victorian Poetics and
      the Theory of Knowledge.   Vict Studies 23 (Spring) 293-
      324.   Relationships between visual images and knowledge
      in Victorian poetry theory.

2734 Simon, John.   Traduttore, Traditore or the Tradition of
      Traducing.   Poetry 136 (Apr.) 40-58.   Problems of trans-
      lation.

2735 Smith, W. D.   The Black Self-Concept.   J Black Stud 10
      (Mar.) 355-66.   Historical and theoretical reflections of
      the development of self-concepts: 18 propositions.

2736 Speer, J. H.   Cowboy Chautauqua: An Account of Its Origins
      in Central Texas, 1885-1890.   Sthn Spch Comm J 45
      (Spring) 282-96.   Role of early Chautauqua in elocution.

2737 Spiegel, D. L., & Carol Rogers.   Teacher Responses to
      Miscues During Oral Reading by Second Grade Students.
      J Educ Research 74 (Sept./Oct.) 8-12.   Categories of re-
      sponse analyzed and only 5 percent of teacher response
      related to meaning.

2738 Stafford, W. T., ed.   John Dos Passos: Special Issue.
      Mod Fict Stud 26 (Autumn).   Articles plus book reviews
      and checklists.

2739 Steinman, L. M.   A Dithering of Presences: Style and
      Language in Stevens' Essays.   Contemp Lit 21 (Winter)
      100-17.   Includes Stevens' idea of poet as actor.

2740 Stephenson, R. H.   On the Widespread Use of an Inappropri-
      ate and Restrictive Model of the Literary Aphorism.   Mod
      Lang Rev 75 (Jan.) 1-17.   Known as maxims or apothegms,
      this literary form has the capacity to communicate a
      thought stimulus, is used throughout critical lit, has flex-
      ible functioning, and has the power to center attention on
      language itself.

2741 Stern, C. S.   Some Recent Writings on Victorian Theatre.
      Vict Studies 23 (Spring) 389-98.   Review of new books on
      Victorian theatre.

2742 Stern, D. A.   Teaching and Acting: A Vocal Analogy.
      Comm Educ 29 (July) 259-63.   Expressive speaking style
      needed for effective communication in lecture/performing/
      speaking situations.

2743 Suto, Andras.   Star at the Stake.   Mod Intl Drama 13
      (Spring) 54-97.   Contemporary Hungarian drama translated
      by Jena Brogyanyi.

2744 Taft-Kaufman, Jill.   A Rhetorical Perspective for Teaching
      the Solo Performance of Shakespearean Dramatic Litera-

ture. Comm Educ 29 (May) 112-24. Suggest combination of rhetorical perspective with developmental teaching strategy for translating Shakespearean dramatic lit into solo performance.

2745 Tintner, A. R. Jamesian Structures in The Age of Innocence and Related Stories. Twenty Cent Lit 26 (Fall) 332-48. Wharton's novel largely dependent on James' works, in technical sense.

2746 Tolomeo, Diane. Home to Her True Country: The Final Trilogy of Flannery O'Connor. Stud in Short Fict 17 (Summer) 335-42. Shock tactics in O'Connor's final three stories.

2747 Twining, M. A. Damas and Two Sea Island Poets. J Black Stud 10 (June) 449-60. Poetry of negritude twisted by dislocated sense of self analyzed in three poems by Damas and others.

2748 Valentine, K. B., & M. Kennedy. The Gender Antonym Replacement Technique (Gart): Computer-Assisted Categorization of Gender Issues in Selected Feminist Literature. J Ariz Comm & Theat Assc 12 (Spring) 29-41. Means for determining sexism in lit.

2749 Van Wert, W. F. Narration in John Hawkes' Trilogy. Lit Rev 24 (Fall) 21-39. Analysis of narration of The Blood Oranges (1971); Death, Sleep and Traveler (1974) and Travesty (1976).

2750 Watson, K. W., & L. R. Barker. Cognitive Response of Oral Interpreters to Literature. Sthn Spch Comm J 45 (Winter) 173-86. Lateralized alpha activity of OI'ers while listening to varied oral messages.

2751 Welch, D. M. Distance and Progress in "In Memoriam." Vict Poetry 18 (Summer) 169-78. Tension of past and future in Tennyson's poem.

2752 Wells, Lynn. Skills Integration for Oral Interpretation: Oral Histories. J Ariz Comm & Theat Assc 12 (Spring) 11-6. Oral history assignment in OI class.

2753 Wentz, R. E. Portrait of an Actor. Christian Cent 97 (Jan.) 18-20. The author (a religious studies professor at Arizona State University) as an actor is a transformed being: sees acting as form of religious experience.

2754 Wilkinson, A. C. Children's Understanding in Reading and Listening. J Ed Psych 72 (Aug.) 561-74. Study of processing content by experimental methods of silent reading vs. listening to oral reader and vs. reading along with an oral reader.

2755 Workman, B. X.   A Semester of Hemingway for Gifted High School Students.   J Reading (Apr.) 598-600.   Course resulted in maximum understanding and effective oral and critical reading and writing research.

2756 Zwillinger, Frank.   Galileo Galilei.   Mod Intl Drama 13 (Spring) 7-51.   Contains German drama in five acts, translated by Franz Haberl.

SPECIALIZED PERIODICALS

INTERPRETATION DIVISION NEWSLETTER

2757 Klyn, M. S.   A Note on Farce in Readers Theatre.   (Nov. 1966) p. 5.   Description of a RT production of three of Chekhov's short farces that prove that farce is appropriate for RT and that timing is vital to farce.

2758 Jisha, H. J.   Editing Literature for Oral Interpretation. (Mar. 1967).   n. p.

2759 Simpson, V. L.   A Readers Theatre Production of The Comedy of Errors.   (Nov. 1967) pp. 5-6.   Description of production and problems encountered in production.

2760 Schneider, R. J.   Readers Theatre: Experiment in Intimate Literature.   (Mar. 1968) pp. 5-7.   Compiled script on alienation, I, Diary using intimate non-fiction, disconnected presentational form and symbolic set to emphasize theme of alienation.

2761 Bowen, E. R.   A Chamber Theatre Production.   (Nov. 1968) pp. 19-20.   A production of Kop's The Dissent of Dominick Shapiro at Central Michigan University.

2762 Quarnstrom, I. B.   A Choral Theatre Production.   (Nov. 1968) pp. 20-21.   Production of O'Neill's Lazarus Laughed at Central Michigan University in which voice choir proved successful.

2763 Bacon, W. A.   Research in Interpretation.   (Spring 1970) pp. 10-11.   Bacon finds fault with some of Sloan's suggestions and sees importance in historical view.

2764 Editors.   Oral Interpretation for the Blind.   (Spring 1970) pp. 6-7.   Special projects class at University of Utah discovers the problems facing OI for the blind.

2765 Hayden, Rebecca.   The Paradox of the Sonnet.   (Spring 1970) pp. 3-6.   Sonnet with its paradox of control and freedom will continue to be medium for vital poetic expression.

2766 Kleinau, Marion. Guidelines for Research of Oral Interpretation: A Symbolic Interaction Approach. (Spring 1970) pp. 12-6. Researchers in OI can no longer afford unexamined assumptions concerning what happens in process of OI, but must question each one from an empirical point of view.

2767 Loesch, K. T. Report on Research in Linguistics for the Committee on Guidelines for Research in Interpretation. (Spring 1970) pp. 11-12. Necessary to preserve and enlarge awareness of ways in which OI may suitably engage with other fields.

2768 Sloan, T. O. Guidelines for Research in Literature. (Spring 1970) pp. 9-10. Research should be more rhetorical in orientation and needs to take overt cognizance of current work in hermeneutics.

2769 McLaughlin, Frank. A Recipe for Triggering Relevance. (Fall 1970) pp. 3-4. To engage students with tasks they will feel meaningful, author suggests closing textbooks and tuning in radio and other modern media spheres.

2770 Poindexter, J. W. The Trapped Idealists. (Summer 1971) pp. 2-5. Author suggests that the words of the title describe the educational publisher, teachers and authors; he suggests some guidelines that should be followed by prospective OI textbook authors.

2771 Bacon, W. A. Research in Interpretation. (Fall 1971) p. 2. Suggestions for research.

2772 Hardwick, M. R. It Is Time. (Fall 1971) p. 3. Need to study style until it can be identified in terms of appropriateness for individual OI performances.

2773 Mazzaferri, Annette. Increase Our Creativity in Readers Theatre. (Fall 1971) p. 4. Developing realization in performance and its effect on students.

2774 McHughes, J. L. The Contemporary Poet as Jongleur. (Fall 1971) pp. 4-6. How James Dickey came to terms with performance demands made on him.

2775 Yordan, Judy. Concrete Poetry and Oral Performance. (Fall 1971) pp. 6-7. Performance values of concrete poetry.

2776 Bacon, W. A. A Response to T. O. Sloan. (Spring 1972) p. 7. In OI act of performing text is central.

2777 Hardy, M. N. A Readers Theatre Lighting System for Under $100. (Spring 1972) pp. 2-5. How to build a RT light system for special demands of RT.

2778 Homewood, Ed, & Roselyn Schiff. An Experiment in Teaching Writing and Oral Interpretation. (Spring 1972) pp. 4-6. The student as writer and interpreter.

2779 Gura, T. J. Some Notes on the Structure and Performance of the Poetry of Gerard Manley Hopkins. (Fall 1972) pp. 4-7. Illustrates some tricks of Hopkins and some solutions to Hopkins' problems.

2780 Pattison, S. D. Listeners Theatre: Perhaps Naming Is Explaining. (Fall 1972) pp. 7-8. Emphasis in RT is not on reader but on listener.

2781 Roloff, L. H. The Field of Interpretation: Instructive Wonder. (Spring 1973) pp. 7-9. Four suggestions where the energies of a professional can be taken, and where a student can be led.

2782 Hunsinger, Paul. Public Reading of Poetry in Britain: An American View. (Fall 1973) pp. 1-5. Historical perspective of OI in Britain which is enjoying a renaissance, and a brief discussion of new style of the art which is emerging, more conversational than declamatory in nature.

2783 Svore, J. L. Oral Interpretation: An Act of the Mind. (Fall 1973) pp. 5-7. Subject matter of OI discussed; concludes that it is activity of mind, an act of creativity.

2784 Jeffrey, R. C. Toward Developing a Professional Conscience. (Spring 1974) pp. 5-8. Personal reminiscences about problems and discoveries in developing a professional conscience.

2785 Williams, D. A. Literature, Performance and the Law. (Spring 1974) pp. 8-10. Copyright laws as apply to OI.

2786 Forrest, W. C. Abstract and Experiential Meaning in the Verbal Artwork. (Fall 1974) pp. 6-7.

2787 Jansen, W. H. Truth in Oral Performance. (Spring 1975) pp. 9-11. Fine line between believability and disbelief in performance.

2788 Pattison, S. D. The Oral Critique of Interpretative Readings: Levels of Criticism & Evaluation in the Classroom. (Spring 1975) pp. 12-3. Discussion of classroom purposes and evaluation environment.

2789 Schneider, R. J. Report on Learning Resources in Oral Interpretation. (Spring 1975) pp. 6-7. Summary of results of survey of learning resources currently used by teachers of OI.

2790 Maher, M. Z. Backstage at the Bicentennial. (Fall 1975) pp. 4-5. Bicentennial events make interpreters aware of audience.

ORAL ENGLISH

2791 Forrest, W. C., & Cornelius Novelli. About Oral English. 1 (Winter 1972) 1-3. Aim and scope of oral English.

2792 Geiger, Don. Performance as the Act of Understanding Literature. 1 (Winter 1972) 3-6. Performance is explication.

2793 Noon, W. T. Distant Music in Finnegans Wake. 1 (Winter 1972) 6-9. Oral approach is way to open students' eyes and ears to this musically charming book.

2794 Rickert, A. E. Production Notes for a Staged Reading of Othello. 1 (Winter 1972) 9-13. Planning a reading forces one to look at lit critically; out of such a view, both understanding and enjoyment is increased.

2795 Sloyer, Shirlee. Show on the Road: Oral Performers as Reading Motivators. 1 (Winter 1972) 13-5. Hearing oral readings can motivate students to become interested in lit.

2796 Bacon, W. A. Act of Interpretation. 1 (Spring 1972) 1-6. Importance of teaching OI in lit courses, as opposed to pure criticism; poetry reading as action and translation.

2797 Boudreau, Gordon. Henry Thoreau's Sound Sense. 1 (Spring 1972) 7-12. Explains how Thoreau's sense of sound is reflected in his choice of words in Walden.

2798 Haas, Richard. Oral Interpretation as Discovery Through Persona. 1 (Spring 1972) 13-4. Character of speaker gives insight.

2799 Esolen, Gary. Advantages of the Oral Study of Literature. 1 (Summer 1972) 1-7. Why it is worthwhile to attempt to teach lit by involving students actively in oral performance.

2800 Cargas, H. J. Four Hours and Forty-Eight Voices: Whitman's Leaves of Grass on Television. 1 (Summer 1972) 7-8. How Leaves was produced for TV.

2801 Schrero, E. M. Intonation and Moral Insight: Reading Henry James Aloud. 1 (Summer 1972) 8-13. Intonation, stress and rhythm essential to language meaning.

2802 Swander, H. D. MLA Seminar: Performance and the Teaching of Drama. 1 (Summer 1972) 13-4. Invitation sent out by Swander for the '72 MLA meeting--includes some questions that the seminar confronted.

2803 Farrell, T. J. From Orality to Literacy: Teaching Writing to the Disadvantaged. 1 (Fall 1972) 1-5. Outline of process of oral-chirographic approach to teaching composition to disadvantaged but highly oral students.

2804 Bozek, M. D. Some Oral Techniques in Teaching Literature to Upward Bound Students. 1 (Fall 1972) 5-7. Using oral approaches to lit for special students.

2805 Loesch, K. T. Towards an Ontology of Literature in Performance. 1 (Fall 1972) 8-14. Behavior of performer controlled by schematic structure of lit.

2806 Forrest, W. C., & Neil Novelli. Getting Started with the Oral Study of Literature. 1 Supplement (Fall 1972) 1-17. Intended for teachers who want to try oral approaches to lit and could use a map for their initial efforts.

2807 Havelock, Eric. Orality & Literacy, Ancient & Modern: An Interview of Eric Havelock. 2 (Winter 1976) 1-9. Plato's hostility to oral culture and advocacy of logic and abstract thinking examined in preface to Plato.

2808 Mertes, B. F. Oral Interpretation of Literature: The Basic Class Revisited. 2 (Winter 1976) 10-2. Impressions of teacher coming back to basic course.

2809 Babula, William. The Shaped Sound of Faith: George Herbert's "Easter Wings." 2 (Winter 1976) 13-4. Points out oral/aural pattern of poem in readers' preparation for oral delivery.

2810 Richards, I. A. The Eye and the Ear. 2 (Spring 1976) 2-6. Reprint from English Leaflet (May 1948) 65-72. Expressive speech necessary models in classrooms.

2811 Russo, J. P. I. A. Richards' Poetries: Their Media and Ends, ed. by Trevor Eaton. 2 (Spring 1976) 6-9. Review of collection of 17 essays by Richards which are educational, theoretical, and practical criticism.

2812 Anastos, Perry. Oral Performance in the Seventh Grade. 2 (Spring 1976) 9-12. Shows how energy that flows through bodies of 7th graders is used as a means of experience in reading various types of lit.

2813 Proffitt, Edward. The Mystery of Voice: The Place of Oral Interpretation in Teaching The Prelude. 2 (Spring 1976) 12-3. To integrate OI with interpretation of theme, imagery, metaphor, and structure of The Prelude. Followed by Q/A with Proffitt.

2814 Forrest, W. C., & Cornelius Novelli. Present at the Birth of a Poem. 2 (Summer 1976) 1-2. Introduction to very successful northwest Modern Language Association meeting, Boston, 1973, which describes high level of excitement and interest taken by the audience.

2815 Walsh, Chad. Poem on the Spot. 2 (Summer 1976) 2-7. Walsh describes method of creating poetry with tape recorder rather than ball point and gives demonstration.

2816 Lord, A. B. Oral Improvisation of Poetry with Traditional Formulas and Without. 2 (Summer 1976) 8-14. Lord discusses Walsh's demonstration of a tapepoem and is later joined by others.

2817 Walsh, Chad. Afterwords. 2 (Summer 1976) 14-6. Walsh amplifies an earlier point that poetry may split into several autonomous parts.

2818 Lord, A. B. Afterword. 2 (Summer 1976) 16. Lord emphasizes the distinction between orally improvised poetry and oral traditional poetry.

2819 Forrest, W. C., & K. T. Loesch. Chamber Theatre & the Dramatization of Narrative: An Interview with Robert Breen. 2 (Fall 1976) 1-12. CT retains narrative element while using theatrical elements.

2820 White, M. R. Readers Theatre: To Memorize or Not to Memorize. 2 (Fall 1976) 12-4. May or may not memorize but consistency is essential.

2821 Adams, W. A. Readers Theatre in the Public School Curriculum: A Synergistic Force. 2 (Fall 1976) 15-21. RT develops rapidly as tool that can motivate and implement learning of any subject.

2822 Bowen, E. R. Non-Drama in the Theatre. 2 (Fall 1976) 21-4. Description of anthology show an evening of irreverence presented at Central Michigan University.

2823 Coger, L. I. Directing Narrative Fiction for Performance. 2 (Fall 1976) 24-34. Director studies lit to decide line divisions, interpretations, and staging.

ISSUES IN INTERPRETATION

2824 Kelly, Michael, ed. Issues in Interpretation 1 (1976) No. 1. What Should Be the Role for Drama in Oral Interpretation? Issue contains responses from six scholars plus summary response by the editor; contents listed below.

2825 Schneider, R. J. What Should Be the Role for Drama in Oral Interpretation? pp. 3-4. OI awakens intellectual as well as emotional sensibilities beyond parameters of play.

2826 Stern, C. S. pp. 5-6. Illusion created by OI different from staged production and each offers own kind of pleasure.

2827 Okey, L. L. pp. 7-8. Solo performance allows amplification of self; recreation of experience through language and discovery of author's rhetorical strategies.

2828 Bennett, Suzanne. pp. 8-9. Through solo or group reading student realizes voices speaking, controlling structure, and cyclic communicative situation of audience reacting.

2829 Gura, T. J. pp. 10-11. Why must exclusivity be for any mode of performance for any genre?

2830 Maher, M. Z. pp. 12-4. In a word: Shakespeare.

2831 Rossi, P. C. , ed. Issues in Interpretation 1 (1976) No. 2. Adaptation of Dickens' Hard Times. Seven scholars adapt first chapter. Response to adaptation at end of issue; contents listed below.

2832 Breen, R. S. pp. 3-4.

2833 Frederickson, R. Q. pp. 4-6.

2834 Espinola, J. C. pp. 6-7.

2835 Potts, M. L. pp. 8-9.

2836 Bowen, E. R. pp. 13-11.

2837 Cribbs, R. C. pp. 11-13.

2838 Parisien, Robert. pp. 13-15. Rossi response: skilled adaptor must exercise same degree of expertise and control inherent in the finest artists.

2839 Kelly, Michael, ed. Issues in Interpretation 1 (1976) No. 3. Issue: The Myth of the Manuscript. Response by five scholars. Editor response at end of issue; more questions raised than supplied--further investigation needed. Contents listed below.

2840 Marlor, C. S. Manuscript restraining element on both performer and audience.

2841 Rickert, W. E. pp. 3-5. To require manuscript for all performances seems very arbitrary.

2842 Overstreet, Robert. pp. 5-7. Decision may be determined by lit and performance situation rather than convention.

2843 Thompson, D. W. pp. 7-8. It is not the manuscript per se, but how it is utilized.

2844 Hudson, Lee. pp. 9-10. Functional use of manuscript does not aesthetically fulfill convention; choice in performance is a creative imperative.

2845 McCloud, George. pp. 15-17. Response to Timothy Gura's essay in Vol. 1, No. 1. McCloud argues that advisability of including drama in an interpretation course must be informed by needs and features of real-life academic department that the course is intended to serve.

2846 Lentz, Tony, ed. Issues in Interpretation 2 (1977) No. 1. Issue: Genre. For all its positive virtues, has the study of literary genre diverted us from the greatest challenge we face: that of understanding interpretation and its non-generic standards of excellence? Contents listed below.

2847 Bacon, W. A. pp. 2-3. OI is committed to study of performance, which involves study of text performed, study of performer, audience and art of the writer plus a study of elements which enter into the total process.

2848 Salper, D. R. pp. 3-4. OI in major part is committed to study of lit, and one way of grouping lit is by genre.

2849 Williams, D. A. pp. 5-6. By building wisely on our useful knowledge of lit theory, and discovering performance potentials in lit, OI will be contributing to both lit and performance theory--beyond genre.

2850 Hardwick, M. R. pp. 6-7. To know the nature of genre is to integrate information technically while the lit enterprise is kept sacred.

2851 Bolton, Janet. pp. 7-9. Effectiveness of OI performance is not assured by knowledge of lit forms and genres.

2852 Campbell, P. N. pp. 9-10. First, it is not clear that generic approach is workable; it ignores dramatistic approach and the vital distinction between verse and prose.

2853 Lentz, Tony. pp. 11-12. Editorial Response: Study of genres is not only useful tool for OIer. If we are to proceed beyond genre, we must develop critical tools to explore complex constructs of behaviors, both real and potential, that are part of performance event.

2854 Floyd, V. H. pp. 13-14. Re: Manuscript Vol. 1 (1976) No. 3. Whether manuscript is physically present or not, must serve up to performer and to audience a universe that exists by virtue of imposing its own reality upon them-- en patuite.

2855 Williams, J. W. p. 14. Re: Drama Vol. 1 (1976) No. 1. Drama not to be made idol or scapegoat, but viewed as major genre of lit and as flexible, multi-faceted and creative force in OI.

2856 Kelly, Michael, ed. Issues in Interpretation 2 (1977) No. 2. The Issue: Audience. Why has the audience been given passing interest? Contents listed below.

2857 Brandes, P. D. Discusses series of transactions the OIer makes in adjusting to audience.

2858 Sloan, T. O. We should approach an issue like audience by facing directly ontological question: every act of OI is potentially or in effect an argument or ontology.

2859 Gaede, C. J. Examines the different positions the audience member occupies within the world of literature in each literary mode.

2860 Pattison, S. D. Audience will demand a focus on rhetorical problem of matching an idea with an audience; requiring the OI to develop proper mood for experiencing the lit.

2861 Long, B. W. A knowing audience informs the performer and is in a position to be informed in a rich way by the performed text.

2862 Parrella, Gilda. Important for OIer is the awareness of a kind of dialogue between performer and audience which parallels original oral relationship that story-teller had with audience.

2863 Kelly, Michael. Editorial Response: We need to sharpen theoretical positions on role of audience.

2864 Kelly, Michael, & Wendy Oschmann, eds. Issues in Interpretation 2 (1977) No. 3. The Issue: The Audience in Oral Interpretation: Literature. Editors use four sonnets by C. C. Long as basis for responses. Contents listed below.

2865 Loesch, K. T. Analyses shifting roles of audiences present at OI events and clarifies what OI accomplishes.

2866 McGeever, C. J. Primary relationship between personae of all quality lyric poetry and all reasonably sensitive audiences is voyeuristic.

2867 Trauernicht, M. M. Discovers audience in each poem and shows how each audience might be handled.

2868 Boyce, W. A. In regarding OI as art form we must consider the aesthetic aspects of written text which form basis for OI act.

2869 Kelly, Michael, & Wendy Oschmann. Editorial Response: The more concrete the fictive audience becomes, the more evidence of response the persona must seem to receive from that fictive audience.

2870 Oschmann, Wendy, ed. Issues in Interpretation 3 (1978) No. 1. The Issue: The Audience in Interpretation: Performance. Contents listed below.

2871 Valentine, K. B. OIer's ever conscious concern must be what happens when this group of people meets this interpreter embodying this text at this point in time.

2872 Wells, Lynn. OIer determines the style of performance and prepares mentally for various reactions to performance beforehand.

2873 Hunsinger, Paul. Major concern with audience in moment of performance is the effect of listeners on OI during the transactional process.

2874 Stone, Marlene. Audience feedback is delayed, but that feedback is extremely valuable for performance.

2875 Pearse, J. A. Examines response of OIer to mass-audience public performance.

2876 Oschmann, Wendy. Editor's Response: Seems OI has number of techniques to use to gain response, but when and to what extent one uses them is still a mystery--perhaps it should remain so.

2877 Kelly, Michael, & Tony Lentz, eds. Issues in Interpretation 3 (1978) No. 2. The Issue: The Future: Where Do We Go from Here? Contents listed below.

2878 Campbell, P. N. Proper direction for OI is toward rich mixture of aesthetics and language theory.

2879 Haas, Richard. OI does not exist outside academics, we have no role models out there.

2880 Edwards, Paul. We must refine and redefine the basic course.

2881 Cheney, Lois. Four suggestions for improving health of OI.

2882 Hudson, Lee, & B. W. Long. Thirteen predictive claims for OI, mostly positive.

2883 Martin, H. R. Future secure if we do two things: offer artistic contributions of merit to community and focus research on the art form itself.

2884 Lentz, Tony. Editor's Response: We must expose students to OI, not hide it under a basket.

2885 Kelly, Michael, & Tony Lentz, eds. Issues in Interpretation 3 (1978) No. 3. The Issue: What Are the Enduring Values of Your Endeavor, Those Personal and Public Benefits Which Drive You to Keep Doing What You Do? Contents listed below.

2886 Okey, L. L. Okey describes the views from his window, from which he sees value of OI, friends, knowledge, illumination and understanding.

2887 McGeever, C. J. Sees OI as ceremony.

2888 Rossi, P. C. Using OI skills and performance training in writing for TV and working with program talent.

2889 Martin, H. R. Literature has come alive and puts him in good company.

2889a Bowen, E. R. In the theatre, especially Chamber Theatre, interpretative forms offer unsurpassed opportunity to genuine creativity.

2890 Bahn, Eugene. Acquisition of knowledge, philosophical insight, and spiritual enlightenment.

2891 Sundstrom, Aileen. The legacy of OI and its richness.

2892 Brooks, Keith. OI allows one a close encounter with life and living, plus development of fourfold skill acquisitions: vocal responsiveness, physical responsiveness, lit analysis, and social analysis of audience.

2893 Haushalter, W. R. The possibility of discovering worlds which are to be found in lit.

2894 Rickert, W. E. To sustain that connection with a poem's voice, to preserve and clarify the voices of lit, and to participate in the poetic coming.

2895 Maher, M. Z. Constant fulfillment and releasing in students what they want to find in themselves.

2896 Lentz, Tony. Editorial Response: Value is personal growth.

2897 Lentz, Tony, ed. Issues in Interpretation 3 (1978) No. 4. The Issue: Performance Which Is Not Recognized as a Critical Concern in OI. Contents listed below.

2898 Bennett, Suzanne. To ask if it is time to direct attention to performance is to ignore OI's history and intent as well as modern directions in interpretation.

2899 [No entry.]

2900 Williams, D. A. Performance is a form of explication by real participation. Lit is not an object and our response to it is not objective; subjectivity is no longer a dirty word.

2901 Wells, Lynn. OIers should stop talking among themselves about ontology of performance and spend some time educating the general public.

2902 Lentz, Tony. Editor's Response: OI should invest more time and prestige in performance and criticism of performance. At the same time field should focus on development of critical theories and vocabularies for study of lit in performance not for performance.

2903 Perry, M. A. Voice in Poetry: An Argument for the pursuance of a modern oral tradition. First in five-part series investigating voice in poetry.

2904 Lentz, Tony, ed. Issues in Interpretation 4 (1979) No. 1. The Issue: Success: What Are the Key Characteristics of the Programs in Oral Interpretation That Continue to Grow and Prosper? Contents listed below.

2905 Elsea, J. G., & K. B. Valentine. Suggest a successful curriculum and note five characteristics of program success.

2906 Bowen, E. R. Need to sell OI more especially to administration.

2907 Meyer, J. J. Continual engagement with colleagues; more inter-disciplinary contact.

2908 Haushalter, W. R. Strong interpretation program can defend itself it it meets certain conditions.

2909 Doll, H. D. Three issues to insure academic support: focus, variety, and scholarship.

2910 Conquergood, Dwight. Liberal arts education in general and OI in particular are threatened by two currents: undertow of marketability and rising tide of scientism.

2911 Long, B. W. List of attributes that appear to keep and add new courses and faculty: attracting and graduating majors, receiving fair share of funding, and enjoying measure of stability.

2912 Lentz, Tony. Editorial Response: Questions Remain: Is OI a performance art? If so, does it need that vast audience that some believe is waiting for us?

2913 Perry, M. A. Voice in Poetry: An Argument for the Pursuance of a Modern Tradition Part II. Discovers OI has regard for performance of lit that emphasizes not only understanding but enjoyment of fullness of verbal technique.

READERS THEATRE NEWS

2914 Taylor, M. S. I'm OK, You're OK, Readers Theatre Is OK. 1 (Dec. 1973) 7. RT has caught imagination of educators in elementary and secondary school as reading enrichment.

2915 Noll, A. J. Readers Theatre in Education. 1 (Dec. 1973) 8. Introduction of RT overcomes student's aversion to textbooks and stimulates study of lit.

2916 Adams, J. A. The Great Conversion. 1 (Dec. 1973) 9. Twelve suggestions for converting schools to a faith in RT. RT viable form requiring as much creativity as plays.

2917 Wilson, Pat. Helpful Hints for Beginners. 1 (Dec. 1973) 11. Do: Choose lit with dialogue, lit not dependent on visual effects, lit that contains vivid situations and characters. Don't: Choose first person point of view or heavy action.

2918 Frank, Elle. Readers Theatre for the Observer. 1 (Dec. 1973) 12. Rehearsal observers get more as class members, non-participating, from watching rehearsal than audience members get from performance.

2919 Gregory, Paul. Paul Gregory Speaks. 2 (Winter 1974) 3 & 5. Interview with Gregory and his thoughts on RT and its use.

2920 Moorehead, Agnes. Staging Don Juan in Hell. 2 (Winter 1974) 6. One of the original performers describes production of first modern RT presentation.

2921 MacLay, J. H. The Character of the Narrator. 3 (Spring 1975) 3. Persona key to understanding lit and storyteller should be characterized in terms of style.

2922 Gregory, Paul. Awareness. 3 (Spring 1975) 4. Cultivate the mind to keep it active.

2923 Breen, R. S. Readers Theatre and the Audience. 3 (Spring 1975) 6. RT communicates more directly with audience than traditional theatre.

2924 Coger, L. I. Kinesics in Interpreters Theatre. 3 (Spring 1975) 6-7. Body language can be used to deintensify, overintensify, neutralize and hide emotions as well as communicate immediacy, power, responsiveness.

2925 Bacon, W. A. Readers Theatre as a Humanizing Process. 3 (Fall 1975) 3 & 11. Relationship between performer and text is sharing relationship.

2926 Gregory, Paul. The Secret of Individual Progress in Art. 3 (Fall 1975) 9 & 11. Three important elements in mind --intelligence, impersonality, intention--which must be used constantly.

2927 MacLay, J. H. Translating the Literary Form into a Performance Form. (Spring 1976) 3-4, 10. Value of studying lit through interpretation rather than interpretation through lit and various types of narration to be found in lit.

2928 Williams, D. A. Readers Theatre: The Heuristic Feast. (Spring 1976) 5, 11. Problems encountered in teaching RT and adjustments made in attempt to solve the problems.

2929 Johnson, J. L. Readers Theatre and Evening School: A Perfect Match. (Spring 1976) 7-8. RT at Modesto Jr. College.

2930 Crain, Iz, & W. F. Smith. Readers Theatre Reaches the Young. 4 (Fall 1976) 3-4, 22-3. Basic techniques in RT with special use for youth.

2931 Hidden, Norman. Oral Sharing of Poetry. 4 (Fall 1976) 6, 18. Return and importance of poetry performed.

2932 Gura, T. J. Report from the SCA Summer Conference on the Performance of Literature. 4 (Fall 1976) 9, 18.

Summary of conference which laid emphasis on group performance.

2933 Hardy, M. N. CRT--A Professional Touring Readers Theatre. 4 (Fall 1976) 9, 19. History, trials and tribulations of forming professional touring RT company.

2934 Nutial, Mark. Another Professional Readers Theatre Group: The Peanut Butter Readers of Gorham, Maine. 4 (Fall 1976) 19-20. Brief history and outline of future plans.

2935 Pickering, J. V. Readers Theatre as Theatre. 4 (Spring 1977) 1, 18. RT is always theatre.

2936 Richardson, Ralph. Gleanings from London. 4 (Spring 1977) 2-3. Need for delving into subconscious when creating character for a performance.

2937 Gielgud, John. Gleanings from London. 4 (Spring 1977) 2. Importance of voice quality in performance.

2938 Stoppard, Tom. Gleanings from London. 4 (Spring 1977) 3-4. Playwright answers student's questions about his working methods when writing a play.

2939 Cronley, Connie. Confessions of a Poetry Reader. 4 (Spring 1977) 7-8. The Tiger's Eye Quartet, a poetry reading company, a résumé.

2940 Ackerman, Sam; Carol Henegar; & William Adams. Readers Theatre Discography. 4 (Spring 1977) 13, 15. Guide to commercial RT productions, recordings of lit adapted for group performance and commercial RT productions for which there is no recording information available.

2941 Turpin, T. J. Readers Theatre Goes to Sweden. 4 (Spring 1977) 17-8. Introduction of new art form to Swedish.

2942 Bacon, W. A. Readers Theatre: A Few Caveats and Several Personal Responses. 5 (Spring 1978) 1, 26. Bacon notes problem of defining RT, claims RT should ultimately be used for pleasure.

2943 Hunsinger, Paul. Readers and Chamber Theatre: A Possibility for Therapy. 5 (Spring 1978) 2. Sees need for further exploration of therapeutic aspects of RT and possibility of clinics and research and training grants in this area.

2944 Bowen, E. R. Informal Conversations with the Leaders of Readers Theatre. 5 (Spring 1978) 3-4. Primary merit of RT is as excellent form of theatre for superior audiences.

2945 Galati, F. J. Informal Conversations with the Leaders of
Readers Theatre. 5 (Spring 1978) 4-6. Galati talks of
his career and of directing Beckett's Endgame in which
author directions play a major part.

2946 Provenmire, E. K. Informal Conversations with the Leaders of Readers Theatre. 5 (Spring 1978) 6-8. Provenmire discusses in detail his creation of the verse choir.

2947 White, M. R. Informal Conversations with the Leaders of
Readers Theatre. 5 (Spring 1978) 8-10. Sees future of
RT as prosperous so long as it is not passed off as the-
atre.

2948 Adams, W. J. Informal Conversations with the Leaders of
Readers Theatre. 5 (Spring 1978) 10-1. Interview with
Pamela Adams. W. Adams charts successful future of
RT.

2949 Crowe, John. The Grapes of Wrath: American Premiere
Review. 5 (Spring 1978) 12. Praise for institute of RT's
production first presented at London RT workshop in 1976.

2950 Abbott, Philip. Highlights from the '77 National Summer
Workshop. 5 (Spring 1978) 13-4. Abbott's speech in
which he emphasizes actor's involvement with character.

2951 Bradbury, Ray. Highlights from the '77 National Summer
Workshop. 5 (Spring 1978) 14-5. Writer approves of RT
interpretations of his work and describes his own career.

2952 Cooley, Thomas. An Experimental Production.... 5 (Spring
1978) 29. Description of RT production of The Night
Thoreau Spent in Jail which comprised some scenes being
read and others being acted.

2953 Corwin, Norman. Highlights from the '77 National Summer
Workshop. 5 (Spring 1978) 20-1. Corwin, the father of
RT, describes his career and answers audience questions.

2954 Sills, Paul. Highlights from the '77 National Summer Workshop. 5 (Spring 1978) 21-2. Discussion of story theatre
and adaptation of stories for RT, notes his intent is that
story theatre should play like improvisational theatre.

2955 Cunningham, C. C. From Classroom Interpreter to Successful Actor. 5 (Spring 1978) 23-6. Cunningham's last
public address in which he maintains that a performer's
most important resource is emotion.

2956 Todd, Bob. Readers Repertory Theatre of Modesto: Coffee,
Culture and Caring.... 5 (Spring 1978) 30. RT company
uses a coffee house as its theatre and soon becomes the
craze.

2957 Gillmon, Rita. Message Theatre: At Work on a Problem of Inequity. 5 (Spring 1978) 30. Staging Sascha Garson's script which works toward social security reform. Garson's hope is to see day when age and sex won't be used to judge person's qualifications for performance.

2958 Corwin, Norman. Reminiscences of a Nominated Father. 6 (Fall 1978) 3-30. Detailed description of Corwin's production of World of Carl Sandburg. Remembers that it was stilted reading but dramatic experience.

2959 Roloff, L. H. Readers Theatre: Spatio-Temporal Interpretation. 6 (Fall/Winter 1978) 5, 46-7. Defines RT as probe by performers in time and space, and gives some kind of presentational form to material that is usually designated as literature.

2960 Crain, Iz; Richard Feist; & Alba Pickslay. Foreign Language Instruction Through Bilingual Readers Theatre. 6 (Fall/Winter 1978) 11-2, 51-2. Introduction of RT into language class makes students who once stumbled in oral reading more alert and fluent.

2961 Pattison, S. D. Informal Conversation. 6 (Fall/Winter 1978) 13, 14, 49-50, 53. RT must broaden its academic and educational spectrum to include children and senior citizens.

2962 Downs, Bernard. Directing the Metaphoric Mind. 6 (Fall/Winter 1978) 15-6. Downs finds Spolin's approach to directing which honors sacredness of intuitive behavior practical and pleasurable.

2963 Wells, Lynn. Oral Interpretation Festival: Background and Groundwork. 6 (Fall/Winter 1978) 17-8. Traces theatre festivals through ages and follows the divergent path taken by OI festival. Concludes that it takes time, money, organization, student and school cooperation and a good deal of energy to put on successful festival.

2964 Adams, J. A. Readers Theatre: A Shot in Literature's Arm. 6 (Fall/Winter 1978) 19-20. RT removes the lethargy from lit classes.

2965 Rudisill, A. S. Touring Readers Theatre: The Imagination Players. 6 (Fall/Winter 1978) 21-3. Company inspired by RT workshop at San Diego State whose goal was to introduce RT to elementary and junior high school students.

2966 Kleinau, Marion. Informal Conversation. 6 (Fall/Winter 1978) 48-9. Kleinau sees bright future for RT as long as there is understanding of its aesthetic identification.

2967 Bacon, W. A., et al. Valedictory and Reminiscences. 6 (Spring/Summer 1979) 3-5, 18 & 24. Retrospective coverage of Bacon's career on the occasion of his retirement from teaching.

2968 Valentine, K. B. Interpretation Trigger Scripting: An Effective Communication Strategy. 6 (Spring/Summer 1979) 7-8, 41, 46, 47. Use of carefully selected scripts of lit intended to kindle planned-for responses from specialized audiences, its benefits, strategies for use and ethical and evaluative dimensions.

2969 Marlor, C. S. Informal Conversation. 6 (Spring/Summer 1979) 15, 44-46. Marlor finds most satisfactory definition in OI to be Coger's Theatre of the Mind.

2970 Roloff, L. H. Informal Conversation. 6 (Spring/Summer 1979) 15, 47-9. Describes current interest in new course called "Interpretation of Literature Through Media."

2971 MacLeod, Molly. Recreating the Message: Readers Theatre in the Worship Setting. 6 (Spring/Summ 1979) 17 & 46. RT provides exciting and effective medium for recreating the message of the church.

2972 Pacilio, Bob. Forensics and Readers Theatre. 6 (Spring/Summer 1979) 20. Reasons why RT and forensics are compatible: RT helps unify speech squad, provides showcase for talent, can become a fund raiser and provides outlet for creativity.

2973 Schneider, R. J. Staging the Subtext: The Visceral Metaphor. 6 (Spring/Summer 1979) 21-3, 35 & 42. Texts that overtly reveal primal tensions find staged forms that awaken similar feelings of intense and mythic awe in an audience.

2974 Thorpe, Phyllis. Fitting Readers Theatre into the Secondary Drama Program. 6 (Spring/Summer 1979) 25. High school teacher finds RT opens up wide range of interesting material for examination and discovery.

2975 McBain, Olivia. Readers Theatre: A Reading Motivation for Educable Mentally Retarded Students. 6 (Spring/Summer 1979) 28. EMR students pleased/excited by RT because of motivational factor of surprise.

2976 Soares, Kenneth. Graduation Readers Theatre Speech? 6 (Spring/Summer 1979) 28 & 42. RT successful alternative to regular graduation speech.

2977 Poschman, William. College. 6 (Spring/Summer 1979) 36. Notes the sad appearance of differences between OI festivals and tournaments.

2978   Sparks, Donna.   College.   6 (Spring/Summer 1979) 36-7.
       Praise for forensics tournaments.

2979   Pearse, J. A.   College.   6 (Spring/Summer 1979) 38.
       Praise for festivals because they offer learning, mingling,
       and individual growth of each attendant.

2980   Robertson, G. L.   College.   6 (Spring/Summer 1979) 38-9.
       Finds no dichotomy between festivals and tournaments; both
       are compatible and offer outlets for all.

2981   Schener, Don.   Highbrow Violence on Television.   6 (Spring/
       Summer 1979) 50.   Why no complaints when a TV station
       airs Robinson Jeffers' poem "The Roan Stallion," the
       theme of which is the death of God?

2982   Hartman, Beth, & Burton Alho.   The Power of Common Ex-
       perience: The Living Text.   7 (Fall/Winter 1979) 5-6,
       18 & 48.   Description of RT anthology script arranged
       and performed by six disabled persons.

2983   McCoy, Robert.   John Updike's Buchanan Dying: A Chamber
       Theatre Production.   7 (Fall/Winter 1979) 7-8, 37.   De-
       scription of concept for production of text employing both
       RT and cinema.

2984   Kittleson, Ole, & Blake-Robert Maas.   Magnet Program and
       Readers Theatre.   7 (Fall/Winter 1979) 9 & 52.   Program
       which tries to bring about voluntary desegregation finds RT
       rewarding/challenging.

2985   Poschman, William.   The Premiere of Under Milk Wood.
       7 (Fall/Winter 1979) 11-12, 41-3.   Interviews with two
       actors in original production: Roy Poole and Al Collins.

2986   Elsea, J. G.   Oral Interpretation and the 1980's: Recharg-
       ing the Discipline.   7 (Fall/Winter 1979) 13 & 52.   Need
       is for more dynamic and creative teaching.

2987   Rudisill, Sue.   Secondary.   7 (Fall/Winter 1979) 15-6, 46-8.
       Three secondary school teachers share experience with RT
       and discuss methods of teaching and grading.

2988   Ratliff, G. L.   Reflections of Bertolt Brecht and Readers
       Theatre: Alienation as a Tool of Communication.   7
       (Fall/Winter 1979) 19-20, & 53.   Random reflections and
       historical perspectives on Brecht in theory and perform-
       ance.

2989   Anastos, Perry.   The Use of Oral Reading and Teaching
       Le Petit Prince.   7 (Fall/Winter 1979) 21-2, 45-6, & 52.
       Approach used in some episodes of Le Petit Prince in
       high school French class.

2990 Poschman, William. College Department: Copyright. 7
(Fall/Winter 1979) 23-4, 50-1. Interview with lawyer Bob
Chickoring on issue of copyright.

2991 Schneider, R. J. Informal Conversation. 7 (Fall/Winter
1979) 25 & 37. Schneider sees future in oral tradition of
folk literature but concerned for RT as valid art form.

2992 Marlor, C. S. Readers Theatre Bibliography. 7 (Fall/
Winter 1979) 28-30. Bibliography of research and productions, 1978-79.

2993 Taylor, Sharon. Keeping the Oral Tradition Alive. 7
(Spring/Summer 1980) 2-4, 35 & 46. Art of storytelling
examined, finds RT and storytelling akin, meets storyteller Ray Hicks.

2994 Lentz, Tony. The Spirits Beyond the Letter. 7 (Spring/
Summer 1980) 5-6. Brief summary of Greek view of
writing, lit being a spoken art form.

2995 Rickert, W. E. Readers Theatre on Wheels. 7 (Spring/
Summer 1980) 7-8, 34. Rewards and problems encouraging handicapped to perform RT; adaptations necessary in
production style.

2996 Alton, Lyndee. Elementary: Introducing the Chet F. Harrit
Readers Theatre Company. 7 (Spring/Summer 1980) 9,
42. RT company of third graders encourages reading and
self confidence.

2997 Haenny, Doris. Elementary: It Happens in the Library.
7 (Spring/Summer 1980) 9, 44 & 48. Elementary teacher
finds library ideal setting for RT and sees off-stage focus
as more involving.

2998 MacLay, J. H. Readers Theatre Honors Eudora Welty. 7
(Spring/Summer 1980) 11-12. Welty awarded honorary
doctorate and sees two of her short stories performed at
University of Illinois.

2999 Pentilescu, Marc. An Intimate Look at a Traveling Readers
Theatre Troupe. 7 (Spring/Summer 1980) 13-4, & 39.
Investigation of Peanut Butter Readers, one aimed at chil-
dren's audience.

3000 Johnson, Jim. Secondary Schools: Timeless Tales from
Greek Mythology. 7 (Spring/Summer 1980) 15, 27, 32,
33, 36, 37, 38. Portion of script and production notes
from RT production of some Ovid short stories at Modesto
Jr. College.

3001 Adams, W. J., et al. Readers Theatre on Video: Capturing Sound and Color on Tape. 7 (Spring/Summer 1980) 16-8, & 40-1. Adapting RT for video tape.

3002 Sauro, D. A. The Nuts and Bolts of Readers Theatre. 7 (Spring/Summer 1980) 19-20, & 37. Guidelines for classroom use of RT, using Serendipity Readers as example.

3003 Poschman, William. College: Criticism: Giving and Taking. 7 (Spring/Summer 1980) 21-2. How can we avoid the subjective of so much criticism and establish more workable criteria?

3004 Messinger, Bonnie. College: Theatre of Interpretation as a Japanese Tea Room. 7 (Spring/Summer 1980) 21, 26, 38. RT as a way to be finely aware and conscious, to develop new or renewed sense of the other.

3005 Williams, D. A. College: Chi Square: Critic Meets Last. 7 (Spring/Summer 1980) 21 & 23. In criticism perhaps the last word is that there is no last word, but sees evaluation as time to share and compare.

3006 Metcalf, L. D. College: Judging on the Forensics Circuit. 7 (Spring/Summer 1980) 21-2, 26-7. Essence of OI is how effectively student brings the lit to life, not how realistically the lit brings the student to life.

3007 Long, B. W. Informal Conversation With.... 7 (Spring/Summer 1980) 24 & 28. Long describes new magazine Literature in Performance and warns that RT must be careful not to cut too much from the original text.

3008 Pearse, J. A. Informal Conversation with.... 7 (Spring/Summer 1980) 24, 28-9, & 38. Production must have three elements to be called RT: script, sense of place and off-stage focus.

3009 McGeever, C. J. Informal Conversation with.... 7 (Spring/Summer 1980) 24 & 29. Sees biggest area of growth in RT in children's lit.

3010 Hardy, M. N. Informal Conversation with.... 7 (Spring/Summer 1980) 25, 29, 30. Explains formation and concept of professional RT group. Sees RT going in two directions: RT concepts becoming absorbed in professional theatre and colleges/universities leading the way in discovering new techniques.

3011 Frederickson, R. Q. Informal Conversations with.... 7 (Spring/Summer 1980) 25, 30, 31. Unproductive to define RT as apart from theatre in general and cautions that RT must avoid schisms with theatre departments.

3012 Crannell, K. C.   Informal Conversation with. ...   7 (Spring/ Summer 1980) 25, 31-2.   Raises interesting concept of role distribution in performance.

3013 Allison, Barbara.   Elementary: Readers Theatre for the Underachiever.   7 (Spring/Summer 1980) 42, 45, & 46. RT aid to remedial readers.

3014 Vogler, Dottie.   Elementary: Utilizing Readers Theatre for the Gifted.   7 (Spring/Summer 1980) 43, 45, 48.   RT backbone for class of gifted and talented students.

3015 Corwin, Norman.   Text and Passion.   8 (Fall/Winter 1980) 2-4, 36-9.   RT creation of time, many atmospheres and characters; suspends disbelief and educates--making it stand high among various dramatic forms.

3016 Bolar, G. M.   Responses to a Choreopoem.   8 (Fall/Winter 1980) 5-6, 41-3.   A description of the production and critics' reactions to For Colored Girls Who Have Considered Suicide When the Rainbow Is Enuf.

3017 Shouse, Elaine.   Linguistic Texture in an Afrocentric Mode. 8 (Fall/Winter 1980) 7-8.   Afro-American possesses a rich and zesty vocabulary, a unique trust for rhythm, and a bold and special spirit for word usage providing an opportunity for rich expression.

3018 Singer, Jackie.   Bridging the Age Gap--Elementary to Secondary.   8 (Fall/Winter 1980) 9-10.   San Diego's Kearny High School presents a fast-paced RT collage of lit with much success.

3019 Leight, Jan.   Readers Theatre--A Total Classroom Approach. 8 (Fall/Winter 1980) 10, 39, 48.   Technique of dividing up parts among all pupils means that everyone can become excited about reading and about RT, too.

3020 Williams, D. A.   Metaphor--The Gift of Performance.   8 (Fall/Winter 1980) 11-2.   A derivation and discussion of the importance of metaphor in poetry.   The gift of performance is in the voicing of the metaphor.

3021 Crouch, I. M.   The Roving Critic.   8 (Fall/Winter 1980) 15. Giving feedback to performance by students is task that must be exercised with much skill.

3022 Visel, Adele.   Elders Take to Readers Theatre.   8 (Fall/ Winter 1980) 16-7.   Four products are presented with much success with only a week's rehearsal at Elderhostel.

3023 Anderson, J. S.   Actors in Consort.   8 (Fall/Winter 1980) 17.   English actor's description of first attempt at RT.

3024 Fletcher, Marilyn. California School Marks Decade of Readers Theatre. 8 (Fall/Winter 1980) 18. Brief history of success of McKinleyville High School work with RT.

3025 Thorpe, Phyllis. Readers Theatre--A Plus for the Secondary School Theatre Program. 8 (Fall/Winter 1980) 20, 45, 48. RT in all its forms brings lit to life and audiences, too, at the secondary school level.

3026 McBain, Olivia. Readers Theatre for Educable Mentally Retarded Students. 8 (Fall/Winter 1980) 21, 44-5. Script called <u>Narcissa Whitman, Pioneer Girl</u>, which keeps pupils' interest by active involvement.

3027 Poschman, William. Readers Theatre and the ATA: A Moral Tale. 8 (Fall/Winter 1980) 24, 26, 28. Where OI stands in respect to ATA and SCA with statements from M. F. Hopkins, Vincent Brann, Jeanette Myers, and J. A. Wray.

3028 Holden, D. O. The First 200 Years: Black Bicentennial. 8 (Fall/Winter 1980) 29-35. Description of production and script, which traced history of black man from American appearance to 1968.

THESES AND DISSERTATIONS

1918

3029   Saxton, J. A.   The Correlation of the Departments of English and Expression.   M. A.   Ohio Wesleyan U.

1919

3030   West, C. F.   The Psycho-Genetic Nature of Expression, A Discussion of the Meaning of Expression.   M. A.   Ohio Wesleyan U.

1920

3031   Flemming, E. G.   A Study of Silent Reading in Classes in Speech.   M. A.   U. Wisc.

1922

3032   Burford, E. A.   Some Fundamental Considerations in the Oral Interpretation of Literature.   M. A.   Ohio Wesleyan.

3033   Parrish, W. M.   A Study in Oratorical Prose Rhythm. M. A.   Cornell U.

1923

3034   Buehler, E. C.   The Creation of Atmosphere by the Reader. M. A.   Northwestern U.

3035   Ericson, E. S.   Specific Difficulties of Silent and Oral Narrative Reading.   M. A.   U. Minn.

3036   Lowrey, Sara.   The Vocal Interpretation of Literature. M. A.   Baylor.

1924

3037 Cunningham, C. C.   An Analysis of the Technique of Henrik Ibsen's Social Dramas and a Comparison of This Technique with That of Certain Other Drama Forms.   M. A.   Northwestern.

3038 Fry, H. D.   The Place of Recall in the Whole Method of Learning Material for Oral Interpretation.   M. A.   Northwestern.

3039 Haugh, L. E.   The Bible Story in Religious Education.   M. A.   U. Southern Calif.

3040 Hoover, M. E.   Inner Speech and Its Functions in Oral Interpretation.   M. A.   Northwestern.

3041 Park, K. N.   The Effect of Rhythm on the Rate of Oral Reading.   M. A.   U. Chicago.

3042 Welch, Constance.   Speech Rhythm as Correlated with Various Human Emotions.   M. A.   Northwestern.

1925

3043 Bowman, C. A.   A Study of the Curry System of Training in Expression.   M. A.   Northwestern.

3044 Leverton, G. H.   The Philosophy of the Human Voice by James Rush: An Analysis and Evaluation.   M. A.   Northwestern.

3045 Stone, L. E.   Silent vs. Vocal Presentation of Memory Material for Oral Interpretation.   M. A.   Northwestern.

3046 Whitaker, E. B.   Interpretative Reading.   M. A.   U. Iowa.

1926

3047 Havinghurst, M. M.   Respiration in Oral Reading.   M. A.   U. Wisc.

3048 Keppel, V. J.   Representative Critics and Actors on Oral Expression.   M. A.   Cornell U.

3049 McNabb, L. C.   Modern Tendencies in Dramatic Interpretation.   M. A.   Ohio Wesleyan U.

3050 Perego, I. M.   The Function of Imagery in the Appreciation and Interpretation of Poetry.   Diss.   U. Wisc.

3051 Wilson, H. E. A Study of Content and Aims of Courses in Interpretative Reading in Academic Institutions of the United States. M. A. U. Wisc.

1927

3052 Bradley, H. A. A Study of the Structure of a Selected Group of Webster's Speeches. M. A. Cornell.

3053 Constance, M. R. An Analysis of the Poetry of Robert Frost to Determine Its Value for Public Reading Programs. M. A. Northwestern.

3054 Corley, M. E. The Identification of Various Emotional Qualities in the Oral Reading of a Foreign Language. M. A. U. Wisc.

3055 Haney, E. V. Incipient Motor Responses in Oral Interpretation. M. A. Northwestern.

3056 Higgins, H. H. A Critical Study of Selected Books on Reading Published in the United States Before 1861. M. A. U. Iowa.

3057 Horsman, M. J. A Study of the Delsarte System of Expression. M. A. Northwestern.

3058 Lewis, M. A. Children's Interpretation of Reading Material. M. A. U. Wisc.

3059 Spadine, E. J. A Critique of the Teachings of François Delsarte in Terms of an Objective Attitude Toward Mind. M. A. Cornell.

1928

3060 Blanks, A. F. An Introduction Study in the History of the Teaching of Public Speaking in the United States. Diss. Stanford U.

3061 Fritz, C. A. The Content of the Teaching of Speech in the American Colleges Before 1850. Diss. N. Y. U.

3062 Fushs, I. C. Audience Judgements as to the Effectiveness of Various Postures Used During Public Reading and Interpretation. M. A. U. Iowa.

3063 Marsh, G. E. A Study of the Effect of Various Directions on Rate in the Oral Reading of Oratorical Prose. M. A. Northwestern.

3064 Rittenberg, Fanny. A Study of the Effect of Oral Reading Versus Silent Reading on Children's Preferences. M. A. Syracuse.

3065 Roach, D. I. Ruskin's Art Principles Applied to Dramatic Interpretation. M. A. U. Wisc.

1929

3066 Berkstresser, K. E. Mental Hygiene Through Dramatics and Interpretative Reading. M. A. U. Wisc.

3067 Bradley, Catherine. Costumes and Costuming in the Interpretation of Drama. M. A. Ohio Wesleyan U.

3068 Ewing, W. H. Vividness of Imagery in Single and Multiple Silent and Oral Readings of Familiar and Unfamiliar Selections. M. A. Northwestern.

3069 Hendrickson, H. O. A Comparative Study of Art Definitions and Their Application to the Art of Oral Interpretation. M. A. U. Wisc.

3070 Kuehne, Catherine. Reading Abridgements of Contemporary Novels. M. A. U. Wisc.

3071 Mattern, Grace. The Biography of Robert McLean Cumnock. M. A. Northwestern.

3072 Miller, M. O. A Critique of S. S. Curry's Conception of Mind. M. A. U. Iowa.

3073 Parrish, W. M. Richard Whately's Elements of Rhetoric, Parts I and II: A Critical Edition. Diss. Cornell U.

3074 Ward, G. B. A Critique of Studies in Reading Rates, Silent & Oral. M. A. Iowa St.

3075 Williams, H. M. Judgement of Emotion and Dramatic Characterization from Pictures. M. A. Northwestern.

1930

3076 Gilbert, Edna. An Evaluation and Classification of Literature Suitable for Dramatization. M. A. Northwestern U.

3077 Kaump, E. A. Reading for High School Speech Courses. Diss. U. Wisc.

3078 Keuhne, Catharine. Reading Abridgements of Contemporary Novels. M. A. U. Utah.

1931

3079 Cogswell, E. M. A Description and Application of the Significant Contribution of Psychology to the Problems of Interpretative Reading. M. A. U. Southern Calif.

3080 Dailey, A. M. Assignments for the Teaching of Reading Aloud in an Elementary Course in Speech Training. M. A. U. Iowa.

3081 Gross, B. M. Interpretation as a Fine Art. M. A. Northwestern.

3082 Koepke, W. C. Pupil Development Through Oral Reading. Diss. Marquette U.

1932

3083 Fisher, E. B. The Origin and Sources of the Moscow Art Theatre. M. A. Northwestern.

3084 Hilde, N. V. A Study of the Life of Sarah Siddons: An Estimate of Her Ability as Oral Interpreter of Literature. M. A. Northwestern.

3085 Lynch, G. E. Objective Study of Time, Pitch and Intensity Factors in the Reading of Emotional and Unemotional Materials by Experienced and Inexperienced Readers. Diss. U. Iowa.

3086 Mueller, M. H. An Experiment in the Measurement of the Effectiveness of Oral Reading. M. S. Purdue. (Also listed as 1938.)

3087 Ray, J. H. A Study of Choral Verse Speaking. M. A. U. Southern Calif.

3088 Wirka, Mildred. The Poetry of Amy Lowell, An Appraisal from the Point of View of Public Reading. M. A. U. Wisc.

1933

3089 Becker, Rebecca. The Relationship Between Speech Power and Personality--A Case Study of Lamb and Dickens. M. A. U. Wisc.

3090 Buck, L. E. A Study from a Psychological Viewpoint of the Basic Attitudes Motivating the Language Symbols Used in the Plays of Eugene Gladstone O'Neill and Suggestions for the Oral Interpretation of the One-Act Play Ile. M. A. U. Minnesota.

3091 Krause, A. E. A Study of Creative Imagination. M. A. Northwestern.

3092 Thurston, Rozetta. Choric Speech as an Aid to Worship. M. A. U. Denver.

1934

3093 Anderson, H. R. An Experiment in Oral and Written English. M. A. Northwestern.

3094 Bertermann, H. A. A Record of Growth in Oral and Silent Reading as a Basis for Rating Primary Children. M. A. U. Conn.

3095 Christmore, E. C. Oral vs. Silent Reading for Literary Appreciation, An Experimental Study. M. A. U. Southern Calif.

3096 Jones, J. P. The Poets' Use of Color. M. A. U. Wisc.

3097 Porter, L. F. Voice Training and Interpretive Reading for High School Pupils. M. A. Colo. State Teachers College.

3098 Richardson, L. H. Principles of Story-Telling for Adults. M. A. U. Southern Calif.

3099 Swanson, D. E. Common Elements in Silent and Oral Reading. Diss. Iowa St. U.

3100 Wokurka, R. A. An Attitude Scale for Measuring the Effectiveness of an Oral Reading. M. A. U. Minn.

1935

3101 Coulton, T. E. Trends in Speech Education in American Colleges 1835-1935. Diss. N. Y. U.

3102 Foots, A. R. An Understanding of Poet's Structure as a Basis for the Speaking of Poetry. M. A. U. Southern Calif.

3103 Greenfield, V. T. Analysis of Speech Needs and Abilities of College Freshmen with Previous Training in Declamation. M. A. U. Iowa.

3104 Humphrey, J. S. Delsarte's Synthetic Philosophy of Expression. M. A. Cornell U.

3105- Latimer, Mary. The English Domestic Prose Tragedy of the
6 Eighteenth Century. Diss. U. Wisc.

3107 Lough, Mary. Effects Upon High School Students of a Speech Approach as Compared with the Conventional Approach in Teaching Literature. M. A. U. Denver.

3108 Lutz, M. E. Choral Reading--Its Application to the Teaching of Speech. M. A. L. S. U.

3109 Merrill, Vivian. The Relative Effectiveness of Presenting Children's Literature over the Radio and in the Classroom. M. A. U. Wisc.

3110 Peterson, Ellen. A Study of the Imagery in Rupert Brooke's Poems from the Standpoint of the Interpreter. M. A. Northwestern.

3111 Ray, H. M. A Study of the Prosody of Henry Wadsworth Longfellow to Determine the Sources of His Popularity. M. A. Northwestern.

3112 Redd, Marion. A Comparative Study of Techniques Employed by Ten Outstanding Authorities in the Field of Interpretation. M. A. Northwestern.

3113 Schaeffer, L. M. The Electra Character in Dramatic Literature. M. A. Northwestern.

3114 Williams, G. M. A Study of James Whitcomb Riley as an Interpretive Reader. M. A. Northwestern.

1936

3115 Beckey, R. E. A Critical Study of Certain Exercises in Interpretative Reading Based on the Novel. M. A. U. Iowa.

3116 Clasen, Gratia. An Interpretive Analysis of Keats' "The Eve of St. Agnes." M. A. Northwestern.

3117 Conger, M. W. Poetry for Use in Children's Reading. Diss. U. Wisc.

3118 Cowen, J. M. Pitch, Intensity, and Rhythmic Movements in American Dramatic Speech. Diss. U. Iowa.

3119 Dement, Frances. A Critical Study of Certain Exercises in Interpretive Reading Based on the Short Story. M. A. U. Iowa.

3120 Domigan, Maxine. Status of Teaching of Speech in the Universities and Colleges of the United States. M. A. Ohio Wesleyan.

3121 Eccles, Dorothy. A Study of Various Means of Stimulating the Imagination of the Oral Interpreter. M. A. Northwestern.

3122 Hill, Florynce. Experiments with the Oral and Written Methods of Teaching Medieval History, European History, and American Literature. M. A. Northwestern.

3123 Hilts, I. S. An Interpretive Study of George Eliot's Romola. M. A. Northwestern.

3124 Ives, A. B. The Interpretation of Tennyson's "Launcelot and Elaine." M. A. Northwestern.

3125 Jerome, E. K. A Comparison of Adolescent Males Undergoing Change of Voice as to Chronological, Mental and Skeletal Ages. M. A. Northwestern.

3126 Kendall, L. M. Critical Analysis of Specific Works of Five Leading Authorities in the Field of Interpretation. M. A. U. Southern Calif.

3127 Leonard, M. V. Oral Monologues of Early Californian Life Based on Historical Research. M. A. U. Southern Calif.

3128 Millsapps, L. S. The Role of Specific Words in the Distribution of Stuttering Moments During Oral Reading. M. A. U. Iowa.

3129 Perrin, P. G. The Teaching of Rhetoric in the American Colleges Before 1750. Diss. U. Chicago.

3130 Snyder, Mary. An Interpretive Study of Rosalind in As You Like It. M. A. Northwestern.

1937

3131 Beene, Rosalind. Tennyson's Images of Water. M. A. Stanford U.

3132 Breen, R. S. A Production of John Webster's The Duchess of Malfi. M. A. Northwestern U.

3133 Flack, Z. O. The Technique of the Dramatic Monologue. M. A. L. S. U.

3134 Gordon, E. C. Analysis of Oral Reading Ability of Elementary School Children. M. A. U. Mich.

3135 Grossenbacher, Helene. The Interpretation of Swinburne's Hertha. M. A. Northwestern.

3136 Jacobs, L. A. Sarah Siddons: As a Shakespearean Interpreter. M. A. Cornell U.

3137 Oliver, R. T. Re-Evaluation of the Oratory of Burke, Fox, Sheridan and Pitt. Diss. U. Wisc.

3138 Richey, E. B. An Interpretation of Edgar Allan Poe's The Fall of the House of Usher. M. A. Northwestern.

3139 Sarby, C. B. Evaluation of Research Findings on Errors in Oral Reading with Implication for the Teaching of Speech. M. A. U. Iowa.

3140 Shaver, Claude. The Delsarte System of Expression as Seen Through the Notes of Steele MacKaye. Diss. U. Wisc.

3141 Smith, Thelma. A Comparison of Standard Techniques of Acting and Interpretation as Applied to Wilde's Lady Windermere's Fan. M. A. L. S. U.

1938

3142 Baker, M. L. An Experiment in the Use of Radio Dramatization in High School History Classrooms. M. A. U. Wisc.

3143 Carmichael, H. E. A Comparative Evaluation of Oral and Written Methods of Teaching Tenth Grade English. M. A. Wayne U.

3144 Current, L. M. A Study of S. H. Clark as a Teacher of Interpretive Speech. M. A. Northwestern.

3145 Gracie, R. S. Six Original Monodramas on Pioneer Women of the West with Technique and History of Monodrama. M. A. U. Denver.

3146 Inness, Marjory. A Statistical Analysis of the Effect of Word Content Versus the Situation on Stuttering During Oral Reading. M. A. U. of Iowa.

3147 Kimball, M. L. A Study of the Development of Some Theories of Oral Interpretation. M. A. U. Wash.

3148 King, C. A. The Effectiveness of Group Speaking on the Acquisition of Certain Speech Skills. Diss. L. S. U.

3149 Lance, H. E. Projects in Reading Aloud for Junior High School Students Emphasizing Voice Improvement. M. A. U. Iowa.

3150 McKenna, Muriel. Study of Development, Present Status, and Performance of Monologue. Diss. U. Wisc.

3151 Moore, C. E. A Study of the Emotional Effects of Letter Sounds. Diss. U. Wisc.

3152 Ogg, H. L. Critique of Oral and Silent Reading of Poetic Literature. Diss. U. C. L. A.

3153 Park, Marie. Diagnostic Study of Development in Rehearsal and Performance of Students in Dramatic Interpretation. Diss. U. Iowa.

3154 Pettygrove, Phyllis. An Objective Study of Audience Comprehension of Standardized Reading Test Material When Presented Orally. M. A. U. Minnesota.

3155 Plummer, Harry. Determination of Correlation Between Oral/Silent Reading Ability of 100 University of Utah Students Selecting a Course in Oral Reading. M. A. U. Utah.

3156 Potter, Gail. Methodology of the Construction of an Historical Monologue. M. A. U. Southern Calif.

3157 Ritter, Esther. Remedial Treatment of Oral Reading Difficulties in Junior & Senior High Schools. M. A. U. Southern Calif.

3158 Sorenson, F. C. Meter and Rhythm in English Prosody. Diss. Stanford.

3159 Thomsen, A. M. Original Monodramas Adapted from Biographies Selected by Institute of Character Research. M. A. U. Southern Calif.

3160 Warden, C. R. The Effect of the Absence of Visual Stimuli of a Speaker Upon Audience Attitudes. M. A. Ohio St. U.

1939

3161 Burke, H. L. A Study in Pitch of Oral Reading of 4th Grade Children. M. A. Boston U.

3162 Gibbs, G. E. A Critical Study of the Constitutional Regulations Governing Declamatory Contests in the High Schools of the United States. Diss. U. Wisc.

3163 Harwell, R. L. Interpretative Principles as Revealed by a Study of the Classicists. M. A. U. Wisc.

3164 Hoffman, M. E. Pedagogical Implications in the Writings of Charles Henry Woolbert. M. A. U. Wisc.

3165 Martin, L. A. A Two Year Experiment in Teaching Interpretive Reading in High School with Case Records of Individual Progress. M. A. U. Iowa.

3166 Miller, M. K. An Analysis of Aesthetic Principles: Their Application to the Art of Interpretation. M. A. L. S. U.

3167 Rickard, P. B. An Evaluation of Various Types of Oral Presentation in Terms of Audience Comprehension. M. A. Wayne U.

3168 Ross, Irene. An Interpretative Study of Portia in William Shakespeare's The Merchant of Venice. M. A. Northwestern.

3169 Smith, R. G. A Study of Certain Forms of Antithetic Emphasis in Oral Interpretation from a Recorded Speech of Difficult Prose. M. A. Indiana U.

3170 Snell, A. H. A Study of Negro Poetry for Its Value to the Interpreter. M. A. U. Wisc.

1940

3171 Anderson, Lillian. An Interpretative Study of the Character of Lady Macbeth in William Shakespeare's Tragedy Macbeth. M. A. Northwestern.

3172 Burke, C. M. Experiment in the Comparison of the Amount of Appreciation Gained for Poetry Read Silently as Compared with That Gained from Hearing the Same Poetry Interpreted Orally. M. A. Baylor.

3173 Carter, Bertha B. A Study of the Oral Reading Disabilities of a Sixth, Seventh and Eighth Grade Group Deficient in Silent Reading. M. A. Iowa State.

3174 Cook, M. L. Significant Implications for the Interpreter in the Writings of James Russell Lowell and Amy Lowell. M. A. U. Wisc.

3175 Darley, F. L. A Normative Study of Oral Reading Rate. M. A. U. Iowa.

3176 Hicks, L. M. Comparison of the Arts of Interpretation and Acting. Diss. U. Wisc.

3177 Holmes, O. A. A Comparative Study of Early and Recent Textbooks in Interpretive Reading. M. A. Iowa St. U.

3178 Hugo, J. D. Milton's Rhetoric in Satan's Speeches. M. A. U. Missouri.

3179 Kaump, E. A. An Analysis of the Structural Differences Between the Oral and Written Language of One Hundred Secondary School Students. Diss. U. Wisc.

3180 Krulevitch, Walker. Short Story Adaptations for Radio. M. A. U. Wisc.

3181 Levy, E. L. Delsarte's Cours d'Esthetique Appliquee, Based on an Original Notebook. M. A. L. S. U.

3182 McGuire, L. M. The Style of Mrs. Siddons and Her Characterization of Lady Macbeth. M. A. Yale U.

3183 Newbitt, H. D. A Compendium of the Objectives and Methods of the Contemporary Authorities in Teaching the First Course in Interpretive Reading on the College Level. M. A. Penn. St. U.

3184 Partridge, A. E. Emerson and Woolbert. M. A. U. Michigan.

3185 Pierce, L. A. Rhythm in Literature Parallels the Scale of Specificity of Speech Development: A Biolinguistic Study. M. A. U. Michigan.

3186 Tate, Marjorie. The Relationship of Status and Growth in the Quality of Oral Reading to Comprehension and Speed and to Total Growth of the Child. M. A. U. Mich.

3187 Temple, M. F. The Function of Imagination in Interpretation as Applied to the Teaching of High School Students. M. A. U. Wisc.

3188 Van Metre, J. M. A Comparison of the Eye Movements of Good and Poor Oral Readers. M. A. U. Denver.

1941

3189 Anderson, M. G. The Relative Effectiveness of Storytelling and Dramatization in Primary School Broadcasting. M. A. U. Wisc.

3190 Enfield, C. G. Five Original Monodramas in a Series Entitled "The Honorable Cynthia Houston." M. A. U. Southern Calif.

3191 Hahn, E. F. Study of Influence of Variations in the Social Complexity of Oral Reading Situations, of Phonetic and Grammatical Factors, and of Remedial Treatment Upon Stuttering Frequency. Diss. U. C. L. A.

3192 Hallinan, M. J. A Study of Six of the Most Widely Used Translations of Dante's Inferno to Determine Their Relative Suitability for Oral Interpretation. M. A. U. Utah.

3193 Kretsinger, E. A. An Interpretative Analysis of Browning's "Andrea del Sarto." M. A. U. Oklahoma.

3194 Morris, Virginia. The Influence of Delsarte Philosophy of Expression as Revealed Through the Lectures of Steele MacKaye. M. A. L. S. U.

3195 Price, Navalyne. The Delsarte Philosophy of Expression as Seen Through Certain Manuscripts of the Rev. William R. Alger. M. A. L. S. U.

3196 Riddle, T. E. Characterization as Evolved by the Poet and Dramatist: A Comparative Study. M. A. U. Wisc.

3197 Robb, M. M. The Teaching of Oral Interpretation in the Colleges and Universities of the United States. Diss. Columbia U. Teachers College.

3198 Robertson, M. C. An Interpretive Analysis of Euripides' Trojan Women. M. A. U. Okla.

3199 Stephens, Elmyra. The Role of Oral Reading in Secondary Education. M. A. Wayne U.

3200 Wilson, M. L. Comparison of Oral Reading and Extemporaneous Speaking Rates of Elementary School Children. M. A. U. Denver.

1942

3201 Bloodstein, O. N. A Study of Oral Reading Rates of Stutterers in Relation to Frequency of Stuttering. M. A. Iowa State.

3202 Connell, V. E. The Interpretation of Lady Macbeth by Siddon, Cushman, and Ristori. M. A. U. Michigan.

3203 Glasgow, G. M. The Effects of Variations of Quality, Pitch, Rate, and Enunciation on the Comprehension and Appreciation of Prose and Poetry by High School Sophomores. Diss. N. Y. U.

3204 Hale, L. L. Reevaluation of the Vocal Philosophy of Dr. James Rush as Based on a Study of His Sources. Diss. L. S. U.

3205 Hymel, M. C. Fanny Kemble: Dramatic Reader. M. A. L. S. U.

3206   Lantz, R. C.   Choral Reading for Churches.   M. A.   U. Mich.

3207   Moothart, P. L.   An Analysis and Evaluation of Oral Reading Testing Materials.   M. A.   Iowa St.

3208   Morison, Josephine.   Oral Interpretation of the Poetry of Alfred Noyes.   M. A.   Baylor.

3209   Neely, G. A.   The School of Delsarte.   M. A.   L. S. U.

3210   Otwell, E. L.   The Monologue, A Medium for Training in Bodily Action and Imaginative Growth.   M. A.   U. Wisc.

3211   Peckenpaugh, J. C.   The Relationship of Oral Interpretation to Dramatic Art.   M. A.   St. College of Washington.

3212   Phillips, H. K.   The Influence of Samuel Silas Curry on Modern Interpretation Textbooks.   M. A.   U. Ala.

3213   Pittelman, R. K.   A Comparative Study of Oral Reading Rate of Superior, Normal and Stuttering Speakers.   M. A. Purdue.

3214   Rasmussen, M. L.   Aural Sensitivity Developed Through Choric Speech.   M. A.   U. Southern Calif.

3215   Stephens, R. J.   Charles Dickens, Oral Reader.   M. A.   U. Okla.

1943

3216   Berlin, A. J.   Rating the Intelligibility of Oral Reading. M. A.   U. Wisc.

3217   Drake, A. C.   Elocution Theories of S. S. Curry and Their Application.   M. A.   L. S. U.

3218   Emerson, M. L.   A Study of Changes in the Use of Voice in Projecting Meaning from the Printed Page.   M. A.   U. Iowa.

3219   Hyatt, A. V.   The Place of Oral Reading in the School Program.   Diss.   Columbia U. Teachers Coll.

3220   Jayne, B. M.   The Interpretation of Stories.   M. A.   U. Mich.

3221   McKee, A. L.   Choral Problems Involved in the Production of Aeschylus' "The Orestian Trilogy."   M. A.   U. Iowa.

3222   Pines, William.   An Interpretative Study of Old-Time Negro Preaching.   Diss.   U. Mich.

3223 Saxton, L. R. Interpretative Reading from the Classical
      Novel Adapted for Radio. M. A. W. Tex. St. Coll.

1944

3224 Grantham, F. E. Oral Reading in the General Reading Pro-
      gram in the Secondary School. M. A. U. Okla.

3225 Vergara, Allys. A Critical Study of a Group of College
      Women's Responses to Poetry. Diss. Columbia U.

1945

3226 Crenshaw, I. E. A Comparative Study of the Use of Imagery
      in the Works of Robert Frost and Emily Dickinson: Signif-
      icant Values for the Interpreter. M. A. U. Wisc.

3227 Harang, M. W. The Public Career of François Delsarte.
      M. A. Louisiana St. U.

3228 Hobbs, D. M. The Spoken Art of Mark Twain. M. A. U.
      Oklahoma.

3229 Lee, C. I. Prosodic Analysis and Oral Interpretation of the
      Poetry of Paul Verlaine. Diss. Northwestern.

3230 Minor, G. M. Contributing Factors to the Decline of Oral
      Interpretation in the Great Age of Roman Literature.
      M. A. U. Missouri.

3231 Newman, D. L. Literature for Declamation. M. A. U.
      Mich.

3232 Parris, W. B. Interpretation, Monodrama: The Rampant
      Victorian--Life of Florence Nightingale. M. A. Bob
      Jones U.

1946

3233 Dillport, R. W. The Pupils of Delsarte. M. A. L. S. U.

3234 Donner, S. T. The Speaking and Reading of Mark Twain.
      Diss. Northwestern.

3235 Farma, W. J. A Study of Comparative Speech Forms of
      Delivery with Reference to Interpretative Reading. Diss.
      U. Wisc.

3236 Lord, Betty. A Study of the Life and Writings of Emily
      Dickinson in the Preparation for a Dramatization of Her
      Life. M. A. Smith College.

3237 Montgomery, J. R. Developing the Technique of Choral Speaking. M. A. U. Mich.

3238 Pafford, R. B. Amy Lowell, Oral Interpreter. M. A. U. Okla.

3239 Ray, Elaine. A Study of Trends in Methods of Teaching Oral Interpretation. M. A. Stanford U.

3240 Tousey, G. J. The Elocutionary Teaching of William Holmes McGuffey. M. A. Louisiana St. U.

1947

3241 Barber, E. S. Analysis for Oral Interpretation of the Dramatic Elements in Milton's Paradise Lost. Diss. Northwestern.

3242 Barry, J. J. Ralph Brownell Dennis, Lecturer, Interpreter and Dean of the School of Speech. M. A. Northwestern.

3243 Cavall, F. M. An Investigation into the Method of Teaching Oral Interpretation. M. A. Iowa St.

3244 Dixon, C. C. The Amount and Rate of Adaptation of Stuttering in Different Oral Reading Situations. M. A. Iowa St.

3245 Hamilton, R. G. Oral Interpretation of Literature in the Elementary Schools. M. A. Emerson Coll.

3246 Hammond, J. M. An Objective Study of the Pitch Characteristics of Eight-Year-Old Girls During Oral Reading. M. A. Iowa St.

3247 Hough, G. B. Student Workbook for Oral Interpretation. M. A. Kansas St. College.

3248 Lowrey, Jean. An Approach to the Study of the Effect of Training in Oral Interpretation on Speech and Comprehension in Silent Reading. M. A. L. S. U.

3249 Palangio, J. H. Five Historical Monodramas of Famous Women. M. A. U. Denver.

3250 Panattoni, F. I. Principles in the Selection, Adaptation, and Presentation of the Play Sun Up for the Lecture Recital. M. A. U. Mich.

3251 Seedorf, E. H. An Experimental Study of the Amount of Agreement Among Judges in Evaluating Oral Interpretation Contests. Diss. U. Wisc.

3252 Siebert, R. F. A Study of the Interpretation of Ibsen's
Hedda Gabler. M. A. U. Mich.

1948

3253 Barnett, Wynette. An Experimental Study in the Teaching
of Voice and Diction Through Ear Training, Phonetic and
Oral Reading Approaches. Diss. U. Wisc.

3254 Ciliberto, M. B. Interpretation, Monodrama: The Orchid,
Concerning the Famous Empress of China. M. A. Bob
Jones U.

3255 Donnell, M. G. The Theory and Practice of Booth Lawrey
as a Teacher of Speech. M. A. L. S. U.

3256 Ewbank, H. L. , Jr. A Preliminary Historical Study of the
American Lyceum from 1826 to 1840. M. A. U. Wisc.

3257 Flick, C. E. Using Motion Pictures to Teach Bodily Action. M. A. U. Nebraska.

3258 Hamilton, M. L. The Lyceum in New Orleans 1840-1860.
M. A. L. S. U.

3259 Hatch, Alene. Spoon River: A Lyric Choral Drama. M. A.
U. Denver.

3260 Henning, E. S. Portraits in Contemporary Poetry: A Medium for the Interpreter's Growth. M. S. U. Wisc.

3261 Hethmon, Robert. Dramatic Theory of William Butler
Yeats. M. A. Cornell U.

3262 Morris, M. V. Comparison of the Outcomes of the Oral
Interpretation Experience in the High School with Some
Stated Aims as Suggested by Leading Texts. M. A. U.
Wash.

3263 Penland, V. D. An Experimental Study to Measure Effectiveness in Oral Reading by Means of a Rating Scale Technique. Diss. U. Southern Calif.

3264 Wiksell, M. J. Social Aspects of Nineteenth Century American Elocution. Diss. L. S. U.

3265 Zimmerman, Joe. An Experimental Study of the Psychological Characteristics of a Group of Superior College
Actors. Diss. Northwestern.

1949

3266 Beardsley, P. W.   Listening Versus Listening and Reading:
      A Study of the Appreciation of Poetry.   M. A.   U. Okla.

3267 Branley, C. W.   Expressive Power Through the Oral Inter-
      pretation of Greek Tragedy. M. A.   U. Wisc.

3268 Britt, Betty.   Interpretation Monodrama: The Witch's Web,
      About Salem Witchcraft.   M. A.   Bob Jones U.

3269 Brooks, Keith.   Hypnotic Poetry--A Study.   M. S.   U. Wisc.

3270 Cain, Wendell.   A High School Course of Study in Inter-
      pretation.   M. A.   W. Tex. St. Coll.

3271 Cole, Ailene.   The Theory and Practice of Choral Reading.
      M. A.   U. Minn.

3272 Davis, C. L.   An Enriched Reading Program in Operation.
      M. A.   W. Tex. St. Coll.

3273 Davis, P. B.   An Investigation of the Suggestion of Age
      Through Voice in Interpretive Reading.   M. A.   U. Denver.

3274 Fuller, M. W.   An Interpretive Analysis of Three Plays and
      Their Stage Settings: Les Mouches by Jean-Paul Sartre,
      Tobias and the Angel by James Bridle, and Spook Sonata
      by August Strindberg.   M. A.   U. Southern Calif.

3275 Huff, N. M.   An Investigation of the Results of Sound Ef-
      fects Upon the Reading of Emotional Poetry.   M. A.
      Indiana U.

3276 Huhn, Florence.   An Analysis of the Theories of T. S.
      Eliot and W. H. Auden on Poetic Drama.   M. A.   Catholic
      U.

3277 Kamp, L. J.   A Study of Maxwell Anderson's Experiment
      in Poetic Drama.   M. A.   U. Mich.

3278 Kolch, F. L.   The Philosophies of Elocution in the Nine-
      teenth Century.   M. A.   Wayne St. U.

3279 Laur, M. V.   A Study of the Dramatic Monologue: Its Value
      for the Student of Oral Interpretation.   M. S.   U. Wisc.

3280 Lord, A. B.   The Singer of Tales: Study in the Processes
      of Composition of Yugoslav, Greek and Germanic Oral
      Narrative Poetry.   Diss.   Harvard.

3281 Morris, M. V.   Survey of the Status and an Analysis of the
      Outcome of the Oral Interpretation Experience in Certain

High Schools in the State of Washington. M. A. U. Washington.

3282 Nelson, Laverne. Dramatic Production, Choral Speaking Play, the Song of Deliverance from the Bible. M. A. Bob Jones U.

3283 Richeson, E. M. An Experimental Study of the Visual and Aural Perception of Selected Modern Poetry. M. A. U. Ala.

3284 Roberts, P. P. Speech Sound Time and Oral Reading Time of College Stutterers and Non-Stutterers. M. A. Purdue.

3285 Vandraegen, Daniel. The Natural School of Oral Reading in England: 1748-1828. Diss. Northwestern.

1950

3286 Breen, R. S. Symbolic Action in the Oral Interpretation of Robinson Jeffers' "Roan Stallion." Diss. Northwestern.

3287 Cass, D. L. A Study of Audience Preferences for Varying Degrees of Metrical Obviousness in Oral Interpretation. M. A. U. Okla.

3288 Crandall, W. T. An Experimental and Descriptive Study of the Comparative Effectiveness of Two Religious Radio Broadcasts. M. A. U. Southern Calif.

3289 Ellis, R. E. Some Audience Centered Problems of Shake-spearean Productions. M. A. U. Michigan.

3290 Gilbert, E. E. An Experimental Study of the Effects of Training in Oral Reading on Silent Reading Skills. Diss. U. Wisc.

3291 Hancock, M. M. A Study of Two Methods of Teaching the Interpretation of Radio Continuity. M. A. U. Nebr.

3292 Hunter, I. C. Analytical Approach to the Oral Interpretation of Three Old Testament Stories. M. A. U. Wash.

3293- Johnston, E. C. The Oral Interpretation of the Book of
4 Job. M. A. U. Mich.

3295 McCarthy, M. M. Interpretative Reading Behavior: Study of Selected Factors. Diss. U. Wisc.

3296 Mewshaw, J. B. Elocution and Oral Interpretation. M. A. U. Mich.

3297 Newman, J. B. Joshua Steele: Prosody in Speech Education. Diss. N. Y. U.

3298 Powers, V. M. An Interpretive Analysis of Robinson Jeffers' Medea. M. A. U. Okla.

3298a Renshaw, Edyth. Three Schools of Speech: The Emerson College of Oratory, The School of Expression, and The Leland Powers School of The Spoken Word. Diss. Columbia U.

3299 Roach, H. P. History of Speech Education at Columbia College 1754-1940. Diss. Columbia U.

3300 Sanders, L. J. The Writings of Carl Sandburg: An Appraisal of Their Value to the Public Reader. M. A. U. Wisc.

3301 Weisman, H. M. An Investigation of the Methods and Techniques in the Dramatization of Fiction. Diss. Denver U.

1951

3302 Boast, W. M.; J. A. Buchanan; M. F. Casmen; & W. I. Norling. Suggested Units of Study in Oral Interpretation at the College Level. M. A. U. Denver.

3303 Bohyer, J. A. The Sentimental Comedy of James Mathew Barrie for the Oral Reader. M. A. U. Mich.

3304 Booth, W. C. The Analysis and Comparison of Vocal Technique of the Delivery of Hamlet's Soliloquy (Act II, Scene II) as Recorded by John Barrymore and Maurice Evans. M. A. U. Mich.

3305 Bosmajian, Haig. Origin and Development of the Art of Oral Interpretation of Verse in the United States. M. A. Coll. of Pacific.

3306 Colvin, C. R. A Study of the Problems in Interpretation, Character Analysis and Projection of the Author's Intent in Preparing the Lecture Recital for Public Presentation. M. A. Kent St. U.

3307 Edne, E. G. An Experimental Study of the Effects of Training in Oral Reading on Silent Reading Skills. Diss. U. Wisc.

3308 Hehner, O. D. A Series of Lesson Plans in Oral Reading and the Dramatic Interpretation of Literature. M. A. St. Louis U.

3309 Herbst, Irwin. An Experimental Study of the Effects of
Room Characteristics and Noise Upon the Rate and Accuracy of Reading Familiar Material. M. A. Ohio St. U.

3310 Houlihan, M. E. An Analysis of Dramatic Literature for
Speech Improvement in the Secondary Schools. M. Ed.
Boston U.

3311 Hunsinger, Paul. Study of the Oral Interpretation of King
James Version of the Bible as the Scripture Lesson in the
Sunday Morning Worship Services of the Protestant
Churches. Diss. Northwestern.

3312 Kelly, Irene. Ruth Draper--One Woman Theatre. M. A.
U. Mich.

3313 Loney, G. M. Edith Sitwell: A Study. M. A. U. Wisc.

3314 Marr, Gaylord. A Study of Methods of Adapting Stage Drama
and Prose Fiction to the Radio Medium. M. A. U.
Nebraska.

3315 Marsh, Robert. Modern Poetry in Oral Interpretation: A
Study of the Extent to Which Contemporary Poetry Is Used
in College Level Oral Interpretation Classes with Consideration of Selected Related Factors as Possible Conditions
Governing Its Use. M. S. U. Oregon.

3316 Okey, L. L. A Descriptive Biographical Study of Thomas
Clarkson Trueblood. Diss. U. Mich.

3317 Pickett, W. W. An Experiment to Determine Comparative
Audience Response to the Reading of Shakespearian Drama-
tic Verse with and Without Musical Accompaniment. M. A.
U. Mich.

3318 Sandboe, A. P. Hamlet: A Production Book. M. F. A.
Fordham U.

3319 Schwerman, E. L. An Analysis for the Oral Interpreter,
of Rainer Maria Rilke's "Duineser Elegien" and "Sonnette"
and "Orpheus." Diss. Northwestern.

3320 Skendi, Stavro. Albanian and South Slavic Oral Epic Poetry.
Diss. Columbia.

3321 Summers, M. C. An Interpretive Analysis of Euripides'
Medea. M. A. Baylor U.

3322 Wargo, D. M. A Survey of the Public Performance Interpretative Reading Program in Pennsylvania Colleges and
Universities. M. A. Penn. St. Coll.

3323 Whitehair, B. M. Original Dramatic Reading with a Critical Analysis of Staging and Lighting for College Use. M. A. U. Wash.

3324 Wigley, J. A. A Study of Students' Response to Recording of Poetry Recorded by Its Authors and by Other Interpreters. M. A. U. Wash.

3325 Williams, Georgia. An Analysis of Poetry for the Improvement of Speech in the Secondary Schools. M. Ed. Boston U.

1952

3326 Beaver, Doris. The Oral Interpretation of Coleridge's Christabel. M. A. U. Okla.

3327 Beighley, K. C. The Effects of Four Attributes of Speech on the Comprehension of Prose. Diss. Ohio St. U.

3328 Bowyer, F. E. James E. Murdock, The Elocutionist. M. A. U. Colo.

3329 Brady, J. B. History and Analysis of Oral Interpretation Activities. M. A. Baylor U.

3330 Burns, Kenneth. A Survey of the Contemporary Outlook Relative to the Basic Aspects of Oral Interpretation as It Is Evidenced in Selected Writings in the Field: 1915-50. Diss. Northwestern U.

3331 Coger, L. I. A Comparison for the Oral Interpreter of the Teaching Methods of Curry & Stanislavsky. Diss. Northwestern.

3332 Compere, M. S. A Study in the Teaching of Poetry. Diss. Mich. St. U.

3333 Floyd, H. W. A Comparative Study of Seneca's and Robinson Jeffers' Versions of Medea as Related to the Medea of Euripides. M. A. U. Southern Calif.

3334 Giese, P. P. A Study of the Preparation Involved in the Selection and Preparation of Materials (Poems, Stories & Plays) for Public Presentation with Consideration to Needs of Specific Types of Audiences. M. A. Kent St.

3335 Gobrecht, E. F. A Descriptive Study of the Potential Use of Poetry in Television Programming. M. A. Ohio St. U.

3336 Goldstein, B. J. The Comprehension of Poetry: A Study of Two Hundred College Women's Response to Poetry. Diss. Columbia U. Tchrs. Coll.

3337 Golladay, Gertrude. The Singed Wings: Poetry and Explication, Introduced by a Discussion of Method. M. A. U. Denver.

3338 Hart, R. L. Public Reading in New York City from 1851 to 1861. M. A. L. S. U.

3339 Jordon, E. P. A Comparative Investigation of Impromptu Speaking and Oral Reading Under Conditions of Delayed Auditory Feedback. M. A. U. Ill.

3340 Kuykendall, R. B. The Reading and Speaking of Vachel Lindsay. Diss. Northwestern.

3341 Laird, Dugan. American and English Theories in the Natural Tradition of Oral Reading: 1880-1915. Diss. Northwestern.

3342 Wickersham, J. M. The Use of Oral Interpretation in a Speech Therapy Program of Children with Cerebral Palsy. M. A. U. Fla.

3343 Young, James. An Experimental Study of Relative Effects Upon Vocabulary Growth of Silent Reading, Listening and Reading Aloud. Diss. U. Southern Calif.

1953

3344 Bone, E. M. Problems in Selecting Material for Reading Festivals. M. A. U. Wisc.

3345 Caswell, Troy. The Concept of Aesthetic Distance in Oral Interpretation. M. A. U. Okla.

3346 Clemenci, R. B. A Compilation of Methods and Instructional Materials for Teaching Oral Expressions in a Sixth Grade. M. Ed. Boston U.

3347 Cole, O. F. Scholarship and Milton: A Study in the Method of the Oral Interpreter. M. A. U. Okla.

3348 Edwards, A. L. Whitman: 1920. M. A. UNC-Chapel Hill.

3349 Fitze, Arlene. A Survey of Curricular and Extracurricular Instruction in the High Schools of Pennsylvania. M. A. Penn. St. U.

3350 Gahagan, H. P. The Dramatization of Short Stories for the Understanding and Appreciation of Literature at the Ninth Grade. M. Ed. Boston U.

3351 Hallauer, J. W. Some Problems of Dramatization. Diss. Ohio St. U.

3352 Hansen, L. A., Jr. A Lyric Theatre Adaptation of Robert Browning's "Pippa Passes." M. S. Boston U.

3353 Hill, J. B. The Circle by W. Somerset Maugham. M. F. A. Art Institute of Chicago.

3354 Kidder, R. R. The Preparation and Use of Recordings in the Study of Interpretative Speech. Diss. Wayne St. U.

3355 Luetenegger, R. R. A Study of Adaptation and Recovery in the Oral Reading of Stutterers. M. A. St. U. Iowa.

3356 Maheu, Sister A. M. A Dramatistic Approach to a Rhetorical Study of the Sermon on the Mount. M. A. U. Hawaii.

3357 Manion, O. G. An Application of Readability Formulas to Oral Communication. Diss. U. Mich.

3358 McGraw, W. R., Jr. An Analysis and Production Book of The Fan by Carlo Goldoni. M. A. Ohio St. U.

3359 McKee, M. J. An Oral Reading Syllabus for Elementary School Teachers. M. A. St. Louis U.

3360 Norris, M. S. Musical Stories--A Series of Thirteen Tape-Recorded Programs Presenting Folk Stories and Their Music. M. S. Boston U.

3361 Roberts, H. P. Problems in Adapting the Dramatic Short Story for Television. M. A. U. Southern Calif.

3362 Roland, P. T. A Study of the Problems in the Production of Folk Fantasy. M. A. Bowling Green St. U.

3363 Stamm, Dee. A Logical and Emotional Approach to the Song of Songs with Lecture Recital. M. A. U. Mich.

3364 Vaughan, J. W. A Critical Analysis of the Problems in a Practical Application of the Principles of Interpretation, Direction, and Design in Producing Shakespeare's Macbeth. M. A. Indiana U.

3365 Weintraub, S. A. The Paralleling of Principles & Methods in Oral Interpretation of Literature. Diss. Columbia.

3366 Wieand, B. J. The Book of Ruth: Comparative Study and Lecture Recital. M. A. U. Mich.

3367 Zucchero, W. H. An Historical Study of the Proceedings of the National Association of Elocutionists. M. A. U. Mich.

1954

3368 Adams, W. W.   Relationships Between the Principles of
Acting and Rhetorical Delivery in 18th-Century England.
Diss.   U. of Ill., Urbana.

3369 Aserlind, Leroy.   The Association of Auditory Musical Discrimination and Interpretative Reading Ability.   M. S.   U.
Oregon.

3370 Beloof, R. L.   E. E. Cummings: The Prosodic Shape of
His Poems.   Diss.   Northwestern.

3371 Cunningham, E. T.   Suggestions and Audio-Visual Aids for
Reading the Bible Aloud.   M. A.   U. Mich.

3372 Dehaas, M. J.   S. S. Curry's Theory of Oral and Bodily
Expression.   M. A.   U. Ill.

3373 Dickenson, D. D.   A Study of First Grade Children's Oral
Verbal Expression as Related to Reading Readiness.
M. A.   U. Redlands.

3374 Ely, J. B.   The Canterbury Pilgrims, An Epic Film Play
Set in 14th-Century England.   M. A.   U. Calif. at L. A.

3375 Fairies, C. J.   The Philosophy of Oral Interpretation of
Poetry According to Edith Sitwell.   M. A.   U. Mich.

3376 Forbes, Charlotte.   Recital: Six Characters in Search of an
Author, The Misanthrope, Cymbeline.   M. F. A.   Columbia
U.

3377 Jensen, Paul.   A Study of Perceived Harshness as a Function or Oral Reading Time.   M. A.   Iowa St.

3378 Kahan, Gerald.   A Shakespeare Production Handbook for
Non-Professionals.   Diss.   U. Wisc.

3379 Lerea, Louis.   An Exploratory Study of the Effects of Experimentally Induced Success and Failure Upon Oral Reading Performance and the Levels of Aspiration of Stutterers.
Diss.   U. Pittsburgh.

3380 Loney, G. M.   Dramatizations of American Novels, 1900-
1917.   Diss.   Stanford U.

3381 Mattingly, A. S.   The Mechanical School of Oral Reading in
England, 1761-1821.   Diss.   Northwestern.

3382 Merill, A. A.   A Compilation of Religious and Inspirational
Literature.   M. A.   Fresno St. Coll.

3383 Mills, M. J. A Study of the Use of Radio Dramatization in the High School English Classroom and Its Effects on the Student's Comprehension of Literature. M. A. U. Mich.

3384 Newman, P. W. A Comparative Study of Self-Formulated Speech and Oral Reading with Reference to Adaption and Recovery of the Stuttering Response. Diss. U. Iowa.

3385 Platt, J. H. Study of Personality Factors Common to Speaking, Listening, Writing and Reading. Diss. U. Denver.

3386 Rizzo, Sister M. J. Lily C. Whitaker: Founder of the New Orleans College of Oratory and Elocution. Diss. U. Wisc.

3387 Schrup, M. K. A Production Study and Text of William Shakespeare's Macbeth as Produced by the Speech and Drama Department of the Catholic University in March of 1952. M. F. A. Catholic U. of America.

3388 Smoot, J. S. Platform Theatre: Theatrical Elements of the Lyceum-Chautauqua. Diss. U. Mich.

3389 Stoesser, M. R. Production Study and Text of The Traitor. M. F. A. Catholic U. of America.

3390 Varnado, A. F. The Reverend Gilbert Austin's Chironomia. Diss. L. S. U.

1955

3391 Armstrong, R. A. A Descriptive History of Scenic Design in Speech Department Productions at the University of Michigan from 1928-1953. M. A. U. Mich.

3392 Bennett, M. C. An Analysis of Concepts of Technique for the Communication of Literature in Selected Modern Works on Oral Interpretation. M. A. U. Ala.

3393 Bredendick, R. R. A Survey of the Art of Storytelling. M. S. U. Wisc.

3394 Brookshire, Helen. Typical Programs of the Oral Readers as Reflected in Werner's Magazine. M. A. L. S. U.

3395 Caron, Gerard. Oral Interpretation of the Sunday Gospels. M. A. Emerson College.

3396 Christopher, Nancy. Life in Literature. M. Ed. U. Texas.

3397 Cohelo, Richard. Some Factors Contributing to the Integration and Time-Binding Behavior of the Oral Interpreter

Obtained by Means of an Investigation of the Theories of George H. Mead, Suzanne Langer and Kurt Levin. Diss. U. Denver.

3398 Daley, M. P. Therese: A Dramatization of François Mauriac's Novel Therese Desqueyrous. M. A. Catholic U. of America.

3399 Day, J. E. The Development of a Traditional Folk Ballad as a Dance-Drama for Television. M. A. Mich. St. U.

3400 Dimasia, Ilda. Original Stories Integrating the Teaching of Articulation with Social Studies and Reading in the Second Grade. M. Ed. Boston U.

3401 Doolittle, Joyce. Fifty Stories for Creative Dramatics. M. A. Indiana U.

3402 Evans, E. F. Some Contemporary Concepts of Bodily Action as Related to the Oral Reader. M. A. U. Mich.

3403 Farrell, Nancy. A Survey of Opinions and Reports on Narration for Selected Interpretive Films. M. A. U. South Carolina.

3404 Fredericks, Virginia. A Study of the Oral Interpretation of Selected Poems by Edward Arlington Robinson. M. A. U. Minn.

3405 Gillis, H. R. The American College and University Literary Societies at Selected Institutions of the Mid-Atlantic Area 1875-1950. Diss. Wstn. Reserve U.

3406 Jisha, H. J. An Interpretive Analysis of Shelley's "Julian and Maddalo. " M. A. Baylor.

3407 Jones, Lloyd. Trends in Oral Interpretation as Seen Through the Professional Journals from 1940-1955. Diss. U. Denver.

3408 Longley, P. C. Creative Dramatics: A Technique for the Teaching of Literature. M. A. Texas State College for Women.

3409 Lundeen, D. J. An Investigation of the Relationship of Vertical Mandibular Movement to Loudness and Rate of Speech and to Aspects of Individual Variation. Diss. U. Minn.

3410 McGinty, M. D. The Oral Interpretation of The Book of Daniel. M. A. U. Okla.

3411 Mohrmann, G. P. Aesthetic Concepts in Selected Oral Interpretation Textbooks. M. A. U. Wash.

3412 Olson, B. G. The Interpretation of the Book of Psalms. M. A. U. Okla.

3413 Owens, Rosemary. A Character Analysis from the Standpoint of the Oral Interpreter of the Four Principle Characters in Edwin Arlington Robinson's Poem, "Tristram." Diss. U. Denver.

3414 Pearson, T. A. An Analysis of The Adventures of Huckleberry Finn for oral interpretation. M. A. Baylor.

3415 Pennington, R. B. The Oral Interpretation of Selected Sonnets of Sir Thomas Wyatt. M. A. U. Okla.

3416 Rebillot, E. P. A Theatrical Adaptation of Beowulf for the High School Stage. M. A. U. Mich.

3417 Ross, V. M. A Study of the Problems of Dramatization of Three Narratives. M. A. Ohio St. U.

3418 Schaus, Lucibel. Original Dramatic Adaptations Supplementary to the Scott, Foresman Series in First Grade. M. A. Boston U.

3419 Simpson, K. B. The Happy Prince, A Dramatization of the Oscar Wilde Fairy Tale. M. A. U. Wash.

3420 Virnelle, Yvonne. Three Original Dramatic Adaptations of Children's Stories with Prompt Books and Suggestions for Their Production. M. S. Kansas St. C.

3421 Watkins, M. L. The Writing and Production of a Children's Plays Based Upon Thackeray's The Rose and the Ring. M. A. Mich. St. U.

3422 Worrell, Elizabeth. The Short Works of Virginia Woolf: A Study for the Oral Interpreter. Diss. Northwestern.

1956

3423 Alluisi, M. B. The Relationship Between Vocal Characteristics in Oral Reading and the Relative Information of Selected Phrases. Diss. Ohio State.

3424 Campbell, Stephanie. The Dramatic Effect of the Lyric Poetry in Three Plays by Christopher Fry. M. A. Catholic U. of America.

3425 Challgren, Patricia. A Systematic Approach for the Teaching of Dialects for Oral Interpretation and Acting. M. A. Occidental Coll.

3426 Cleary, J. W. <u>Chirologia</u> ... <u>Chironomia</u> A Facsimile
Edition with Introduction and Notes. Diss. U. Wisc.

3427 Dauner, Sister M. A. The Use of Poetry Recordings in
English and Speech. M. A. U. Mich.

3428 Davis, D. A. Early Minstrel Production. M. A. U. Mich.

3429 Gumpert, Gary. The Problems Involved in the Television
Adaptation of Katherine Anne Porter's <u>Noon Wine</u>. M. A.
Mich. St. U.

3430 Hadley, D. S. Oral Interpretation at the Chautauqua Institution & the Chautauqua School of Expression 1874-1900.
Diss. Northwestern.

3431 Hannon, K. M. An Adaptation of "The Necklace" for Television. M. A. Mich. St. U.

3432 Kiefer, M. T. Adapting the Novel <u>Fabiola</u> to Dramatic
Production. M. A. St. Louis U.

3433 Leach, Wilford. Gertrude Stein and the Modern Theatre.
Diss. U. Ill.

3434 Lee, K. K. A Translation of the Korean Classic <u>Choon
Hyang Chun</u> for Oral Interpretation. M. A. Stanford U.

3435 Lins, Kathryn. An Interpretive Study of Selected Poetry of
Genevieve Taggard. M. A. U. Hawaii.

3436 Logsdon, J. M. Original Verse Created, Devised and
Adapted for Choral Reading on the Various Educational
Levels. M. A. Marquette.

3437 Low, D. R. The Speeches, Lectures and Readings of
Charles Dickens and William M. Thackeray in the United
States, 1842-1868. Diss. Northwestern.

3438 Mikle, R. L. Selecting and Adapting Literary Material for
the Lecture Recital Form of Presentation. M. A. U.
Mich.

3439 Neely, Marguerite. Contemporary Theory Concerning Purposes for College Courses in Oral Interpretation. M. A.
Stanford U.

3440 Newman, Robert. A Dramatic Adaptation for Television of
Pushkin's <u>Prose Tale--an Amateur Peasant Girl</u>. M. A.
U. Mich.

3441 Servine, Margaret. Fundamentals of Oral Reading: A Textbook in Oral Reading for Secondary Schools. Diss.
Columbia Tchrs. Coll.

3442 Staub, A. W. Shakespeare's Inner Stage. M. A. L. S. U.

3443 Swall, M. R. An Analysis of Selected Dramatic Monologues in Preparation for Oral Interpretation. M. A. U. Hawaii.

3444 Wigley, J. A. An Analysis of the Imagery of William Faulkner's Absalom, Absalom! Diss. Northwestern.

1957

3445 Boudreaux, J. R. A Study of Consonantal Sounds in Beginning Reading Literature. M. A. W. Va. U.

3446 Bowes, A. S. Speech Reading Lessons with Poetry. M. A. Emerson Coll.

3447 Boyle, J. F. A Syllabus in Oral Interpretation of Literature. M. A. St. Louis U.

3448 Bradley, P. M. An Experiment in Teaching the Oral Interpretation of Literature. M. A. St. Louis U.

3449 Cheney, L. A. A Correlating of the Stanislavsky Acting Techniques with the Medium of Oral Interpretation. M. A. Kent St. U.

3450 Evans, G. H. An Analysis and Interpretation of The Scarecrow by Percy MacKaye. M. A. Sacramento St. Coll.

3451 Evans, Hugh. Comic Aspects of Shakespeare's Henry V. M. A. Stanford U.

3452 Evans, P. M. Oral Interpretation in Anglo-Saxon England. Diss. Northwestern.

3453 Feuerman, Helene. An Experimental Story of Amount of Anticipated Difficulty in Oral Reading as a Function of Amount of Exposure to Delayed Auditory Feedback. M. S. Penn. St. U.

3454 Foster, E. A. A Critical Study of the Recorded Interpretive Readings of Selected Modern Poets Reading Their Own Works. M. A. U. Ill.

3455 Fulsem, R. E. An Investigation of the Structural Aspects of Free Verse as They Affect the Oral Reader. Diss. Northwestern.

3456 Hoffman, S. V. A Creative Study of the Presentational Technique for Especial Literary Selections Through Oral Interpretation. Diss. Pepperdine C.

3457 Hoopes, Ned. Review of Criteria for Evaluation of Literature to Be Used in Oral Interpretation. M. A. Brigham Young U.

3458 Leonardo, M. M. The Teaching of Imagery in Selected Books Dealing with Oral Interpretation Published from 1756-1956. M. A. L. S. U.

3459 Loge, E. R. An Experimental Study of the Comparative Effectiveness of the Oral and Traditional Methods of Teaching High School Literature. M. A. U. N. Dakota.

3460 Mann, G. W. An Historical Evaluation of the Character of Thomas Beckett as Shown by T. S. Eliot in Murder in the Cathedral and Alfred Lord Tennyson in Beckett. M. A. U. Ga.

3461 Mezvinsky, S. S. The Heroines of Medea, Phaedra, Ghosts, and Summer and Smoke: Subjects for Oral Interpretation. M. A. U. Wisc.

3462 Miller, M. H. The Collected Speeches of Charles Dickens with Introduction and Notes. Diss. U. Wisc.

3463 Moldenhauer, J. F. An Analysis and Annotation of Articles on Teaching Oral Interpretation in the Quarterly Journal of Speech for 1915 Through 1954. M. A. Iowa St.

3464 Norman, R. A. Reading Aloud and Extemporaneous Speaking on the Radio. Diss. Columbia U.

3465 Palmer, B. A. An Analysis of the University of Michigan Storytime Programming over WPAO-TV. M. A. U. Mich.

3466 Paulson, R. S. A Comparison of Oral Interpretation Theories, 1850-1950. M. A. Fresno St. C.

3467 Rooney, Boyd. A Study in Methods of Adapting Prose Literature for Television. M. A. U. Nebraska.

3468 Ryder, Viola. An Analysis of the Process of Adapting from the Narrative Work to the Dramatic Form. M. A. Smith C.

3469 Strickland, Sylvia. A Study of the Problems Involved in a Readers Theatre Production of At Midnight on the 31st of March. M. A. U. Ala.

3470 Walton, J. F. A Readability Analysis of Selected Facts, Forum Radio Programs. M. A. U. Colo.

3471 Watson, C. A. An Original Television Adaptation and Production Thesis of Ethan Frome. M. A. St. C. Wash.

<u>1958</u>

3472 Anderson, R. G.   The Oral Interpretation of Southwestern
      Folklore.   M. A.   Baylor U.

3473 Averett, Fran.   An Analysis for the Oral Interpretation of
      The Lady's Not for Burning by Christopher Fry.   M. A.
      U. Wash.

3474 Bahn, Pat.   A Study of the Monologue and One Woman Show,
      Production Based on Red Wine First by N. Tyre.   M. A.
      Southern Ill. U.

3475 Boyce, W. A.   Melancholy in Shakespeare's Comedies.
      M. A.   U. Denver.

3476 Cain, D. R.   The Adaptation and Live Production of a
      Short Story on Education Television Facilities.   M. S.
      U. Wisc.

3477 Carnes, E. H.   Principal Roles of Leading American Actors.
      M. A.   U. Wash.

3478 Finch, L. L.   A Subjective Evaluation of Choral Reading
      as a Method of Instruction.   M. A.   Miss. Southern
      College.

3479 Gjerset, Ava.   An Interpretive Analysis and Comparison
      of The Plain Dealer by William Wycherly and Le Mis-
      anthrope by Jean Baptiste Poquelin Molière.   M. F. A.
      U. Okla.

3480 Gray, W. A.   Listeners and Readers Responses to Poetry.
      Diss.   Columbia U.

3481 Hunter, Ruth.   Interpretive Reading as an Art.   M. A.
      Wayne St. U.

3482 Johnson, G. O.   The Oral Interpretation of Virgil's Aeneid.
      M. A.   U. Okla.   (1959?)

3483 Kane, Edward.   The Oral Interpretation of Opera with a
      Study of the Oral Interpretation of Menotti's The Consul
      with Full Production Notes and the Complete Script for a
      Readers Theatre Production.   M. A.   Southern Ill. U.

3484 [No entry]

3485 McCormick, B. D.   A Creative Interpretation of the Book
      of Judith: A Recital.   M. S.   U. Pittsburgh.

3486 Merrill, M. L.   Production Book of Billy Budd.   M. F. A.
      Catholic U. of Am.

3487 Nicholson, L. E. Oral Techniques in the Composition of Expanded Anglo-Saxon Verses. Diss. Harvard.

3488 Rambo, D. E. An Analysis for the Oral Interpreter of "Four Quartets" by T. S. Eliot. Diss. Northwestern.

3489 Sill, J. T. Oral Interpretation of The Letters of Abraham Lincoln with Production Notes on a Group Reading of Lincoln's Letters. M. A. Southern Ill. U.

3490 Taeschner, R. E. Production Text and Introduction to the Reader's Theatre Version of The Day Lincoln Was Shot. M. F. A. Catholic U. of Am.

3491 Thompson, Ronald. An Interpretation of the Role of Hamlet. M. F. A. U. Okla.

3492 Trauernicht, M. M. The Life and Work of Charles Henry Woolbert. Diss. U. Wisc.

3493 Von Szeliski, J. J. A Comparative Analysis of Two Major Types of Shakespearean Villains, in the Characters Iago and Richard III. M. A. Purdue.

3494 Williams, E. M. An Aristotelian Analysis of the Rhetoric of Selected Shakespearean Passages. M. A. Mich. St. U.

3495 Zimmerman, P. W. Shakespeare's Treatment of Love in Three Comedies: Much Ado About Nothing, As You Like It, and Twelfth Night. M. S. St. U. of Iowa.

1959

3496 Allison, J. H. The Development of a Tape Recording of Appreciative Listening to Choral Speaking in the Fourth Grade. M. Ed. Boston U.

3497 Aly, L. F. John G. Neihardt as Speaker and Reader. Diss. U. Missouri.

3498 Amram, F. M. An Exploration and Redefinition of the Term Empathy and an Application of the Concept to Speech Theory with Special Attention to Oral Interpreters. M. A. U. Minn.

3499 Bales, Allen. The Study of Point of View in the Novels of Nathaniel Hawthorne. Diss. Northwestern.

3500 Bedard, G. T. An Analysis of the Statements of Purpose in Teaching Oral Interpretation. M. A. Ind. U.

3501 Biewirth, E. B. A Rhetorical and Semantic Study of Charles Hillman Brough's Major Chautauqua Addresses. M. A. U. Ark.

3502 Campbell, P. N.   An Experimental Study of the Retention
      and Comprehension of Poetry Resulting from Silent Read-
      ing and from Oral Interpretation.   Diss.   U. Southern
      Calif.

3503 Collins, R. E.   An Experimental Investigation of the Com-
      prehension of Prose Materials When Read Silently and
      When Read Aloud.   Diss.   U. Southern Calif.

3504 Creech, H. B.   The Duration of the Syllable in Oral Read-
      ing.   M. A.   Ohio St. U.

3505 Denny, C. K.   Prose as a Medium of Expression in the
      Theatre.   M. A.   Smith C.

3506 Goulding, B. J.   The Preparation and Performance of a
      Solo Drama.   M. A.   Ohio U.

3507 Hedges, F. L.   Selecting, Abridging, and Arranging Humor-
      ous Prose for Oral Interpretation by High School Students.
      M. A.   Iowa St. U.

3508 Holt, A. M.   The Process of Adapting Children's Literature
      into Short Plays for Use in the Early Junior High Years.
      M. A.   Tex. Women's U.

3509 Johnson, G. O.   The Oral Interpretation of Virgil's Aeneid.
      M. A.   U. Okla.   (1958?)

3510 Kidder, R. R.   The Preparation and Use of Recordings in
      the Study of Interpretative Reading.   Diss.   Wayne U.

3511 Lane, M. R.   An Anthology of Poems from American Liter-
      ature for Choral Reading in the Elementary Grades.
      M. Ed.   Boston U.

3512 Lineberger, James.   From Story to Play: An Analysis of
      the Development of a Full-Length Play from an Original
      Short Story.   M. A.   U. Minnesota.

3513 Marcoux, J. P.   The Integration of Speaking and Listening
      with Twelfth Grade Literature in Calais, Maine.   M. Ed.
      Boston U.

3514 McGraw, R. T.   Criteria for Adapting Narrative Literature
      into Group Oral Reading Form.   M. A.   Bowling Green
      St. U.

3515 Mintor, W. W.   Study of Invocational Formulae in Early
      Greek Oral Poetry.   Diss.   Columbia U.

3516 Monaghan, R. R.   Oral Interpretation of H. D. Thoreau as
      Applied to Radio.   M. A.   Stanford U.

3517 Napiecinski, T. H. The Dramatization of the American
      Serious Novel, 1926-1952. Diss. U. Wisc.

3518 Raines, M. C. The Creative Process in Acting. M. A.
      Baylor U.

3519 Rivera, R. S. An Analytical Study of the Selected Works
      of Charles Warren Stoddard in Preparation for an Inter-
      pretive Reading Program. M. A. U. Hawaii.

3520 Shirley, J. K. The Teaching of Interpretative Reading in
      the Theological Seminaries of Two Protestant Churches.
      M. A. Wayne U.

3521 Silvestri, V. N. A Comparison of Retention and General
      Understanding of Poetry Prepared for Oral Interpretation
      and Poetry Studied Silently. M. S. Emerson Coll.

3522 Smith, S. G. Acting and Interpretation Problems in The
      Orestia. M. A. St. Louis U.

3523 Soule, Donald. Irony in Early Critical Comedy. M. A.
      Stanford U.

3524 Starnes, M. E. Ophelia: A Survey of Interpretation from
      the Restoration to the Present. M. F. A. Yale U.

3525 Statham, C. M. The Application of Prevailing Principles
      of Elocution to Theatrical Criticism of American Action:
      1815-1840. Diss. U. Fla.

3526 Trisolini, A. G. Analysis of the Structure of Hart Crane's
      "The Bridge." M. A. Northwestern.

3527 Wintersole, W. R. Production of a Series of Radio Scripts
      Written for Children and Based on American Folk Songs
      from 1775 to 1891. M. A. U. C. L. A.

1960

3528 Baker, W. A. Comparative Study of Six Textbooks in Oral
      Interpretation. M. A. Bowling Green St. U.

3529 Bradley, J. F. A Reading Theatre Adaptation of David Cop-
      perfield for High School Students. M. A. Mich. St. U.

3530 Catmull, J. F. An Interpretation of the Book of Job.
      M. F. A. U. Utah.

3531 Crum, J. M. A Project for the Use of Oral Interpretation
      in High School Literature and Language Arts Classes in
      the State of Washington. M. A. U. Wash.

3532 Dickinson, Loren. Public Address Theatre and Interpretation at the Epworth League Assembly in Lincoln, Nebraska. M. A. U. Nebr.

3533 Dodez, M. L. Robinson Jeffers' "Roan Stallion": Analysis and Appraisal for the Oral Interpreter. M. A. Ohio St. U.

3534 Heise, R. C. A Study of the Oral Interpretation of a Play as Exemplified by a Group Play Reading of The Relapse by Sir John Van Brough. M. A U. Wisc.

3535 O'Neill, W. A. Oral-Formulaic Structure in Old English Elegiac Poetry. Diss. U. Wisc.

3536 Reynolds, N. J. A Historical Study of the Oral Interpretation Activities of the Circuit Chautauqua: 1904-32. Diss. U. Southern Calif.

3537 Rude, R. V. Consideration of Jung's Concept of the Self as an Aid to the Understanding of Character in Prose Fiction. Diss. Northwestern.

3538 Schramm, A. N. The Construction and Evaluation of Objective Test Items in Oral Interpretation. M. A. Ohio St. U.

3539 Thompson, Patricia. Basic Techniques for the Staging of Poetry. M. A. Penn. St. U.

1961

3540 Attanasio, F. G. Duration of Oral Reading Times and Sound Pressure Level Under Conditions of Delay and Intensity of Auditory Side-Tone Transmission. Diss. Ohio U.

3541 Boden, Anneke-Jan. Original Arrangements of Biblical Literature for Readers Theatre. Diss. U. Denver.

3542 Conham, Nanette. Production Techniques in Adapting Children's Literature to Chamber Theatre. M. A. Occidental C.

3543 Cowan, Clairenell. A Dramatic Recital of Ibsen's A Doll's House. M. A. Penn. St. U.

3544 Elkins, N. C. Teaching Oral Interpretation in the Junior High School. M. A. U. Texas.

3545 Emerick, A. P. William Faulkner's Humor in Selected Stories: Its Significance to Oral Interpreter. M. A. U. Ariz.

3546 Fredericks, Virginia. An Approach to the Teaching of Oral Interpretation in Terms of Dramatic Action. Diss. U. Minn.

3547 Goodrich, J. R. Recording of Poetry for Use in High School. M. A. Sacramento St. C.

3548 Loesch, K. T. Prosodic Patterns in the Poetry of Dylan Thomas. Diss. Northwestern.

3549 Loganbill, G. B. Cornelia Otis Skinner and Her Art Form of Monologue-Drama. Diss. Mich. St. U.

3550 Manburg, Sandra. Children's Literature on TV: A Production Study. M. A. Ohio St. U.

3551 Marlor, C. S. Preparing Plays for Oral Interpretation: A Handbook for College Courses in Advanced Oral Interpretation. Diss. N. Y. U.

3552 McLelland, Sylvia. A History of the Significant Eras of Bodily Motion in Oral Interpretation. M. A. U. Boston.

3553 Nicholson, Catherine. The Chorus as a Ritual Element in Greek Tragedy. Diss. Northwestern.

3554 Peabody, H. B. Hesiod's Works and Days: An Exemplar of the Ancient Greek Oral Style. Diss. Harvard.

3555 Sivier, Evelyn. A Study of Interpretative Speech in England. Diss. Wayne St. U.

3556 Sozen, J. C. Anna Morgan: Reader, Teacher and Director. Diss. U. Illinois.

3557 Woodward, E. C. Recordings of Literary Selections Co-ordinated for Use with California Adopted Seventh Grade Literature Text. M. A. Sacramento St. C.

3558 Wray, J. E. Theories and Methods of Representative Contemporary Poets as Readers of Their Own Poetry. Diss. U. Wisc.

1962

3559 Bonham, W. D. Mark Twain's "The Mysterious Stranger": A Study in the Adaptation of Narrative Prose Material to Readers Theatre. M. A. Southern Ill. U.

3560 Christensen, A. E. The Teaching of Oral Interpretation at the College Level. Diss. Penn. State U.

3561 Davidson, C. M. Some Historical and Critical Foundations for a Concept of Rhythm in Dramatic Theory. Diss. U. Iowa.

3562 Goodman, R. F. The Effective Reading of the Epistle and Gospel at Sunday Mass. M. A. Catholic U. Amer.

3563 Gray, V. D. Interpretation in Western Speech. M. A. L. S. U.

3564 Hanks, W. E. A Study of Voice Control in the 19th Century with Rules and Principles Applied to Literary Selections of the Period. M. A. Miami U.

3565 Johnson, A. R. There Is a Willow. Diss. U. Denver.

3566 Johnson, Larry. A Readers Theatre Presentation of Roman Catholic Playwrights--Phillip Barry, Graham Greene, and Federico [García] Lorca. M. F. A. U. Portland.

3566a Long, B. W. John Ciardi: Poet-Critic on Oral Reading. M. A. L. S. U.

3567 Matlon, R. J. The Life and Elocutionary Teaching of Jonathan Barber. M. A. Purdue.

3568 Ramblin, Bill. The Inventions and Innovations of Steele MacKaye. M. A. L. S. U.

3569 Reynolds, J. D. A Study of the Oral Interpretation of the Philosophical Novel The Fall by Albert Camus. M. A. Baylor.

3570 Ropp, A. L. An Investigation of Poetry Which Captures the Interest of High School Students. M. A. Iowa St. U.

3571 Scott, V. L. Letter to Corinth 1:1. M. F. A. Iowa St. U.

3572 Swingle, E. E. A Scale for the Measurement of Empathic Effect in Terms of Emotional Impact. M. A. Ohio St. U.

3573 Tally, Joyce. An Experimental Reading Production: The World We Live In. M. A. Miss. Southern Coll.

3574- Wallace, R. D. An Analytical/Historical Study of the Factors
5   Contributing to the Success of Mark Twain as an Oral Interpreter. Diss. U. Southern Calif.

3576 Wulftange, I. M. An Experimental Study of Audience Response to the Oral Interpretation of Literature as Perceived Through Different Media. Diss. Ohio St.

1963

3577 Arant, P. M. Comparative Techniques of the Russian Oral Epic: The Bylina. Diss. Harvard.

3578 Barry, Kristin. The Development of an Interpretive Program for the Poems and Letters of Emily Dickinson. M. A. U. Wash.

3579 Brady, Julie. The Use of Indigenous Material in Readers Theatre Productions, with Specific Emphasis on the History of Southern Illinois. M. A. Southern Ill. U.

3580 Cannon, Jo Ann. Interpretative Analysis of the Fiction of Ernest Hemingway. M. A. Baylor.

3581 Colson, T. D. An Analysis of Selected Poems of Gerard Manley Hopkins for Oral Interpretation and a Study of His Poetic Theories. Diss. U. Okla.

3582 Culley, R. C. Oral Formulaic Language in the Biblical Psalms. Diss. U. Toronto.

3583 Didez, M. L. An Examination of the Theories and Methodologies of John Walker (1732-1807) with Emphasis on Gesturing. Diss. Ohio State U.

3584 Doyle, E. M. The Nature of Verse in Drama, with Special Reference to J. B., A Play in Verse by Archibald McLeish. Diss. Northwestern.

3585 Dubofsky, Joan. An Investigation of Sex Differences in Oral Reading Adaptation to Delayed Sidetone as Measured by Fluency and Duration. M. A. Northern Ill. U.

3586 Dunlavy, J. F. An Interpretation Study of Three Roles. M. A. Iowa St. U.

3587 Espinola, J. C. Concepts of Imagery in the New Criticism and Implications for the Oral Interpreter of Poetry. M. A. U. Okla.

3588 Fullerton, M. C. A Study of the Musical Approach to Dramatic Interpretation. M. F. A. Texas Christian U.

3589 Gruner, C. R. An Experimental Study of Effectiveness of Oral Satire in Modifying Attitudes. Diss. Ohio St. U.

3590 Hartung, Nancy. The Contributions of Hiram Corson to the Field of Oral Interpretation. M. A. Wayne St. U.

3591 Kepke, A. N. A Study of Communications of Perception of Character Among Actors, Director and Audience Using Q Methodology. Diss. Mich. St. U.

3592 Lowewer, E. A. Characterization, Old Mortality, and the Oral Interpreter. M. A. U. Oklahoma.

3593 Lukanitsch, R. M. The Relationship of the Figures of Sound to the Rhythm in Certain Poems of Gerard Manley Hopkins. Diss. Northwestern.

3594 Matter, George. The Relationship of Rhetorical Discourse and Poetry, A Critical Analysis. M. A. U. Pittsburgh.

3595 Mohrmann, G. P. The Impact of Oral Theory and Practice Upon the Poetry of Walt Whitman. Diss. U. Fla.

3596 Monroe, E. A. Group Reading of Drama: Essence and Aesthetic Principles. Diss. U. Wisc.

1964

3597 Abernethy, R. L. A Study of Existing Practices and Principles of Storytelling for Children in the United States. Diss. Northwestern.

3598 Bailey, Dorothy. An Analysis of the Status and Value of Humorous Literature as a Vehicle for Study and Performance in the Oral Interpretation Area of Speech Education. M. A. Kent St. U.

3599 Bynum, D. E. A Taxonomy of Oral Narrative Song: The Isolation and Description of Invariables in Serbo-Croatian Tradition. Diss. Harvard.

3600 Carrington, R. H. Archibald MacLeish: A Study of His Prosody for the Oral Interpreter. Diss. U. Wisc.

3601 Edwards, J. L. An Interpreter's Analysis of Selected Stories by Kay Boyle. M. A. U. Ariz.

3602 Graff, G. E. The Dramatic Theory of Poetry. Diss. Stanford U.

3603 Grimm, E. C. A Critical Analysis of Readers Theatre. M. A. U. Maryland.

3604 Haas, C. E. A Structural Analysis of Selected Sonnets of Gerard Manley Hopkins. Diss. U. Denver.

3605 Henderson, G. A. A Comparison of the Oral Interpretation Techniques of Charles Dickens, Mark Twain and Robert Frost. M. A. Bowling Green St. U.

3606 Jones, R. G. Readers Theatre Production: A Portrait of the Artist as a Young Man. M. A. Ohio St. U.

3607 Kirkland, A. S. The Elocutionary Theory and Practice of James Edward Murdoch. Diss. Wayne St. U.

3608 Kittelsen, R. E. Interpretation of 20th-Century Poetic Drama. M. A. Miami U.

3609 Lamb, J. H. John Walker: Elocutionist and Student of the English Language. Diss. St. U. Iowa.

3610 Larson, W. A. An Investigation of the Reader's Theatre Production Style. M. A. U. N. Dakota.

3611 Linn, J. R. Historical Study of Oral Interpretation in London: 1951-62 as a Form of Professional Theatre. Diss. U. Southern Calif.

3612 Macksoud, R. S. Literary Theories of Kenneth Burke and the Discovery of Meanings in Oral Interpretation. Diss. U. C. L. A.

3613 Marcoux, J. P. Analysis of Current Trends Concerning Basic Aspects of Oral Interpretation as Evidenced in Selected Writings in the Field, 1950-63, with Implications for Speech Education. Diss. Northwestern.

3614 Porter, A. L. The Construction and Testing of a Forced Choice Scale for Measuring Achievement in Oral Interpretation. Diss. Ohio St. U.

3615 Rockey, J. R. Effects of Directive and Non-Directive Criticism on Changes in Semantic Compatibility During the Preparation of a Readers Theatre Production. M. A. Southern Ill.

3616 Salper, D. R. A Study of an Oral Approach to the Appreciation of Poetry. Diss. U. of Minn.

3617 Scott, W. C. The Oral Nature of the Homeric Simile. Diss. Princeton.

3618 Sundstrom, A. L. The Influence of the Traditional Schools of Interpretation on the Contemporary Eclectic Philosophy of Reading Aloud. Diss. Wayne St. U.

3619 Torsey, K. E. The Application of the Tenets of Austin, Rush, and Curry by Writers of Representative Collegiate Speech Texts, 1925-1955. Diss. U. Fla.

3620 Watts, A. C. Swutol Sang Scopes: A Study of Oral Tradition in Old English Poetry. Diss. Yale.

3621 White, V. S. A Readers Theatre Presentation of an Adaptation of Stephen Vincent Benet's "Western Star." M. S. Kansas St. Tchrs. Coll.

3622 Witt, D. M. A Comparative Analysis of Audience Response
      to Realistic and Anti-Realistic Drama When Perceived
      Through Acting Readers Theatre and Silent Reading.
      Diss. U. Denver.

1965

3623 Barton, M. B. The Selection Adaptation and Presentation
      of Three Local Color Short Stories for a Readers Theatre
      Program. M. A. U. Houston.

3624 Brizzi, J. L. An Experimental Study of Chamber Theatre
      as a Teaching Device in a Ninth-Grade Literature Class.
      M. A. Kent St. U.

3625 Carver, J. C. Semantic Compatibility Among Interpreters
      During the Production of an Original Play. M. A. Mich.
      St. U.

3626 Cole, E. J. The Sound of Poetry: Two Parallels. M. A.
      L. S. U.

3627 DeGracia, C. P. Selection of Literature for Use in Oral
      Interpretation in Philippine Junior College English and
      Speech Classes. M. A. U. Wash.

3628 Desantis, F. A. James Steele MacKaye's Adaptation of the
      Delsarte System of Expression for the Spectatorium.
      M. A. Mich. St. U.

3629 Fish, R. S. The Oral Interpretation of Horror Stories of
      H. P. Lovecraft. M. A. U. Okla.

3630 Frederickson, R. Q. Maude May Babcock and the Depart-
      ment of Elocution at the University of Utah. M. A. U.
      Utah.

3631 Garry, J. J. Permit Me Voyage: A Study of a Dramatic
      Adaptation of the Works of James Agee. M. A. Ohio St.
      U.

3632 Hahn, R. D. Poetry of Emily Dickinson: Analysis for
      Oral Interpretation. M. A. Ohio St. U.

3633 Hawkins, J. L. A Study of the Relationship of Point of
      View to the Structure of the Alexandria Quartet by Law-
      rence Durrell. Diss. Northwestern.

3634 Henning, W. K. The Significance to the Oral Interpreter
      of the Pause in the Published Stage Plays of Harold Pinter.
      M. A. U. Ariz.

3635 Heston, L. A. A Study of Point of View in Three Novels by Henry James: The Spoils of Poynton, The Wings of the Dove, The Golden Bowl. Diss. Northwestern.

3636 Hollatz, E. A. The Development of Literary Societies in Selected Illinois Colleges in the 19th Century and Their Role in Speech Training. Diss. Northwestern.

3637 Horton, J. F. A Study of Empathy and Its Relation to Aesthetic Experience and Oral Interpretation. M. A. Auburn.

3638 Jisha, H. J. The Development of Imagery as an Integral Element in Interpretative Reading. Diss. Wayne St. U.

3639 Lockard, S. K. Public Readings in New York City from 1865 to 1870. M. A. L. S. U.

3640 Mello, E. C. Mark Twain's Writing on Oral Interpretation. M. S. N. Texas St. U.

3641 Monaghan, M. O. An Adaptation for Readers Theatre of François Mauriac's Woman of the Pharisees. M. F. A. Catholic U. of Amer.

3642 Payne, D. M. The Roles of Imagined Speaker and Listener in Selected Poems of E. E. Cummings. M. A. U. Minn.

3643 Puppe, J. A. A Comparison of Articulation, Oral Reading, & Comprehension Vocabulary of Sixth Graders. M. A. U. Nebr.

3644 Reid, E. T. Interprctive Analysis of the Writing of Tennessee Williams. M. A. Baylor U.

3645 Salgado, R. H. Robert Browning: An Interpreter's Analysis of Selected Monologues. M. A. U. Ariz.

3646 Simpson, V. L. A Readers Theatre Production of Sophocles' Electra. M. A. Texas Tech. Coll.

3647 Snyder, E. H. Historical Backgrounds and Development of Chorus Speaking in Germany: 1918-1964. Diss. Northwestern.

3648 Svore, J. L. An Investigation of Audience Response to Prose Literature When Perceived Through Silent Reading, Oral Interpretation, and Readers Theatre. M. A. U. Montana.

3649 Tinsley, N. M. An Experimental Analysis of Narrative Poetry to Be Used for Oral Interpretation. M. A. Iowa St. U.

3650 Turek, J. E. Poetry for Choral Reading Categorized by
School Grade Level Difficulty of Reading. M. A. Miami
U.

1966

3651 Ashburn, S. J. The Evolutionary Patterns in the Dialogue
of Novels by John Steinbeck. M. A. W. Tex. St. U.

3652 Blodgett, B. G. A Study of Dylan Thomas' Public Reading,
His Poetic Theory as It Relates to Oral Interpretation and
an Analysis of Selected Works. M. A. Auburn U.

3653 Bradford, Lawrence. The Use of an Operant Procedure in
Reducing Rate of Oral Reading and Impromptu Speaking.
Diss. U. Kansas.

3654 Broadway, J. A. An Experimental Study of the Comprehen-
sion and Retention of Expository Prose Resulting from
Silent Reading and from Listening to Oral Reading. M. A.
Auburn U.

3655 Busch, C. T. Oral Interpretation in American Colleges and
Universities from 1930-1965. Diss. U. of Utah.

3656 Byerly, G. K. Compounds and Other Elements of Poetic
Diction Derived from an Oral/Formulaic Tradition: A
Comparison of Aeschylus and the Beowulf Poet. Diss.
U. Penn.

3657 Case, R. Y. An Artistic Philosophical Comparison of the
Early Poetry of T. S. Eliot and the Plays of Samuel
Beckett. M. A. Syracuse U.

3658 Chaney, Tom. The Poetry of Robert Penn Warren: An
Analysis for Interpretation. M. A. Baylor U.

3659 Clyde, G. E. An Oral Interpreter's Approach to the Poetry
of Gwendolyn Brooks. Diss. Southern Ill.

3660 Compton, H. W. The Reading and Study of Poetry in the
Secondary Schools: A Survey of Articles in The Quarterly
Journal of Speech, The Speech Teacher, Speech Mono-
graphs, and The English Journal from 1954 through 1964.
M. A. W. Virginia U.

3661 Fry, D. K. Aesthetics of Oral-Formulaic Theory: Judith.
Diss. U. Calif. Berkeley.

3662 Garliner, M. S. The Preparation of an Educational Film
Script Dealing with Readers Theatre. M. A. Ohio St. U.

3663 Gray, P. H. The Origins of Expression: Principle Sources of Samuel Silas Curry's Theory of Expression. Diss. L. S. U.

3664 Hogan, J. C. The Oral Nature of the Homeric Simile. Diss. Cornell.

3665 Klyn, M. S. Webster on the Seventh of March. Diss. Northwestern.

3666 Koperski, R. J. An Analysis of Selected Dramatic Poems of Robert Frost. Diss. U. Missouri.

3667 McIntosh, D. M. A Study of the Relationship of Classroom Instruction and Contest Practices of Characterization in Oral Interpretation. M. A. Bowling Green U.

3668 Neilson, I. E. A Comparative Analysis and Practical Application of the Theories of Samuel Curry, Charlotte Lee and Martin Cobin. M. A. U. Ga.

3669 Norman, Norma. Parrish's Interpretation of the Principles of Gestalt Psychology as Applied in Representative Oral Interpretation Texts, 1932-1963. M. F. A. Texas Christian U.

3670 Park, L. G. Poet of Perspectives: The Style of W. H. Auden. Diss. Northwestern.

3671 Patterson, R. E. Thomas Sheridan: Pioneer in British Speech Technology. Diss. Ohio St. U.

3672 Reynolds, J. D. Attitude Change by the Stimulus of Oral Interpretation of Poetic Literature. Diss. Ohio State.

3673 Shirley, J. K. The Teaching of Oral Reading in the Protestant Theological Seminaries. Diss. Wayne St. U.

3674 Smith, J. W. A Study of Selected Professional Reading Programs in the United States: 1950-1960. M. A. Tex. Christ. U.

3675 Talbot, Carl. Woolbert's Theories of Oral Interpretation, Their Origins, Influence and Present Significance. Diss. U. C. L. A.

3676 Terango, Larry. Pitch and Duration Characteristics of the Oral Reading of Males in a Masculinity-Femininity Dimension. Diss. Case Western Reserve.

3677 Warland, Stephen. An Experimental Study of the Effect of Visual Delivery Upon Listener Response to the Oral Interpretation of Literature. M. A. U. Nebraska.

3678 Woodward, L. E. A Study to Determine the Value of Speech Proficiency to Prospective School Teachers and More Specifically the Value of Oral Interpretation Training to the High School Literature or Poetry Teacher. M. A. Brigham Young U.

1967

3679 Amberg, Walter. A Comparative Study of Individual Speech Contest Events in Public High Schools of the Thirteen States in the Central States Speech Association. M. A. Mankato St. Coll.

3680 Alexander, E. L. An Experimental Investigation of Four Methods of Teaching Vocal Emphasis in Oral Interpretation. M. A. U. Hawaii.

3681 Baugh, P. W. A Readers Theatre Production of Mark Twain's Personal Recollections of Joan of Arc. M. A. U. Houston.

3682 Benton, Johnny. An Interpretative Analysis of Robinson Jeffers' "The Woman at Point Sur." Diss. U. Okla.

3683 Bindert, Kathleen. A Critical Study Through Oral Interpretation of the Poems of James Dickey. M. A. Syracuse U.

3684 Brooks, L. L. A Study of the Procedure That Should Be Followed in Preparing a Public Recital Interpreting the Poetry of T. S. Eliot. M. A. L. A. Polytech. Inst.

3685 Burmingham, Kim. An Examination of Empathy and Its Role in Interpretation. M. A. U. Ariz.

3686 Butler, R. R. A Study of Readers Theatre in the Colleges and Universities of the United States. M. A. U. Nebr.

3687 Calder, N. D. An Historical Interpretation of the Uncle Remus Stories. M. A. U. Utah.

3688 Chase, L. C. The Concept of Elocution in Common School Readers Used in the United States Between 1820-1960. Diss. U. C. L. A.

3689 Flamer, M. A. A Systematic Approach to Image Analysis. M. A. Ohio St. U.

3690 Ganbacini, Alcyne. An Oral English Curriculum Guide for Use in Project Head Start in Derby, Connecticut. M. A. Southern Conn. St. Coll.

3691 Hayden, E. A. Satire: An Appraisal of Its Use in Oral Interpretation. M. A. Ohio St. U.

3692 Hecht, P. A. A Historical Study and Evaluation of the Delsarte System of Acting in the United States. M. A. Catholic U. of Amer.

3693 Herrington, M. A. A Visual Mode of Instruction for the Teaching of Oral Interpretation to High School Students on the Junior and Senior Level. M. A. Mich. St. U.

3694 Hess, J. A. Child Audience Attitudes Toward Two Interpretations of Long John Silver. M. A. U. Kansas.

3695 Hobar, Donald. The Oral Tradition in Malory's Morte d'Arthur. Diss. U. Pitt.

3696 Jellicorse, J. L. The Poet as Persuader: A Rhetorical Explication of the Life and Writing of Walt Whitman. Diss. Northwestern.

3697 Kern, J. B. A Readers Theatre Television Production Based on the Poetry of Robert Frost. M. A. Tex. Tech. Coll.

3698 Lewis, L. T. Emanuel: A Program for Choric Interpretation. M. A. St. Louis U.

3699 Logan, E. A. A Study of Robert L. Flynn's Journey at Jefferson, An Adaptation of William Faulkner's As I Lay Dying. M. A. Tulane.

3700 Markwood, S. H. The Like-Dislike Response to Poetry at the Eighth Grade Level: A Controlled Classroom Study. M. A. Bowling Green U.

3701 McGeever, C. J. An Anthology for Use in the Beginning Classes of Interpretation. M. A. Kansas St. U.

3702 Moses, M. A. An Adaptation for Readers Theatre of Ernest Hemingway's A Farewell to Arms. M. A. N. Dakota St.

3703 Mraz, Thomas. An Analysis of Written Comments Given to Selected Students of Burnsville High School in Oral Interpretation Contests. M. A. Mankato St. Coll.

3704 Roland, Paul. An Exploratory Study of Sex as a Factor Influencing Appropriateness in the Reader-Literature Complex. Diss. Southern Ill. U.

3705 Roloff, L. H. Critical Study of Contemporary Aesthetic Theories and Precepts Contributing to an Aesthetic of Oral Interpretation. Diss. U. Southern Calif.

3706 Rood, D. P. The Birth of a State--A Series of Reading Programs and Dramatic Productions for Elementary and Secondary Schools in Nebraska--1966-67. M. A. U. Nebr.

3707 Schmid, B. P. Selected Novels Adapted to Ninety-Minute Television Programs. M. A. Miami U. of Ohio.

3708 Schmidt, P. L. An Examination of the Selected Persuasive Features of Three Poems by Lawrence Ferlinghetti. M. A. Penn. St. U.

3709 Schramm, A. N. The Semantic Differential in Oral Interpretation Research. Diss. Ohio St. U.

3710 Smith, A. Y. An Application of Kenneth Burke's Critical Methods to Oral Interpretation. M. A. U. Utah. (1968?)

3711 Snow, K. G. The Changing Principles of Bodily Action in Oral Interpretation in America from 1886-1966. M. A. U. Utah.

3712 Snyder, B. P. A Readers Theatre Production Drawn from Various Writings of George Bernard Shaw. M. A. Syracuse U.

3713 Stulik, S. B. How to Present Prose, Poetry, and Plays as Readings: A Handbook for the Director of Readers Theatre. M. A. Emerson Coll.

3714 Thomas, Pamela. The Sound and Sense of a Private Poet: The Oral Interpretation of Emily Dickinson. M. A. U. Wyoming.

3715 Whitaker, B. J. Distance in the Performance of Literature. Diss. L. S. U.

1968

3716 Barclay, M. T. Major American Emphases in Theories of Oral Interpretation from 1890 to 1950. Diss. U. Minn.

3717 Behnke, Dorothy. Guide to Selecting and Adapting Materials for Readers Theatre in the Secondary Schools. M. A. Kansas St. Tchrs. Coll.

3718 Callahan, C. R. The Plays of D. H. Lawrence: A Theatrical Reading. M. A. U. Oregon.

3719 Catterson, S. K. An Experimental Study of the Effect of Exposure to Oral Interpretation Models Upon Student Performance in Oral Interpretation. M. A. U. Nebr.

3720 Comerford, John. An Investigation of the Composition and the Functions of the Lyrics of Frank Loesser. M. A. Catholic U. of America.

3721 Dalan, N. C. A Comparative Analysis of Audience Response to Use of Offstage Focus and Onstage Focus in Readers Theatre. Diss. U. Denver.

3722 Erickson, K. V. Opinions Held and/or Techniques Practiced in Readers Theatre by College Level Instructors, Directors of Readers Theatre and New York City Professional Readers. M. A. Penn. St. U.

3723 Eubank, M. H. The Redpath Lyceum Bureau from 1868 to 1901. Diss. U. Mich.

3724 Fick, Linda. Utilizing Readers Theatre in the Elementary Schools. M. A. N. Eastern Ill. St. Coll.

3725 Gix, D. J. A Creative Study of Selections from Walt Whitman's Drum Taps. M. A. Miami U.

3726 Herndon, R. M. Oral Reading Instruction in Bible Colleges. M. A. Texas Christ. U.

3727 Hickey, N. C. An Analysis and Production of Selections from the Chautauqua Performances by Elinor Lincoln. M. A. U. Southern Calif.

3728 Hopkins, M. F. Descriptive Analysis of Philology of Selected Poems by Andrei Voznesensky. Diss. L. S. U.

3729 Jarrell, S. T. A Study Concerning the Procedure Necessary to Prepare Under Milk Wood for a Readers Theatre Performance Prior to Casting. M. A. Louisiana Polytch. Inst.

3730 Jaswal, A. J. Oral Interpretation as a Form of Professional Theatre on New York Stage from 1945 to 1965. Diss. Mich. St. U.

3731 Jewell, J. C. Analysis and Adaptation of Life and Works of Sylvia Plath for Readers Theatre. M. A. Indiana St. U.

3732 Johnson, J. G. Soviet Literature 1953-1963: The Power to Persuade. M. A. Northwestern.

3733 Kelly, Christine. The Once and Future King: An Interpreter's Theatre Adaptation and Production for a Child Audience. M. A. Kansas St. Tchrs. Coll.

3734 Kelly, M. L. Methods and Principles of Literary Adaptation for Readers Theatre. M. A. U. Iowa.

3735 Kolsti, J. S. The Bilingual Singer: A Study in Albanian and Serbo-Croatian Oral Epic Traditions. Diss. Harvard.

3736 Kropf, Anne. The Relationship Between Auditory Discrimination Abilities and Problems of General Articulation and Oral Reading Ability. M. A. Hofstra U.

3737 Laing, G. A. Lecture and Demonstration of Six Styles of Oral Interpretation. M. A. Calif. St. Coll.

3738 Matsen, P. P. Hesiod's Works and Days and Homeric Oral Poetry. Diss. Bryn Mawr.

3739 McFarling, L. L. Study of Stress Caused by Delayed Auditory Feedback on the Oral Reading Rates of Males and Females. M. A. St. Cloud St. Coll.

3740 Ochrymowycz, R. O. Aspects of Oral Style in the Romances Juglarescos of the Carolingian Cycle. Diss. U. Iowa.

3741 Oliver, M. R. A Readers Theatre Adaptation of George Orwell's Animal Farm. M. A. Marquette U.

3742 Osborn, Anabel. An Investigation of Audience Response to Dramatic Poetic Literature When Perceived Through Silent Reading and Oral Group Reading. M. A. U. Montana.

3743 Prather, L. A. A Matter of Wilderness: An Interpreter's Approach to the Study of Contemporary Women Poets. M. A. Southern Methodist U.

3744 Salter, Mordic. Kahlil Gibran: The Prophet. M. A. Miami U. of Ohio.

3745 Savage, M. S. Wallace Stevens: Poetry as Religion. Diss. Northwestern.

3746 Screiber, Elsie. Beyond the Sun Set: A Readers Theatre Production of Columbus. M. A. Sacramento St. Coll.

3747 Smith, A. Y. An Application of Kenneth Burke's Critical Methods to Oral Interpretation. M. S. U. Utah. (1967?)

3748 Smith, J. H. A Readers Theatre Adaptation and Production of Archy and Mehitabel for Special High School Audiences. M. A. Kansas St. Tchrs. Coll.

3749 Tresner, J. T. The Tree Witch by Peter Viereck: A Study for Readers Theatre. M. A. U. Okla.

3750 West, J. C. An Analysis of 1912-1967 English Journal Articles Concerning Teaching Oral English in High School. M. A. Cent. Missouri St. Coll.

3751 Williams, D. W.   Oral Interpreter's Index to The Dialogues of Plato.   M. A.   L. S. U.

3752 Wilson, M. W.   A Pilot Study of the Effect of Oral Reading of Literature, Chosen to Arouse Pity and Fear for Cathartic Effect, on the Inappropriate Behavior of a Group of Emotionally Handicapped Children.   M. A.   U. Utah.

3753 Young, J. D.   An Analysis of Three Modes of Group Interpretation in the Speech Arts Curriculum.   M. A.   N. Texas St. U.

1969

3754 Ackley, B. G.   Platform Reading in America, 1650-1775. Diss.   U. Southern Calif.

3755 Anderson, M. D.   Religious Themes in the Works of Robert Lowell.   Diss.   U. Missouri.

3756 Clark, V. F.   The Rhetoric of W. H. Auden's Verse Plays. Diss.   U. Wash.

3757 Coffey, J. E.   The Evolution of an Oral Formulaic Tradition in Old and Middle English Alliterative Verse.   Diss. State U. of N. Y. at Buffalo.

3758 Coote, M. P.   The Singers Use of Theme in Composing Oral Narrative Song in the Serbo-Croatian Tradition. Diss.   Harvard.

3759 Dart, R. E.   The Search for Dylan Thomas and Some Other Characters.   M. A.   Humbolt St. Coll.

3760 Davis, L. L.   A Readers Theatre Production of the Poetry of Rod McKuen.   M. A.   Tex. Christian U.

3761 Dolphin, C. Z.   An Adaptation to Readers Theatre of I Never Promised You a Rose Garden.   M. A.   Marquette U.

3762 Eler, B. J.   A Chamber Theatre Production and Production Notebook of Virginia Woolf's To the Lighthouse.   M. A. Ill. St. U.

3763 Engelkes, Faith.   A Study of Gesture in Elocution and Oral Interpretation During the Years 1870 to 1930 in the United States.   M. A.   U. Northern Iowa.

3764 Espinola, J. C.   Point of View in Selected Novels by Virginia Woolf.   Diss.   Northwestern.   (1970?)

3765 French, Alice. The Life and Writing of Thomas Wolfe: A Program for Readers Theatre. M. A. U. Okla.

3766 Gribben, K. K. The I of Cummings: An Approach to the Oral Interpretation of the Poetry of E. E. Cummings. M. A. U. Wyoming.

3767 Hartman, M. D. The Chautauqua Speaking of Robert La Follette. Diss. U. Minn.

3768 Haushalter, W. R. The Programming of Platform Artists at the University of Michigan, 1912-1961. Diss. U. Mich.

3768a Heck, S. J. An Analysis and Adaptation of Evelyn Waugh's Vile Bodies for Chamber Theatre Presentation. M. A. U. South Fla.

3769 Hill, S. I. A Readers Theatre High School Program and Sample Scripts for Use in the Classroom. M. A. Kent St. U.

3770 Hornsby, C. L. A Study of the Circuit Chautauqua in Lake Charles, Louisiana, 1916-1931. M. A. L. S. U.

3771- Hudson, Lee. An Application of the Operations of Meta-
2 phorical Expression to the Process of Oral Interpretation. M. A. U. Ill.

3773 James, P. R. Oral Reading in New Orleans from 1890-1900. M. A. L. S. U.

3774 Kasle, Daniel. Charles Laughton's Techniques of Oral Interpretation. M. A. Indiana U.

3775 Kirby, K. R. Public Reading in Chicago from 1912 Through 1916. M. A. L. S. U.

3776 Knoblock, C. L. Adaptation and Production Book of A. A. Milne's Winnie the Pooh. M. A. U. Maryland.

3777 Martin, S. G. Caldecott Medal Award Books, 1938-68, Their Literary and Oral Characteristics as They Relate to Story Telling. Diss. Wayne St. U.

3778 Parrella, Gilda. The Concept of Empathy: A Study in Discovery, Definition, and Design with Application to Literature and Its Performance. Diss. U. Wash.

3779 Passey, J. C. An Application of Bertolt Brecht's Theory of Alienation to Modern Performance Theory in Oral Interpretation. M. A. U. Wash.

3780 Pattison, S. D. An Analysis of Readers Theatre Based on Selected Theatre Theory with Special Emphasis on Characterization. Diss. U. Minn.

3781 Paynter, L. F. The Novel as Readers Theatre: Thornton Wilder's Heaven's My Destination. M. A. Fresno St. Coll.

3782 Peebles, Ramona. Richard Brinsley Sheridan: Drury Lane. M. A. Tex. Tech. U.

3783 Phillips, J. P. T. S. Eliot's Murder in the Cathedral: A Readers Theatre Production. M. A. U. Tex. at Austin.

3784 Radliff, S. P. A Study of the Techniques of Adapting Children's Literature to the Stage. Diss. Bowling Green St. U.

3785 Rohrer, Daniel. Young Ladies' Literary Society of Oberlin College: 1835-1860. M. A. U. Wisc.

3786 Rude, J. A. Production Thesis: "And Things That Go Bump in the Night." M. A. Indiana U.

3787 Schlicher, J. E. Emily: A Study of Emily Dickinson for Oral Interpretation. M. A. Indiana U.

3788 Sheffield, K. W. Selected Theories of Comedy and Their Application to the Oral Performance of Literature. M. A. Auburn U.

3789 Silvestri, M. A. The Concept of Taste: An Examination and Comparison of the Views of Hugh Blair and Current Oral Interpretation Textbooks. M. A. Emerson Coll.

3790 Smith, R. E. An Analysis of the Function of Place in the Short Story "With Way Up in the Air" and Other Stories. Diss. U. Missouri.

3791 Steck, R. C. An Analytic Study and Adaptation of Conrad's The Secret Agent for a Chamber Theatre Presentation. M. A. U. South Fla.

3792 Swink, H. M. The Oral Tradition of Yoknapatawpha County. Diss. U. Virginia.

3793 Sysel, R. A. Andrew Comstock: Elocutionary Theories. M. A. Colo. St. U.

3794 Wagner, P. R. An Evaluation of the Suitability of Walt Whitman's Poetry to Oral Interpretation Utilizing an Analysis of "Out of the Cradle Endlessly Rocking." M. A. U. Cinn.

3795 Wesley, R. J. A Study of Instruction for Liturgical Reading in Roman Catholic Diocesan Seminaries in the United States. Diss. Wayne St. U.

3796 Williams, J. L. Readers Theatre and Chamber Theatre: A Survey of Definitions. M. A. U. Utah.

1970

3797 Bensch, B. B. The Once and Future King: An Adaptation for the Blind. M. A. Brigham Young U.

3798 Brown, P. A. Oral Interpretation in the King County High Schools: A Survey with Curriculum Guidelines. M. A. U. Wash.

3799 Crannell, K. C. A Prosodic Analysis of Selected Dramatic Narratives of Robert Frost. Diss. Northwestern.

3800 Doll, H. D. An Experimental Investigation into the Effectiveness of Readers Theatre and Silent Reading in Communicating the Meaning of Unfamiliar Dramatic Literature. Diss. Ohio U.

3801 Duffy, P. F. The Oral Interpretation of Scripture for Ministerial Students. M. A. Baylor U.

3802 Ellopulos, James. A Rhetorical-Poetic Description of the Verbal Forms of Samuel Beckett's Dramatic Language. Diss. Ohio St. U.

3803 Espinola, J. C. Point of View in Selected Works by Virginia Woolf. Diss. Northwestern. (1969?)

3804 Fish, R. S. A Dramatic and Rhetorical Analysis of "The Man Against the Sky" and Other Selected Poems of A. E. Robinson. Diss. U. Okla.

3805 Franklin, W. G. An Experimental Study of the Acoustic Characteristics of Simulated Emotion. Diss. Penn. St. U.

3806 Gray, J. W. John Masefield's Lecture Tours and Public Readings in the United States in 1916 and 1918. Diss. L. S. U.

3807 Hairston, E. H. An Analysis of the Use of Oral Interpretation as a Psychotherapeutic Technique. Diss. Ohio St. U.

3808 Harlien, R. C. Cutting and Adapting Prose and Poetry for Oral Interpretation. M. A. N. Tex. St. U.

3809 Hullum, V. J. An Analytical Study of the Poetry of Langston Hughes: Interpretative Reader's Approach. M. A. Wayne St. U.

3810 Jenson, J. R. A History of Chautauqua Activities at Lakeside, Ohio: 1873-1970. Diss. Bowling Green St. U.

3811 Lanham, M. L. The Effect of a Blind Director on an Oral Interpreter's Performance. M. A. Bowling Green St. U.

3812 MacBride, D. G. John Ciardi: Poet, Literary Critic, Oral Interpreter: His Literary Concepts and Their Significance for the Field of Oral Interpretation. Diss. U. C. L. A.

3813 McMinn, Marjorie. Kahlil Gibran: A Dramatic Adaption and Interpretation of The Fifth Season. M. A. Abilene Christ. Coll.

3814 Onwuemene, Michael. A Controlled Oral-Formulaic Analysis of the Old English Vernacular Riddles. Diss. U. Kansas.

3815 Ramsey, B. A. Applied Literature: A Theoretical and Experimental Investigation of Persuasive Effect of Oral Interpretation. Diss. U. Colo.

3816 Reihm, J. B. E. E. Cummings' Stylistic Devices: Aids to the Oral Interpreter. M. A. Purdue.

3817 Rhode, J. K. A Dramatic Analysis of Selected Poems of James Dickey. M. A. U. Tex. at Austin.

3818 Rienstra, P. J. No Sense of Decency: A Readers Theatre Production Based on the Army-McCarthy Hearings. M. A. U. Tex. at Austin.

3819 Robinson, J. L. A Production Thesis: Readers Theatre Production of an Original Production of an Original Children's Musical Fantasy John and the Magic Ring. M. A. U. Tenn.

3820 Rogers, P. J. A Readers Theatre Presentation Based on Literary and Documentary Materials of the Great Depression of the 1930's. M. A. U. Houston.

3821 Smith, Gary. The Tools and Methods Used to Create and Sustain a Mood in Oral Interpretation. M. A. Kent St. U.

3822 Stevens, P. B. A Study of Kinesthetic Imagery in Selected Poetry of Theodore Roethke. Diss. Northwestern.

3823 Vinson, C. M. Imagery in the Short Stories of Eudora Welty. Diss. Northwestern.

3824 Williams, M. E.   A Compilation of Choral Reading Materials Suitable for Use in Language Arts Classes in the Secondary School.   M. A.   E. Tex. St. U.

3825 Witt, D. L.   Theatre for Children: Children's Stories Become Children's Drama.   M. A.   E. Tex. St. U.

3826 Wood, J. B.   A Study of a Readers Theatre Production of a Documentary.   M. A.   U. Nebr. at Lincoln.

1971

3827 Ackerman, F. S.   The Interrelationship in Joseph Heller's Catch-22 in Light of Albert Camus' Philosophy of the Absurd.   M. A.   Penn. St. U.

3828 Adams, M. C.   Image Patterns in Theodore Roethke's "Meditations of an Old Woman."   M. A.   U. Wash.

3829 Agnew, B. A.   Readers Theatre Production: Brecht on Brecht.   M. A.   Purdue.

3830 Arrington, R. J.   Speech Activities in Tahlequa, Cherokee Nation, During the Seventies.   Diss.   L. S. U.

3831 Atkinson, L. D.   The Career of Elia Kazan.   M. A.   Chico St. Coll.

3832 Baily, E. J.   Francis Anne Kemble and the American Audience.   M. A.   Tex. Tech. U.

3833 Barksdale, Cynthia.   A Readers Theatre Program Exploring the Black Aesthetic.   M. A.   Adelphi U.

3834 Barton, L. S.   The Development of a Code to Describe Reader-Director Interaction in Readers Theatre Rehearsals.   M. A.   U. Tex. at Austin.

3835 Bates, M. H.   An Interpretative Analysis of Nikos Kazantzakis' The Odyssey: A Modern Sequel.   M. A.   Baylor U.

3836 Batson, G. T.   The Theatrical History of the Lyceum Theatre of Memphis: 1911-1935.   M. A.   U. Mississippi.

3837 Boyce, S. N.   A Readers Theatre Production Reflecting a Study of the 1884-1885 Reading Tour of Mark Twain.   M. A.   U. N. C. -Chapel Hill.

3838 Brill, M. J.   Randall Jarrell: A Study Through Oral Interpretation.   M. A.   Syracuse U.

3839 Burke, Rosalie. An Experimental Study of the Effects Upon
the Audience of Presentations of Readers Theatre. M. A.
U. Nebr.

3840 Carlsen, J. W. A Descriptive Study of the Relationship of
Value Traits to the Oral Interpretation of Literature.
Diss. U. of Calif.

3841 Carr, Kathleen. An Experimental Investigation of the Re-
sponse to Obscene Language in Literature When Presented
Through Silent Reading and Oral Interpretation. M. A.
Bowling Green St. U.

3842 Cohen, Edwin. Woody Guthrie and the American Folk Song.
Diss. U. Southern Calif.

3843 Coleman, E. L. Langston Hughes: As American Dramatist.
Diss. U. Oregon.

3844 Congdon, M. G. A Study of the Dramatic Chorus and Its
Application to Readers Theatre. Diss. U. Mich.

3845 Cowen, M. M. Practical Experimentation with the Oral
Interpretation of Literature. M. A. DePauw U.

3846 Crane, Joshua. An Investigation of Cast and Audience Semantic Agreement in Readers Theatre Productions. Diss.
Ohio State U.

3847 Cummings, A. J. The Rhetoric of John Donne's "Devotions
Upon Emergent Occasions." Diss. Northwestern.

3848 Dayoub, B. J. Nothing Gold Can Stay: A Readers Theatre
Production Thesis. M. A. SW. Missouri St. Coll.

3849 Del Polito, C. M. A Journey Through Darkness: Readers
Theatre Production of the Poetry of Anne Sexton. M. A.
Purdue.

3850 Eoyang, E. C. Word of Mouth: Oral Story-Telling in the
Pien-Wen. Diss. Indiana U.

3851 Fetter, Joanne. An Interpretative Analysis of John Dos
Passos' U. S. A. M. A. Baylor U.

3852 Frost, W. L. Novel into Play: An Examination and Illus-
tration of Techniques Used in the Adaptation of Selected
American Novels for Stage Performance. Diss. U. Minn.

3853 Fujimoto, E. K. The Comparative Communicative Power of
Verbal and Non-Verbal Symbols. Diss. Ohio St. U.

3854 Galati, F. J. A Study of Mirror Analogues in Vladimir
Nabokov's Pale Fire. Diss. Northwestern.

3855 Gay, J. A. An Original Script for Readers Theatre: Pardon, but Your Generation Gap Is Showing. M. A. Chico St. Coll.

3856 Gibson, J. S. The Broadcast Interpretation of Ted Malone. Diss. U. Okla.

3857 Gilbert, C. A. A Theoretical Approach to Oral Interpretation as Communication. Diss. Purdue.

3858 Glenn, R. W. Rhetoric and Poetics: The Case of Leftist Fiction and Criticism During the Thirties. Diss. Northwestern.

3859 Gordon, L. O. Readers Theatre Adaptation and Production of The Magic Mountain by Thomas Mann. M. A. San Fran. St. Coll.

3860 Haas, Richard. Visual Perception of Literature as a Dimension in the Oral Interpretation of Poetry. Diss. U. Utah.

3861 Hawthorne, L. S. A Rhetoric of Human Rights as Expressed in the Simple Columns by Langston Hughes. Diss. Penn. St. U.

3862 Heath, R. L. Kenneth Burke's Theory of Language. Diss. U. Ill.

3863 Hoban, J. L. The Structure of Myth in Rhetorical Criticism. Diss. U. Ill.

3864 Hoffman, A. P. A Readers Theatre Production Analysis of Joseph Heller's We Bombed in New Haven. M. A. Calif. St. Coll.

3865 Hold, K. C. A Study of the Lecture Recital as a Form of Interpretation Through a Presentational Investigation of Theodore Roethke. M. S. Syracuse U.

3866 Hughes, P. R. A Survey Study of Oral Interpretation Within the California State Colleges, 1970. M. A. Calif. St. Coll.

3867 Jefferson, Bonnie. A Study Comparing Individual ... Group Instructional Methods in Oral Interpretation. M. A. Ohio U.

3868 Jones, J. E. Robert W. Service--The Yukon Troubadour. M. A. U. Utah.

3869 Kierman, G. M. Charles Dickens and His American Audience--1842: A Study in Ethos. Diss. Ohio St. U.

3870 Kneupper, Charles. The Adaptation of the Novel for Readers Theatre. M. A. Bowling Green St. U.

3871 Lane, T. K. Love Is the Answer: A Creative Thesis Production Combining Multi-Media and Oral Interpretation. M. A. N. Tex. St. U.

3872 Loving, M. L. Here Is a Place: An Application of the Group Involvement Approach to a Readers Theatre Production of Southwest Literature. M. A. Tex. Tech. U.

3873 Manchester, B. B. An Experimental Investigation of the Effects of Persuasive Interpretation on Attitude Change, Evaluation of Quality, and Speaker Credibility. Diss. Purdue.

3874 Marsh, Brian. An Adaptation of Dostoyevsky's Notes from the Underground into Playscript Form. M. A. Bowling Green St. U.

3875 Marshall, K. K. The Career of Hiram Corson, with Emphasis on His Teaching of Literature by the Method of Oral Interpretation. M. S. Syracuse U.

3876 McCammon, L. A. Battle of the Sexes: As a Comic Device and a Theme for a Readers Theatre Program. M. A. U. Tenn.

3877 McGuire, S. A. The End of the Beginning--A Thesis on a Readers Theatre Production of Trips to the Moon Literature. M. S. Syracuse U.

3878 Nichols, J. J. A Study of the Application of Henri Bergson's Time-Concept in the Dramatic Writings of Gertrude Stein. M. A. U. Maine at Orono.

3879 Null, P. M. "The Gift of the Magi": A Tagmemic Analysis. M. A. Kansas St. U.

3880 Osentowski, Mary. An Oral Interpreter's Approach to Selected Poetry of Langston Hughes. M. S. N. Tex. St. U.

3881 Pickering, J. V. Medieval English Folk Drama. Diss. U. Calif. at Davis.

3882 Pollard, P. A. A Readers Theatre Production of W. H. Auden's For the Time Being: A Christmas Oratorio. M. A. U. Tex.

3883 Pullan, B. H. Brigham Young, The Patriot--A Readers Theatre Script. M. A. Brigham Young U.

3884 Rice, H. E. The Relationship of Bertolt Brecht's Critical Writings, Theories and Methods to Oral Interpretation. Diss. Purdue.

3885 Richardson, J. G. Division on the Groundwork: Edward Albee's Adaptation of Carson McCullers' The Ballad of the Sad Cafe. M. A. U. Fla.

3886 Rickert, W. E. A Survey and Synthesis of Precepts for the Oral Interpretation of the Bible. M. A. Cent. Mich. U.

3887 Ross, W. R. Poetry: Theatre in the Mind. Diss. U. Utah.

3888 Sturges, Christine. The Effects of a Narrator's Presence on High School Audiences to Character in the Staging of Narrative Literature. Diss. Northwestern.

3889 Taylor, F. J. Readers Theatre: An Investigation of Its Philosophy and Practice with Recommendations for Michigan Forensics. M. A. Wayne St. U.

3890 Thomas, V. P. An Adaption for Readers Theatre of Five Tales from Chekhov. M. A. Calif. St. Coll. -Fullerton.

3891 Tomscha, T. J. A Readers Theatre Production of an Original Adaptation of The Adventures of Huckleberry Finn for High School Students. M. A. U. of South Dakota.

3892 Vickers, B. A. "Thurso's Landing": Robinson Jeffers. M. A. San Fran. St. Coll.

3893 Wellbaum, Sam. The Oral Interpretation of Stream of Consciousness Fiction. Diss. U. Southern Calif.

3894 Wessel, Janet. Oral Interpretation in Worship. M. A. U. Nebr.

3895 Weybright, M. D. A Study of Tensiveness in Selected Novels of William Faulkner. Diss. Northwestern.

3896 Williams, D. A. The Effects of Positive and Negative Audience Response on the Oral Interpreter: A Multiple Indicator Approach. Diss. U. Utah.

3897 Wilsey, D. N. Innocence to Innocence: Poems of Blake. M. A. Colo. St. U.

1972

3898 Ackley, G. A Comparative Study of Acting and Oral Interpretation Theory and Practice as Revealed in Selected

American College Texts: 1900-1970. Diss. U. Southern Calif.

3899 Atkinson, M. L. A Readers Theatre Script for a Religious Experience. M. A. Wstn. Ill. U.

3900 Bass, R. J. One Handful of Dream-Dust: An Analysis of the Use of the Blues in Selected Poetry of Langston Hughes. M. A. U. Wash.

3901 Bell, C. H. An Original Adaption and Production Study of William Golding's Lord of the Flies for a Readers Theatre Production. M. A. Bowling Green St. U.

3902 Borger, B. A. Selected Poems by Felix N. Stelfanile: An Oral Interpreter's Analysis. M. A. Purdue.

3903 Burkette, Eugene. A Study of the Ballad Characteristics in Carson McCuller's The Ballad of the Sad Cafe Through Chamber Theatre Adaption and Presentation. M. A. U. South Fla.

3904 Capo, L. G. Only Dead People Don't Cry--A Creative Thesis (Chamber Theatre). M. A. Cent. Mich. U.

3905 Crouch, H. W. A Readers Theatre Production of Selected Works of E. E. Cummings. M. A. U. Cinn.

3906 Crouch, I. M. Joan of Arc and Four Playwrights: A Rhetorical Analysis for Oral Interpretation. Diss. Southern Ill. U.

3907 Dejulio, M. J. Altering the Medium Can Alter the Message: Interpretations Resulting from Common Typographic Variations. M. A. U. Penn.

3908 Denithorne, M. R. The Effects of Oral Interpretation of Selected Black Literature on Audience Attitudes. M. A. U. Maine at Orono.

3909 Dial, V. L. A Descriptive Study of the Tradition of Oral Reading in the Benedictine Order. Diss. U. Mich.

3910 Dohrenburg, A. P. The Poetic Development of George Meredith from The Monthly Observer to "Modern Love." Diss. Northwestern.

3911 Elkins, W. D. The Development of Criteria for the Design of an Ideal Environment for Interpretation. M. A. N. Tex. St. U.

3912 Freeman, F. A. Functional Ambiguity in Early Poems by W. H. Auden. Diss. Northwestern.

3913 Golden, H. A.   A Study of Games Played in Ada or Ardor: A Family Chronicle by Vladimir Nabokov.   Diss.   Northwestern.

3914 Greenway, M. B.   The Wind in the Willows: A Chamber Theatre Production for Children.   M. A.   U. Tex. at Austin.

3915 Heady, D. E.   Charles Wesley Emerson: A Theory of Oral Interpretation.   Diss.   Wayne St. U.

3916 Henning, W. K.   A Semantic for Oral Interpretation: A Wheelwrightean Perspective.   Diss.   U. Southern Calif.

3917 Heslop, M. L.   Readers Theatre: Production of John Knowles' Novel: A Separate Peace.   M. A.   U. Utah.

3918 Hicks, L. C.   An Examination of Tone in the Greenhouse Poetry of Theodore Roethke.   M. A.   U. Ariz.

3919 Horner, Jack, & C. J. Policy.   Love, Life, and Other Illusions: An Original Two-Actor Concert Utilizing the Techniques of Oral Interpretation, Readers Theatre, and Acting.   M. A.   U. Akron.

3920 Keaveney, M. M.   Narrative Viewpoint in Two Novels by Alain Robbe-Grillet.   Diss.   U. Ill.

3921 Kingsley, J. C.   The Effect of Marshall McLuhan's Concept of Perception on the Oral Interpretation of Literature.   Diss.   U. Calif.

3922 Lindley, Carlyn.   The Effect of Three Modes of Oral Interpretation of Literature on Empathic Audience Response.   M. A.   U. South Fla.

3923 McHughes, J. L.   A Phenomenological Analysis of Literary Time in the Poetry of James Dickey.   Diss.   Northwestern.

3924 Osborne, William.   A Descriptive-Creative Study Involving the Social Implications of a Chamber Theatre Adaption of Watermelon Man.   M. A.   U. South Fla.

3925 Parody, R. C.   An Experiment in Multi-Media Readers Theatre.   M. A.   Ohio St. U.

3926 Powell, S. G.   The Psychology of Madmen: A Perspective on Readers Theatre.   M. A.   U. of Calif. at Santa Barbara.

3927 Robinette, J. A.   The Adaptive-Creative Process in Readers Theatre: Three Original Manuscripts.   Diss.   Southern Ill. U.

3928 Rose, Jane. The Function of Alienation Effect in the Concept of Aesthetic Distance of Readers Theatre. M. A.
Murry St. U.

3929 Sandifer, C. M. The Metamorphosis of Fiction: A Study
of Methods and Techniques of Adapting Literature and
Especially Novels to Readers Theatre. Diss. Purdue.

3930 Schmider, C. L. Precision Which Creates Movement: The
Stylistics of E. E. Cummings. Diss. U. Denver. (1973?)

3931 Shipment, I. K. Chamber Theatre Production of Ken Kesey's
One Flew Over the Cuckoo's Nest. M. A. U. Maryland.

3932 Simpson, V. J. A Study of Selected Radio Plays by Norman
Corwin for Adaptation to Readers Theatre. Diss. Wayne
St. U.

3933 Sladkus, Paul. The Little Prince (Tape). M. A. Fairfield U.

3934 Smiley, J. D. Meaning in Selected Stories of Joyce Carol
Oates. M. A. U. Missouri at Columbia.

3935 Somer, R. F. Archibald MacLeish, Spokesman for Democracy: A Rhetorical Study of His Advocacy of the American
Dream. Diss. U. Ill.

3936 Spadacene, Karen. An Analysis of a Screenplay for a Chamber
Theatre Adaption and Presentation: Ingmar Bergman's Smiles
of a Summer Night. M. A. U. South Fla.

3937 Strine, M. S. The Novel as Rhetorical Act: An Interpretation
of the Major Fiction of William Styron. Diss. U. Wash.

3938 Teneyck, J. A. Gestalt Psychology as Applied to Interpreters Theatre. M. A. S-West Missouri St. U.

3939 Thurman, L. E. A Group Interpretation Production of Jules
Verne's Twenty Thousand Leagues Under the Sea. M. S.
N. Tex. St. U.

3940 Tobias, D. R. A Pluralistic Approach to Walt Whitman's
"Song of the Open Road" for the Oral Interpreter: Ex-
plicative, Archetypal, and Rhetorical Analysis. M. A.
U. Houston.

3941 Tungate, J. L. Romantic Images in Popular Songs: 1950-
1959. Diss. Northwestern.

3941a Waechter, Martin. A Methodology for a Functional Analysis
of the Relationship Between Oral Reading Comprehension
in Beginning Readers. Diss. U. Oregon.

3942 Waite, M. D. A History of Readers Theatre in the Colleges of the State of Utah from Its Beginnings to 1968. M. A. U. Utah.

3943 Zafran, R. L. A Group Interpretation Production of Selected Literature of Leonard Cohen. M. A. N. Tex. St. U.

1973

3944 Anderson, Diane. Charting the Quest of Demian Through the Medium of Interpreters Theatre. M. A. S-West Missouri St. U.

3945 Anderson, T. D. The Role of Point of View in the Adaptation Process. Diss. Southern Ill. U.

3946 Arnfield, N. J. The Contributions of Gertrude Johnson to the Philosophical and Practical Development of the Teaching of Oral Interpretation: An Analysis and Appraisal. Diss. Wayne St. U.

3947 Arnold, J. H. Narrative Structure in the Collected Tales of E. M. Forster. Diss. U. Ill.

3948 Barley, S. M. Visions of Death: A Staging and Analysis of an Original Narrative Poem. U. South Fla.

3949 Griffin, K. H. A Comparative Analysis of Audience Response to Readers Theatre Technique. M. A. Wake Forest U.

3950 Harms, P. W. C. S. Lewis as Translator. Diss. Northwestern.

3951 Herndon, R. T. A Symbolic Interactional Theory of Reader-Poetry Encounter: A Process Description of the Reader's Interaction with New Poetry. Diss. Southern Ill. U. (1975?)

3952 Hoffman, D. J. The Novelist as Rhetorician: Characterization and Vision in the Short Fiction of Bernard Malamud. Diss. U. Wash.

3953 Hudson, Lee. Beat Generation Poetics and the Oral Tradition of Literature. Diss. U. Tex. at Austin.

3954 Jensen, L. J. A Psycholinguistic Analysis of the Oral Reading Behavior of Selected Proficient, Average and Weak Readers Reading the Same Material. Diss. Mich. St. U.

3955 Jones, J. S. Metaphor and Poetic Structure in the Prepara-
tory Meditations by Edward Taylor. Diss. Northwestern.

3956 Lande, Margot, & Alan Mirabelli. Conversion from Theatre
to Videotape. M. A. Fairfield U.

3957 Maher, M. Z. A Rhetorical Analysis of Shakespeare's
Troilus and Cressida. Diss. U. Mich.

3958 Martin, Annette. Readers Theatre: Audience Response to
Increased Use of Theatrical Techniques and Devices in
Performance. Diss. U. Mich.

3959 McElroy, Hilda-Njoki. Traditional Wit and Humor in Pan-
Afrikan Drama. Diss. Northwestern.

3960 Pazereskis, John. The Narrators of Evelyn Waugh: A
Study of Five Works of Fiction. Diss. Northwestern.

3961 Pearse, J. A. Montage in Modern Fiction: A Cinemato-
graphic Approach to the Analysis of Ironic Tone in Joyce
Cary's The Horse's Mouth. Diss. U. Ariz.

3962 Pelham, S. H. Kinesics as Applied to Interpreters Theatre.
M. A. S-West Missouri St. U.

3963 Potts, M. L. The Genesis and Evolution of the Creative
Personality: A Rankian Analysis of the Diary of Anaïs
Nin, Volumes I-V. U. Southern Calif.

3964 Ryan, J. H. The Teaching of Oral Interpretation in Roman
Catholic Seminaries in the United States. Diss. U. Missouri at Columbia.

3965 Schmider, C. L. Precision Which Creates Movement: The
Stylistics of E. E. Cummings. Diss. U. Denver.

3966 Scobie, N. C. Readers Theatre for Children: An Approach
and Evaluation. M. A. U. Wisc. at Eau Claire.

3967 Stafford, M. A. Oral Interpretation of Literature in the Los
Angeles Community Colleges: A Proposed Program to
Meet the Needs of Black Students. Diss. U. Southern
Calif.

3968 Taylor, T. A. Woody Guthrie-Child of Dust: A One Man
Show. M. A. U. Tex. at Austin.

3969 Valentine, K. B. A Patterned Imagination: William Morris' Use of Pattern in Decorative Design and the Last
Prose Romances, 1883-1896. Diss. U. Utah.

3970 Vanvalkenberg, L. L. The History of Oral Interpretation in
Selected State Universities. Diss. Wayne St. U.

3971 Wilcox, E. E. Shades of Gray in the Red, White and Blue. M. A. New Mexico St. U.

1974

3972 Bindert, Kathleen. Ethos as Mask: A Study of Character in the Plays of Luigi Pirandello. Diss. Northwestern.

3973 Bozarth-Campbell, A. R. An Incarnational Aesthetic of Interpretation. Diss. Northwestern.

3974 Calk, J. A. A Lecture Recital Illustrating the Southern Influence on the Poetry of Robert Penn Warren. M. A. N. Tex. St. U.

3975 Callas, J. H. Classical Greek Literature as an Aural Experience. Diss. U. Texas-Austin.

3976 Caswell, J. R. A Comparative Analysis of the Dramatic Structures of American and Japanese Film. M. A. San Diego St. U.

3977 Claytor, S. E. Lawrence Ferlinghetti: His Poetic Style and Oral Values. M. A. Univ. N. C. -Ch.

3978 Ditto, L. D. The Effects of Language Characteristics in Oral Reading. Diss. Mich. State U.

3979 Dorris, C. A. A Rhetorical Analysis of the Manipulation of Distance in Kurt Vonnegut, Jr. 's Breakfast of Champions. M. A. Southern Ill. U.

3980 Dunn, M. H. An Exploratory Study of the Effects of a College Level Creative Drama Course on Creative Thinking, Risk Taking, and Social Group Acceptance. Diss. Southern Ill. U.

3981 Elder, J. T. An Experimental Study of the Effect that Different Presentations Have Upon Audience Response to Aesthetic Distance. M. A. Penn. St. U.

3982 Gaede, C. J. Feedback in the Oral Interpretation Classroom: The Development and Application of a Communications Model to the Structure of the Verbal Feedback of the Critique Sessions. Diss. Southern Ill. U.

3983 Gura, T. J. The Function of the Hero in Shakespeare's Last Tragedies. Diss. Northwestern.

3984 Isbell, T. L. A Critique of Language Assumptions Beneath Prevalent Theories of Oral Interpretation from the Perspectives of Roland Barthes' Literary Structuralism. Diss. Southern Ill.

3985 Kearns, W. G.   An Examination of Materials and Methods Used in Professional Educational Readers Theatre Productions from 1867-68 to 1971-72.   Diss.   Ohio U.

3986 Kerr, B. R.   An Oral Interpretation Program of Selected Navajo Literature.   M. S.   N. Texas St. U.

3987 Lawrence, K. E.   Black vs. Bourgeois in the Novels of the Harlem Renaissance: A Study of Literary Conflict.   Diss. U. Ill.

3988 Lazaro, P. B.   A Survey of Approaches in Philippine Oral Literature Scholarship.   Diss.   Northwestern.   (1975?)

3989 Lewis, T. V.   Traditions of Group Reading in Religious Worship.   M. A.   Ohio St. U.

3990 Manry, Diorah.   An Experimental Study of Rating Charts Used in Evaluation of Oral Interpretation.   M. A.   Brigham Young U.

3991 Mosley, G. R.   An Historical Study of Unity's Spoken Word Tradition and Charles Fillmore's Metaphysical Interpretation of Biblical Literature.   M. A.   Wayne St. U.

3992 Rickert, W. E.   The Sound, Structure, and Meaning of Rhyme: An Oral Correlative Study in Modern Poetry. Diss.   U. Mich.

3993 Roberts, J. D.   Identification of Oral Reading Errors and Functional Levels on Informal Reading Inventories.   Diss. U. Northern Colo.

3994 Root, M. M.   Kenneth Burke's Concept of the Criticism of Literature as Rhetoric.   Diss.   U. Ill. -Urbana.

3995 Smith, K. D.   Women of the Nobility in Shakespeare's English History Plays.   Diss.   Northwestern.

3996 Steiner, L. L.   The Use of Poetic Self-Actualization as a Stimulus for Rehabilitation and Reintegration Within the Penal System.   M. S.   Southern Ill. U.

3997 Turpin, T. J.   The Cheyenne World View as Reflected in the Oral Traditions of the Culture Heroes: Sweet Medicine, and Erect Horns.   Diss.   U. Southern Calif.

3998 York, P. A.   Standardizing the Doll Empathic Response Scale for Oral Interpretation.   M. A.   U. N. C. -Chapel Hill.

1975

3999 Arnold, V. O. Narrative Structure and the Readers Theatre
Staging of Nothing Like the Sun by Anthony Burgess.
Diss. U. Ill. -Urbana.

4000 Chard, G. E. Flannery O'Connor's Fiction: Materials and
Selected Structures. Diss. Northwestern.

4001 Cosentine, D. J. Patterns in Domeisia: The Dialectics of
Mende Narrative Performance. Diss. U. Wisc.

4002 Creed, Bruce. Performative Attitudes Toward Real or
Imagined Events in Scenes of Passion and Despair by
Joyce Carol Oates. M. A. Wstn. Ky. U.

4003 Davis, D. A. An Adaptation and Production of The Hiding
Place for Readers Theatre. M. A. Baylor U.

4004 Gimple, D. A. The Performance of Folktales as a Communicative Act: A Descriptive Study of Two North Carolina
Folk Narrators. M. A. U. N. C. -Chapel Hill.

4005 Harriet, S. H. An Experimental Study of Listener Response
to Sequencing Poetry as Perceived on Radio. Diss. U.
Oregon.

4006 Harris, A. A. Analysis of Point of View in the Novels of
Kurt Vonnegut, Jr. , as Applied to Oral Interpretation.
M. A. N. Tex. St. U.

4007 Herndon, R. T. A Symbolic Interactionist Theory of Reader-
Poetry Encounter: A Process Description of the Reader's
Interaction with New Poetry. Diss. Southern Ill. U.

4008 Hester, S. K. An Attitude Survey of Current Texas High
School Teachers Towards Oral Interpretation Contests in
the University Interscholastic League. M. S. N. Tex.
St. U.

4009 Hipps, D. C. Charles Dickens as an Oral Interpreter.
M. A. U. N. C. -Chapel Hill.

4010 Hurdis, S. M. Multimedia, Mixed-Media, and Intermedia:
Their Utilization in the Oral Interpretation of Literature.
M. A. N. Tex. St. U.

4011 Lazaro, P. B. A Survey of Approaches in Philippine Oral
Literature Scholarship. Diss. Northwestern. (1974?)

4012 Lea, J. K. Methods of Instruction in the Basic or Only
Oral Interpretation of Literature Course at the College
Level: A Survey. Diss. U. Maryland.

4013 Mayberry, D. R. A Comparison of Three Techniques of Teaching Literature: Silent Reading, Solo Performance and Readers Theatre. Diss. N. Tex. St. U.

4014 McCloud, G. E. Plot as a Staging Determinant for Chamber Theatre. Diss. U. Mich.

4015 McGeever, C. J. Toward a Theory of Chamber Theatre Production: The Function of First Person. Diss. U. Mich.

4016 Parker, W. E. Creativity and Memory: A Study of the Creative Process Involved in the Writing of the Interpreters Theatre Script "From These Sterile Hills." Diss. Southern Ill. U.

4017 Passey, J. C. An Interpretive Analysis of the Interaction of Illusion and Reality in Selected Verse of James Dickey from 1951-1971. Diss. U. Ill. -Urbana.

4018 Phillips, M. J. The Dissenting Voice: A Rhetorical Analysis of Denise Levertov's Engaged Poetry. Diss. U. Tex. -Austin.

4019 Skinner, J. F. Implications of Play Theory for the Performance of Literature. M. A. U. Tex. -Austin.

4020 Stack, Patricia. Kenneth Burke's Dramatic Pentad Used as an Analytic Tool for Determining Dimensions of Meaning for the Oral Interpretation of Selected Prose Works of Nikos Kazantzakis. Diss. N. Y. U.

4021 Turney, J. T. The Writing, Production, and Direction of an Original Readers Theatre Script: "A Toast to Gods." M. A. N. Tex. St. U.

4022 Watkins, Bonnie. The Performance of Experimental Prose Fiction. M. A. U. Tex. -Austin.

4023 Welton, J. L. Interpretive Movement: A Training Approach for Performers of Literature. Diss. Southern Ill. U.

4024 Wicker, P. E. Jamesian Women: A Readers Theatre Adaptation from Selected Novels of Henry James. M. S. N. Tex. St. U.

4025 Wonzong, R. L. A Structural Analysis of Arthur Miller's Plays. Diss. Northwestern.

4026 Zastrow, S. V. The Structure of Selected Plays by American Women Playwrights: 1920-1970. Diss. Northwestern.

1976

4027 Bartine, David. Meanings in Critical Theory: A Study of the Modern Conflation of Rhetoric and Poetics. Diss. U. Calif. at Berkeley.

4028 Benson, P. L. An Historical and Attitudinal Study of the Oral Interpretation Events in the Arkansas State Speech Festival. M. S. N. Tex. St. U.

4029 Dunitz, C. A. An Analysis of the Effects of Varying Modes of Prose Presentation on Comprehension and Aesthetic Appreciation. Diss. Wayne St. U.

4030 Dunnagan, Karen. Vocal Quality and Audience Appreciation. M. A. Indiana St. U.

4031 Ellsworth, C. E. The Application of Selected Acting Techniques to a Critical Analysis of Characterization in Oral Interpretation. M. A. U. N. C. -Chapel Hill.

4032 Gordon, V. L. The Role of the Director in Readers Theatre: An Extrapolation from Conventional Theatre. M. A. U. N. C. -Chapel Hill.

4033 Hall, D. R. Oral Interpretation of Literature: An Approach to Teaching Middle School English. M. A. N. Tex. St. U.

4034 Hauschild, S. K. A Bibliography of Dramatic Recordings in the Studio Library of the University of Texas at Austin Cross-Referenced by Titles, Authors, Performers, and Directors. M. A. U. Texas at Austin.

4035 James, L. B. Black Orality and Actionality: Their Development and Influence on Contemporary Black Poetry. Diss. Wayne St. U.

4036 Jeffrey, P. R. Diane Wakoski: An Expressive Voice in Contemporary American Poetry. Diss. U. Texas at Austin.

4037 Keener, C. D. The Effect of Literature with an Affective Message on the Attitudes of Performers of Oral Interpretation and the Relationship of Performer's Attitudes to Involvement with Persona. Diss. Southern Ill. U. at Carbondale.

4038- Kwal, T. S. An Experimental Study of Sex as a Factor In-
9   fluencing Audience Evaluation of Reader Effectiveness and Audience Comprehension of Performance for Selected Dramatic Monologues. Diss. N. Y. U.

4040 Marder, B. A.   Group Interpretation of Biblical Literature:
        Eight Original Scripts for Use in Church. M. A. N. Tex.
        St. U.

4041 McManus, B. K.   Literary Comedy to Concert Comedy: The
        Achievements of Artemus Ward, Petroleum v. Nasby, and
        Josh Billings. Diss. U. Texas at Austin.

4042 Moseley, M. L.   The Canterbury Tales: A Production The-
        sis. M. A. Calif. St. U. at Chico.

4042a Plax, P. M.   Guidelines for Interpretive Performance of
        Four Narrative Genres: Commentator, Dramatized Nar-
        rator, Scenic Narration, and Internal Narration.   Diss.
        U. Southern Calif.

4043 Saldivar, Ramon.   Reading and Rhetoric: Studies in the In-
        terpretation of Modern Narrative. Diss. Yale U.

4044 Schneider, C. F.   Music for Literature: A Descriptive
        Study of Literary Program Music for Use in the Teaching
        and Performance of Literature. Diss. U. Texas at
        Austin.

4045 Simpson, C. E.   "Orpheus" and the Dramatic Performance
        of Poetry. Diss. U. Minn.

4046 Williams, D. A.   Evaluation of Performance: An Adaptation
        of George Santayana's Standard of Excellence for Poetry.
        Diss. U. Southern Calif.

1977

4047 Abarry, A. S.   Rhetoric and Poetics of Oral African Liter-
        ature: A Study of the Ga of Ghana. Diss. S. U. N. Y. at
        Buffalo.

4048 Bailey, P. M.   The Effect of Oral Interpretation and Other
        Methods of Exposure to a Poem upon Literary Comprehen-
        sion and Appreciation. M. Ed. Ind. St. U.

4049 Brock, Carolyn.   Production of John Knowles' A Separate
        Peace. M. A. Southern Meth. U.

4050 Broderick, S. M.   The Tori: Structure, Aesthetics and
        Time in Krio Oral Narrative-Performance. Diss. U.
        Wisc.

4051 Burrus, J. L.   Charlotte's Web: An Analysis and Proposal
        for Production. M. A. U. Texas at Austin.

4052 Carpenter, B. G. The Prose Fiction of Donald Bartheleme: A Compendium of Critical Commentary and Suggestions for Staging. M. A. U. Texas at Austin.

4053 Cater, R. R. A Production of Frederick Gaines' The Legend of Sleepy Hollow. M. A. Calif. St. U.

4054 Collier, M. B. Love and Friendship: An Evening with Jane Austen. M. A. Calif. St. U.

4055 Conquergood, L. D. The Anglo-Saxon Boast: Structure and Function. Diss. Northwestern.

4056 Davis, M. D. The Rationale, Values, and Course Guide for a Senior High Oral Interpretation Course. Diss. Carnegie-Mellon U.

4057 De Lecour, C. A. "The Phantom Tollbooth": A Chamber Theatre Production for Children. M. A. U. Texas at Austin.

4058 Dorward, Jack. A Study of Dark-Light Imagery in Sherwood Anderson's Winesburg, Ohio. M. A. U. Wash.

4059 Farnsworth, G. L. Alienation in Contemporary American Poetry: A Group Interpretation Script. M. S. N. Tex. St. U.

4060 Frederickson, R. Q. Rhetoric in Howard Nemerov's Poetry of Wit. Diss. Utah.

4061 Garrett, W. J. Shades of Sterling Brown: An Analysis and Readers Theatre Production of Sterling Brown. M. A. U. N. C. -Chapel Hill.

4062 Glover, J. S. The History and Development of Choric Theatre and Its Application to the Selected Works of Theodore Roethke. M. A. Southwest Missouri St. U.

4063 Greene, S. S. The Scop and Tradition: The Critical Implications of the Oral-Formulaic Theory for Old English Studies. Diss. Columbia.

4064 Hight-McMurray, M. J. Readers Theatre for Senior Citizens. M. A. U. N. C. -Chapel Hill.

4065 House, S. K. Effectiveness of Chamber Theatre Compared to Acting for the Understanding of Literature. Diss. U. Tulsa.

4066 Jackson, J. F. Speech-Act Theory and Reader-Response Criticism. Diss. U. Minn.

4067 Jones, J. W. Performance of the Narration in James
Joyce's Ulysses. Diss. U. Wash.

4068 Keener, C. D. A Study of the Relationships Among Performer Attitudes, Involvement with Personae, and the
Performance of Literature. Diss. Southern Ill. U.

4069 Kelly, M. L. The Theory of Oral Interpretation: The
Functions of Audience. Diss. U. Mich.

4070 Kempton, D. R. The Social Determination of Narrative
Performance in Three Canterbury Tales. Diss. U. Calif.

4071 Korinek, J. T. The Interpretive-Rhetorical Situation: A
Framework for Post Performance Analysis of Interpretation. M. A. Wstn. Ky. U.

4072 Lambert, L. L. A Group Interpretation Script Based on the
Life, Works, and Times of Dante Alighieri. M. A. N.
Tex. St. U.

4073 Livingston, R. A. Making the Whole Most Musicall: A
Study of Prosodic Elements and Patterns of Sound in the
Poetry of Henry Vaughn. Diss. Northwestern.

4074 Logan, C. A. Adaptation of Narrative Fiction to Readers
Theatre Performance. Diss. U. Southern Calif.

4075 Loxley, R. B. Environments for Oral Interpretation: The
Design and Use of Space for the Performance of Literature. Diss. Southern Ill. U.

4076 MacLeod, M. A. An Interpreters Theatre Production of A
Colossal Hoax of Clocks and Calendars. M. A. Calif. St.
U. at Long Beach.

4077 Martin, H. R. Analysis of the Dramatic Speaking Voice: A
Practical System and Methodology. Diss. U. Mich.

4078 Marz, C. H. John Dos Passos: The Performing Voice.
Diss. Brandeis U.

4079 McNabb, Michael. Sinclair Lewis: A Biographical Portrait.
M. A. N. Tex. St. U.

4080 Mesinger, B. M. Dissonance and Indeterminancy in the
Critical Writings and Fiction of Joyce Carol Oates: Implications for the Interpreter. Diss. Wayne St. U.

4081 Meyers, J. W. A Perceptual Process View of the Reader-
Text Relationship in the Interpretative Performance Experience. Diss. U. Mich.

4082 Minister, K. A. The Perception of Literature by Silent Readers and Oral Interpreters: A Theory and an Exploratory Experimental Study. Diss. Northwestern.

4083 Nash, Carman. Calypso in Interpreters Theatre: Performance as Social Criticism. M. A. Ariz. St. U.

4084 Neiman, Jack. Stanislavski: His Acting Principles and Their Significance for the Field of Oral Interpretation. Diss. U. Calif. at L. A.

4085 Nord, M. H. A People's Voice: The Rhetorical Art of Tennyson's Public Poetry. Diss. Vanderbilt.

4086 Pelias, R. J. In the Whirl of Today. M. A. Southern Meth. U.

4087 Peyton, D. K. Style, Structure and Performance: A Study of John Fowles' The French Lieutenant's Woman. M. A. Calif. St. U.

4088 Sauceda, J. S. Readers Theatre Derived from the Literature of James Joyce. M. A. Florida St. U.

4089 Scott, P. E. An Interpreter's Approach to the Language Behavior of Literary Speakers: A Sociolinguistic Analysis of Joyce Carol Oates' Poetry. Diss. Southern Ill. U.

4090 Seguine, A. M. A System of Analysis for Defining the Folk Performing Arts as an Interdisciplinary Study. Diss. Columbia Tchrs. Coll.

4091 Simeone, E. G. The Paper Courtship: The Correspondence Between Ellen Terry and George Bernard Shaw: A Performance of Their Letters. M. A. U. Texas at Austin.

4092 Smith, A. Y. A Comparison of Two Instructional Methods for Teaching Communicative Skills of Oral Interpretation. Diss. Brigham Young U.

4093 Stafford, Larry. Eugene Field: Public Reader. M. A. L. S. U.

4094 Sturdivant, P. S. A Socio-Biographical Study Designed to Develop a Performable Persona for William Cowper's Letters. Diss. U. Texas at Austin.

4095 Svore, J. L. An Ontological Perspective Applied to the Interpretation of Saul Bellow's Henderson the Rain King. Diss. U. Ariz.

4096 Taylor, J. S. Adapting and Producing Eudora Welty's "A Piece of News" for Chamber Theatre and Television. M. A. U. Texas at Austin.

4097 Thompson, J. C. Oral Interpretation and Joycean Epiphany: A Study of the Literary Concept in Relation to the Interpreter's Performance Task. Diss. Purdue.

4098 Trantham, A. C. A Readers Theatre Script Based on the Writings of William A. Owens. M. A. N. Tex. St. U.

4099 Watson, K. W. An Investigation of the Lateralized Alpha Activity of Oral Interpreters While Listening to Selected Stimulus Materials. M. A. Auburn.

4100 Welden, L. F. Hiram Corson: Interpretative Reader, English Teacher, Literary Scholar. Diss. L. S. U. Agri. / Mech. Coll.

4101 Wieland, Janice. All the Lonely People. M. A. Southern Meth. U.

4102 Yordon, J. E. The Double Motif in the Fiction of Flannery O'Connor. Diss. Southern Ill. U.

1978

4103 Bennett, Suzanne. The Lyrical Novel: A Structural Analysis and Performance Perspective. Diss. U. Missouri.

4104 Bowden, E. A. Performed Literature: Words and Music by Bob Dylan. Diss. U. Calif.

4105 Boyd, G. R. Ohio's Poets-in-the-Schools. M. A. U. Texas at Austin.

4106 Breitwieser, D. E. Silent Reading as Dramatic Experience: Literary Perspective Through Participation. Diss. Southern Ill. U.

4107 Brown, P. J. Jazz Poetry: Definition, Analysis and Performance. U. Southern Calif.

4108 Brown, S. H. An Experimental Study in the Preservation of Poetry Shape. M. A. Auburn.

4109 Capo, K. E. Redeeming Words: A Study of Confessional Rhetoric in the Poetry of Anne Sexton. Diss. Northwestern.

4110 Chapman, W. A. Strategies for Silence: W. S. Merwin's Disembodied Voice. Diss. Utah.

4111 Di Luzio, Giovanni. How Can We Know the Dancer from the Dance: A Readers Theatre Production. M. A. Calif. St. U.

4112 Edelnant, J. A. Nabokov's Black Rainbow: An Analysis of the Rhetorical Function of Color Imagery in Ada or Ardor: A Family Chronicle. Diss. Northwestern.

4113 Evans, V. S. Thomas Pynchon's Gravity's Rainbow as Modernist Paradigm. M. A. Utah.

4114 Fine, E. C. The Folklore Text: A Performance-Centered Approach. Diss. U. Texas at Austin.

4115 Gray, C. G. Syntactic Analysis and the Performance of Poetry: A Transformational-Generative Method. Diss. U. Texas at Austin.

4116 Hudson, J. G. Contemporary Native American: A Group Interpretation Script Based upon Vine Deloria Jr.'s God Is Red, N. Scott Momaday's The Way to Rainy Mountain and Hyemeyost's Storm of Seven Arrows. M. S. N. Tex. St. U.

4117 Lacaze, K. M. The Influence of the Rev. Jenkin Lloyd Jones on the Browning Movement in the Middle West from 1882 to 1890. M. A. L. S. U.

4118 Le Wilhelm, N. I. The Last Temptation of Christ--An Example of a Cutting of a Novel of Extreme Length into a Script of Playable Length. M. A. Southwest Missouri St. U.

4119 Marshall, K. L. A Study, for Oral Interpretation, of Selected Poetry by Contemporary American Women. Diss. Syracuse U.

4120 McCue, Mark. Readers Theatre as Criticism of D'Annunzio's Sogni delle Stagioni. M. A. Ariz. St. U.

4121 McDonnell, W. E. A Study for the Oral Interpreter of Problems in the Performance of Shakespeare's Plays. Diss. Northwestern.

4122 McNabb, M. L. A Group Interpretation Script, Sinclair Lewis: A Biographical Portrait. M. A. N. Tex. St. U.

4123 Mutswairo, S. M. Oral Literature in Zimbabwe: An Analytico-Interpretative Approach. Diss. Howard U.

4124 O'Brien, J. L. The Humanism of Bernard Malamud in Four Selected Novels. Diss. U. of Ill. at Urbana-Champaign.

4125 Parris, S. C. An Empirical Study in the Measurement of Theatrical Dimensions. M. A. U. N. C. at Chapel Hill.

4126 Rein, L. M. A Rhetorical Study of Lew Sarett. Diss. Northwestern.

4127 Roden, S. A. A Comparison of Three Techniques of Teaching Literature: Silent Reading, Readers Theatre, and Video-Tape Readers Theatre. Diss. N. Texas St. U.

4128 Speer, J. H. Folkloristics and the Performance of Literature. Diss. U. Texas at Austin.

4129 Strong, W. F. An Analysis of Mark Twain's Oral Interpretation on the Reading Tour of 1884-1885. M. S. N. Tex. St. U.

4130 Tapia, J. E. Circuit Chautauqua's Promotional Visions: A Study of Program Brochures, Circa 1904-1932. Diss. U. Ariz.

4131 Waisman, Charlotte. Collective Identity and the Archetype of the Common Man and Woman in the Poetry of Howard Nemerov. Diss. Northwestern.

4132 Wysong, P. A. An Appraisal of Oral Interpretation Theory in Light of Recent Psychological Research on Mental Imagery. Diss. U. Texas at Austin.

1979

4133 Becker, B. S. The Time Consciousness of Performance: A Phenomenological Exploration of the Relationship Between Performer and Text in the Performance of Literature. Diss. Northwestern.

4134 Becker, James. The Poetics of Good and Evil: A Study of Plot and Character in the Later Plays of Charles Williams. Diss. U. Wash.

4135 Corbett, D. L. Oral Interpretation: An Experimental Text for Junior High School Students in a Rural Area. M. Ed. Brigham Young U.

4136 Dewester, J. D. Spiritual Isolation: A Readers Theatre Production of Carson McCuller's Novel The Heart Is a Lonely Hunter. M. A. Purdue.

4137 Elliot, A. G. A Dramatistic Analysis of Two Tales from Afro-American Folklore. M. A. Wayne St. U.

4138 Geist, P. R. A Comparative Study of the Performer's Empathic Process in the Arts of Interpretation and Modern Dance. M. A. U. Northern Iowa.

4139 Hathaway, J. A. The Use of Appalachian Culture and Oral Tradition in the Teaching of Literature to Adolescents. Diss. Ohio St. U.

4140 Highnam, Sandra. An Information Processing Approach to Group Performance of Poetry: Implications for Adaptation and Audience Research. M. A. U. Northern Iowa.

4141 Lentz, Tony. The Oral Tradition of Interpretation: Reading in Hellenic Greece as Described by Ancient Authors. Diss. U. Mich.

4142 Manley, K. F. Literary Criticism and the Oral Narrative. Diss. Indiana U.

4143 Mathis, J. W. The Phenomenology of Movement in the Poetry of Richard Wilbur. Diss. Northwestern.

4144 Parrish, Patricia. The Novel as Rhetoric: A Study of William S. Burroughs' Naked Lunch. M. A. Utah.

4145 Pelias, R. J. Oral Interpretation as a Method for Increasing Perspective-Taking Abilities. Diss. U. Ill.

4146 Ryburn, N. E. A Study of the Circuit Chautauqua in Pine Bluff, Arkansas, 1914-1926. M. A. L. S. U.

4147 Singer, S. S. Laurence Olivier Directs Shakespeare: A Study in Film Authorship. Diss. Northwestern.

4148 Sloyer, Shirlee. Readers Theatre: Handbook for Teachers of Grades Four Through Six. Diss. N. Y. U.

4149 Sturges, R. S. Interpretation as Action: The Reader in Late Medieval Narrative. Diss. Brown U.

4150 Wendt, T. A. A Study of Peter Brook's Interpretations of Shakespeare's Plays, 1945-1975. Diss. Northwestern.

4151 Woodard, D. J. The Effect of Written Analysis on the Oral Interpretation of Poetry. M. Ed. Ill. St. U.

1980

4152 Bell, E. E. A Proposed Staging of Wole Soyinka's A Dance of the Forests: An Aristotelian Analysis and Study of Yoruba Oral Traditions. M. A. U. Texas at Austin.

4153 Berman, M. A. An Experimental Study of Chamber Theatre Dramatization as an Aid to Understanding Literature. M. A. Calif. St. U.

4154 Edwards, M. L. The Rhetoric of Afro-American Poetry: A Rhetorical Analysis of Black Poetry and the Selected Poetry of Margaret Walker and Langston Hughes. Diss. U. Kansas.

4155 Edwards, P. C. The Treatment of Taste in Selected Elocution and Expression Texts: A Comparative Analysis. Diss. U. Texas at Austin.

4156 Howson, B. J. Chamber Theatre: A Comparative Study of Interpretation Texts and Articles. M. A. Wayne St. U.

4157 Karcher, J. H. A Rhetorical Situation Analysis of the Suicide Poems of Sylvia Plath and Anne Sexton. M. A. Miami U.

4158 Miller, C. A. A Phenomenological Analysis of Literary Experience: The Oral Interpreter's Preparation of Lyric Poetry for Performance. Southern Ill. U. at Carbondale.

4159 Mullins, S. R. A Report on Oral Interpretation in the Secondary Classroom and Relationships Discovered in Reading Achievement and Self-Concept Changes. Diss. U. Arkansas.

4160 Paris, Richard. Walt Whitman's Rhetoric: An Analysis of Intentions and Techniques. Univ. of Calif. at Berkeley.

4161 Reid, G. G. A Readers Theatre Production of Women on Women: Facing Adulthood. M. A. Purdue.

4162 Sauceda, J. S. The Wordloosed Soundscript: Formulating an Oral Interpretation of James Joyce's Finnegans Wake. Diss. U. Southern Calif.

4163 Sauro, D. A. Subjective Criticism: A Supplemental Technique for Teaching the Oral Interpretation of Literature. M. A. U. Ariz.

4164 Schooley, B. J. Anna Cora Mowatt: Public Reader. M. A. L. S. U.

4165 Schwalm, D. L. Narrator Reliability in the Creative Autobiography: An Approach for the Solo Interpreter. M. A. Wstn. Ky. U.

4166 Sedano, M. V. Chicanismo in Selected Poetry from the Chicano Movement 1969-1972: A Rhetorical Study. Diss. U. Southern Calif.

4167 Souza, N. G. Man and Superman--The Dream Interlude. M. A. Calif. St. U. at Chico.

4168 Tallant, C. E. Theory and Performance of Narrative Ambiguity in Selected Novels by John Hawkes. Diss. L. S. U.

4169 Tapia, R. L. A Perfection of Thought: Wallace Stevens and His Reader. Diss. U. Wash.

4170 Taylor, J. S. Narrative Strategies in Fiction and Film: An Analysis of the American Short Story Series. Diss. U. Texas at Austin.

4171 Timpson, D. D. A Rhetorical Study of Selected F. Scott Fitzgerald Stories. M. A. Utah.

4172 Van Oosting, James. An Original Novel, Snow Angels, and a Critical Commentary upon the Writing Process. Diss. Northwestern.

4173 Zweig, E. M. Performance Poetry: Critical Approaches to Contemporary Intermedia. Diss. U. Mich.

FILMSTRIPS

4174   Allen, Woody. Woody Allen: An American Comedy. Allen discusses how and why he writes, reads, and how he uses his reading. We learn of the craft that creates apparent looseness of his comic genius. Allen notes how important discipline and risk are. Films for the Humanities, Inc., Box 2053, Princeton, N. J. 30 mins. Purchase $400; rent $42. 50.

4175   Bacon, W. A. A Sense of the Other. Students shown preparing for and performing in Bacon's Shakespeare class at Northwestern. Comments by Bacon provide framework for this investigation of the process and benefits of study of lit in performance. Northwestern U. 16mm, 33 mins., color. Purchase $375; $30 rental.

4176   Bass, Saul. Notes on the Popular Arts. Saul Bass has created several that are standards in investigating man's creative adjustment to his world. A series of concisely scripted sketches which explore effects of film, TV, pop music, and novel on modern society and related attempts of academicians to describe these various phenomena. Pyramid Films, Box 1048, Santa Monica, Calif. 90406. 20 mins. Purchase $350; rent inquire.

4177   Borges, J. L. The Inner World of Jorge Luis Borges. Borges and Joseph Wiseman narrate program dedicated to picturing Borges in his world. Dual nature of fictive world he creates is reflected in film as we see and hear Borges discuss his familial heritage and lit sources. Films for the Humanities, Box 2053, Princeton, N. J. 08540. 28. 5 mins. Purchase $375; rental $37. 50.

4178   Colette. Ruby Dee narrates program presenting passages of Colette's observations. Numerous photos. Directed by Edouard Berne. Perspective Films, 369 West Erie, Chicago 60610. 12. 5 mins. Purchase $282; rent $25.

4179   Cummings, E. E. An American Original: E. E. Cummings. First Poetry Quartet sits at sidewalk cafe in Greenwich Village and dramatizes several Cummings poems. Also available in video-cassette. Nebraska ETV Network. $350, 16mm; $250, video-cassette.

4180 Dickinson, Emily. Emily Dickinson: A Certain Slant of Light. Julie Harris narrates and guides viewer through Amherst home site of Dickinson. Pyramid Films. $375, 16mm; $280, video-cassette. 29 mins.; apply for rental.

4181 Editors. The American Dream. Henry Fonda joins First Poetry Quartet in performing poems (Sandburg, Frost, et al.) which deal with the American Dream. Great Plains National ITV Library. 16mm; 30 mins., color $350; videocassette $275; rental $78.50.

4182 Editors. The American Experience in Literature: The Romantic Age. Five strips accompanied by five audio cassettes and study guide. Writers include Poe, Hawthorne, Melville, Thoreau and Emerson. Also analysis of works of these writers as well as comments on lives and times. Encyclopaedia Britannica $82.95.

4183 Editors. The American Experience in Literature: Nineteenth-Century Poets. Series includes four scripts accompanied by four audio cassettes and study guide. Poets include Longfellow, Whittier, Holmes, Lowell, Whitman and Dickinson. Includes biographical data, emotional and political influences and readings from their works. Classical music minimally supports readings. Encyclopaedia Britannica $71.50.

4184 Editors. American Folklore Films and Videotapes: An Index. Listing of over 1800 films and videotapes indexed and annotated. Available from Center for Southern Folklore, 1216 Peabody Avenue, Box 4081, Memphis, Tenn. 38104. 350 pages $15.

4185 Editors. Modern American Poetry. Two parts. Interaction between artist and environment explored in poetry of Frost, Sandburg, Robinson, Ginsberg and others. Educational Dimensions Corp.

4186 Editors. Modern American Literature. Strip traces American lit from end of WW II through early 70's. Numerous quotations from contemporary authors strong point of strip. Educational Audio-Visual.

4187 Editors. Poems of the Sea. Thematic anthology of compiled poems by First Poetry Quartet. Nebraska ETV Network, 16mm, 30 mins. $350; videocassette $225, rental $25.

4188 Ezra Pound: Poet's Poet. Pound in his 80's reading own poetry and discussing his literary life from boyhood in Idaho to Philadelphia to England prior to WW I and Paris in the 20's. Films for the Humanities, Inc., P. O. Box

2053, Princeton, N. J. 08540. 28. 5 mins/bw. Purchase $300; rent $30.

4189 Faulkner, William. William Faulkner: A Life on Paper. Malcolm Cowley, Lauren Bacall, Jill Faulkner Summers and others discuss the life and writings of Faulkner in two-hour film narrated by Raymond Burr. Film is full of informed gossip that expands one's understanding of Faulkner. Contact Mississippi Authority for Educational Television.

4190 Frost, Robert. The Death of the Hired Man. A rendering of the atmosphere of early 20th-century New England farm life which frames the action of narrative poem by Frost. Encyclopaedia Britannica, 16mm, 22 mins. color, $350; rental $21.

4191 Jeffers, Robinson. Tor House. Burgess Meredith performs Jeffers' poetry as voice over while we see land that in-spired Jeffers' work--California's Big Sur and Monterey Peninsula. Directed by James Hatch. Indiana St. U. Audio-Visual Center, Terre Haute, Ind. 47809. 24. 5 mins. Purchase $340; rental $12. 50.

4192 Knopf, A. A. A Publisher Is Known by the Company He Keeps. Narrated by Knopf, this film is case study of relationship between author and publisher in second and third decades of this century. Features reminiscences of Thomas Mann and Willa Cather. Phoenix Films, $20, 16mm, 25 mins. , b/w.

4193 Knopf, A. A. , & Mrs. Knopf. Dialogue. Film comprised of personal thoughts of Knopfs and includes photo records of literary figures of 20th-century, including Camus and Updike. Phoenix Films. $17. 00 rental, 16mm, b/w.

4193a Oates, J. C. In the Region of Ice. Academy Award win-ning adaptation of Oates' story of relationship between nun and male student. Phoenix Films. $35 rental, 16mm, 38 mins. , b/w.

4194 O'Connor, Flannery. The Comforts of Home. 40-min. color adaptation of short story by O'Connor. Stockard Channing. Phoenix Films. $47. 50 rental.

4195 O'Connor, Flannery. Good Country People. Adaptation of Short Story. Jeff Jackson Films. 16mm, 32 mins.

4196 O'Connor, Flannery. The River. O'Connor's story of ef-fects of river bank Fundamentalist religious service in award-winning film. Phoenix Films. 16mm, 29 mins. , color. Rental $40.

4197 Rogers, Paul. Stanislavsky: Maker of the Modern Theatre. Rogers looks at evolution of Stanislavsky as actor, director, and founder of Moscow Art Theatre. In one section of film, we see Stanislavsky meet with actors to discuss psychological requirements of a characterization. Also recalled is opening night of Seagull. Films for the Humanities, Inc., Box 2053, Princeton, N.J. 08540. 28.5 mins./bw. Purchase $300; rent $30.

4198 Sandburg, Carl. The World of Carl Sandburg. Film based on Norman Corwin's stage presentation of the same name features Uta Hagen and Fritz Weaver. Phoenix Films. 16mm 59 mins., b/w. Rental $40.

4199 Steffens, Roger, & Ben Shedd. Poetry for People Who Hate Poetry. Recorded in theatre with stool and volumes of poetry and other books as props, these films rely on Steffens' stage presence to produce vitality of the lit package of three films: About Words, E. E. Cummings, Shakespeare. 12-17 mins. Churchill Films, 662 N. Robertson Blvd., Los Angeles, Calif. 90069. Purchase $680. Apply for rental.

4200 Steinbeck, John. The Red Pony. Feature length film adaptation stars Henry Fonda and Maureen O'Hara. Phoenix Films. 16mm, 101 mins., color. $100 rental.

4201 Roloff, L. H. Son of the Sad Fall: The Poetry of Robinson Jeffers. 16mm film available, Public Relations Office, Occidental College, Los Angeles, Calif. 90041. Video tape: KNBC Los Angeles.

4202- Welty, Eudora. Eudora Welty. Viewer shown Welty's world
3   of Jackson, Mississippi and photos made during course of her life there. Welty reads from her fiction and discusses craft and responsibilities of author. Perspective Films. $420, 16mm, color; $357 videocassette; $40 rental.

VIDEOTAPES

4204 Beasley, Marty. Audience-Role Considerations in Writing
      for Reader's Theatre. TV-taped lecture, La. Tech.
      U. and La. Writer's Conference, 1976.

4205 Editors. The American Short Story. Series of dramatized
      stories. Includes "Soldier's Home," "Almos' a Man,"
      "The Music School," "I'm a Fool," "The Golden Honey-
      moon," and others. Teacher's guides and viewer's guides
      available as well as paperback editions of the stories in
      the series. Contact Perspective Films.

4206 Editors. The Fact in Fiction. Flannery O'Connor's "A Good
      Man Is Hard to Find" and Truman Capote's In Cold Blood
      compared in terms of their literary use of fact. 29 mins.
      Rental information: contact National Instructional TV
      Center.

4207 Editors. The Historical Novel. Using William Styron's
      The Confessions of Nat Turner, this 29-minute program
      discusses the historical novel as an attempt to reconstruct
      the life of a previous era. Rental information: National
      Instructional TV Center.

4208 Editors. Three Artists in the Northwest. Through words
      and works of three artists (painter Guy Anderson, sculptor
      George Tsuta Kawa and late poet Theodore Roethke), this
      program explores relationship between environment and
      creative experience. 29 mins. Rental $68; contact Public
      Television Library.

4209 Faulkner, William. Tales of Yoknapatawpha. Also part of
      Climate of Genius Series on Mississippi artists in context,
      this videotape features Faulkner. Program taped on
      grounds and inside Faulkner's Oxford home, Rowan Oak.
      Discussion of Faulkner's humor and fiction by Shelby
      Foote, Blyden Jackson, Louis Rubin, Jr., Lewis Simpson,
      and T. Daniel Young. Contact Mississippi Authority for
      Education Television.

4210 Kleinau, Marion, & J. L. McHughes. Sensory Approaches
      to Literature. Videotape produced by the Illinois Office of
      Education.

4211 Welty, Eudora. A Conversation with Eudora Welty. Welty seen in conversation with her friend Frank Hains, Arts Editor of Jackson Daily News. Discussion of Welty's early experiences as writer, reactions to readers and critics, her inspirations, aspirations and personal working techniques. Contact Mississippi Authority for Educational Television.

4212 Welty, Eudora. A Season of Dreams: The Vision of Eudora Welty. This program first seen in 1970 opens with Welty reading from her work, "A Memory." Characters and places from several of her stories are presented through readings, songs, and simply staged scenes. Scenes are taken from "Lily Daw," "Ponder Heart," "Piece of News," "Petrified Man," "Robber Bridegroom," and "Wide Net." Contact Mississippi Authority for Educational Television.

4213 Welty, Eudora. A Time and a Place. Part of the Climate of Genius Series on Mississippi artists in context, this videotape features Welty. Narrated by Cicely Tyson, it features discussion of Welty's fiction by Peggy Prenshaw, Louis Rubin, Jr., Lewis Simpson, Elizabeth Spencer, and T. Daniel Young. Contact Mississippi Authority for Educational Television.

A LISTING OF RECORDED LITERATURE

This listing is in two parts. Part 1, the main section, lists recordings alphabetically by author of the literary piece recorded. Recordings of pieces by different authors (as in poetry anthologies) are listed under the "author" entry word "MANY." The format is as follows:

> AUTHOR
> Performer(s)
> Title
> Production company
> Type of recording

Performers' names have often been shortened to last names, and only primary performers are listed. The items are predominantly sound recordings, though videotapes and films have also been included.

Following the main listing is Part 2, a title index, which includes authors' names in parentheses as the key back to the main listing.

For information concerning specific recordings, write to the appropriate production company:

ARGO SPOKEN WORD RECORDINGS
Houghton-Mifflin Company
Department M-70
1 Beacon Street
Boston, Mass. 02107

CAEDMON RECORDS
505 Eighth Avenue
New York, N. Y. 10018

CASSETTE CURRICULUM
Everett/Edwards, Inc.
P. O. Box 1060
Deland, Fla. 32720
(Most entries in this category
   represent literary analyses of
   the listed work suitable for
   class use)

COLUMBIA MASTERWORKS
Columbia Records
51 West 52nd Street
New York, N. Y. 10019

FILMS FOR THE HUMANITIES
P. O. Box 2053
Princeton, N. J. 08540

HOUGHTON MIFFLIN COMPANY
Department M
1 Beacon Street
Boston, Mass. 02107

JABBERWOCKY
Cassette Classics Department 197
P. O. Box 6727
San Francisco, Calif. 94101
(Complete scripts available on re-
   quest)

PACIFICA TAPE LIBRARY
Department L T 3
5316 Venice Blvd.
Los Angeles, Calif. 90019

PROFILES IN LITERATURE
Temple University
Office of Television Services
Tomlinson Hall 214
Philadelphia, Pa. 19122

AARDEMA, Verna
  Dee, Ruby; Davis, Ossie
  Zulu, Other African Folktales
  Caedmon
  Cassette, Record

AESCHYLUS
  Cavender, Kenneth
  Agamemnon
  Cassette Curriculum
  Cassette

AESCHYLUS
  Not Named
  Agamemnon
  Jabberwocky
  Cassette

AESCHYLUS
  Cavander, Kenneth
  Choephori
  Cassette Curriculum
  Cassette

AESCHYLUS
  Cavander, Kenneth
  Eumenides
  Cassette Curriculum
  Cassette

AESCHYLUS
  Cavander, Kenneth
  Prometheus Bound
  Jabberwocky
  Cassette

AESOP
  Karloff, Boris
  Fables
  Caedmon
  Cassette, Record

AGEE, James
  Agee, James; Flye, Father
  Portrait
  Caedmon
  Cassette, Record

AGEE, James, & W. Evans
  Dee; Grizzard
  Let Us Now Praise Famous Men
  Caedmon
  Cassette, Record

AIKEN, Conrad
  Aiken, Conrad
  Reading Conrad Aiken
  Caedmon
  Cassette, Record

ALBEE, Edward
  Rhome, Frances
  American Dream, The Sandbox
  Cassette Curriculum
  Cassette

ALBEE, Edward
  Hepburn, Scofield
  A Delicate Balance
  Caedmon
  Cassette, Record

ALBEE, Edward
  Pease, Donald
  Tiny Alice
  Cassette Curriculum
  Cassette

ALBEE, Edward
  Bigsby, C. W. E.
  Who's Afraid of Virginia Woolf?
  Cassette Curriculum
  Cassette

ALCOTT, Louisa May
  Harris, Julie
  Little Women
  Caedmon
  Cassette, Record

ALEICHEM, Sholom
  Skulnik, Menasha
  Sholom Aleichem
  Caedmon
  Cassette, Record

ALEXANDER, Lloyd
Shachter, Jaqueline
An Interview With ...
Profiles in Literature
Videotape

ANDERSEN, Hans Christian
Redgrave, Michael
Emperor's New Clothes and
    Other Tales
Caedmon
Cassette, Record

ANDERSEN, Hans Christian
Karloff, Boris
Little Match Girl
Caedmon
Cassette, Record

ANDERSEN, Hans Christian
Nesbitt, Cathleen
Little Mermaid
Caedmon
Cassette, Record

ANDERSEN, Hans Christian
McKenna, Siobhan
Poems, The Story of His Life
Caedmon
Cassette, Record

ANDERSEN, Hans Christian
Nesbitt, Cathleen
Snow Queen
Caedmon
Cassette, Record

ANDERSEN, Hans Christian
Not Named
Swinehead
Jabberwocky
Cassette

ANDERSEN, Hans Christian
Not Named
Tinder Box
Jabberwocky
Cassette

ANDERSON, Sherwood
Grebstein, Sheldon
Winesburg, Ohio
Cassette Curriculum
Cassette

ANONYMOUS
Not Named
Aladdin; Or the Wonderful Lamp

Jabberwocky
Cassette

ANONYMOUS
Quayle, Anthony
Ballad of Robin Hood
Caedmon
Cassette, Record

ANONYMOUS
Fairbanks, Douglas, Jr.
Beauty and Beast and Other
    Stories
Caedmon
Cassette, Record

ANONYMOUS
Malone, Kemp
Beowulf
Caedmon
Cassette, Record

ANONYMOUS
Duncan; King; Orr; Rylands
Beowulf
Argo
Record

ANONYMOUS
Bessinger, J. B.
Beowulf and Other Poems
Caedmon
Cassette, Record

ANONYMOUS
Mohyeddin, Zia
Bhagavad-Gita
Caedmon
Cassette, Record

ANONYMOUS
Kitt, Eartha; Gunn, Moses
Black Pioneers in American
    History 1
Caedmon
Cassette, Record

ANONYMOUS
Sands, Diana; Gunn, Moses
Black Pioneers in American
    History 2
Caedmon
Cassette, Record

ANONYMOUS
Marshall, Herbert
Book of Job
Caedmon
Cassette, Record

ANONYMOUS
Anderson; Bloom
Book of Judith, Ruth
Caedmon
Cassette, Record

ANONYMOUS
Rutherford, A.
Byron and Liberty
Cassette Curriculum
Cassette

ANONYMOUS
Ross, Angus
Charles Dickens, Poet, Entertainer
Cassette Curriculum
Cassette

ANONYMOUS
Ives, Burl
Christmas at the White House
Caedmon
Cassette, Record

ANONYMOUS
Harris, Wayne
Discovering Rhythm and Rhyme in Poetry
Caedmon
Cassette, Record

ANONYMOUS
Keach, Stacy
Earth Day
Caedmon
Cassette, Record

ANONYMOUS
Mason, James
Ecclesiastes
Caedmon
Cassette, Record

ANONYMOUS
Meredith, Burgess; Cast
Everyman
Caedmon
Cassette, Record

ANONYMOUS
Mohyeddin, Zia
Fables of India
Caedmon
Cassette, Record

ANONYMOUS
Cusack, Cyril

Fairy Tales of Ireland
Caedmon
Cassette, Record

ANONYMOUS
Verdon, Gwen
Ferdinand and Other Stories
Caedmon
Cassette, Record

ANONYMOUS
Armitage; Butler; Chadwick
Five British Sculptors
Caedmon
Cassette, Record

ANONYMOUS
Fairbanks, Douglas, Jr.
Flying Dutchman, Other Ghost Ship Tales
Caedmon
Cassette, Record

ANONYMOUS
No Name
Folksongs of Britain: Christmas
Caedmon
Cassette, Record

ANONYMOUS
Kitt, Eartha
Folktales of the Tribes of Africa
Caedmon
Cassette, Record

ANONYMOUS
Anderson, Judith
Genesis
Caedmon
Cassette, Record

ANONYMOUS
Seeger, Pete; Brand, Oscar; et al.
Golden Slumbers
Caedmon
Cassette, Record

ANONYMOUS
Bloom, Claire
Goldilocks, Three Bears, Others
Caedmon
Cassette, Record

ANONYMOUS
Price, Vincent
Graveyard of Ghost Tales
Caedmon
Cassette, Record

ANONYMOUS
No Name
Hearing Poetry, Vol. 1
Caedmon
Cassette, Record

ANONYMOUS
No Name
Hearing Poetry, Vol. 2
Caedmon
Cassette, Record

ANONYMOUS
Many
History Reflected, Vol. 1
Argo
Record

ANONYMOUS
Many
History Reflected, Vol. 2
Argo
Record

ANONYMOUS
Many
History Reflected, Vol. 3
Argo
Record

ANONYMOUS
Redgrave; Tutin; Holm
History Reflected, Vol. 4
Argo
Record

ANONYMOUS
Rylands; Sinden; Redgrave
History Reflected, Vol. 5
Argo
Record

ANONYMOUS
Scales; King; Tutin
History Reflected, Vol. 6
Argo
Record

ANONYMOUS
Grimes, Tammy
Hurray for Captain Jane!
    Other Stories
Caedmon
Cassette, Record

ANONYMOUS
Lerner, Laurence
Intro to the Ring and the Book

Cassette Curriculum
Cassette

ANONYMOUS
Cusack, Cyril
Irish Fairy Tales
Caedmon
Cassette, Record

ANONYMOUS
Weizmann; Chaim; Others
Israel Is Born
Caedmon
Cassette, Record

ANONYMOUS
Ross, Angus
Johnson and Boswell
Cassette Curriculum
Cassette

ANONYMOUS
Thorlby, A. K.
Keats and Romanticism 1
Cassette Curriculum
Cassette

ANONYMOUS
Thorlby, A. K.
Keats and Romanticism 2
Cassette Curriculum
Cassette

ANONYMOUS
Karloff; Harris
Let's Listen
Caedmon
Cassette, Record

ANONYMOUS
Brombert, Victor
Les Liaisons Dangereuses
Cassette Curriculum
Cassette

ANONYMOUS
Cusack, Cyril
Little Flower of St. Francis
Caedmon
Cassette, Record

ANONYMOUS
Lerner, Laurence
Madness and the Corruptions
    of Christian
Cassette Curriculum
Cassette

ANONYMOUS
Richardson, Ian
Malleus Maleficarum
Caedmon
Cassette, Record

ANONYMOUS
Anderson; Begley
Meditations for Modern Class-
room
Caedmon
Cassette, Record

ANONYMOUS
Ritchard; Karloff; Holm
Mother Goose
Caedmon
Cassette, Record

ANONYMOUS
Thorndike, Dame Sybil
Mrs. Pankhurst
Argo
Record

ANONYMOUS
Olivier, Laurence
On the Death of King George
Caedmon
Cassette, Record

ANONYMOUS
Begley; Brand
Paul Bunyon in Story and Song
Caedmon
Cassette, Record

ANONYMOUS
Bessinger, J. B.; Borrof
Pearl Poet: Gawain, Dialogues,
etc.
Caedmon
Cassette, Record

ANONYMOUS
Harris; Karloff; Wayne
Pony Engine, Other Stories
Caedmon
Cassette, Record

ANONYMOUS
Anderson, Judith
Psalms and David
Caedmon
Cassette, Record

ANONYMOUS
Swift Eagle

Pueblo Indians
Caedmon
Cassette, Record

ANONYMOUS
Randel, William
Sarah Orne Jewett
Cassette Curriculum
Cassette

ANONYMOUS
Silvera; McGavin; Cast
Second Shepherds' Play
Caedmon
Cassette, Record

ANONYMOUS
Medcalf, Stephen
Sir Gawain and the Green Knight
Cassette Curriculum
Cassette

ANONYMOUS
Ross, Angus
Sir Thomas More's Tudor Eng-
land
Cassette Curriculum
Cassette

ANONYMOUS
Quayle, Anthony
Song of Roland
Caedmon
Cassette, Record

ANONYMOUS
Bloom; Rains
Song of Songs/Abelard & Heloise
Caedmon
Cassette, Record

ANONYMOUS
Redgrave; Richardson
Soul of an Age
Caedmon
Cassette, Record

ANONYMOUS
Conrad, William
Spirits and Spooks for Halloween
Caedmon
Cassette, Record

ANONYMOUS
Johns, Glynis
Story of Peter Pan
Caedmon
Cassette, Record

ANONYMOUS
No Name
Story of the Music Box
Caedmon
Cassette, Record

ANONYMOUS
Price, Vincent
Tales of Witches, Ghosts and
Goblins
Caedmon
Cassette, Record

ANONYMOUS
Karloff, Boris
Three Little Pigs
Caedmon
Cassette, Record

ANONYMOUS
Dee; Davis
Tough Poems for Tough People
Caedmon
Cassette, Record

ANONYMOUS
Bloom, Claire
Tristan and Iseult
Caedmon
Cassette, Record

ANONYMOUS
Silvera, Frank; Cast
Wellsprings of Drama
Caedmon
Cassette, Record

ANONYMOUS
Harris; Holbrook; Others
White House Saga
Caedmon
Cassette, Record

ANONYMOUS
Price, Vincent
Witches' Tales, A Coven of
Caedmon
Cassette, Record

ANTONINUS, Brother
Antoninus, Brother
Brother Antoninus Reads His
Poetry
Caedmon
Cassette, Record

ARISTOPHANES
Cavander, Kenneth

Clouds
Cassette Curriculum
Cassette

ARISTOPHANES
Many
Ecclesiazusae
Films for the Humanities
Film

ARISTOPHANES
Cavender, Kenneth
Frogs
Cassette Curriculum
Cassette

ARISTOPHANES
Gingold; Holloway
Lysistrata
Caedmon
Cassette, Record

ARISTOPHANES
Cavender, Kenneth
Lysistrata
Cassette Curriculum
Cassette

ARISTOTLE
Von Staden, Heinrich
Poetics
Cassette Curriculum
Cassette

AUBREY, John
Dotrice, Roy
Brief Lives
Argo
Record

AUDEN, W. H.
Auden, W. H.
Poems
Argo
Record

AUDEN, W. H.
Auden, W. H.
W. H. Auden Reading His Poetry
Caedmon
Cassette, Record

AUSTIN, Mary
Lyday, Jo
Works of Mary Austin
Cassette Curriculum
Cassette

BALL, William
Gielgud, Sir John; Leighton,
    Margaret
Homage to Shakespeare
Columbia Masterworks
Cassette, Record

BALZAC, Honoré
Brombert, Victor
Works of Balzac
Cassette Curriculum
Cassette

BARBOUR, Philip
Barbour, Philip; Cast
Jamestown Saga
Caedmon
Cassette, Record

BARBOUR, Philip
Barbour, Philip; Cast
Pilgrim Saga
Caedmon
Cassette, Record

BARTHELME, Donald
Griffin, Robert
Come Back, Dr. Caligari
Cassette Curriculum
Cassette

BAUDELAIRE, Charles Pierre
LeFallienne, Jordan
Les Fleurs du Mal
Caedmon
Cassette, Record

BAUDELAIRE, Charles Pierre
Gaudon, Jean
Works of Baudelaire
Cassette Curriculum
Cassette

BAUM, Frank L.
Not Named
Wizard of Oz
Jabberwocky
Cassette

BECKETT, Samuel
Cusack, Cyril
Samuel Beckett
Caedmon
Cassette, Record

BECKETT, Samuel
Lahr; Marshall; Kasznar
Waiting for Godot

Caedmon
Cassette, Record

BECKETT, Samuel
Gordon, Lois
Waiting for Godot
Cassette Curriculum
Cassette

BECKETT, Samuel
O'Shea, Milo
Waiting for Godot
Films for the Humanities
Film

BECKETT, Thomas
Kern, Edith
Works of Beckett
Cassette Curriculum
Cassette

BELLOC, Hilaire
Speaight, Robert
Poems
Argo
Record

BELLOW, Saul
Tuttleton, James W.
Adventures of Augie March
Cassette Curriculum
Cassette

BELLOW, Saul
Grebstein, Sheldon
Herzog
Cassette Curriculum
Cassette

BELPRE, Pura
Shachter, Jaqueline
An Interview With ...
Profiles in Literature
Videotape

BEMELMANS, Ludwig
Channing, Carol
Madeline
Caedmon
Cassette, Record

BEMELMANS, Ludwig
Channing, Carol
Madeline and the Gypsies, Other
    Stories
Caedmon
Cassette, Record

BENDICK, Robert & Jeanne
Shachter, Jaqueline
An Interview With ...
Profiles in Literature
Videotape

BENET, Stephen
Stapleton; Hingle
Book of Americans
Caedmon
Cassette, Record

BENET, Stephen
Wiseman, Joseph
Nightmare at Noon, Other Poems
Caedmon
Cassette, Record

BENET, Stephen Vincent
Power; Anderson; Massey
John Brown's Body
Columbia Masterworks
Cassette, Record

BENET, Stephen Vincent
Benét, Stephen Vincent
Poetry of Stephen Vincent Benét
Caedmon
Cassette, Record

BERGER, Terry
McNeil, Claudia
Black Fairy Tales
Caedmon
Cassette, Record

BERRIGAN, Daniel
Berrigan, Daniel
Daniel Berrigan Raps
Caedmon
Cassette, Record

BERRIGAN, Daniel
Center Theater Group
Trial of Catonsville 9
Caedmon
Cassette, Record

BERRY, Erick
Tupou, Manu
South Sea Island Tales
Caedmon
Cassette, Record

BERRYMAN, John
Ramsey, Paul
John Berryman
Cassette Curriculum
Cassette

BETJEMAN, John
Betjeman, John
Summoned by Bells
Argo
Record

BIERCE, Ambrose
McCallum, David
Occurrence at Owl Creek Bridge;
The Damned Thing
Caedmon
Cassette, Record

BIERHOST, John
Silverheels, Jay
Indian Fire Plum Legends
Caedmon
Cassette, Record

BLAKE, William
Bates; Bonnamy; Devlin
Poems
Argo
Record

BLAKE, William
Richardson, Ralph
Poetry of William Blake
Caedmon
Cassette, Record

BLUME, Judy
Shachter, Jaqueline
An Interview With ...
Profiles in Literature
Videotape

BLY, Robert
Bly, Robert
Poems of Robert Bly
Cassette Curriculum
Record

BOGAN, Louise
Ramsey, Paul
Louise Bogan
Cassette Curriculum
Cassette

BOMANS, Godfried
Ritchard, Cyril
Wily Wizard and Wicked Witch
Caedmon
Cassette, Record

BONTEMPS, Arna
Shachter, Jaqueline
An Interview With ...

Profiles in Literature
Videotape

BORGES, Jorge Luis
Borges, Jorge Luis
Inner World of Jorge Luis
Borges
Films for the Humanities
Film

BORNSTEIN, Diane
Bessinger, J. B.
History of English Language
Caedmon
Cassette, Record

BOSWELL, James
Quayle, Anthony
In Search of a Wife
Caedmon
Cassette, Record

BOSWELL, James
Quayle, Anthony
London Journal
Caedmon
Cassette, Record

BRADBURY, Ray
Nimoy, Leonard
Martian Chronicles; Soft Rains;
Usher II
Caedmon
Cassette, Record

BRADFORD, Roark
Moreland, Mantan
Ol' Man Adam
Caedmon
Cassette, Record

BRATHWAITE, Edward
Brathwaite, Edward
Islands
Argo
Record

BRATHWAITE, Edward
Brathwaite, Edward
Masks
Argo
Record

BRATHWAITE, Edward
Brathwaite, Edward
Rights of Passage
Argo
Record

BRAUTIGAN, Richard
Rosenberg, Marc
Trout Fishing in America
Cassette Curriculum
Cassette

BRECHT, Bertolt
Demetz, Peter
Galileo
Cassette Curriculum
Cassette

BRECHT, Bertolt
Demetz, Peter
Mother Courage and Her Children
Cassette Curriculum
Cassette

BRECHT, Bertolt
Clark; Jackson; Lenya; Lindfors
Brecht on Brecht
Columbia Masterworks
Cassette, Record

BRECHT, Bertolt
Bently, Eric; Richards, Paul;
Others
Exception and the Rule
Columbia Masterworks
Cassette, Record

BRECHT, Bertolt
No Name
Man's a Man
Columbia Masterworks
Cassette, Record

BRONTE, Charlotte
Bloom; Quayle; Nesbitt; Rose
Jane Eyre
Caedmon
Cassette, Record

BROOKS, Gwendolyn
Brooks, Gwendolyn
Gwen Brooks Reading Her Poetry
Caedmon
Cassette, Record

BROWN, Murray
Rose, George
Poetry, Prose, Life of R. L.
Stevenson
Caedmon
Cassette, Record

BROWNING, Elizabeth
Cornell; Quayle

Sonnets; Barretts of Wimpole
Street
Caedmon
Cassette, Record

BROWNING, Robert
Lerner, Laurence
Italian Renaissance
Cassette Curriculum
Cassette

BROWNING, Robert
Mason, James
My Last Duchess, Other Poems
Caedmon
Cassette, Record

BROWNING, Robert
Not Named
Pied Piper of Hamelin
Jabberwocky
Cassette

BROWNING, Robert
Baxter, Keith
Pied Piper, Other Stories
Caedmon
Cassette, Record

BROWNING, Robert
Bates; McCarthey; Adrian
Poems, Vol. 1
Argo
Record

BROWNING, Robert
Watson; Adrian; King
Poems, Vol. 2
Argo
Record

BROWNING, Robert
Mason, James
Poetry of Robert Browning
Caedmon
Cassette, Record

BROWNING, Robert
Lerner, Laurence
Versions of Christianity
Cassette Curriculum
Cassette

BURGESS, Anthony
Burgess, Anthony
Burgess Reads from Clockwork
Orange
Caedmon
Cassette, Record

BURGESS, Anthony
Burgess, Anthony
Eve of Saint Venus; Nothing
Like the Sun
Caedmon
Cassette, Record

BURNS, Robert
Blover; McIntyre; Blair
Poems
Argo
Record

BURNS, Robert
Worlock; Brookes
Poetry of R. Burns; Border
Ballads
Caedmon
Cassette, Record

BYRON, George Gordon, Lord
Johnson; Ashcroft; Richer
Don Juan
Argo
Record

BYRON, George Gordon, Lord
Rutherford, A.
Don Juan
Cassette Curriculum
Cassette

BYRON, George Gordon, Lord
Orr, Duncan
Poems
Argo
Record

BYRON, George Gordon, Lord
Power, Tyrone
Poetry of Byron
Caedmon
Cassette, Record

CALDERON DE LA BARCA, P.
Calderón de la Barca, P.
El Alcalde de Zalamea
Caedmon
Cassette, Record

CALDERON DE LA BARCA, P.
Calderón de la Barca, P.
La Vida Es Sueño
Caedmon
Cassette, Record

CAMERON, Eleanor
Shachter, Jaqueline
An Interview With ...

Chinese Fairy Tales
Caedmon
Cassette, Record

CHANG, Isabelle
McKenna, Siobhan
Tales of China and Tibet
Caedmon
Cassette, Record

CHAUCER, Geoffrey
Medcalf, Stephen
Art of Self-Consciousness
Cassette Curriculum
Cassette

CHAUCER, Geoffrey
Bessinger, J. B.
Canterbury Tales Prologue
Caedmon
Cassette, Record

CHAUCER, Geoffrey
Bessinger, J. B.
Miller's Tale; Reeve's Tale
Caedmon
Cassette, Record

CHAUCER, Geoffrey
Ross, Robert
Nun's, Priest's, Pardoner's
Tales
Caedmon
Cassette, Record

CHAUCER, Geoffrey
Coghill; Cavis; Burrow
Nun's Tale; Priest's Tale
Argo
Record

CHAUCER, Geoffrey
MacLiammoir; Holloway
Pardoner's Tale; Miller's Tale
Caedmon
Cassette, Record

CHAUCER, Geoffrey
Bessinger, J. B.
Parliament of Fowls, Six
Other Poems
Caedmon
Cassette, Record

CHAUCER, Geoffrey
Coghill, Neville
Prologue to Canterbury Tales
Argo
Record

CHAUCER, Geoffrey
Medcalf, Stephen
Troilus and Criseyde
Cassette Curriculum
Cassette

CHAUCER, Geoffrey
Watson; Prunella; Scales; Orr
Troilus and Criseyde
Argo
Record

CHAUCER, Geoffrey
Ashcroft, Peggy
Wife of Bath
Caedmon
Cassette, Record

CHEKHOV, Anton
Tandy; Minnesota Theatre Co.
Cherry Orchard
Caedmon
Cassette, Record

CHEKHOV, Anton
McKenna; Cuasack
Three Sisters
Caedmon
Cassette, Record

CHEKHOV, Anton
Casson; Thorndike; Olivier
Uncle Vanya
Caedmon
Cassette, Record

CHEKHOV, Anton
Olivier, Laurence
Uncle Vanya
Films for the Humanities
Film

CHEKHOV, Anton
Wallach, Eli
Writers's Life
Films for the Humanities
Film

CHURCHILL, Winston
Churchill, Winston
W. Churchill in His Own Voice
Caedmon
Cassette, Record

CHURCHILL, Winston
Welles, Orson, et al.
Finest Hours
Columbia Masterworks
Cassette, Record

CIARDI, John
  Ciardi, John
  Poems of John Ciardi
  Cassette Curriculum
  Record

CLARK, Walter
  Westbrook, Max
  Works of Walter Van Tilburg
    Clark
  Cassette Curriculum
  Cassette

CLEVERDON, Hobbs
  Squire, William
  John Donne
  Argo
  Record

COCTEAU, Jean
  Bergman, Ingrid
  Human Voice
  Caedmon
  Cassette, Record

COCTEAU, Jean
  Leighton; Brett; Cilento; Magee
  Infernal Machine
  Caedmon
  Cassette, Record

COCTEAU, Jean
  Cocteau, Jean
  Reading by Jean Cocteau
  Caedmon
  Cassette, Record

COCTEAU, Jean
  Cocteau, Jean
  Reading Jean Cocteau
  Caedmon
  Cassette, Record

COCTEAU, Jean
  Cocteau, Jean
  Self Portrait
  Caedmon
  Cassette, Record

COLERIDGE, Samuel
  Prickett, Stephen
  Biographia Literaria
  Cassette Curriculum
  Cassette

COLERIDGE, Samuel
  Prickett, Stephen
  Christabel

Cassette Curriculum
Cassette

COLERIDGE, Samuel
  Bonnamy; Burton; Devlin
  Poems
  Argo
  Record

COLERIDGE, Samuel
  Richardson, Ralph
  Poetry of Samuel Coleridge
  Caedmon
  Cassette, Record

COLERIDGE, Samuel
  Prickett, Stephen
  Rime of the Ancient Mariner
  Cassette Curriculum
  Cassette

COLETTE
  Colette
  Reading Colette
  Caedmon
  Cassette, Record

COLETTE
  Colette
  Readings by Colette
  Caedmon
  Cassette, Record

COLLODI, Carlo
  Ritchard, Cyril
  Pinocchio
  Caedmon
  Cassette, Record

COLUM, Padraic
  Dullea, Keir
  Children of Odin, Book of
    Northern Myths
  Caedmon
  Cassette, Record

COLUM, Padraic
  Quayle, Anthony
  Twelve Labors of Heracles
  Caedmon
  Cassette, Record

COLWELL, C. Carter
  Colwell, C. Carter
  Hamlet: Character and Theme
  Cassette Curriculum
  Record

COLWELL, C. Carter
Colwell, C. Carter
Hamlet: Plot and Structure
Cassette Curriculum
Record

COLWELL, C. Carter
Colwell, C. Carter
Measure for Measure as a
Problem Play
Cassette Curriculum
Record

COLWELL, C. Carter
Colwell, C. Carter
Study of King Lear
Cassette Curriculum
Record

COLWELL, C. Carter
Colwell, C. Carter
Study of Macbeth
Cassette Curriculum
Record

COLWELL, C. Carter
Colwell, C. Carter
Study of Midsummer Night's
Dream
Cassette Curriculum
Record

COLWELL, C. Carter
Colwell, C. Carter
Study of Othello
Cassette Curriculum
Record

COLWELL, C. Carter
Colwell, C. Carter
Study of Romeo and Juliet
Cassette Curriculum
Record

COLWELL, C. Carter
Colwell, C. Carter
Study of The Tempest
Cassette Curriculum
Record

CONGREVE, William
National Theatre of Great
Britain
Way of the World
Caedmon
Cassette, Record

CONKLING, Hilda
Conkling, Hilda

Poems by a Little Girl
Caedmon
Cassette, Record

CONRAD, Joseph
Quayle, Anthony
Heart of Darkness
Caedmon
Cassette, Record

COOPER, James Fenimore
Mason, James; Cast
Last of the Mohicans
Caedmon
Cassette, Record

COWARD, Noel
Coward; Leighton
Apple Cart and Poems
Caedmon
Cassette, Record

COWARD, Noel
Coward; Leighton
Dialogues
Caedmon
Cassette, Record

COZZENS, James G.
Schneider, Robert L.
Guard of Honor
Cassette Curriculum
Cassette

CRABBE, George
Holm; Rose; Woolf
Poems
Argo
Record

CRANE, Hart
Weber, Brom
Hart Crane 1
Cassette Curriculum
Cassette

CRANE, Hart
Weber, Brom
Hart Crane 2
Cassette Curriculum
Cassette

CRANE, Hart
Williams, Tennessee
Tennessee Williams Reads Hart
Crane
Caedmon
Cassette, Record

CRANE, Stephen
Not Named
Bride Comes to Yellow Sky
Jabberwocky
Cassette

CRANE, Stephen
French, Warren
Maggie
Cassette Curriculum
Cassette

CRANE, Stephen
French, Warren
Open Boat
Cassette Curriculum
Cassette

CRANE, Stephen
French, Warren
Red Badge of Courage
Cassette Curriculum
Cassette

CRANE, Stephen
O'Brien, Edmond
Red Badge of Courage
Caedmon
Cassette, Record

CRANE, Stephen
French, Warren
Western Stories
Cassette Curriculum
Cassette

CREELEY, Robert
Creeley, Robert
Poems of Robert Creeley
Cassette Curriculum
Record

CRESWICK, Paul
Quayle, Anthony
Adventures of Robin Hood,
    Vol. 1
Caedmon
Cassette, Record

CRESWICK, Paul
Quayle, Anthony
Adventures of Robin Hood,
    Vol. 2
Caedmon
Cassette, Record

CRESWICK, Paul
Quayle, Anthony

Adventures of Robin Hood,
    Vol. 3
Caedmon
Cassette, Record

CRESWICK, Paul
Quayle, Anthony
Adventures of Robin Hood,
    Vol. 4
Caedmon
Cassette, Record

CULLEN, Countee
Dee; Davis
Poetry of Countee Cullen
Caedmon
Cassette, Record

CUMMINGS, E. E.
Cummings, E. E.
Collected Poetry '20-'40 and
    Prose
Caedmon
Cassette, Record

CUMMINGS, E. E.
Cummings, E. E.
E. E. Cummings Reading His
    Poetry
Caedmon
Cassette, Record

CUMMINGS, E. E.
Cummings, E. E.
E. E. Cummings Reads His
    Poetry and Prose
Caedmon
Cassette, Record

CUMMINGS, E. E.
Friedman, Norman
E. E. Cummings 1
Cassette Curriculum
Cassette

CUMMINGS, E. E.
Friedman, Norman
E. E. Cummings 2
Cassette Curriculum
Cassette

CUMMINGS, E. E.
Cummings, E. E.
Making of a Poet
Films for the Humanities
Film

CUMMINGS, E. E.
Cummings, E. E.

Nonlecture 1
Caedmon
Cassette, Record

CUMMINGS, E. E.
Cummings, E. E.
Nonlecture 2
Caedmon
Cassette, Record

CUMMINGS, E. E.
Cummings, E. E.
Nonlecture 3
Caedmon
Cassette, Record

CUMMINGS, E. E.
Cummings, E. E.
Nonlecture 4
Caedmon
Cassette, Record

CUMMINGS, E. E.
Cummings, E. E.
Nonlecture 5
Caedmon
Cassette, Record

CUMMINGS, E. E.
Cummings, E. E.
Nonlecture 6
Caedmon
Cassette, Record

DA VINCI, Leonardo See
LEONARDO DA VINCI

DABERMAN, Martin
No Name
In White America
Columbia Masterworks
Cassette, Record

DAHL, Roald
Dahl, Roald
Charlie and the Chocolate
Factory
Caedmon
Cassette, Record

DANTE
Freccero, John
Divine Comedy
Cassette Curriculum
Cassette

DE ANGELI, Marguerite
Shachter, Jaqueline

An Interview With ...
Profiles in Literature
Videotape

DE BRUNHOFF, Jean
Jourdan, Louis
Story of Babar and Travels of
Babar
Caedmon
Cassette, Record

DEFOE, Daniel
McKenna; Siobhan
Moll Flanders
Caedmon
Cassette, Record

DE LA MARE, Walter
Redgrave, Lynn
Animal Stories
Caedmon
Cassette, Record

DE LA MARE, Walter
Bloom, Claire
Cinderella, Other Fairy Tales
Caedmon
Cassette, Record

DE LA MARE, Walter
Bloom, Claire
Red Riding Hood, Dancing
Princess
Caedmon
Cassette, Record

DE LA MARE, Walter
De La Mare, Walter
Walter De La Mare Speaking,
Reading
Caedmon
Cassette, Record

DE MAUPASSANT, Guy See
MAUPASSANT, Guy De

DE QUINCEY, Thomas
Quayle, Anthony
Confessions of an English Opium
Eater
Caedmon
Cassette, Record

DE SADE, Marquis See SADE,
Marquis De

DE TOCQUEVILLE, Alexis See
TOCQUEVILLE, Alexis De

DEVITO, Joseph
DeVito, Joseph
Allness
Cassette Curriculum
Cassette

DICKENS, Charles
Ross, Angus
Bleak House
Cassette Curriculum
Cassette

DICKENS, Charles
Not Named
Christmas Carol
Jabberwocky
Cassette

DICKENS, Charles
Richardson; Scofield; Cast
Christmas Carol
Caedmon
Cassette, Record

DICKENS, Charles
Ross, Angus
Dombey and Son
Cassette Curriculum
Cassette

DICKENS, Charles
Williams, Emlyn
Emlyn Williams as Charles
Dickens
Argo
Record

DICKENS, Charles
Not Named
Great Expectations
Jabberwocky
Cassette

DICKENS, Charles
Ross, Angus
Great Expectations
Cassette Curriculum
Cassette

DICKENS, Charles
Not Named
Oliver Twist
Jabberwocky
Cassette

DICKENS, Charles
Ross, Angus
Our Mutual Friend
Cassette Curriculum
Cassette

DICKENS, Charles
Karloff; Casson
Pickwick Papers
Caedmon
Cassette, Record

DICKENS, Charles
Ross, Angus
Pickwick Papers
Cassette Curriculum
Cassette

DICKEY, James
Calhoun, Richard
Deliverance
Cassette Curriculum
Cassette

DICKEY, James
Dickey, James
James Dickey Reads His Poetry
and Prose
Caedmon
Cassette, Record

DICKEY, James
Calhoun, Richard
James Dickey 1
Cassette Curriculum
Cassette

DICKEY, James
Calhoun, Richard
James Dickey 2
Cassette Curriculum
Cassette

DICKINSON, Emily
Anderson, Charles R.
Emily Dickinson 1
Cassette Curriculum
Cassette

DICKINSON, Emily
Anderson, Charles R.
Emily Dickinson 2
Cassette Curriculum
Cassette

DICKINSON, Emily
Harris, Julie
Poems of Emily Dickinson
Caedmon
Cassette, Record

DICKINSON, Emily
  Harris, Julie
  Self Portrait of Emily Dickinson
  Caedmon
  Cassette, Record

DOBIE, J. Frank
  Pilkington, William T.
  Works of J. Frank Dobie
  Cassette Curriculum
  Cassette

DONNE, John
  Johnson; Orr; Squire
  Love Poems
  Argo
  Record

DONNE, John
  Burton, Richard
  Love Poems of John Donne
  Caedmon
  Cassette, Record

DONNE, John
  Lerner, Laurence
  Love Poetry
  Cassette Curriculum
  Cassette

DONNE, John
  Lerner, Laurence
  Love Poetry, The Range
  Cassette Curriculum
  Cassette

DONNE, John
  Lerner, Laurence
  Religious Poetry
  Cassette Curriculum
  Cassette

DONNE, John
  Marshall, Herbert
  Sermons and Meditations
  Caedmon
  Cassette, Record

DONNE, John
  Lerner, Laurence
  Subsequent Poetry
  Cassette Curriculum
  Cassette

DOS PASSOS, John
  Dos Passos; Begley; Torn
  USA
  Caedmon
  Cassette, Record

DOS PASSOS, John
  Dos Passos; Grizzard; Begley
  USA
  Caedmon
  Cassette, Record

DOS PASSOS, John
  Gurko, Leo
  USA
  Cassette Curriculum
  Cassette

DOSTOYEVSKY, Feodor
  Jackson, Robert
  Crime and Punishment
  Cassette Curriculum
  Cassette

DOSTOYEVSKY, Feodor
  Jackson, Robert
  Notes from Underground
  Cassette Curriculum
  Cassette

DOYLE, Arthur Conan
  Not Named
  Hound of the Baskervilles
  Jabberwocky
  Cassette

DOYLE, Arthur Conan
  Rathbone, Basil
  Redheaded League
  Caedmon
  Cassette, Record

DOYLE, Arthur Conan
  Rathbone, Basil
  Scandal in Bohemia
  Caedmon
  Cassette, Record

DOYLE, Arthur Conan
  Rathbone, Basil
  Silver Blaze
  Caedmon
  Cassette, Record

DOYLE, Arthur Conan
  Rathbone, Basil
  Speckled Band, Final Problem
  Caedmon
  Cassette, Record

DREISER, Theodore
  Lehan, Richard
  An American Tragedy
  Cassette Curriculum
  Cassette

DREISER, Theodore
Grebstein, Sheldon
Sister Carrie
Cassette Curriculum
Cassette

DRYDEN, John
Ross, Angus
Absalom and Achitophel, Medal
Cassette Curriculum
Cassette

DRYDEN, John
Ross, Angus
All for Love, Spanish Fryar
Cassette Curriculum
Cassette

DRYDEN, John
Ross, Angus
Dryden the Critic
Cassette Curriculum
Cassette

DRYDEN, John
Scofield, Paul
Poetry of John Dryden
Caedmon
Cassette, Record

DRYDEN, John
Ross, Angus
Religio Laici, Hind, Panther
Cassette Curriculum
Cassette

DUMAS FILS, Alexandre
Legallienne, Cast
Camille
Caedmon
Cassette, Record

DUVOISIN, Roger
Harris, Julie
Petunia
Caedmon
Cassette, Record

EBERHART, Richard
Engel, Bernard F.
Richard Eberhart
Cassette Curriculum
Cassette

EBERHART, Richard
Eberhart, Richard
Richard Eberhart Reads His
Poetry

Caedmon
Cassette, Record

EISENHOWER, Dwight D.
Eisenhower; Others
Eisenhower in His Own Voice,
Others
Caedmon
Cassette, Record

ELIOT, George
Anderson; Rathbone; Nesbit
Silas Marner
Caedmon
Cassette, Record

ELIOT, T. S.
Robson; Scofield; Thorndike;
Wef
Family Reunion
Caedmon
Cassette, Record

ELIOT, T. S.
Eliot, T. S.
Four Quartets
Caedmon
Cassette, Record

ELIOT, T. S.
Speaight, Robert
Four Quartets
Argo
Record

ELIOT, T. S.
Scofield; Cusack; McCowen;
Hiller
Murder in the Cathedral
Caedmon
Cassette, Record

ELIOT, T. S.
Eliot, T. S.
Old Possum's Book of Practical
Cats
Argo
Record

ELIOT, T. S.
Speaight, Robert
Poems
Argo
Record

ELIOT, T. S.
Eliot, T. S.
T. S. Eliot Reads Poems and

Choruses
Caedmon
Cassette, Record

ELIOT, T. S.
Eliot, T. S.
Waste Land and Other Poems
Caedmon
Cassette, Record

ELLISON, Ralph
Turner, Darwin T.
Invisible Man
Cassette Curriculum
Cassette

EMERSON, Ralph Waldo
MacLeish, Archibald
Essay on Education and Self-
Reliance
Caedmon
Cassette, Record

EMERSON, Ralph Waldo
Randel, William
Poetry of Emerson
Cassette Curriculum
Cassette

EMERSON, Ralph Waldo
MacLeish, Archibald
Poetry of R. W. Emerson
Caedmon
Cassette, Record

ERASMUS
Greene, Thomas M.
Praise of Folly
Cassette Curriculum
Cassette

ESTES, E., & McElderry, M.
Shachter, Jaqueline
An Interview With ...
Profiles in Literature
Videotape

ETULAIN, Richard
Etulain, Richard
Mountain Man in Literature
Cassette Curriculum
Cassette

EURIPIDES
Cavander, Kenneth
Bacchae
Cassette Curriculum
Cassette

EURIPIDES
Cavander, Kenneth
Hippolytus
Cassette Curriculum
Cassette

EURIPIDES
Anderson; Quayle
Medea
Caedmon
Cassette, Record

EURIPIDES
Cavander, Kenneth
Medea
Cassette Curriculum
Cassette

EURIPIDES
Cavander, Kenneth
Trojan Woman
Cassette Curriculum
Cassette

EVANS, W. See AGEE, James

FARJEON, Elenor
Richardson, Ian
Mighty Men
Caedmon
Cassette, Record

FAULKNER, William
Holman, Hugh
Absalom, Absalom!
Cassette Curriculum
Cassette

FAULKNER, William
Fiedler, Leslie
Bear
Cassette Curriculum
Cassette

FAULKNER, William
Widmer, Kingsley
Light in August
Cassette Curriculum
Cassette

FAULKNER, William
Faulkner, William
Reading William Faulkner
Caedmon
Cassette, Record

FAULKNER, William
Young, Philip

Sound and the Fury
Cassette Curriculum
Cassette

FEELINGS, Tom & Muriel
Shachter, Jaqueline
An Interview With ...
Profiles in Literature
Videotape

FERLINGHETTI, Lawrence
Kahn, Sy
Lawrence Ferlinghetti
Cassette Curriculum
Cassette

FERLINGHETTI, Lawrence
Ferlinghetti, Lawrence
Poems of Lawrence Ferlinghetti
Cassette Curriculum
Record

FERRIL, Thomas Hornsby
Scherting, John
Works of Thomas Hornsby
Ferril
Cassette Curriculum
Cassette

FIELD, Eugene
Harris, Julie
Wynken, Blynken and Nod, Other
Poems
Caedmon
Cassette, Record

FISHER, Vardis
Grover, Dorys
Works of Vardis Fisher
Cassette Curriculum
Cassette

FITZGERALD, Edward
Drake, Alfred
Rubaiyat
Caedmon
Cassette, Record

FITZGERALD, F. Scott
Miller, James E.
Great Gatsby
Cassette Curriculum
Cassette

FITZGERALD, F. Scott
Stern, Milton
Tender Is the Night
Cassette Curriculum
Cassette

FLAUBERT, Gustave
Brombert, Victor
Madame Bovary
Cassette Curriculum
Cassette

FLEMING, Ian
Gingold, Hermoine
Chitty Chitty Bang Bang
Caedmon
Cassette, Record

FORBES, Esther
Marshall, E. G.; Cast
Johnny Tremain
Caedmon
Cassette, Record

FORSTER, Edward Morgan
Forster, Edward Morgan
Poems
Argo
Record

FRANKLIN, Benjamin
Begley, Ed
Autobiography of Benjamin
Franklin
Caedmon
Cassette, Record

FRASER, Lady Antonia
No Names
Mary, Queen of Scots
Argo
Record

FRENCH, Warren
French, Warren
Lecture on Greetings, A Film
Cassette Curriculum
Record

FRENCH, Warren
French, Warren
Lecture on Hiroshima, Mon
Amour
Cassette Curriculum
Record

FRENCH, Warren
French, Warren
Lecture on Intolerance
Cassette Curriculum
Record

FRENCH, Warren
French, Warren

Lecture on Red Desert
Cassette Curriculum
Record

FRENCH, Warren
French, Warren
Lecture on the Cabinet of Dr.
Caligari
Cassette Curriculum
Record

FRENCH, Warren
French, Warren
Lecture on The Grapes of Wrath
Cassette Curriculum
Record

FRENCH, Warren
French, Warren
Lecture on 8 1/2
Cassette Curriculum
Record

FRITZ, Jean
Shachter, Jaqueline
An Interview With ...
Profiles in Literature
Videotape

FROST, Robert
Frost, Robert
First Acquaintance
Films for the Humanities
Film

FROST, Robert
Frost, Robert
Reading Robert Frost
Caedmon
Cassette, Record

FROST, Robert
Cox, James M.
Robert Frost 2
Casette Curriculum
Cassette

FROST, Robert
Frost, Robert
The Road Not Taken & Others
Caedmon
Cassette, Record

GAINES, Ernest
McNeil, Claudia
Autobiography of Miss Jane
Pittman
Caedmon
Cassette, Record

GARCIA LORCA, Federico
Douglas, Maria; Dantes, Raul
Poesía, Drama
Caedmon
Cassette, Record

GARLAND, Woodward
No Name
John Clare
Argo
Record

GENET, Jean
Brown; Magee; Cusack; Culver
Balcony
Caedmon
Cassette, Record

GENET, Jean
Genet, Jean
Selected Works of Jean Genet
Caedmon
Cassette, Record

GENET, Jean
Kern, Edith
Two Works of Genet
Cassette Curriculum
Cassette

GEORGE, Jean
Shachter, Jaqueline
An Interview With ...
Profiles in Literature
Videotape

GILBERT, W. S.
Grenfell; Holloway
Bad Ballads, Cautionary Tales
Caedmon
Cassette, Record

GINSBERG, Allen
Merrill, Thomas F.
Allen Ginsberg
Cassette Curriculum
Cassette

GINSBERG, Allen
Ginsberg, Allen
Poems of Allen Ginsberg
Cassette Curriculum
Record

GIRAUDAUX, Jean
Rhome, Frances
Madwoman of Chaillot
Cassette Curriculum
Cassette

GITTINS, Anne
  Tupou, Manu
  Tales from the South Pacific
  Caedmon
  Cassette, Record

GOBLE, Paul & Dorothy
  Junaluska, Arthur S.
  Custer's Last Battle, Red
    Hawk's Account
  Caedmon
  Cassette, Record

GOFF, Beth
  Harris; Wiseman
  Stories About Divorce to Aid
    Children
  Caedmon
  Cassette, Record

GOLDSMITH, Oliver
  Sim; Bloom; Debanzie
  She Stoops to Conquer
  Caedmon
  Cassette, Record

GRAHAM, Lorenz
  Shachter, Jaqueline
  An Interview With ...
  Profiles in Literature
  Videotape

GRAHAME, Kenneth
  Karloff, Boris
  Reluctant Dragon
  Jabberwocky
  Cassette, Record

GRAHAME, Kenneth
  McCallum, David
  Wind in the Willows
  Caedmon
  Cassette, Record

GRAHAME, Kenneth
  Goolden; Shelley; Church
  Wind in the Willows
  Argo
  Record

GRASS, Günter
  Freedman, Ralph
  Works of Günter Grass
  Cassette Curriculum
  Cassette

GRAVES, Robert
  Graves, Robert

Poems
Argo
Record

GRAVES, Robert
  Graves, Robert
  Robert Graves Reads His Poetry
  Caedmon
  Cassette, Record

GRAY AND COLLINS
  Bebb; Neville; Rylands; Squire
  Poems
  Argo
  Record

GRAY, Simon
  Bates, Alan
  Butley
  Caedmon
  Cassette, Record

GRAY, Thomas
  Mason, James
  Elegy Written in a Country
    Churchyard
  Caedmon
  Cassette, Record

GREGG, Hubert
  Gregg, Hubert
  Hubert Gregg as Jerome S.
    Jerome
  Argo
  Record

GRIMM, Jacob & Wilhelm
  Bloom, Claire
  Hansel and Gretel, Other Tales
  Caedmon
  Cassette, Record

GRIMM, Jacob & Wilhelm
  Schildkraut, Joseph
  Tom Thumb, Rumpelstiltskin
    Others
  Caedmon
  Cassette, Record

GRIMM'S FAIRY TALES
  Not Named
  Fisherman and His Wife
  Jabberwocky
  Cassette

GRIMM'S FAIRY TALES
  Not Named
  Hansel and Gretel

Jabberwocky
Cassette

GRIMM'S FAIRY TALES
Not Named
Rumpelstiltskin
Jabberwocky
Cassette

GRIMM'S FAIRY TALES
Not Named
Snow White and the Seven Dwarfs
Jabberwocky
Cassette

GUTHRIE, A. B., Jr.
Guthrie, A. B., Jr.
Big Sky
Caedmon
Cassette, Record

HAINES, John
Haines, John
Poems of John Haines
Cassette Curriculum
Record

HALE, Edward Everett
Robinson, Edward G.
Man Without a Country
Caedmon
Cassette, Record

HALE, Lucretia
Nesbitt, Cathleen
Peterkin Papers
Caedmon
Cassette, Record

HAMILTON, Virginia
Hamilton, Virginia
Virginia Hamilton Reads from
    Zeelly
Caedmon
Cassette, Record

HAMILTON, Virginia
Hamilton, Virginia
Zeely
Caedmon
Cassette, Record

HANDKE, Peter
D'Andrea, Paul
Kaspar
Cassette Curriculum
Cassette

HANSBERRY, Lorraine
Hansberry, Lorraine
Black Experience in the Crea-
    tion of Drama
Films for the Humanities
Film

HANSBERRY, Lorraine
Hansberry, Lorraine
Lorraine Hansberry Speaks Out
Caedmon
Cassette, Record

HANSBERRY, Lorraine
Dee; Davis; Sands; McNeil
Raisin in the Sun
Caedmon
Cassette, Record

HANSBERRY, Lorraine
Bigsby, C. W. E.
Raisin in the Sun
Cassette Curriculum
Cassette

HANSBERRY, Lorraine
Jones; Baxley; McNeil; Sattin
To Be Young, Gifted and Black
Caedmon
Cassette, Record

HARDY, Thomas
Holm; Jefford; Pasco
Poems, Vol. 1
Argo
Record

HARDY, Thomas
Holm; Jefford; King; Pasco
Poems, Vol. 2
Argo
Record

HARDY, Thomas
Burton, Richard
Poetry of Thomas Hardy
Caedmon
Cassette, Record

HARTE, Bret
Begley, Ed
Luck of Roaring Camp; The Out-
    casts of Poker Flats
Caedmon
Cassette, Record

HARTE, Bret
Morrow, Patrick

Works of Bret Harte
Cassette Curriculum
Cassette

HASLAM, Gerald
Haslam, Gerald
American Indian Literature
Cassette Curriculum
Cassette

HAWTHORNE, Nathaniel
Fossum, Robert
Birthmark, The Artist of the
Beautiful
Cassette Curriculum
Cassette

HAWTHORNE, Nathaniel
Fossum, Robert
Celestial Railroad, Maypole of
Merry Mount
Cassette Curriculum
Cassette

HAWTHORNE, Nathaniel
Fossum, Robert
Goodman Brown, Minister's
Black Veil
Cassette Curriculum
Cassette

HAWTHORNE, Nathaniel
Not Named
Great Short Stories
Jabberwocky
Cassette

HAWTHORNE, Nathaniel
Nesbitt, Cathleen
Jason and the Golden Fleece
Caedmon
Cassette, Record

HAWTHORNE, Nathaniel
Fossum, Robert
My Kinsman, Roger Malvin's
Burial
Cassette Curriculum
Cassette

HAWTHORNE, Nathaniel
Fossum, Robert
Scarlet Letter
Cassette Curriculum
Cassette

HAWTHORNE, Nathaniel
Rathbone, Basil

Stories Vol. 1
Caedmon
Cassette, Record

HAWTHORNE, Nathaniel
Rathbone, Basil
Stories, Vol. 2
Caedmon
Cassette, Record

HAWTHORNE, Nathaniel
Quayle, Anthony
Tanglewood Tales: Theseus
Caedmon
Cassette, Record

HAWTHORNE, Nathaniel
Quayle, Anthony
Tanglewood Tales: Pluto and
Prosperina
Caedmon
Cassette, Record

HAZEAM, Lou
Cobb, Lee J.; Gabel, Martin
Van Gogh: A Self Portrait
Columbia Masterworks
Cassette, Record

HEANEY, Seamus
Heaney, Seamus
Poet in Limboland
Films for the Humanities
Film

HECHT, Ben
Ryan; Cass; Convy; Hamilton
Front Page
Caedmon
Cassette, Record

HELLER, Joseph
Heller, Joseph
Catch-22
Caedmon
Cassette, Record

HELLER, Joseph
Pease, Donald
Catch-22
Cassette Curriculum
Cassette

HEMINGWAY, Ernest
Young, Philip
Farewell to Arms
Cassette Curriculum
Cassette

HEMINGWAY, Ernest
  Grebstein, Sheldon
  For Whom the Bell Tolls
  Cassette Curriculum
  Cassette

HEMINGWAY, Ernest
  Hemingway, Ernest
  Reading Ernest Hemingway
  Caedmon
  Cassette, Record

HEMINGWAY, Ernest
  Young, Philip
  Sun Also Rises
  Cassette Curriculum
  Cassette

HENRY, O. (W. S. Porter)
  Harris, Begley
  Gift of Magi, Other Stories
  Caedmon
  Cassette, Record

HESSE, Hermann
  Demetz, Peter
  Magister Ludi/Glass Bead Game
  Cassette Curriculum
  Cassette

HESSE, Hermann
  Freedman, Ralph
  Works of Hermann Hesse
  Cassette Curriculum
  Cassette

HITCHCOCK, George
  Hitchcock, George
  The Poems of George Hitchcock
  Cassette Curriculum
  Record

HOBAN, Tana
  Shachter, Jaqueline
  An Interview With ...
  Profiles in Literature
  Videotape

HOLMES, Oliver Wendell
  Begley, Ed
  Old Ironsides, Other Poems
  Caedmon
  Cassette, Record

HOMER
  Quayle, Anthony
  Iliad
  Caedmon
  Cassette, Record

HOMER
  Dimock, George
  Iliad Part 1
  Cassette Curriculum
  Cassette

HOMER
  Dimock, George
  Iliad Part 2
  Cassette Curriculum
  Cassette

HOMER
  Not Named
  Odyssey
  Jabberwocky
  Cassette

HOMER
  Quayle, Anthony
  Odyssey
  Caedmon
  Cassette, Record

HOMER
  Dimock, George
  Odyssey 1
  Cassette Curriculum
  Cassette

HOMER
  Dimock, George
  Odyssey 2
  Cassette Curriculum
  Cassette

HOPKINS, Gerard Manley
  Daiches, David
  G. M. Hopkins 1
  Cassette Curriculum
  Cassette

HOPKINS, Gerard Manley
  Daiches, David
  G. M. Hopkins 2
  Cassette Curriculum
  Cassette

HOPKINS, Gerard Manley
  Jefford; Pasco; Redgrave
  Poems
  Argo
  Record

HOPKINS, Gerard Manley
  Cusack, Cyril
  Poetry of G. M. Hopkins
  Caedmon
  Cassette, Record

HORACE
  Commager, Steele
  Works of Horace
  Cassette Curriculum
  Cassette

HOUSMAN, A. E.
  Mason, James
  Shropshire Lad and Other Poems
  Caedmon
  Cassette, Record

HUGHES, Langston
  Turner, Darwin
  Langston Hughes
  Cassette Curriculum
  Cassette

HUGHES, Langston
  Jones, James Earl
  Poems from Black Africa
  Caedmon
  Cassette, Record

HUGHES, Langston
  Davis, Ossie
  Simple Stories
  Caedmon
  Cassette, Record

HUGO, Victor
  Gaudon, Jean
  Les Contemplations
  Cassette Curriculum
  Cassette

HUNT, James H. L.
  Mason, James
  Abou Ben Adhem
  Caedmon
  Cassette, Record

HUTCHINSON, W. H.
  Hutchinson, W. H.
  Cowboy in Literature
  Cassette Curriculum
  Cassette

HUXLEY, Aldous
  Huxley, Aldous
  Speaking Personally
  Caedmon
  Cassette, Record

IBSEN, Henrik
  Bloom; Madden
  Doll's House
  Caedmon
  Cassette, Record

IBSEN, Henrik
  Lincoln Center Rep. Co.
  Enemy of the People
  Caedmon
  Cassette, Record

IBSEN, Henrik
  Plowright; Nesbitt; Quayle
  Hedda Gabler
  Caedmon
  Cassette, Record

IBSEN, Henrik
  Worth, Irene
  Hedda Gabler
  Films for the Humanities
  Film

IBSEN, Henrik
  Redgrave; Smith; Adrian; John-
    son
  Master Builder
  Caedmon
  Cassette, Record

IBSEN, Henrik
  Reinert, Otto
  Wild Duck
  Cassette Curriculum
  Cassette

IONESCO, Eugene
  McKenna; Cusack; Ionesco
  Chairs
  Caedmon
  Cassette, Record

IONESCO, Eugene
  Pease, Donald
  Chairs
  Cassette Curriculum
  Cassette

IONESCO, Eugene
  Mostel, Zero
  Rhinoceros
  Caedmon
  Cassette, Record

IONESCO, Eugene
  Kern, Edith
  Works of Ionesco
  Cassette Curriculum
  Cassette

IRVING, Washington
  Not Named
  Legend of Sleepy Hollow

Jabberwocky
Cassette

IRVING, Washington
Begley, Ed
Legend of Sleepy Hollow
Caedmon
Cassette, Record

IRVING, Washington
Begley, Ed
Rip Van Winkle
Caedmon
Cassette, Record

JACKSON, Jesse
Shachter, Jaqueline
An Interview With ...
Profiles in Literature
Videotape

JACKSON, Mahalia
Jackson, Mahalia
Life I Sing About
Caedmon
Cassette, Record

JACOBS, W. W.
Quayle, Anthony
Monkey's Paw
Caedmon
Cassette, Record

JAMES, Henry
Gurko, Leo
Ambassadors
Cassette Curriculum
Cassette

JAMES, Henry
Not Named
Turn of the Screw
Jabberwocky
Cassette

JAMES, Henry
Anderson, Judith
Turn of the Screw
Caedmon
Cassette, Record

JARRELL, Randall
Jarrell, Randall
Bat Poet
Caedmon
Cassette, Record

JARRELL, Randall
Jarrell, Randall

Gingerbread Rabbit
Caedmon
Cassette, Record

JARRELL, Randall
Jarrell, Randall
Poems Against War
Caedmon
Cassette, Record

JARRELL, Randall
Calhoun, Richard
Randall Jarrell
Cassette Curriculum
Cassette

JEFFERS, Robinson
Anderson, Judith
Poetry of Robinson Jeffers
Caedmon
Cassette, Record

JEFFERS, Robinson
Everson, William
Robinson Jeffers
Cassette Curriculum
Cassette

JIMENEZ, Juan Ramón
Jimenez, Juan Ramón
Readings by Juan Ramón Jiménez
Caedmon
Cassette, Record

JIMENEZ, Juan Ramón
Jiménez, Juan Ramón
Reading Juan Jiménez (Spanish)
Caedmon
Cassette, Record

JOHNSON; GOLDSMITH; COWPER
Neville; Rylands; Squire
Poems
Argo
Record

JOHNSON, Samuel
Ross, Angus
Johnson the Critic
Cassette Curriculum
Cassette

JOHNSON, Samuel
Ross, Angus
Johnson the Poet
Cassette Curriculum
Cassette

JOHNSON, Samuel
Ross, Angus
Man and Manners
Cassette Curriculum
Cassette

JONES, David
Jones, David
Poems
Argo
Record

JONES, James
Burress, Lee
From Here to Eternity
Cassette Curriculum
Cassette

JONSON, Ben
Salgado; Gamini
Jonson as Critic
Cassette Curriculum
Cassette

JONSON, Ben
Salgado; Gamini
Jonson the Dramatist
Cassette Curriculum
Cassette

JONSON, Ben
Salgado; Gamini
Jonson the Poet
Cassette Curriculum

JONSON, Ben
Mack, Maynard, Jr.
Volpone
Cassette Curriculum
Cassette

JOYCE, James
McKenna; Cusack
Finnegans Wake
Caedmon
Cassette, Record

JOYCE, James
Staples, Hugh
James Joyce 1
Cassette Curriculum
Cassette

JOYCE, James
Staples, Hugh
James Joyce 2
Cassette Curriculum
Cassette

JOYCE, James
Cusack, Cyril
Poems Pennyeach
Caedmon
Cassette, Record

JOYCE, James
Staples, Hugh
Portrait of an Artist
Cassette Curriculum
Cassette

JOYCE, James
Cusack, Cyril
Portrait of the Artist
Caedmon
Cassette, Record

JOYCE, James
Joyce, James
Reading James Joyce
Caedmon
Cassette, Record

JOYCE, James
Jefford; O'Shea; Roeves
Ulysses
Caedmon
Cassette, Record

JOYCE, James
McKenna; Marshall
Ulysses
Caedmon
Cassette, Record

JOYCE, James
Staples, Hugh
Ulysses 1
Cassette Curriculum
Cassette

JOYCE, James
Staples, Hugh
Ulysses 2
Cassette Curriculum
Cassette

JOYCE, James
Hanratty, Lawrence; Dunn, J.
Tyler
Ulysses: Hades
Columbia Masterworks
Cassette, Record

JOYCE, James
No Name
Ulysses: Lestrygonians

Columbia Masterworks
Cassette, Record

JOYCE, James
No Name
Ulysses: Lotus Eaters
Columbia Masterworks
Cassette, Record

JOYCE, James
No Name
Ulysses: Sirens
Columbia Masterworks
Cassette, Record

JUVENAL
Commager; Steele
Works of Juvenal
Cassette Curriculum
Cassette

KAFKA, Franz
Rolleston, James L.
Castle
Cassette Curriculum
Cassette

KAFKA, Franz
Rolleston, James L.
Metamorphosis, Other Stories
Cassette Curriculum
Cassette

KAFKA, Franz
Lenya, Lotte
Tales of Franz Kafka
Caedmon
Cassette, Record

KAFKA, Franz
Rolleston, James L.
Trial
Cassette Curriculum
Cassette

KAFKA, Franz
Vonnegut, Kurt, Jr.
Trials of Franz Kafka
Films for the Humanities
Film

KAULA, Edna Mason
Peters; Sands
African Village Folk Tales,
Vol. 1
Caedmon
Cassette, Record

KAULA, Edna Mason
Peters; Sands
African Village Folk Tales,
Vol. 2
Caedmon
Cassette, Record

KAULA, Edna Mason
Peters; Sands
African Village Folk Tales,
Vol. 3
Caedmon
Cassette, Record

KAULA, Edna Mason
Dee, Ruby
Rain God's Daughter and Other
Stories
Caedmon
Cassette, Record

KEATS, Ezra Jack
Shachter, Jaqueline
An Interview With ...
Profiles in Literature
Videotape

KEATS, John
Gittings, Robert
Endymion
Cassette Curriculum
Cassette

KEATS, John
Gittings, Robert
Eve of St. Agnes
Cassette Curriculum
Cassette

KEATS, John
Gittings, Robert
Hyperion
Cassette Curriculum
Cassette

KEATS, John
Gittings, Robert
Isabella and Lamia
Cassette Curriculum
Cassette

KEATS, John
Gittings, Robert
Odes
Cassette Curriculum
Cassette

KEATS, John
Church; Godfrey; Johnson
Poems
Argo
Record

KEATS, John
Richardson, Ralph
Poetry of John Keats
Caedmon
Cassette, Record

KEATS, John
Gittings, Robert
Short Poems
Cassette Curriculum
Cassette

KESEY, Ken
Widmer, Kingsley
One Flew Over the Cuckoo's
  Nest
Cassette Curriculum
Cassette

KIPLING, Rudyard
Karloff, Boris
Cat That Walked by Herself
Caedmon
Cassette, Record

KIPLING, Rudyard
Karloff; Others
Gunga Din and Other Poems
Caedmon
Cassette, Record

KIPLING, Rudyard
Quayle, Anthony; Karloff, Boris
How Alphabet Was Made, and
  Other Just So Stories
Caedmon
Cassette, Record

KIPLING, Rudyard
Karloff, Boris
Jungle Book: How Fear Came
Caedmon
Cassette, Record

KIPLING, Rudyard
Karloff, Boris
Jungle Book: Toomai of the
  Elephants
Caedmon
Cassette, Record

KIPLING, Rudyard
Karloff, Boris

Just So Stories, Vol. 1
Caedmon
Cassette, Record

KIPLING, Rudyard
Karloff, Boris
Just So Stories, Vol. 2
Caedmon
Cassette, Record

KIPLING, Rudyard
Johnson; Jefford; Hordern
Just So Stories, Vol. 1
Argo
Record

KIPLING, Rudyard
Johnson; Jefford; Hordern
Just So Stories, Vol. 2
Argo
Record

KIPLING, Rudyard
Quayle, Anthony
Man Who Would Be King
Caedmon
Cassette, Record

KIPLING, Rudyard
Johnson; Wymark; Bates
Poems
Argo
Record

KIPLING, Rudyard
Quayle, Anthony
Poetry
Caedmon
Cassette, Record

KIPLING, Rudyard
Quayle, Anthony
Red Dog, Jungle Book
Caedmon
Cassette, Record

KIPLING, Rudyard
Quayle, Anthony
Wee Willie Winkie, Rikki-Tikki-
  Tave
Caedmon
Cassette, Record

KIPLING, Rudyard
Quayle, Anthony
White Seal
Caedmon
Cassette, Record

KIPPHARDT, Heinar
  Lincoln Center Rep. Co.
  Matter of J. Robert Oppen-
    heimer
  Caedmon
  Cassette, Record

KNIGHT, Eric
  McCallum, David
  Lassie Come Home
  Caedmon
  Cassette, Record

KOPIT, Arthur
  Frieling, Ken
  Indians
  Cassette Curriculum
  Cassette

KOSINSKI, Jerzy
  Rosenberg, Marc
  Steps
  Cassette Curriculum
  Cassette

KRUMGOLD, Joseph
  Shachter, Jaqueline
  An Interview With ...
  Profiles in Literature
  Videotape

KRUSH, Joe and Beth
  Shachter, Jaqueline
  An Interview With ...
  Profiles in Literature
  Videotape

LAMB, Mary
  Harris, Julie
  Tales from Shakespeare--
    Tempest, etc.
  Caedmon
  Cassette, Record

LAND, Andrew
  Bloom, Claire
  Snow White and Other Fairy
    Tales
  Caedmon
  Cassette, Record

LAND, Andrew
  Johns, Glynis
  Snow White and Rose-Red
  Caedmon
  Cassette, Record

LANGFORD, William
  Pasco; King; Bonnamy; Orr

  Visions from Piers Plowman
  Argo
  Record

LAWRENCE, D. H.
  Brown, Pamela
  Lady Chatterley's Lover
  Caedmon
  Cassette, Record

LEAR, Edward
  Bloom, Claire
  Nonsense Stories and Poems
  Caedmon
  Cassette, Record

LEE, Hector
  Lee, Hector
  Roots of Western Literature
  Cassette Curriculum
  Cassette

L'ENGLE, Madeleine
  Shachter, Jaqueline
  An Interview With ...
  Profiles in Literature
  Videotape

LEONARDO DA VINCI
  Drake, Alfred
  Fables of Leonardo da Vinci
  Caedmon
  Cassette, Record

LESTER, Julius
  Dee, Ruby; Davis, Ossie
  To Be a Slave
  Caedmon
  Cassette, Record

LEVERTOV, Denise
  Molesworth, Charles
  Denise Levertov
  Cassette Curriculum
  Cassette

LEWIS, Richard
  Shachter, Jaqueline
  An Interview With ...
  Profiles in Literature
  Videotape

LEWIS, Sinclair
  Griffin, Robert
  Arrowsmith
  Cassette Curriculum
  Cassette

LEWIS, Sinclair
  Lewis, Michael
  Babbitt
  Caedmon
  Cassette, Record

LEWIS, Sinclair
  Grebstein, Sheldon
  Babbitt
  Cassette Curriculum
  Cassette

LEWIS, Sinclair
  Grebstein, Sheldon
  Elmer Gantry
  Cassette Curriculum
  Cassette

LEWIS, Sinclair
  Lewis, Michael
  It Can't Happen Here
  Caedmon
  Cassette, Record

LEWIS, Sinclair
  Grebstein, Sheldon
  Main Street
  Cassette Curriculum
  Cassette

LEWSEN, Charles
  Lewsen, Charles
  Edward Lear
  Argo
  Record

LEXAU, Joan
  Shachter, Jaqueline
  An Interview With ...
  Profiles in Literature
  Videotape

LINDSAY, Vachel
  Lindsay, Vachel
  Reading Vachel Lindsay
  Caedmon
  Cassette, Record

LOBEL, Arnold
  Shachter, Jaqueline
  An Interview With ...
  Profiles in Literature
  Videotape

LONDON, Jack
  Begley, Ed
  Call of the Wild
  Caedmon
  Cassette, Record

LONDON, Jack
  Spinner, Jonathan
  Call of the Wild
  Cassette Curriculum
  Cassette

LONDON, Jack
  Spinner, Jonathan
  Martin Eden
  Cassette Curriculum
  Cassette

LONGFELLOW, Henry W.
  Holbrook, Hal
  Evangeline
  Caedmon
  Cassette, Record

LONGFELLOW, Henry W.
  Holbrook, Hal
  The Best Loved Poems of Long-
    fellow
  Caedmon
  Cassette, Record

LONGFORD, Pasco
  No Name
  Queen Victoria
  Argo
  Record

LOOS, Anita
  Channing, Carol
  Lorelei's Diary
  Caedmon
  Cassette, Record

LORCA, Federico See GARCIA
  LORCA, Federico

LOVECRAFT, H. P.
  French, Warren
  Intro to H. P. Lovecraft
  Cassette Curriculum
  Cassette

LOVECRAFT, H. P.
  McCallum, David
  Rats in the Walls
  Caedmon
  Cassette, Record

LOWELL, James
  No Name
  Benito Cereno
  Columbia Masterworks
  Cassette, Record

LOWELL, Robert
  Staples, Hugh B.
  Robert Lowell, Vol. 1
  Cassette Curriculum
  Cassette

LOWELL, Robert
  Staples, Hugh B.
  Robert Lowell, Vol. 2
  Cassette Curriculum
  Cassette

LUCRETIUS
  Commager; Steele
  Works of Lucretius
  Cassette Curriculum
  Cassette

McELDERRY, M. See ESTES,
  E.

McGINLEY, Phyllis
  Channing, Carol
  Year Without Santa Clause,
    Other Stories
  Caedmon
  Cassette, Record

MACHIAVELLI
  Freccero, John
  Prince
  Cassette Curriculum
  Cassette

MacLEISH, Archibald
  MacLeish, Archibald
  Archibald MacLeish Reads His
    Poetry
  Caedmon
  Cassette, Record

MacLEISH, Archibald
  Kahn, Sy
  J. B.: A Play in Verse
  Cassette Curriculum
  Cassette

MacLEISH, Archibald
  Geer; Strudwick; Poole
  Scratch
  Caedmon
  Cassette, Record

MacNEICE, Louis
  MacNeice, Louis
  Poems
  Argo
  Record

MAILER, Norman
  Pease, Donald
  Naked and the Dead
  Cassette Curriculum
  Cassette

MALAMUD, Bernard
  Grebstein, Sheldon
  The Assistant
  Cassette Curriculum
  Cassette

MALLARME, Stephane
  Gauson, Jean
  Works of Mallarmé
  Cassette Curriculum
  Cassette

MALONE, Kemp
  Malone, Kemp
  On Old English
  Caedmon
  Cassette, Record

MALORY, Sir Thomas
  Barton; White; Holmstrom
  Le Morte d'Arthur
  Argo
  Record

MALORY, Sir Thomas
  McKenna, Siobhan
  Le Morte d'Arthur, Lancelot,
    Guenevere
  Caedmon
  Cassette, Record

MALRAUX, André
  Brombert, Victor
  Man's Fate
  Cassette Curriculum
  Cassette

MALRAUX, André
  Brombert, Victor
  Works of Malraux
  Cassette Curriculum
  Cassette

MANFRED, Frederick
  Manfred, Frederick
  Writing in the West
  Cassette Curriculum
  Cassette

MANN, Thomas
  Rolleston, James L.
  Confessions of Felix Krull

Cassette Curriculum
Cassette

MANN, Thomas
Rolleston, James L.
Death in Venice, Tonio Kroger
Cassette Curriculum
Cassette

MANN, Thomas
Rolleston, James L.
Magic Mountain
Cassette Curriculum
Cassette

MANN, Thomas
Mann, Thomas
Readings by Thomas Mann
Caedmon
Cassette, Record

MANN, Thomas
Mann, Thomas
Thomas Mann Reads
Caedmon
Cassette, Record

MANSFIELD, Katherine
Johnson, Celia
Stories of Katherine Mansfield
Caedmon
Cassette, Record

MANY
Begley; Harris; O'Neal
American Patriotism in Prose
and Poetry
Caedmon
Cassette, Record

MANY
Sparer, Paul; Randolph, John
American Story Poems
Columbia Masterworks
Cassette, Record

MANY
Richardson, Ian
Art of the Essay
Caedmon
Cassette, Record

MANY
Duncan; King; Rylands; Scales
Battle of Maldon, Other Poems
Argo
Record

MANY
Peters; Heath; Carroll; Laine
Beyond the Blues
Argo
Record

MANY
Many
Brain Trust
Argo
Record

MANY
No Name
Caedmon Treasury of Modern
Poetry
Caedmon
Cassette, Record

MANY
No Name
Cambridge Treasury of English
Prose 1
Caedmon
Cassette, Record

MANY
No Name
Cambridge Treasury of English
Prose 2
Caedmon
Cassette, Record

MANY
No Name
Cambridge Treasury of English
Prose 3
Caedmon
Cassette, Record

MANY
No Name
Cambridge Treasury of English
Prose 4
Caedmon
Cassette, Record

MANY
No Name
Cambridge Treasury of English
Prose 5
Caedmon
Cassette, Record

MANY
Yevtushenko; Carnovsky
Classical Russian Poetry
Caedmon
Cassette, Record

MANY
Albert; Begley; Frost; O'Neal
Classics of American Poetry
    for Elementary Schools
Caedmon
Cassette, Record

MANY
Brett; Cornell; Fraser; Grizzard
Classics of English Poetry for
    Elementary Schools
Caedmon
Cassette, Record

MANY
Voces Romanae of Univ. of
    Texas at Austin
Classics of Latin Poetry and
    Prose
Caedmon
Cassette, Record

MANY
Heller, Erich
Dr. Faustus 16th Century to
    Goethe
Cassette Curriculum
Cassette

MANY
Balcon; Dowie; Holm; Watson
Early Victorian Poetry
Argo
Record

MANY
Watson; Bebb; Orr; Duncan
Edison's Talking Phonograph
Argo
Record

MANY
Adrian; Bloom; Quayle; Others
18th-Century Poetry and Drama
Caedmon
Cassette, Record

MANY
Ashcroft; Holm; Johnson; Stride
Elizabethan and Jacobean Poetry
Argo
Record

MANY
Johnson; Holm; Rylands
Elizabethan Sonneteers and
    Edmund Spenser
Argo
Record

MANY
Cowie; McIntyre; Duncan
English Poets from Chaucer to
    Yeats
Argo
Record

MANY
Bloom; Quayle; etc.
English Romantic Poetry
Caedmon
Cassette, Record

MANY
Begley, Ed
Favorite American Poems
Caedmon
Cassette, Record

MANY
No Name
Folksongs of Britain Vol. 1
Caedmon
Cassette, Record

MANY
No Name
Folksongs of Britain Vol. 2
Caedmon
Cassette, Record

MANY
No Name
Folksongs of Britain Vol. 3
Caedmon
Cassette, Record

MANY
No Name
Folksongs of Britain Vol. 4
Caedmon
Cassette, Record

MANY
No Name
Folksongs of Britain Vol. 5
Caedmon
Cassette, Record

MANY
No Name
Folksongs of Britain Vol. 6
Caedmon
Cassette, Record

MANY
No Name
Folksongs of Britain Vol. 7

Caedmon
Cassette, Record

MANY
No Name
Folksongs of Britain Vol. 8
Caedmon
Cassette, Record

MANY
No Name
Folksongs of Britain Vol. 9
Caedmon
Cassette, Record

MANY
No Name
Folksongs of Britain Vol. 10
Caedmon
Cassette, Record

MANY
Harris; Ritchard; Wayne
Gathering of Great Poetry for
Children 1
Caedmon
Cassette, Record

MANY
Harris; Ritchard; Wayne
Gathering of Great Poetry for
Children 2
Caedmon
Cassette, Record

MANY
Harris; Ritchard; Wayne
Gathering of Great Poetry for
Children, Vol. 3
Caedmon
Cassette, Record

MANY
Harris; Ritchard; Wayne
Gathering of Great Poetry for
Children, Vol. 4
Caedmon
Cassette, Record

MANY
Lehmann, Lotte
German Lyric Poetry
Caedmon
Cassette, Record

MANY
Roosevelt; Wilkie; Truman; etc.
Great American Speeches

Caedmon
Cassette, Record

MANY
Begley; Douglas; Price; Sand-
burg
Great American Speeches 1775-
1896
Caedmon
Cassette, Record

MANY
Begley; Grizzard; Marshall
Great American Speeches 1898-
1918
Caedmon
Cassette, Record

MANY
Kennedy; Nixon; etc.
Great American Speeches 1950-
1963
Caedmon
Cassette, Record

MANY
Keckart; McNeil; Natwick
Great American Women's
Speeches
Caedmon
Cassette, Record

MANY
McNeil; Matlock
Great Black Speeches
Caedmon
Cassette, Record

MANY
Bedford; Magee; Quayle
Great British Speeches 1597-
1695
Caedmon
Cassette, Record

MANY
Bedford; Magee; Quayle
Great British Speeches 1628-
1780
Caedmon
Cassette, Record

MANY
Bedford; Magee
Great British Speeches 1784-
1812
Caedmon
Cassette, Record

MANY
  Bedford; Magee; Others
  Great British Speeches 1867-
    1940
  Caedmon
  Cassette, Record

MANY
  No Name
  Great Short Stories
  Caedmon
  Cassette, Record

MANY
  Wilson, Pearl
  Greek Prose and Poetry
  Caedmon
  Cassette, Record

MANY
  Paxinou, Minotis
  Greek Tragedy
  Caedmon
  Cassette, Record

MANY
  Church; Adrian; Barton
  Hollow Crown
  Argo
  Record

MANY
  No Name
  Immigrants: The American
    Dream
  Caedmon
  Cassette, Record

MANY
  Stapleton; Hingle
  Journeys--Prose by Children
  Caedmon
  Cassette, Record

MANY
  Duncan; Holm; King
  Late Victorian Poetry
  Argo
  Record

MANY
  Harris; McDowell
  Miracles: Poems Written by
    Children
  Caedmon
  Cassette, Record

MANY
  No Name

  Noh Plays
  Caedmon
  Cassette, Record

MANY
  No Name
  Poet Speaks, Vol. 1
  Argo
  Record

MANY
  No Name
  Poet Speaks, Vol. 2
  Argo
  Record

MANY
  No Name
  Poet Speaks, Vol. 3
  Argo
  Record

MANY
  No Name
  Poet Speaks, Vol. 4
  Argo
  Record

MANY
  No Name
  Poet Speaks, Vol. 5
  Argo
  Record

MANY
  No Name
  Poet Speaks, Vol. 6
  Argo
  Record

MANY
  No Name
  Poet Speaks, Vol. 7
  Argo
  Record

MANY
  No Name
  Poet Speaks, Vol. 8
  Argo
  Record

MANY
  No Name
  Poet Speaks, Vol. 9
  Argo
  Record

MANY
No Name
Poet Speaks, Vol. 10
Argo
Record

MANY
Many
Poetry International
Argo
Record

MANY
Bonnamy; King; MacIntyre
Poets from Chaucer to Yeats
Argo
Record

MANY
Many
Poets of the West Indies
Caedmon
Cassette, Record

MANY
Watson; Orr; Robson
The Pre-Raphaelites
Argo
Record

MANY
Church; Marquand; Orr; Squire
Religious Metaphysical Poetry
Argo
Record

MANY
Bebb; Squire; Stride
Restoration and Augustan Verse
Argo
Record

MANY
Donat, Robert
Robert Donat Reads Favourite
    Poetry
Argo
Record

MANY
Donat, Robert
Robert Donat Reads Selected
    Poetry
Argo
Record

MANY
Bonnamy; Holmes; Orr; Stride

Secular Metaphysical Poetry
Argo
Record

MANY
Hardwicke; Newton
17th-Century Poetry
Caedmon
Cassette, Record

MANY
Many
Talking About Theatre
Argo
Record

MANY
Price; Albert; Harris; Begley
300 Years Great American Po-
    etry
Caedmon
Cassette, Record

MANY
Bloom; Portman; Neville
Treasury of English Poetry
Caedmon
Cassette, Record

MANY
Ustinov, Peter
Ustinov Reads Cautionary Verse
Argo
Record

MANY
Adrian; Bloom; Howard
Victorian Poetry
Caedmon
Cassette, Record

MARCEAU, Marcel
Marceau, Marcel
Mime Speaks Out
Caedmon
Cassette, Record

MARLOWE, Christopher
Silvera, Frank; Cast
Dr. Faustus
Caedmon
Cassette, Record

MARLOWE, Christopher
Giamatti, A. Bartlett
Dr. Faustus
Cassette Curriculum
Cassette

MARLOWE, Christopher
Salgado, Gamini
Dr. Faustus
Cassette Curriculum
Cassette

MARLOWE, Christopher
McKellen; West; Fletcher
Edward 2
Argo
Record

MARVELL, Andrew
Lerner, Laurence
Garden
Cassette Curriculum
Cassette

MARVELL, Andrew
Lerner, Laurence
Marvell and the Pastoral Tradi-
tion
Cassette Curriculum
Cassette

MARVELL, Andrew
Lerner, Laurence
Marvell's Wit
Cassette Curriculum
Cassette

MARVELL, Andrew
Lerner, Laurence
Political Poetry
Cassette Curriculum
Cassette

MASEFIELD, John
Masefield, John
Fox's Day
Argo
Record

MASEFIELD, John
Masefield, John
Poems
Argo
Record

MASEFIELD, John
Masefield, John
Sea Fever and Other Poems
Caedmon
Cassette, Record

MASTERS, Edgar Lee
Harris, Julie; Cast
Spoon River Anthology

Caedmon
Cassette, Record

MASTERS, Edgar Lee
Garrett; Elston; Patten; Aidmen
Spoon River Anthology
Columbia Masterworks
Cassette, Record

MAUPASSANT, Guy de
Bloom, Claise
Stories of de Maupassant
Caedmon
Cassette, Record

MAYAKOVSKY, Vladimir
Cullum, John
Poetry of Action
Films for the Humanities
Film

MAYES, Bernard
Not Named
Greek Classics
Jabberwocky
Cassette

MEDCALF
Medcalf, Stephen
Canterbury Tales
Cassette Curriculum
Cassette

MELDRUM, Barbara
Meldrum, Barbara
Images of Women in Western
American Lit
Cassette Curriculum
Cassette

MELVILLE, Herman
Stern, Milton
Bartleby the Scrivener
Cassette Curriculum
Cassette

MELVILLE, Herman
Stern, Milton
Benito Cereno
Cassette Curriculum
Cassette

MELVILLE, Herman
Stern, Milton
Billy Budd
Cassette Curriculum
Cassette

MELVILLE, Herman
Stern, Milton
Moby Dick
Cassette Curriculum
Cassette

MELVILLE, Herman
Dullea; Heston; Rose
Moby Dick (Excerpts)
Caedmon
Cassette, Record

MELVILLE, Herman
Stern, Milton
Moby Dick 2
Cassette Curriculum
Cassette

MELVILLE, Herman
Stern, Milton
Poetry of Herman Melville
Cassette Curriculum
Cassette

MELVILLE, Herman
Stern, Milton
Typee
Cassette Curriculum
Cassette

MELZACK, Ronald
Tupou, Manu
Raven: Creator of the World
Caedmon
Cassette, Record

MENCKEN, Henry
Mencken, Henry
Conversing
Caedmon
Cassette, Record

MERRIAM, Eve
Shachter, Jaqueline
An Interview With ...
Profiles in Literature
Videotape

MERRIAM, Eve
No Name
Catch a Little Rhyme
Caedmon
Cassette, Record

MERWIN, W. S.
Merwin, W. S.
W. S. Merwin Reading His
    Poetry

Caedmon
Cassette, Record

MICHENER, James
Shachter, Jaqueline
An Interview With ...
Profiles in Literature
Videotape

MILLAY, Edna St. Vincent
Millay, Edna St. Vincent
Edna Millay Reading Her Poetry
Caedmon
Cassette, Record

MILLAY, Edna St. Vincent
Millay, Edna St. Vincent
Millay at Steepletop
Films for the Humanities
Film

MILLAY, Edna St. Vincent
Anderson, Judith
Poetry of Edna St. Vincent
    Millay
Caedmon
Cassette, Record

MILLER, Arthur
Rep. Co. of Lincoln Center
After the Fall
Caedmon
Cassette, Record

MILLER, Arthur
Rep. Co. of Lincoln Center
Crucible
Caedmon
Cassette, Record

MILLER, Arthur
Cobb; Dunnock
Death of a Salesman
Caedmon
Cassette, Record

MILLER, Arthur
Gordon, Alan
Death of a Salesman
Cassette Curriculum
Cassette

MILLER, Arthur
Rep. Co. of Lincoln Center
Incident at Vichy
Caedmon
Cassette, Record

MILLER, Arthur
Duval; Voight
View from the Bridge
Caedmon
Cassette, Record

MILNE, A. A.
Grimes, Tammy
Prince Rabbit and Other Stories
Caedmon
Cassette, Record

MILNE, A. A.
Anderson, Judith
When We Were Very Young
Caedmon
Cassette, Record

MILNE, A. A.
Channing, Carol
Winnie-The-Pooh
Caedmon
Cassette, Record

MILTON, John
Squire; Holm; Jefford; Cast
Comus
Argo
Record

MILTON, John
Church; McCarthy; Rawlings
Excerpts from Samson Agonistes
Argo
Record

MILTON, John
Daiches, David
Minor Poems 1
Cassette Curriculum
Cassette

MILTON, John
Daiches, David
Minor Poems 2
Cassette Curriculum
Cassette

MILTON, John
Church; Johnson; Redgrave;
Cast
Paradise Lost Book 1
Argo
Record

MILTON, John
Church; Redgrave; Devlin; Cast
Paradise Lost Book 2

Argo
Record

MILTON, John
Church; Redgrave; McCarthy
Paradise Lost Books 3 & 4
Argo
Record

MILTON, John
Church; Redgrave; Watson; Cast
Paradise Lost Books 5 & 6
Argo
Record

MILTON, John
Church; Redgrave; Johnson
Paradise Lost Books 7 & 8
Argo
Record

MILTON, John
Church; Redgrave; Hordern;
Cast
Paradise Lost Books 9, 10 & 12
Argo
Record

MILTON, John
Daiches, David
Paradise Lost 1
Cassette Curriculum
Cassette

MILTON, John
Daiches, David
Paradise Lost 2
Cassette Curriculum
Cassette

MILTON, John
Quayle, Anthony
Paradise Lost, Books 1, 4
Caedmon
Cassette, Record

MILTON, John
Quayle, Anthony
Paradise Lost, Books 2, 3
Caedmon
Cassette, Record

MILTON, John
Daiches, David
Paradise Regained
Cassette Curriculum
Cassette

MILTON, John
McCarthy; Neville; Holm
Paradise Regained Books 1-4
Argo
Record

MILTON, John
Quayle, Anthony
Poetry of John Milton
Caedmon
Cassette, Record

MILTON, John
Redgrave; Adrien; Cast
Samson Agonistes
Caedmon
Cassette, Record

MILTON, John
Daiches, David
Samson Agonistes
Cassette Curriculum
Cassette

MILTON, John
Redgrave, Michael; Others
Samson Agonistes
Columbia Masterworks
Cassette, Record

MILTON, John
Devlin; Squire; Watson
Shorter Poems
Argo
Record

MOLIERE
Ritchard, Cyril
Misanthrope
Films for the Humanities
Film

MOLIERE
APA Phoenix Production
Misanthrope
Caedmon
Cassette, Record

MOLIERE
Rep. Co. of Lincoln Center
Miser
Caedmon
Cassette, Record

MOLIERE
Bedford, Van Ark; Cast
School for Wives
Caedmon
Cassette, Record

MOLIERE
Guicharnaud, Jacques
Tartuffe
Cassette Curriculum
Cassette

MOLIERE
Stratford Nat. Theatre of Canada
Tartuffe
Caedmon
Cassette, Record

MONTAIGNE
Greene, Thomas M.
Works of Montaigne
Cassette Curriculum
Cassette

MOORE, Marianne
Engel, Bernard F.
Marianne Moore
Cassette Curriculum
Cassette

MOORE, Marianne
Moore, Marianne
Marianne Moore Reading Her
Poetry
Caedmon
Cassette, Record

MORE, Sir Thomas
Ross, Angus
Utopia
Cassette Curriculum
Cassette

MORGENSTERN, Christian
Nash, Ogden
Poetry of--Gallows Song
Caedmon
Cassette, Record

MUCHAUSEN, Baron
Ustinov, Peter
Truly Tall Tales
Caedmon
Cassette, Record

MULOCK, Dinah Maria
Nesbitt, Cathleen
Little Lame Prince
Caedmon
Cassette, Record

NASH, Ogden
Nash, Ogden
Christmas with Ogden Nash

Caedmon
Cassette, Record

NASH, Ogden
Nash, Ogden
Kind of an Ode to Duty and
Others
Caedmon
Cassette, Record

NASH, Ogden
Nash, Ogden
Parents Keep Out
Caedmon
Cassette, Record

NASH, Ogden
Nash, Ogden
Reads Ogden Nash
Caedmon
Cassette, Record

NASH, Ogden
Nash, Ogden
Reflections of a Wicked World
Caedmon
Cassette, Record

NEIHARDT, John G.
Milton, John R.
Works of John G. Neihardt
Cassette Curriculum
Cassette

NERUDA, Pablo
Neruda, Pablo; Quayle, Anthony
I Am Pablo Neruda
Films for the Humanities
Film

NERUDA, Pablo
Neruda, Pablo
Pablo Neruda Reading His Poetry
Caedmon
Cassette, Record

NESBIT, E.
Anderson, Judith
Book of Dragon
Caedmon
Cassette, Record

NESBIT, E.
Jeffries, Lionel
Railway Children
Caedmon
Cassette, Record

NEVILLE, Emily
Shachter, Jacqueline
An Interview With ...
Profile in Literature
Videotape

NEWCOMB, Rank Johnson
Junaluska, Arthur S.
Navajo Bird Tales
Caedmon
Cassette, Record

NIETZSCHE, Friedrich
Heller, Erich
Works of Nietzsche
Cassette Curriculum
Cassette

NORTON, Mary
Bloom, Claire
Borrowers
Caedmon
Cassette, Record

O'CASEY, Sean
McKenna; Cusack
Juno and the Paycock
Caedmon
Cassette, Record

O'CASEY, Sean
O'Casey, Sean
Reading Sean O'Casey Vol. 1
Caedmon
Cassette, Record

O'CASEY, Sean
O'Casey, Sean
Reading Sean O'Casey Vol. 2
Caedmon
Cassette, Record

O'CONNOR, Flannery
Martin; Carter
Works of Flannery O'Connor
Cassette Curriculum
Cassette

O'CONNOR, Frank
O'Connor, Frank
Reading Frank O'Connor
Caedmon
Cassette, Record

ODETS, Clifford
Mendelsohn, Michael
Awake and Sing
Cassette Curriculum
Casette

O'HARA, John
Tuttleton, James W.
Appointment in Samarra
Cassette Curriculum
Cassette

O'NEILL, Eugene
Circle in the Square
Ah, Wilderness
Caedmon
Cassette, Record

O'NEILL, Eugene
Jones, James Earl; Cast
Emperor Jones
Caedmon
Cassette, Record

O'NEILL, Eugene
Miller, Jordan
Emperor Jones
Cassette Curriculum
Cassette

O'NEILL, Eugene
Miller, Jordan
Hairy Ape
Cassette Curriculum
Cassette

O'NEILL, Eugene
Marvin; March
Iceman Cometh
Caedmon
Cassette, Record

O'NEILL, Eugene
Miller, Jordan
Iceman Cometh
Cassette Curriculum
Cassette

O'NEILL, Eugene
Ryan; Keach; Fitzgerald; Croft
Long Day's Journey Into Night
Caedmon
Cassette, Record

O'NEILL, Eugene
Bryer; Jackson
Long Day's Journey Into Night
Cassette Curriculum
Cassette

O'NEILL, Eugene
Quintero, Jose
Long Day's Journey Into Night
Films for the Humanities
Film

O'NEILL, Eugene
Jens; Ryan; Brydon
Moon for the Misbegotten
Caedmon
Cassette, Record

O'NEILL, Eugene
Bergman; Hill; Dewhurst
More Stately Mansions
Caedmon
Cassette, Record

O'NEILL, Eugene
Alexander; Thompson; Cast
Mourning Becomes Electra
Caedmon
Cassette, Record

O'NEILL, Eugene
Miller, Jordan
Mourning Becomes Electra
Cassette Curriculum
Cassette

OSBORNE, John
Miller, Jordan
Look Back in Anger
Cassette Curriculum
Cassette

OSBORNE, John
Keach, Stacy
Luther
Caedmon
Cassette, Record

OVID
Commager; Steele
Works of Ovid
Cassette Curriculum
Cassette

OWEN, Guy
Owen, Guy
Poems of Guy Owen
Cassette Curriculum
Cassette

PARKER, Dorothy
Booth, Shirley
Stories of Dorothy Parker
Caedmon
Cassette, Record

PASTERNAK, Boris
Yevtushenko; Carnovsky
Poetry of Boris Pasternak
Caedmon
Cassette, Record

PATTEN, Brian
  Patten, Brian
  Brian Patten Reading His Poetry
  Caedmon
  Cassette, Record

PERRAULT, Charles
  Not Named
  Cinderella
  Jabberwocky
  Cassette

PERRAULT, Charles
  Not Named
  Sleeping Beauty
  Jabberwocky
  Cassette

PERRINE, Laurence
  Perrine, Laurence
  Knowing What the Poem Means
  Cassette Curriculum
  Cassette

PERRINE, Laurence
  Perrine, Laurence
  Poetry Begins with Words
  Cassette Curriculum
  Cassette

PERRINE, Laurence
  Perrine, Laurence
  Poetry in an Age of Science
  Cassette Curriculum
  Cassette

PERRINE, Laurence
  Perrine, Laurence
  Relevance of Poetry
  Cassette Curriculum
  Cassette

PERRINE, Laurence
  Perrine, Laurence
  Tone and Poetic Meaning
  Cassette Curriculum
  Cassette

PERRINE, Laurence
  Perrine, Laurence
  Why Poetry?
  Cassette Curriculum
  Cassette

PETRY, Ann
  Shachter, Jaqueline
  An Interview With ...
  Profiles in Literature
  Videotape

PINTER, Harold
  Gordon, Lois
  Birthday Party
  Cassette Curriculum
  Cassette

PINTER, Harold
  Cusack; Holm
  Homecoming
  Caedmon
  Cassette, Record

PIRANDELLO, Luigi
  Nelson, Robert
  Henry 4
  Cassette Curriculum
  Cassette

PIRANDELLO, Luigi
  Frankel, Ken
  Six Characters in Search of an
    Author
  Films for the Humanities
  Film

PIRANDELLO, Luigi
  D'Andrea, Paul
  Six Characters in Search of an
    Author
  Cassette Curriculum
  Cassette

PIRANDELLO, Luigi
  Nelson, Robert
  Six Characters in Search of an
    Author
  Cassette Curriculum
  Cassette

PLATH, Sylvia
  Hill, Robert W.
  Sylvia Plath
  Cassette Curriculum
  Cassette

PLATO
  Richardson, Ralph
  Apology
  Caedmon
  Cassette, Record

PLATO
  Von Steen, Heinrich
  Apology, Trial, Death of Socrates
  Cassette Curriculum
  Cassette

PLATO
  Not Named

Phaedo
Jabberwocky
Cassette

POE, Edgar Allan
Levine, Stuart
Fall of the House of Usher
Cassette Curriculum
Cassette

POE, Edgar Allan
Price, Vincent
Gold Bug
Caedmon
Cassette, Record

POE, Edgar Allan
Not Named
Gold Bug, Amontillado, Usher
Jabberwocky
Cassette

POE, Edgar Allan
Price, Vincent
Imp of Perverse, Other Tales
Caedmon
Cassette, Record

POE, Edgar Allan
Levine, Stuart
Ligeia
Cassette Curriculum
Cassette

POE, Edgar Allan
Levine, Stuart
Masque of the Red Death
Cassette Curriculum
Cassette

POE, Edgar Allan
No Name
Poems and Tales
Caedmon
Cassette, Record

POE, Edgar Allan
Rathbone, Basil
Poetry by Poe Vol. 1
Caedmon
Cassette, Record

POE, Edgar Allan
Rathbone, Basil
Poetry by Poe Vol. 2
Caedmon
Cassette, Record

POE, Edgar Allan
Rathbone, Basil
Poetry by Poe Vol. 3
Caedmon
Casette, Record

POE, Edgar Allan
Quayle, Anthony
Poetry by Poe Vol. 4
Caedmon
Cassette, Record

POE, Edgar Allan
Levine, Stuart
Purloined Letter
Cassette Curriculum
Cassette

POE, Edgar Allan
Levine, Stuart
Raven and Other Poems
Cassette Curriculum
Cassette

POE, Edgar Allan
Not Named
Tales by Poe
Jabberwocky
Cassette

POPE, Alexander
Ross, Angus
Critic, Gardener, Letter Writer
Cassette Curriculum
Cassette

POPE, Alexander
Adrian; Duncan; Mitchell
Poems
Argo
Record

POPE, Alexander
Redgrave, Michael
Poetry of Alexander Pope, Vol.
1
Caedmon
Cassette, Record

POPE, Alexander
Adrian, Max; Bloom, Claire
Poetry of Alexander Pope, Vol.
2
Caedmon
Cassette, Record

POPE, Alexander
Ross, Angus

Pope the Satirist
Cassette Curriculum
Cassette

POPE, Alexander
Ross, Angus
Pope's Moral Poetry
Cassette Curriculum
Cassette

POPE, Alexander
Ross, Angus
Rape of the Lock
Cassette Curriculum
Cassette

POPE, Alexander
Rylands; Ashcroft; Hyde
Rape of the Lock
Argo
Record

PORTER, Katherine Anne
Porter, Katherine Anne
Downward Path to Wisdom
Caedmon
Cassette, Record

PORTER, Katherine Anne
Porter, Katherine Anne
Noon Wine
Caedmon
Cassette, Record

PORTER, Katherine Anne
Porter, Katherine Anne
Pale Horse, Pale Rider
Caedmon
Cassette, Record

PORTER, Katherine Anne
Gurko, Leo
Ship of Fools
Cassette Curriculum
Cassette

PORTER, W. S. See HENRY, O.

POTTER, Beatrix
Bloom, Claire
Nursery Rhymes and Tales
Caedmon
Cassette, Record

POTTER, Beatrix
Bloom, Claire
Peter Rabbit and Other Stories
Caedmon
Cassette, Record

POTTER, Beatrix
Bloom, Claire
Squirrel Nutkin and Other Tales
Caedmon
Cassette, Record

POTTER, Beatrix
Bloom, Claire
Tailor of Gloucester
Caedmon
Cassette, Record

POTTER, Beatrix
Bloom, Claire
Tale of Flopsy Bunnies, Other
Stories
Caedmon
Cassette, Record

POTTER, Beatrix
Bloom, Claire
Tale of Little Pig Robinson
Caedmon
Cassette, Record

POUND, Ezra
Pound, Ezra
Ezra Pound Reading His Poetry
Vol. 1
Caedmon
Cassette, Record

POUND, Ezra
Pound, Ezra
Ezra Pound Reading His Poetry
Vol. 2
Caedmon
Cassette, Record

POUND, Ezra
Pound, Ezra
Poet's Poet
Films for the Humanities
Film

PROUST, Marcel
Richardson, Ralph
Remembrance of Things Past
Caedmon
Cassette, Record

PROUST, Marcel
Brombert, Victor
Works of Proust
Cassette Curriculum
Cassette

PURDY, James
French, Warren

Malcolm
Cassette Curriculum
Cassette

PYLE, Howard
Fairbanks, Douglas, Jr.
Blueskin, The Pirate
Caedmon
Cassette, Record

PYLE, Howard
Richardson, Ian
King Arthur and His Knights
Caedmon
Cassette, Record

PYLE, Howard
Not Named
Merry Adventures of Robin Hood
Jabberwocky
Cassette

PYLE, Howard
Richardson, Ian
Tales of King Arthur & Knights:
    Excalibur
Caedmon
Cassette, Record

RABELAIS, François
Greene, Thomas M.
Gargantua
Cassette Curriculum
Cassette

RABELAIS, François
Greene, Thomas M.
Pantagruel
Cassette Curriculum
Cassette

RABELAIS, François
Greene, Thomas M.
Third Book
Cassette Curriculum
Cassette

RACINE, Jean
Gaudon, Jean
Phèdre
Cassette Curriculum
Cassette

RANSOM, John Crowe
Young, T. D.
John Crowe Ransom
Cassette Curriculum
Cassette

RAWLINGS, Marjorie
Wayne; Heckert; Yankee
Yearling
Caedmon
Cassette, Record

REEVES, James
Bloom, Claire
Dick Whittington and His Cat,
    Other Stories
Caedmon
Cassette, Record

REY, H. A.
Harris, Julie
Curious George
Caedmon
Cassette, Record

REY, H. A.
Harris, Julie
Curious George Learns the
    Alphabet
Caedmon
Cassette, Record

RHODES, Eugene Manlove
Hutchinson, W. H.
Works of Eugene Manlove
    Rhodes
Cassette Curriculum
Cassette

RICHTER, Conrad
Marshall, E. G.; Cast
Light in the Forest
Caedmon
Cassette, Record

RILKE, Rainer Maria
Lehmann, Lotte
Poetry of Rilke
Caedmon
Cassette, Record

RILKE, Rainer Maria
Rolleston, James L.
Works of Rilke
Cassette Curriculum
Cassette

RIMBAUD, Arthur
Gaudon, Jean
Works of Rimbaud
Cassette Curriculum
Cassette

RIVERA, Diego
Rivera, Diego

Diego Rivera Speaking
Caedmon
Cassette, Record

RIVERA, Geraldo
Rivera, Geraldo
What Is Puerto Rico? Miguel
   Robles
Caedmon
Cassette, Record

ROBERTSON, Keith
Shachter, Jaqueline
An Interview With ...
Profiles in Literature
Videotape

ROBINSON, Edwin A.
Davis, Charles T.
Edwin A. Robinson, Vol. 1
Cassette Curriculum
Cassette

ROBINSON, Edwin A.
Davis, Charles T.
Edwin A. Robinson, Vol. 2
Cassette Curriculum
Cassette

ROETHKE, Theodore
Roethke, Theodore
Roethke Reads His Poetry
Caedmon
Cassette, Record

ROETHKE, Theodore
Grebstein, Sheldon
Theodore Roethke
Cassette Curriculum
Cassette

ROGERS, Will
Rogers, Will
Wit and Wisdom of Will Rogers
Caedmon
Cassette, Record

ROSS, Pat
Dennis; Keckart; McNeil
Young and Female
Caedmon
Cassette, Record

ROSTAND, Edmund
Richardson; Massey; Fraser
Cyrano de Bergerac
Caedmon
Cassette, Record

ROTH, Philip
Grebstein, Sheldon
Portnoy's Complaint
Cassette Curriculum
Cassette

RUSKIN, John
Quayle, Anthony
King of the Golden River
Caedmon
Cassette, Record

RUSSELL, Bertrand
Russell, Bertrand
Bertrand Russell Speaking
Caedmon
Cassette, Record

SACKLER, Howard
No Name
Book of Job
Columbia Masterworks
Cassette, Record

SADE, Marquise de
Magee, Patrick
Selections from Marquis de
   Sade
Caedmon
Cassette, Record

SAINT-EXUPERY, Antoine de
Ustinov, Peter
Little Prince
Argo
Record

SAKI
Baxter, Keith
Reginald on House Parties,
   Other Stories
Caedmon
Cassette, Record

SAKI
Baxter, Keith
Tobermory, Other Stories
Caedmon
Cassette, Record

SALINGER, J. D.
Miller, James E.
Catcher in the Rye
Cassette Curriculum
Cassette

SALTEN, Felix
Johns, Glynis

Bambi
Caedmon
Cassette, Record

SANDBURG, Carl
Sandburg, Carl
American Songbag
Caedmon
Cassette, Record

SANDBURG, Carl
Sandburg, Carl
Autobiography, Always the
Young Strangers
Caedmon
Cassette, Record

SANDBURG, Carl
Duffey, Bernard
Carl Sandburg
Cassette Curriculum
Cassette

SANDBURG, Carl
Sandburg, Carl
Carl Sandburg Reading His
Poetry
Caedmon
Cassette, Record

SANDBURG, Carl
Sandburg, Carl
Fog and Other Poems
Caedmon
Cassette, Record

SANDBURG, Carl
Sandburg, Carl
Lincoln Album
Caedmon
Cassette, Record

SANDBURG, Carl
Sandburg, Carl
People, Yes
Caedmon
Cassette, Record

SANDBURG, Carl
Sandburg, Carl
Poems for Children
Caedmon
Cassette, Record

SANDBURG, Carl
Sandburg, Carl
Remembrance Rock
Caedmon
Cassette, Record

SANDBURG, Carl
Sandburg, Carl
Rootabaga Stories, Vol. 1
Caedmon
Cassette, Record

SANDBURG, Carl
Sandburg, Carl
Rootabaga Stories, Vol. 2
Caedmon
Cassette, Record

SANDBURG, Carl
Sandburg, Carl
Rootabaga Stories, Vol. 3
Caedmon
Cassette, Record

SANDERLIN, George
Quayle, Anthony
Christopher Columbus, 1492
Caedmon
Cassette, Record

SARTRE, Jean Paul
Brombert, Victor
Nausea
Cassette Curriculum
Cassette

SARTRE, Jean Paul
Pleasence; Jackson; Massey
No Exit
Caedmon
Cassette, Record

SARTRE, Jean Paul
Guicharnaud, Jacques
No Exit
Cassette Curriculum
Cassette

SARTRE, Jean Paul
Miller, Jordan
No Exit
Cassette Curriculum
Cassette

SCHAEFER, Jack
Haslam, Gerald
Works of Jack Schaefer
Cassette Curriculum
Cassette

SCHWARTZ, Alvin
Irving, George S.
Tongue Twisters
Caedmon
Cassette, Record

SEFERIS, George
Seferis, George
George Seferis Reads His Poetry
Caedmon
Cassette, Record

SEFERIS, George
Seferis, George; Keeley, Ed
Poetry in Modern Greek
Caedmon
Cassette, Record

SERVICE, ROBERT W.
Begley, Ed
Poetry of R. W. Service
Caedmon
Cassette, Record

SETON, Ernest Thompson
Begley, Ed
Wild Animals I Have Known
Caedmon
Cassette, Record

SEUSS, Dr.
Conried, Hans
Happy Birthday to You, Other
    Stories
Caedmon
Cassette, Record

SEWELL, Anna
Bloom, Claire
Black Beauty
Caedmon
Cassette, Record

SEXTON, Anne
Sexton, Anne
Anne Sexton Reads Her Poetry
Caedmon
Cassette, Record

SHAKESPEARE See also COLWELL,
    C. Carter

SHAKESPEARE
Robson; Portman; Bloom
All's Well That Ends Well
Caedmon
Cassette, Record

SHAKESPEARE
Scott; Scales; Orr; Hordern
All's Well That Ends Well

Argo
Record

SHAKESPEARE
Brown; Quayle
Antony and Cleopatra
Caedmon
Cassette, Record

SHAKESPEARE
Johnson; Worth; Eddison
Antony and Cleopatra
Argo
Record

SHAKESPEARE
Gielgud, John
Approaches to Hamlet
Films for the Humanities
Film

SHAKESPEARE
Redgrave, V.; Mitchell; Adrian
As You Like It
Caedmon
Cassette, Record

SHAKESPEARE
Suzman; Orr; Gardner; Stride
As You Like It
Argo
Record

SHAKESPEARE
Rylands; Bates; Hart; Richer
Comedy of Errors
Argo
Record

SHAKESPEARE
McCowen; Massey; Corbett
Comedy of Errors
Caedmon
Cassette, Record

SHAKESPEARE
Burton; Tandy; Haigh
Coriolanus
Caedmon
Cassette, Record

SHAKESPEARE
White; Arnott; Beves
Coriolanus
Argo
Record

SHAKESPEARE
Bloom; Brown; Quayle
Cymbeline
Caedmon
Cassette, Record

SHAKESPEARE
Drabble; White; Land; Webb
Cymbeline
Argo
Record

SHAKESPEARE
Thomas, Dylan
Dylan Thomas Reading King
  Lear
Caedmon
Cassette, Record

SHAKESPEARE
Scofield; Walker; Wynward
Hamlet
Caedmon
Cassette, Record

SHAKESPEARE
Giamatti, A. Bartlett
Hamlet
Cassette Curriculum
Cassette

SHAKESPEARE
White; Wymark; Scott; Sterke
Hamlet
Argo
Record

SHAKESPEARE
Richardson; Quayle; Mills
Julius Caesar
Caedmon
Cassette, Record

SHAKESPEARE
Church; Johnson; Squire; Holm
Julius Caesar
Argo
Record

SHAKESPEARE
Duncan; Speaight; Scott
King Henry VIII
Argo
Record

SHAKESPEARE
Holm; Gielgud
King Henry V

Caedmon
Cassette, Record

SHAKESPEARE
Watson; Jones; White; Fuller
King Henry V
Argo
Record

SHAKESPEARE
Andrews; Brown; Evans; Quayle
King Henry IV, Part 1
Caedmon
Cassette, Record

SHAKESPEARE
Andrews; Brown; Evans; Quayle
King Henry IV, Part 2
Caedmon
Cassette, Record

SHAKESPEARE
Watson; Beves; Jacobs
King Henry IV, Part 1
Argo
Record

SHAKESPEARE
Watson; Beves; Jacobs; Squire
King Henry IV, Part 2
Argo
Record

SHAKESPEARE
Marquand; Morris; Devlin
King Henry VI, Part 1
Argo
Record

SHAKESPEARE
Marquand; Morris; Wymark
King Henry VI, Part 2
Argo
Record

SHAKESPEARE
Wofit; Haigh; Harris
King John
Caedmon
Cassette, Record

SHAKESPEARE
Hordern; Jacobs; Church
King John
Argo
Record

SHAKESPEARE
Scofield; Cusack; Stride; Brown

King Lear
Caedmon
Cassette, Record

SHAKESPEARE
Devlin; Balcon; Rawlings
King Lear
Argo
Record

SHAKESPEARE
Gielgud; Michell; McKern
King Richard II
Caedmon
Cassette, Record

SHAKESPEARE
Many
King Richard II
Argo
Record

SHAKESPEARE
Stephens; Ashcroft; Cusack
King Richard III
Caedmon
Cassette, Record

SHAKESPEARE
Wymark; Wordsworth; Garland
King Richard III
Argo
Record

SHAKESPEARE
McEwan; Brett
Love's Labour's Lost
Caedmon
Cassette, Record

SHAKESPEARE
Godfrey; Watson; Eddison
Love's Labour's Lost
Argo
Record

SHAKESPEARE
Quayle; Holloway; Ffrangcon-
   Davies
Macbeth
Caedmon
Cassette, Record

SHAKESPEARE
Mack, Maynard, Jr.
Macbeth
Cassette Curriculum
Cassette

SHAKESPEARE
Church; Worth; Barton; Prior
Macbeth
Argo
Record

SHAKESPEARE
Quayle; Holloway
Macbeth, Great Scenes
Caedmon
Cassette, Record

SHAKESPEARE
Gielgud; Leighton; Richardson
Measure for Measure
Caedmon
Cassette, Record

SHAKESPEARE
Rylands; Richer; Marquand
Measure for Measure
Argo
Record

SHAKESPEARE
Griffith; Tutin; Andrews
Merchant of Venice
Caedmon
Cassette, Record

SHAKESPEARE
Church; Scott; Watson
Merchant of Venice
Argo
Record

SHAKESPEARE
Redgrave, M.; Cast
Merchant of Venice, Minor Cuts
Caedmon
Cassette, Record

SHAKESPEARE
Quayle; MacLiammoir; Redman
Merry Wives of Windsor
Caedmon
Cassette, Record

SHAKESPEARE
Wymark; McEwan; Lehman
Merry Wives of Windsor
Argo
Record

SHAKESPEARE
Scofield; Parker
Midsummer Night's Dream
Caedmon
Cassette, Record

SHAKESPEARE
White; Balcon; Goolden
Midsummer Night's Dream
Argo
Record

SHAKESPEARE
Harrison; Roberts
Much Ado About Nothing
Caedmon
Cassette, Record

SHAKESPEARE
Ashcroft; Gielgud; Squire
Much Ado About Nothing
Argo
Record

SHAKESPEARE
Silvera; Massey; Cusack; Johnson
Othello
Caedmon
Cassette, Record

SHAKESPEARE
Johnson; Calder-Marshall
Othello
Argo
Record

SHAKESPEARE
Scofield; Aylmer; Dench; Laurie
Pericles
Caedmon
Cassette, Record

SHAKESPEARE
Squire; Scales; Duncan
Pericles
Argo
Record

SHAKESPEARE
Olivier, Laurence
Poet's Eye
Films for the Humanities
Film

SHAKESPEARE
Burton; Evans; Wofit
Rape of Lucrece
Caedmon
Cassette, Record

SHAKESPEARE
Church; Ashcroft; Holmes
Rape of Lucrece
Argo
Record

SHAKESPEARE
Bloom; Finney; Evans
Romeo and Juliet
Caedmon
Cassette, Record

SHAKESPEARE
Marquand; Richer; White
Romeo and Juliet
Argo
Record

SHAKESPEARE
Quayle; Brown
Scenes from Antony and Cleo-
patra
Caedmon
Cassette, Record

SHAKESPEARE
Marlowe Dramatic Society
Scenes from the Comedies
Argo
Record

SHAKESPEARE
Marlowe Dramatic Society
Scenes from the Histories
Argo
Record

SHAKESPEARE
Marlowe Dramatic Society
Scenes from the Tragedies Vol.
1
Argo
Record

SHAKESPEARE
Marlowe Dramatic Society
Scenes from the Tragedies Vol.
2
Argo
Record

SHAKESPEARE
No Name
Songs from The Plays of Shake-
speare
Caedmon
Cassette, Record

SHAKESPEARE
Gielgud, John
Sonnets
Caedmon
Cassette, Record

SHAKESPEARE
Rylands; Church; White
Sonnets
Argo
Record

SHAKESPEARE
Howar; Leighton
Taming of the Shrew
Caedmon
Cassette, Record

SHAKESPEARE
Godfrey; Ashcroft; Orr; Richer
Taming of the Shrew
Argo
Record

SHAKESPEARE
Redgrave, M.; Griffith; Massey
Tempest
Caedmon
Cassette, Record

SHAKESPEARE
Hordern; Parry; Rields-Hyde
Tempest
Argo
Record

SHAKESPEARE
Squire; Wood; Redgrave
Timon of Athens
Argo
Record

SHAKESPEARE
Quayle; Audley; Hordern
Titus Andronicus
Caedmon
Cassette, Record

SHAKESPEARE
Devlin; Orr; Balcon
Titus Andronicus
Argo
Record

SHAKESPEARE
White; Worth; Barton; Gibson
Troilus and Cressida
Argo
Record

SHAKESPEARE
Brett; Cilento; Cusack
Troylus and Cressida
Caedmon
Cassette, Record

SHAKESPEARE
McKenna; Scofield; Neville
Twelfth Night
Caedmon
Cassette, Record

SHAKESPEARE
Tutin; Balcon; Scales
Twelfth Night
Argo
Record

SHAKESPEARE
Burton; Marquand; Rylands
Two Gentlemen of Verona
Argo
Record

SHAKESPEARE
Wungarde; Laurie; De Souza
Two Gentlemen of Verona
Caedmon
Cassette, Record

SHAKESPEARE
Bloom; Adrian
Venus and Adonis
Caedmon
Cassette, Record

SHAKESPEARE
Worth; Rylands; Lang
Venus and Adonis
Argo
Record

SHAKESPEARE
Gielgud; Ashcroft
Winter's Tale
Caedmon
Cassette, Record

SHAKESPEARE
Squire; Scott; White; Conroy
Winter's Tale
Argo
Record

SHAPIRO, Karl
Reid, Alfred S.
Karl Shapiro
Cassette Curriculum
Cassette

SHAW-TERRY
Ashcroft; Cusack
Shaw-Terry Letters
Caedmon
Cassette, Record

SHAW, George Bernard
Bloom; Adrian; Anderson
Caesar and Cleopatra
Caedmon
Cassette, Record

SHAW, George Bernard
Boyer; Laughton; Hardwicke
Don Juan in Hell
Columbia Masterworks
Cassette, Record

SHAW, George Bernard
Tandy; Shaw Festival
Heartbreak House
Caedmon
Cassette, Record

SHAW, George Bernard
Mermaid Theatre Prod.
John Bull's Other Island
Caedmon
Cassette, Record

SHAW, George Bernard
Smith; Moerley; Johnson
Major Barbara
Caedmon
Cassette, Record

SHAW, George Bernard
London Mermaid Theatre Prod.
Misalliance
Caedmon
Cassette, Record

SHAW, George Bernard
McCowen; Rigg; Cast
Pygmalion
Argo
Record

SHAW, George Bernard
Redgrave, L.; Redgrave, M.;
Hordern
Pygmalion
Caedmon
Cassette, Record

SHAW, George Bernard
McKenna; Pleasence; Aylmer
Saint Joan
Caedmon
Cassette, Record

SHAW, George Bernard
Jefford; McCowen; Adrian
Saint Joan

Argo
Record

SHELLEY, Percy Bysshe
Holloway, John
Adonais
Cassette Curriculum
Cassette

SHELLEY, Percy Bysshe
Holloway, John
Ode to the West Wind
Cassette Curriculum
Cassette

SHELLEY, Percy Bysshe
Holloway, John
Ozymandias
Cassette Curriculum
Cassette

SHELLEY, Percy Bysshe
Marquand; Watson; Garland
Poems
Argo
Record

SHELLEY, Percy Bysshe
Price, Vincent
Poetry of P. B. Shelley
Caedmon
Cassette, Record

SHELLEY, Percy Bysshe
Holloway, John
Prometheus Unbound
Cassette Curriculum
Cassette

SHELLEY, Percy Bysshe
Holloway, John
To a Skylark
Cassette Curriculum
Cassette

SHERIDAN, Richard B.
Evans; Brown; Donald; Cast
Rivals
Caedmon
Cassette, Record

SHERIDAN, Richard B.
Gielgud; Richardson; McEwan
School for Scandal
Caedmon
Cassette, Record

SILLS, Paul
No Name

Paul Sills' Story Theatre
Columbia Masterworks
Cassette, Record

SINGER, Isaac Bashevis
Singer, Isaac Bashevis
I. B. Singer Reads His Stories
Caedmon
Cassette, Record

SINGER, Isaac Bashevis
Singer, Isaac Bashevis
I. B. Singer Reads in Yiddish
Caedmon
Cassette, Record

SITWELL, Edith
Sitwell, Edith
Edith Sitwell Reads Her Poems
Caedmon
Cassette, Record

SITWELL, Edith
Sitwell; Thomas, Dylan
Sitwell and Dylan Thomas Read
   Her Poetry
Caedmon
Cassette, Record

SITWELL, Osbert
Sitwell, Osbert
Osbert Sitwell Reads His Poetry
Caedmon
Cassette, Record

SNYDER, Gary
Tytell, John
Gary Snyder
Cassette Curriculum
Cassette

SOLZHENITSYN, Alexandr
Wallach, Eli
One Day in the Life of Ivan
   Denisovich
Caedmon
Cassette, Record

SOPHOCLES
Not Named
Antigone
Jabberwocky
Cassette

SOPHOCLES
Tutin; Adrian; Brett; Atkins
Antigone
Caedmon
Cassette, Record

SOPHOCLES
Cavander, Kenneth
Antigone
Cassette Curriculum
Cassette

SOPHOCLES
Cavander, Kenneth
Electra
Cassette Curriculum
Cassette

SOPHOCLES
Cavander, Kenneth
Oedipus at Colonus
Cassette Curriculum
Cassette

SOPHOCLES
Campbell, Cast
Oedipus Rex
Caedmon
Cassette, Record

SOPHOCLES
Not Named
Oedipus the King
Jabberwocky
Cassette

SOPHOCLES
Cavander, Kenneth
Oedipus the King
Cassette Curriculum
Cassette

SOPHOCLES
Quayle, Anthony
Oedipus the King
Films for the Humanities
Film

SOPHOCLES
Cavander, Kenneth
Philoctetes
Cassette Curriculum
Cassette

SPEARE, Elizabeth
Shachter, Jaqueline
An Interview With ...
Profiles in Literature
Videotape

SPENDER, Stephen
Spender, Stephen
Poems
Argo
Record

STEVENS, Wallace
  Riddel, Joseph N.
  Wallace Stevens 2
  Cassette Curriculum
  Cassette

STEVENSON, Robert Louis
  Anderson, Judith
  Child's Garden of Verses
  Caedmon
  Cassette, Record

STEVENSON, Robert Louis
  Not Named
  Dr. Jekyll and Mr. Hyde
  Jabberwocky
  Cassette

STEVENSON, Robert Louis
  Quayle, Anthony
  Dr. Jekyll and Mr. Hyde
  Caedmon
  Cassette, Record

STEVENSON, Robert Louis
  Not Named
  Treasure Island
  Jabberwocky
  Cassette

STEVENSON, Robert Louis
  Richardson, Ian
  Treasure Island
  Caedmon
  Cassette, Record

STOCKTON, Frank
  Anderson, Judith
  Lady and the Tiger
  Caedmon
  Cassette, Record

STOKER, Bram
  McCallum, David; Shelley,
    Carole
  Scenes from Dracula
  Caedmon
  Cassette, Record

STOPPARD, Tom
  Frieling, Ken
  Rosencrantz and Guildenstern
    Are Dead
  Cassette Curriculum
  Cassette

STOUTENBERG, Adrien
  Begley, Ed

American Tall Animal Tales,
  Vol. 1
Caedmon
Cassette, Record

STOUTENBERG, Adrien
  Begley, Ed
  American Tall Animal Tales,
    Vol. 2
  Caedmon
  Cassette, Record

STOUTENBERG, Adrien
  Begley, Ed
  Davy Crockett, Pecos Bill
  Caedmon
  Cassette, Record

STOUTENBERG, Adrien
  Begley, Ed
  John Henry, Joe Magarac
  Caedmon
  Cassette, Record

STOUTENBERG, Adrien
  Begley, Ed
  Johnny Appleseed and Paul
    Bunyon
  Caedmon
  Cassette, Record

STOUTENBERG, Adrien
  Begley, Ed
  Mike Fink and Stormalong
  Caedmon
  Cassette, Record

STOWE, Harriet Beecher
  Jaskoski, Helen
  Uncle Tom's Cabin
  Cassette Curriculum
  Cassette

STRINDBERG, August
  Reinert, Otto
  Dream Play
  Cassette Curriculum
  Cassette

STRINDBERG, August
  Reinert, Otto
  Miss Julie, The Father
  Cassette Curriculum
  Cassette

STUART, Jesse
  Stuart, Jesse
  Poems of Jesse Stuart

Cassette Curriculum
Cassette

STYRON, William
Holma, Hugh
Confessions of Nat Turner
Cassette Curriculum
Cassette

SWIFT, Jonathan
Redgrave, Michael
Gulliver's Travels
Caedmon
Cassette, Record

SWIFT, Jonathan
Quayle, Anthony
Gulliver's Travels
Caedmon
Cassette, Record

SWIFT, Jonathan
Ross, Angus
Gulliver's Travels
Cassette Curriculum
Cassette

SWIFT, Jonathan
Magee, Patrick
Modest Proposal, Tale of a
Tub
Caedmon
Cassette, Record

SWIFT, Jonathan
Ross, Angus
Swift the Poet
Cassette Curriculum
Cassette

SWIFT, Jonathan
Ross, Angus
Swift's Prose
Cassette Curriculum
Cassette

SWIFT, Jonathan
Ross, Angus
Tale of a Tub
Cassette Curriculum
Cassette

SYNGE, J. M.
Cusack, McKenna
Playboy of the Western World
Caedmon
Cassette, Record

TAYLOR, William E.
Taylor, William E.
Poems of William E. Taylor
Cassette Curriculum
Record

TAZEWELL, Charles
Nesbitt, Cathleen
Little Wildrose, Other Lang
Fairy Tales
Caedmon
Cassette, Record

TAZEWELL, Charles
Anderson, Judith
Littlest Angel, Bells of Christ-
mas
Caedmon
Cassette, Record

TENNYSON, Alfred Lord
Quayle, Anthony
Idylls of King: Geraint and
Enid
Caedmon
Cassette, Record

TENNYSON, Alfred Lord
Rathbone, Basil
Idylls of the King, Lancelot,
Passing
Caedmon
Cassette, Record

TENNYSON, Alfred Lord
Church; Duncan; McCarthy
Poems, Vol. 1
Argo
Record

TENNYSON, Alfred Lord
Duncan; Hordern, King
Poems, Vol. 2
Argo
Record

TENNYSON, Alfred Lord
Thorndike, Casson
Poetry of Alfred Tennyson
Caedmon
Cassette, Record

TERKEL, Studs
Terkel, Studs
Hard Times
Caedmon
Cassette, Record

TERRY, Ellen
Thorndike, Dame Sybil
People Past and Present
Argo
Record

THOMAS, Dylan
Thomas, Dylan
Adventures in Skin Trade and
Two Poems
Caedmon
Cassette, Record

THOMAS, Dylan
Thomas, Dylan
Child's Christmas in Wales
Caedmon
Cassette, Record

THOMAS, Dylan
Thomas, Dylan
Dylan Thomas Reads, Vol. 1
Caedmon
Cassette, Record

THOMAS, Dylan
Thomas, Dylan
Dylan Thomas Reads, Vol. 2
Caedmon
Cassette, Record

THOMAS, Dylan
Thomas, Dylan
Dylan Thomas Reads, Vols.
3 & 4
Caedmon
Cassette, Record

THOMAS, Dylan
Thomas, Dylan
Dylan Thomas Reads, Vol. 5
Caedmon
Cassette, Record

THOMAS, Dylan
Thomas, Dylan
Dylan Thomas, Sean O'Casey
& Djuna Barnes
Caedmon
Cassette, Record

THOMAS, Dylan
Williams, Emlyn
Emlyn Williams as Dylan
Thomas
Argo
Record

THOMAS, Dylan
Thomas, Dylan
An Evening with Dylan Thomas
Caedmon
Cassette, Record

THOMAS, Dylan
MacNeice; Griffith; Burton
Homage to Dylan Thomas
Argo
Record

THOMAS, Dylan
Thomas, Dylan
In Country Heaven
Caedmon
Cassette, Record

THOMAS, Dylan
Thomas, Dylan
Personal Anthology
Caedmon
Cassette, Record

THOMAS, Dylan
Burton, Richard
Poems
Argo
Record

THOMAS, Dylan
Thomas, Dylan
Return Journey to Swansea
Caedmon
Cassette, Record

THOMAS, Dylan
Thomas, Dylan
Stories and Humourous Essays
Caedmon
Cassette, Record

THOMAS, Dylan
Thomas, Dylan; Cast
Under Milk Wood
Caedmon
Cassette, Record

THOMAS, Dylan
Burton; Griffith; Maddox; Cast
Under Milk Wood
Argo
Record

THOMPSON, Francis
Mason, James
Hound of Heaven
Caedmon
Cassette, Record

THOMPSON, Vernon
Thompson, Vernon
Character
Cassette Curriculum
Cassette

THOMPSON, Vernon
Thompson, Vernon
Conflict and Plot
Cassette Curriculum
Cassette

THOMPSON, Vernon
Thompson, Vernon
Introduction to Literary Analysis
Cassette Curriculum
Cassette

THOMPSON, Vernon
Thompson, Vernon
Point of View in Fiction
Cassette Curriculum
Cassette

THOMPSON, Vernon
Thompson, Vernon
Setting
Cassette Curriculum
Cassette

THOMPSON, Vernon
Thompson, Vernon
Style
Cassette Curriculum
Cassette

THOMPSON, Vernon
Thompson, Vernon
Symbolism and Allegory
Cassette Curriculum
Cassette

THOMPSON, Vernon
Thompson, Vernon
Theme
Cassette Curriculum
Cassette

THOMPSON, Vernon
Thompson, Vernon
Writing the Critical Essay
Cassette Curriculum
Cassette

THOREAU, Henry David
Randel, William
Civil Disobedience
Cassette Curriculum
Cassette

THOREAU, Henry David
MacLeish, Archibald
Civil Disobedience
Caedmon
Cassette, Record

THOREAU, Henry David
Randel, William
Thoreau and the Middle Land-
scape
Cassette Curriculum
Cassette

THOREAU, Henry David
MacLeish, Archibald
Thoreau's World
Caedmon
Cassette, Record

THOREAU, Henry David
MacLeish, Archibald
Walden
Caedmon
Cassette, Record

THOREAU, Henry David
Randel, William
Walden
Cassette Curriculum
Cassette

THURBER, James
Ustinov, Peter
Great Quillow
Caedmon
Cassette, Record

THURBER, James
Ustinov, Peter
Grizzly and Gadgets, Further
Fables
Caedmon
Cassette, Record

THURBER, James
Ustinov, Peter
Many Moons
Caedmon
Cassette, Record

THURBER, James
Ewell; Cass; Ford; Ghostly
Thurber Carnival
Columbia Masterworks
Cassette, Record

THURBER, James
Ustinov, Peter
Unicorn in Garden, Other

Fables
Caedmon
Cassette, Record

THURBER, James
Ewell; Stritch; Kiley
University Days
Caedmon
Cassette, Record

TOCQUEVILLE, Alexis de
Quayle, Anthony
Democracy in America
Caedmon
Cassette, Record

TOLKIEN, J. R. R.
Williamson, Nicol
Hobbit
Argo
Record

TOLKIEN, J. R. R.
Tolkien, J. R. R.
Hobbit, Fellowship of the Ring
Caedmon
Cassette, Record

TOLKIEN, J. R. R.
Tolkien, J. R. R.
Lord of Rings, Two Towers,
    Return of King
Caedmon
Cassette, Record

TOLKIEN, J. R. R.
Tolkien; Swann; Elvin
Poems and Songs of Middle Earth
Caedmon
Cassette, Record

TOLSTOY, Leo
Richardson, Ian
Fables and Fairy Tales
Caedmon
Cassette, Record

TOOMER, Jean
Turner, Darwin T.
Cane
Cassette Curriculum
Cassette

TOWNSEND, John Rowe
Shachter, Jaqueline
An Interview With ...
Profiles in Literature
Videotape

TRAVERS, P. L.
Smith; Stephens; Cast
Mary Poppins
Caedmon
Cassette, Record

TRAVERS, P. L.
Smith; Stephens; Cast
Mary Poppins and Banks Family
Caedmon
Cassette, Record

TRAVERS, P. L.
Smith; Stephens; Cast
Mary Poppins: Balloons and
    Balloons
Caedmon
Cassette, Record

TRAVERS, P. L.
Smith; Stephens; Cast
Mary Poppins Comes Back
Caedmon
Cassette, Record

TRAVERS, P. L.
Travers; Stephens
Mary Poppins from A to Z
Caedmon
Cassette, Record

TRAVERS, P. L.
Smith; Stephens; Cast
Mary Poppins Opens the Door
Caedmon
Cassette, Record

TURNER, Darwin
Turner, Darwin
Poems of Darwin T. Turner
Cassette Curriculum
Cassette

TWAIN, Mark
Geer, Will
Autobiography of Mark Twain
Caedmon
Cassette, Record

TWAIN, Mark
Not Named
Celebrated Jumping Frog
Jabberwocky
Cassette

TWAIN, Mark
Hill, Hamlin
Connecticut Yankee

Cassette Curriculum
Cassette

TWAIN, Mark
Hill; Hamlin
Huck Finn 1
Cassette Curriculum
Cassette

TWAIN, Mark
Hill; Hamlin
Huck Finn 2
Cassette Curriculum
Cassette

TWAIN, Mark
Not Named
Huckleberry Finn
Jabberwocky
Cassette

TWAIN, Mark
Begley, Ed
Huckleberry Finn
Caedmon
Cassette, Record

TWAIN, Mark
Hill; Hamlin
Later Philosophical Writings
Cassette Curriculum
Cassette

TWAIN, Mark
Begley, Ed
Life on the Mississippi
Caedmon
Cassette, Record

TWAIN, Mark
Hill; Hamlin
Man That Corrupted Hadleyburg
Cassette Curriculum
Cassette

TWAIN, Mark
Geer, Will
Mark Twain's America
Caedmon
Cassette, Record

TWAIN, Mark
Geer, Will
Mark Twain's America
Caedmon
Cassette, Record

TWAIN, Mark
Hill; Hamlin

Puddn'head Wilson
Cassette Curriculum
Cassette

TWAIN, Mark
Wayne, David
Short Stories
Caedmon
Cassette, Record

TWAIN, Mark
Brennan; De Wilde
Stories of Mark Twain
Caedmon
Cassette, Record

TWAIN, Mark
Begley, Ed
Tom Sawyer
Caedmon
Cassette, Record

TWAIN, Mark
Begley, Ed
Tom Sawyer, Adventures with
Injun Joe
Caedmon
Cassette, Record

TWAIN, Mark
Hill; Hamlin
Tom Sawyer, Prince and Pauper
Cassette Curriculum
Cassette

TWAIN, Mark
Hill; Hamlin
Travel Books
Cassette Curriculum
Cassette

UPDIKE, John
Updike, John
Couples, Pigeon Feathers
Caedmon
Cassette, Record

VAN GOGH, Vincent
Cobb, Lee J.; Gabel
Self Portrait of Vincent Van
Gogh
Caedmon
Cassette, Record

VERNE, Jules
No Name
Around the World in Eighty Days
Columbia Masterworks
Cassette, Record

VILLENEUVE, Mme. de
Not Named
Beauty and the Beast
Jabberwocky
Cassette

VINING, Elizabeth Gray
Shachter, Jaqueline
An Interview With ...
Profiles in Literature
Videotape

VIRGIL
Dimock, George
Aeneid 1
Cassette Curriculum
Cassette

VIRGIL
Dimock, George
Aeneid 2
Cassette Curriculum
Cassette

VIRGIL
Lewis, Cecil Day
Georgics
Argo
Record

VOLTAIRE, François
Brombert, Victor
Candide
Cassette Curriculum
Cassette

VOLTAIRE, François
Franc, Robert; Chauvin
Candide
Caedmon
Cassette, Record

VONNEGUT, Kurt, Jr.
French, Warren
Breakfast of Champions
Cassette Curriculum
Cassette

VONNEGUT, Kurt, Jr.
Vonnegut, Kurt, Jr.
Cat's Cradle
Caedmon
Cassette, Record

VONNEGUT, Kurt, Jr.
Vonnegut, Kurt, Jr.
Self-Portrait
Films for the Humanities
Film

VONNEGUT, Kurt, Jr.
Pease, Donald
Sirens of Titan
Cassette Curriculum
Cassette

VONNEGUT, Kurt, Jr.
Pease, Donald
Slaughterhouse-Five
Cassette Curriculum
Cassette

VONNEGUT, Kurt, Jr.
Vonnegut, Kurt, Jr.
Slaughterhouse-Five
Caedmon
Cassette, Record

VONNEGUT, Kurt, Jr.
Vonnegut, Kurt, Jr.
Welcome to the Monkey House
Caedmon
Cassette, Record

VUOLO, Brett Harvey
Dennis, S.; Heckart, E.
Pioneer Women's Journals
Caedmon
Cassette, Record

WABER, Bernard
Verdon, Gwen
Lyle, Lyle, Crocodile, Other
Adventures
Caedmon
Cassette, Record

WALD, George
Wald, George
Generation I: Search of a Fu-
ture
Caedmon
Cassette, Record

WARD, Lynd, & McNeer, May
Shachter, Jaqueline
An Interview With ...
Profiles in Literature
Videotape

WARREN, Robert Penn
Schneider, Robert L.
All the King's Men
Cassette Curriculum
Cassette

WARREN, Robert Penn
Core, George
Robert Penn Warren

Cassette Curriculum
Cassette

WATERS, Frank
Lyon, Thomas
Works of Frank Waters
Cassette Curriculum
Cassette

WEBSTER, John
Jefford; Stephens; McCowen
Duchess of Malfi
Caedmon
Cassette, Record

WEISS, Peter
Royal Shakespeare Co.
Marat /Sade
Caedmon
Cassette, Record

WEISS, Peter
Kahn, Sy
Persecution and Assassination
of Jean Paul Marat
Cassette Curriculum
Cassette

WEISS, Peter
Weiss, Peter
Reading from His Works,
Peter Weiss
Caedmon
Cassette, Record

WELLS, H. G.
Not Named
Time Machine
Jabberwocky
Cassette

WELTY, Eudora
Welty, Eudora
Eudora Welty Reading
Caedmon
Cassette, Record

WELTY, Eudora
Griffin, Robert
Losing Battles
Cassette Curriculum
Cassette

WEST, Nathanael
Widmer, Kingsley
Day of the Locust
Cassette Curriculum
Cassette

WHARTON, Edith
Tuttleton, James W.
Age of Innocence
Cassette Curriculum
Cassette

WHITMAN, Walt
Begley, Ed
Crossing Brooklyn Ferry, Other
Poems
Caedmon
Cassette, Record

WHITMAN, Walt
Randel, William
Drum Taps
Cassette Curriculum
Cassette

WHITMAN, Walt
Begley, Ed
Eyewitness to the Civil War
Caedmon
Cassette, Record

WHITMAN, Walt
Begley, Ed
Leaves of Grass Vol. 1
Caedmon
Cassette, Record

WHITMAN, Walt
Begley, Ed
Leaves of Grass Vol. 2
Caedmon
Cassette, Record

WHITMAN, Walt
Randel, William
Leaves of Grass
Cassette Curriculum
Cassette

WHITMAN, Walt
Davis, Charles T.
Walt Whitman 1
Cassette Curriculum
Cassette

WHITMAN, Walt
Davis, Charles T.
Walt Whitman 2
Cassette Curriculum
Cassette

WHITMAN, Walt
Randel, William
Whitman as a Disciple of

Emerson
Cassette Curriculum
Cassette

WHITTIER, John Greenleaf
Begley, Ed
Barefoot Boy, Other Poems
Caedmon
Cassette, Record

WILBUR, Richard
Wilbur, Richard
Richard Wilbur Reading His
   Poetry
Caedmon
Cassette, Record

WILDE, Oscar
Mason, James
Ballad of Reading Gaol
Caedmon
Cassette, Record

WILDE, Oscar
Quayle, Anthony
Canterville Ghost
Caedmon
Cassette, Record

WILDE, Oscar
Not Named
Happy Prince
Jabberwocky
Cassette

WILDE, Oscar
Rathbone, Basil
Happy Prince, Other Fairy
   Tales
Caedmon
Cassette, Record

WILDE, Oscar
Cooper; Greenwood; McCowen
Importance of Being Earnest
Caedmon
Cassette, Record

WILDE, Oscar
Not Named
Nightingale and the Rose
Jabberwocky
Cassette

WILDE, Oscar
Hatfield, Hurd
Picture of Dorian Gray
Caedmon
Cassette, Record

WILDER, Thornton
Williams, Mary Ellen
Bridge of San Luis Rey
Cassette Curriculum
Cassette

WILDER, Thornton
French, Warren
Eighth Day
Cassette Curriculum
Cassette

WILDER, Thornton
Mendelsohn, Michael
Our Town
Cassette Curriculum
Cassette

WILDER, Thornton
Wilder, Thornton
Readings
Films for the Humanities
Film

WILDER, Thornton
Williams, Mary Ellen
Skin of Our Teeth
Cassette Curriculum
Cassette

WILLIAMS, Tennessee
Bryer; Jackson
Glass Menagerie
Cassette Curriculum
Cassette

WILLIAMS, Tennessee
Clift; Harris; Tandy; Wayne
Glass Menagerie
Caedmon
Cassette, Record

WILLIAMS, Tennessee
Kahn, Sy
Night of the Iguana
Cassette Curriculum
Cassette

WILLIAMS, Tennessee
Stapleton; Guardino; Tucci
Rose Tattoo
Caedmon
Cassette, Record

WILLIAMS, Tennessee
Harris; Farentino
Streetcar Named Desire
Caedmon

Cassette, Record

WILLIAMS, Tennessee
Bryer; Jackson
Streetcar Named Desire
Cassette Curriculum
Cassette

WILLIAMS, Tennessee
Williams, Tennessee
Tennessee Williams Reading His
    Works
Caedmon
Cassette, Record

WILLIAMS, William Carlos
Williams, William Carlos
W. Carlos Williams Reads His
    Poetry
Caedmon
Cassette, Record

WILLIAMS, William Carlos
Wagner, Linda
William Carlos Williams
Cassette Curriculum
Cassette

WILLIAMS-ELLIS, Amabel
Quayle, Anthony
Aladdin and His Lamp
Caedmon
Cassette, Record

WILLIAMS-ELLIS, Amabel
Quayle, Anthony
Ali Baba and the Forty Thieves
Caedmon
Cassette, Record

WILLIAMS-ELLIS, Amabel
Bloom, Claire
Childe Rowland, Other British
    Tales
Caedmon
Cassette, Record

WILLIAMS-ELLIS, Amabel
Rose, George
Fairy Tales Told by Gypsies
Caedmon
Cassette, Record

WILLIAMS-ELLIS, Amabel
Nesbitt, Cathleen
Puss in Boots, Other Fairy
    Tales
Caedmon
Cassette, Record

WILLIAMS-ELLIS, Amabel
Quayle, Anthony
Sinbad the Sailor
Caedmon
Cassette, Record

WILLIAMS-ELLIS, Amabel
Harris, Julie
Tale of Scheherazade
Caedmon
Cassette, Record

WODEHOUSE, P. G.
Terry-Thomas; Livesey
Jeeves
Caedmon
Cassette, Record

WOLFE, Thomas
Holman, Hugh
Look Homeward Angel
Cassette Curriculum
Cassette

WOOLF, Virginia
Johnson, Celia
To the Lighthouse
Caedmon
Cassette, Record

WORDSWORTH, William
Prickett, Stephen
Immortality
Cassette Curriculum
Cassette

WORDSWORTH, William
Bates; Church; Godfrey
Poems, Vol. 1
Argo
Record

WORDSWORTH, William
Bates; Church; Godfrey
Poems, Vol. 2
Argo
Record

WORDSWORTH, William
Hardwicke, Cedric
Poetry of William Wordsworth
Caedmon
Cassette, Record

WORDSWORTH, William
Prickett, Stephen
Prelude
Cassette Curriculum
Cassette

Abou Ben Adhem (Hunt, James
H. L.)
Absalom, Absalom! (Faulkner,
William)
Absalom and Achitophel (Dryden,
John)
Adonais (Shelley, Percy Bysshe)
Adventures in Skin Trade and
Two Poems (Thomas, Dylan)
Adventures of Augie March
(Bellow, Saul)
Adventures of Robin Hood, Vol. 1
(Creswick, Paul)
Adventures of Robin Hood, Vol. 2
(Creswick, Paul)
Adventures of Robin Hood, Vol. 3
(Creswick, Paul)
Adventures of Robin Hood, Vol. 4
(Creswick, Paul)
Aeneid (Virgil)
African Village Folk Tales, Vol.
1 (Kaula, Edna Mason)
African Village Folk Tales, Vol.
2 (Kaula, Edna Mason)
African Village Folk Tales, Vol.
3 (Kaula, Edna Mason)
After the Fall (Miller, Arthur)
Agamemnon (Aeschylus)
Age of Innocence (Wharton, Edith)
Ah, Wilderness (O'Neill, Eugene)
Aladdin and His Lamp (Williams-
Ellis, Amabel)
Aladdin; or the Wonderful Lamp
(Anonymous)
Albert Camus Reading Novels,
Essays (Camus, Albert)
Alcalde de Zalamea (Calderón de
la Barca, P.)
Ali Baba and the Forty Thieves
(Williams-Ellis, Amabel)
Alice in Wonderland (Carroll,
Lewis)
Alice Through the Looking Glass
(Carroll, Lewis)
All for Love, Spanish Fryar
(Dryden, John)
All the King's Men (Warren,

Robert Penn)
All's Well That Ends Well (Shake-
speare)
Allen Ginsberg (Ginsberg, Allen)
Allness (DeVito, Joseph)
Ambassadors (James, Henry)
American Dream, The Sandbox
(Albee, Edward)
American Indian Literature (Has-
lam, Gerald)
American Patriotism in Prose and
Poetry (Many)
American Songbag (Sandburg, Carl)
American Story Poems (Many)
American Tall Animal Tales, Vol.
1 (Stoutenberg, Adrien)
American Tall Animal Tales, Vol.
2 (Stoutenberg, Adrien)
American Tragedy (Dreiser, Theo-
dore)
Animal Stories (De La Mare,
Walter)
Anne Sexton Reads Her Poetry
(Sexton, Anne)
Antigone (Sophocles)
Antony and Cleopatra (Shakespeare)
Apology (Plato)
Apology, Trial, Death of Socrates
(Plato)
Apple Cart and Poems (Coward,
Noel)
Appointment in Samarra (O'Hara,
John)
Approaches to Hamlet (Shake-
speare)
Archibald MacLeish Reads His
Poetry (MacLeish, Archibald)
Around the World in Eighty Days
(Verne, Jules)
Arrowsmith (Lewis, Sinclair)
Art of Self-Consciousness (Chaucer)
Art of the Essay (Many)
As You Like It (Shakespeare)
Assistant (Malamud, Bernard)
Autobiography of Benjamin Frank-
lin (Franklin, Benjamin)
Autobiography of Mark Twain

Graveyard of Ghost Tales
(Anonymous)
Great American Speeches (Many)
Great American Speeches 1775-
1896 (Many)
Great American Speeches 1898-
1918 (Many)
Great American Speeches 1950-
1963 (Many)
Great American Women's Speeches
(Many)
Great Black Speeches (Many)
Great British Speeches 1597-
1695 (Many)
Great British Speeches 1628-
1780 (Many)
Great British Speeches 1784-
1812 (Many)
Great British Speeches 1867-
1940 (Many)
Great Expectations (Dickens,
Charles)
Great Gatsby (Fitzgerald, F. Scott)
Great Quillow (Thurber, James)
Great Short Stories (Hawthorne,
Nathaniel)
Great Short Stories (Many)
Greek Classics (Mayes, Bernard)
Greek Prose and Poetry (Many)
Greek Tragedy (Many)
Grizzly and Gadgets, Further
Fables (Thurber, James)
Guard of Honor (Cozzens, James
G.)
Gulliver's Travels (Swift, Jonathan)
Gunga Din and Other Poems
(Kipling, Rudyard)
Gwen Brooks Reading Her Poetry
(Brooks, Gwendolyn)

Hairy Ape (O'Neill, Eugene)
Hamlet (Shakespeare)
Hamlet: Character and Theme
(Colwell, C. Carter)
Hamlet: Plot and Structure
(Colwell, C. Carter)
Hansel and Gretel (Grimm's
Fairy Tales)
Hansel and Gretel, Other Tales
(Grimm, Jacob & Wilhelm)
Happy Birthday to You, Other
Stories (Seuss, Dr.)
Happy Prince (Wilde, Oscar)
Happy Prince, Other Fairy
Tales (Wilde, Oscar)
Hard Times (Terkel, Studs)
Hart Crane 1 (Crane, Hart)

Hart Crane 2 (Crane, Hart)
Hearing Poetry, Vol. 1 (Anony-
mous)
Hearing Poetry, Vol. 2 (Anony-
mous)
Heart of Darkness (Conrad, Joseph)
Heartbreak House (Shaw, George
Bernard)
Hedda Gabler (Ibsen, Henrik)
Heidi (Spyri, Johanna)
Henry IV (Pirandello, Luigi)
Herzog (Bellow, Saul)
Hippolytus (Euripides)
History of English Language (Born-
stein, Diane)
History Reflected, Vol. 1 (Anony-
mous)
History Reflected, Vol. 2 (Anony-
mous)
History Reflected, Vol. 3 (Anony-
mous)
History Reflected, Vol. 4 (Anony-
mous)
History Reflected, Vol. 5 (Anony-
mous)
History Reflected, Vol. 6 (Anony-
mous)
Hobbit (Tolkien, J. R. R.)
Hobbit, Fellowship of the Ring
(Tolkien, J. R. R.)
Hollow Crown (Many)
Homage to Dylan Thomas (Thomas,
Dylan)
Homage to Shakespeare (Ball,
William)
Homecoming (Pinter, Harold)
Hound of Heaven (Thompson, Fran-
cis)
Hound of the Baskervilles (Doyle,
Arthur Conan)
How Alphabet Was Made, And
Other Just So Stories (Kipling,
Rudyard)
Hubert Gregg as Jerome S. Jerome
(Gregg, Hubert)
Huck Finn 1 (Twain, Mark)
Huck Finn 2 (Twain, Mark)
Huckleberry Finn (Twain, Mark)
Human Voice (Cocteau, Jean)
Hunting of Snark; Pied Piper
(Carroll, Lewis; Browning,
Robert)
Hurray for Captain Jane! Other
Stories (Anonymous)
Hyperion (Keats, John)

I Am Pablo Neruda (Neruda, Pablo)

Poetry of Byron (Byron, George Gordon, Lord)

Poetry of [Christian Morgenstern]--Gallow's Song (Morgenstern, Christian)

Poetry of Countee Cullen (Cullen, Countee)

Poetry of Edmund Spenser (Spenser, Edmund)

Poetry of Edna St. Vincent Millay (Millay, Edna St. Vincent)

Poetry of Emerson (Emerson, Ralph Waldo)

Poetry of G. M. Hopkins (Hopkins, Gerard Manley)

Poetry of Herman Melville (Melville, Herman)

Poetry of John Dryden (Dryden, John)

Poetry of John Keats (Keats, John)

Poetry of John Milton (Milton, John)

Poetry of P. B. Shelley (Shelley, Percy Bysshe)

Poetry of R. Burns; Border Ballads (Burns, Robert)

Poetry of R. W. Emerson (Emerson, Ralph Waldo)

Poetry of R. W. Service (Service, Robert W.)

Poetry of Rilke (Rilke, Rainer Maria)

Poetry of Robert Browning (Browning, Robert)

Poetry of Robinson Jeffers (Jeffers, Robinson)

Poetry of Samuel Coleridge (Coleridge, Samuel)

Poetry of Stephen Vincent Benet (Benet, Stephen Vincent)

Poetry of Thomas Hardy (Hardy, Thomas)

Poetry of William Blake (Blake, William)

Poetry of William Butler Yeats (Yeats, William Butler)

Poetry of William Wordsworth (Wordsworth, William)

Poetry, Prose, Life of R. L. Stevenson (Brown, Murray)

Poet's Eye (Shakespeare)

Poets from Chaucer to Yeats (Many)

Poet's Journey (Yevtushenko, Yevgeny)

Poets of the West Indies (Many)

Poet's Poet (Pound, Ezra)

Point of View in Fiction (Thompson, Vernon)

Political Poetry (Marvell, Andrew)

Pony Engine, Other Stories (Anonymous)

Pope the Satirist (Pope, Alexander)

Pope's Moral Poetry (Pope, Alexander)

Popular Westerns (Wylder, Delbert)

Portnoy's Complaint (Roth, Philip)

Portrait (Agee, James)

Portrait of an Artist (Joyce, James)

Portrait of the African Explorers (Stanley and Livingston)

Portrait of the Artist as a Young Man (Joyce, James)

Praise of Folly (Erasmus)

Prelude, The (Wordsworth, William)

Pre-Raphaelites (Many)

Prince, The (Machiavelli)

Prince Rabbit and Other Stories (Milne, A. A.)

Prologue to Canterbury Tales (Chaucer, Geoffrey)

Prometheus Bound (Aeschylus)

Prometheus Unbound (Shelley, Percy Bysshe)

Psalms and David (Anonymous)

Puddn'head Wilson (Twain, Mark)

Pueblo Indians (Anonymous)

Purloined Letter (Poe, Edgar Allan)

Puss in Botts, Other Fairy Tales (Williams-Ellis, Amabel)

Pygmalion (Shaw, George Bernard)

Queen Victoria (Longford, Pasco)

Railway Children (Nesbit, E.)

Rain God's Daughter and Other Stories (Kaula, Edna Mason)

Raisin in the Sun (Hansberry, Lorraine)

Randall Jarrell (Jarrell, Randall)

Rape of Lucrece (Shakespeare)

Rape of the Lock (Pope, Alexander)

Rats in the Walls (Lovecraft, H. P.)

Raven and Other Poems (Poe, Edgar Allan)

Raven: Creator of the World (Melzack, Ronald)

Reading by Jean Cocteau (Cocteau, Jean)

Reading Colette (Colette)

AUTHOR INDEX

White, E. 1267
Whitman, Walt 1070, 1870, 1890,
  2800, 3348, 3595, 3696,
  3725, 3794, 3940, 4160
Whittemore, Reed 2481
Wilbur, Richard 4143
Wilde, Oscar 3141, 3419
Wilder, Thornton 3781
Williams, Charles 2274, 4134
Williams, David A. 2428
Williams, Emlyn 1155, 1166,
  1173, 1174, 1176, 1177,
  1188, 1203, 1210, 1221,
  1226, 1231, 1233, 1236
Williams, Tennessee 2333, 2349,
  3644
Williams, W. C. 2104, 2658
Winan, J. A. 1390
Wind in the Willows 3914
Winesburg, Ohio 4058
Winged Word, The 2537
Wings of the Dove, The 2585, 3635
Winnie the Pooh 3776
Winters, Ivor 1400, 1698, 2054
Winter's Tale 1970
Wise Blood 2610
Wiseman, Joseph 4177
Wit 2680, 3959
Witch's Web, The 3268
With Way Up in the Air 3790
Wolfe, Thomas 3765
Woman at Point Sur, The 3682
Woman of the Pharisees 3641

Women 2490, 3249, 4161
Women in literature 2363, 4024
Women writers 2403, 2583, 3743
Woolbert, C. H. 1303, 1491,
  1561, 3164
Woolf, Virginia 575, 2598,
  3422, 3762, 3764, 3803
Wordgames 1774
Workbook 3247
Works and Days 2537, 3554, 3738
World of Carl Sandburg, The
  4198
World We Live In, The 3573
Wright, Richard 2447
Wright, Thomas 1995
Writing 1386
  Teaching of 2700
Wuthering Heights 1426
Wyatt, Thomas 1667, 3415
Wycherly, William 3479

Yeats, William Butler 1458,
  1883, 2166, 2230, 2437,
  3261
Yevtushenko, Yevgeny 2142
Young, Brigham 3883
Young Girl, The 2698

Zeami 2188
Zen and the Art of Motorcycle
  Maintenance 2390